CONVERGENT EVOLUTION
IN WARM DESERTS

US/IBP SYNTHESIS SERIES

This volume is a contribution to the International Biological Program. The United States effort was sponsored by the National Academy of Sciences through the National Committee for the IBP. The lead federal agency in providing support for IBP has been the National Science Foundation.

Views expressed in this volume do not necessarily represent those of the National Academy of Sciences or of the National Science Foundation.

CONVERGENT EVOLUTION IN WARM DESERTS

An Examination of Strategies and Patterns
in Deserts of
Argentina and the United States

Edited by

Gordon H. Orians
University of Washington

Otto T. Solbrig
Harvard University

Dowden, Hutchinson & Ross, Inc.
Stroudsburg   Pennsylvania

Copyright © 1977 by **The Institute of Ecology**
Library of Congress Catalog Card Number: 76-56261
ISBN: 0-87933-276-X

79 78 77   1 2 3 4 5
Manufactured in the United States of America.

LIBRARY OF CONGRESS CATALOGING IN PUBLICATION DATA
Main entry under title:
Convergent evolution in warm deserts.
  (US/IBP synthesis series; 3)
  Bibliography: p. 292
  1. Desert ecology—Southwest, New. 2. Desert ecology—Argentine Republic.
3. Evolution. 4. Convergence (Biology) I. Orians, Gordon H. II. Solbrig, Otto T.
III. Series.
QH104.5.S6C66   574.5'265   76-56261
ISBN 0-87933-276-X

Exclusive distributor: **Halsted Press**
A Division of John Wiley & Sons, Inc.
ISBN 0-470-99287-5

FOREWORD

This book is one of a series of volumes reporting results of research by U.S. scientists participating in the International Biological Program (IBP). As one of the 58 nations taking part in the IBP during the period July 1967 to June 1974, the United States organized a number of large, multidisciplinary studies pertinent to the central IBP theme of "the biological basis of productivity and human welfare."

These multidisciplinary studies (Integrated Research Programs), directed toward an understanding of the structure and function of major ecological or human systems, have been a distinctive feature of the U.S. participation in the IBP. Many of the detailed investigations that represent individual contributions to the overall objectives of each Integrated Research Program have been published in the journal literature. The main purpose of this series of books is to accomplish a synthesis of the many contributions for each principal program and thus answer the larger questions pertinent to the structure and function of the major systems that have been studied.

Publications Committee: US/IBP
Gabriel Lasker
Robert B. Platt
Frederick E. Smith
W. Frank Blair, Chairman

PREFACE

The International Biological Program (IBP) was a ten-year project (1965–1974) aimed at increasing the productivity of natural and artificial ecosystems of the world. Among the contributions of the United States (US/IBP) was a series of integrated ecosystem studies. One of these projects, the Structure of Ecosystem Subprogram (SES), tested the hypothesis that given two regions with identical climates, geology, and topography, ecosystems that are identical in structure and function will result, despite differences in the initial floras and faunas, provided there has been sufficient time for natural selection to have produced convergence.

The project was based on the study of ecosystems represented in both the Northern and Southern hemispheres: warm deserts and Mediterranean climate ecosystems were the two selected for intensive investigation.

This book is the general summary of the design and results of the Desert Scrub Project of the Structure of Ecosystems Subprogram. Only enough of the factual details are presented to give substance to the general arguments and interpretations. The complete data are being (and will be) published as research contributions in the standard ecological literature. Since this book is a synthesis, it has been organized not as a series of individually authored papers but as a logical sequence of topics to which varying numbers of investigators have contributed data and ideas. Those investigators who have contributed significantly to a particular chapter are listed alphabetically at the beginning of that chapter after the person who served as chapter coordinator. A complete list of project members is given in Appendix T of the book.

The rationale for our approach, the kinds of questions we have posed, and how the data obtained from our work are different from and complementary to other types of biome studies are outlined in Chapter 1. Since we have treated the physical environment as the key independent variable, Chapter 2 is devoted to an analysis of the current climates and physical settings of the two study areas together with a review of their respective geological histories. This chapter indicates the degree to which we were able to match the two sites and the lengths of time desert-adapted organisms have had to converge in the two areas.

Detection of convergence requires that the floras and faunas of the two sites have reasonably independent evolutionary histories. Within a single planet this condition cannot, of course, be met perfectly, but in Chapter 3, where we analyze the two biotas from the point of view of their evolutionary histories, we show that whereas problems are raised by taxonomic similarities of the biotas, nevertheless there are sufficient differences to permit the detection of convergence if it really has occurred.

Plants are structurally and behaviorally simpler than most animals, and, in addition, they are powerfully and directly influenced by the physical environment. The extent of convergence among the morphological and physiological traits of individual species, the number of convergent species pairs, and similarities in resultant community level patterns in the plant communities are analyzed in Chapter 4. A similar analysis for the major groups of animals studied in our project (mammals, birds, reptiles, amphibians, spiders, solpugids, scorpions, grasshoppers, and ants) is presented in Chapter 5.

In addition to examining specific taxa, we paid particular attention to several resource exploitation systems. These studies were focused around three of the potential food resources produced by photosynthetic plants, namely leaves, seeds, and floral rewards (pollen and nectar). Similarities and dissimilarities in these systems in the two deserts are analyzed in Chapter 6.

Finally, in Chapter 7 we summarize our overall results and assess the degree of convergence found among organisms and groups of organisms in the two deserts, attempt to explain the patterns of convergence and nonconvergence, and indicate what we believe to be the major problems and prospects for this kind of evolutionary ecological research.

The entire book has been integrated so that later chapters build on the ideas and data presented in earlier ones. Thus, the book is intended to be read in its entirety, and the reader will find it difficult to begin reading in the middle without having to refer repeatedly back to previously presented information. Short of this we felt that a truly synthetic integrated treatment of our results could not be achieved.

The Desert Scrub Project was a joint venture between Argentine and United States investigators, supported by their respective governments. We acknowledge the financial assistance of the Consejo de Investigaciones Cientificas of Argentina and the National Science Foundation of the United States. We particularly acknowledge the assistance of Drs. Juan Hunziker, Carlos Naranjo, and Ramón Palacios of the University of Buenos Aires, Dr. Jorge Abalos, Mr. Ismael di Tada of the University of Córdoba, and of Drs. Peter Seeligman, Federico Vervoorst, and Abraham Willink of the University of Tucumán, who assisted us in procuring equipment and handling matters in Argentina. Through the courtesy of Drs. Charles Lowe and Tien Wei Yang, laboratory space was made available at the University of Arizona in Tucson. The unfailing hospitality of Dr. and Mrs. Juan Hunziker and Mr. and Mrs. J. P. Alcock of Buenos Aires helped many bewildered Norteamericanos through their first days in Argentina.

Karen Velmure, Dean Rocky Barrick, Peggy Fiedler, and Fred Likens executed the drawings and figures which add so much to the quality of the book. The entire manuscript was reviewed by David W. Goodall, Eric R. Pianka, and Robert H. Whittaker, all of whom made many valuable suggestions for improvements. The editors also wish to thank the many contributors for enduring our manipulations of their ideas and prose into a coherent volume, and the John Simon Guggenheim Foundation for providing time to execute our editorial functions.

Gordon H. Orians
Otto T. Solbrig

CONTENTS

LIST OF
CONTRIBUTORS

Harry P. Bailey
University of California, Riverside

Michael A. Barbour
University of California, Davis

W. Frank Blair
University of Texas, Austin

Rex G. Cates
University of New Mexico

John Cross
University of Arizona

Frank A. Enders
University of Texas, Austin

Guillermo Goldstein
Universidad de Buenos Aires

David Greegor
University of Arizona

Arthur C. Hulse
Indiana University of Pennsylvania

James H. Hunt
University of Missouri, St. Louis

Charles H. Lowe
University of Arizona

Michael A. Mares
University of Pittsburgh

Andrew Moldenke
University of California, Santa Cruz

Jorge Morello
Universidad de Buenos Aires

Jack Neff
University of California, Santa Cruz

Gordon H. Orians
University of Washington

Daniel Otte
Philadelphia Academy of Science

David F. Rhoades
University of Washington

Michael L. Rosenzweig
University of Arizona

Richard D. Sage
University of California, Berkeley

John C. Schultz
Dartmouth College

Beryl B. Simpson
Smithsonian Institution

Otto T. Solbrig
  Harvard University

Carl S. Tomoff
  Prescott College

Federico Vervoorst
  Universidad de Tucumán

Tien W. Yang
  University of Arizona

CONVERGENT EVOLUTION
IN WARM DESERTS

Chapter 1:
An Evolutionary Approach To Ecosystems

·G.H. Orians, O.T. Solbrig

As European biologists explored the world during the nineteenth century, they discovered that structurally similar vegetations were found in regions with similar climates even though the plants were members of distantly related families (Grisebach, 1845; Humboldt, 1849). The striking convergences were explained as the adaptations of plants to the constraints imposed by the physical environments in the areas (Schimper, 1903). Nearly all current ecology texts have paired maps of world climates and vegetations and, at the level of plant life forms, the descriptive aspects of convergence have been well documented. Surprisingly, however, these "natural experiments" in community evolution were not extensively exploited by animal ecologists to obtain information about patterns of animal community evolution, nor did plant ecologists carry their studies much further than relating general aspects of plant growth forms to climatic conditions. More or less independently-evolved communities in regions with similar climates, but isolated from one another by great expanses of different physical environments that impose barriers to the dispersal of plants and animals, provide unique opportunities to develop and test a variety of theories about the evolution of adaptations and the resultant patterns of community organization. The major objectives of the Structure of Ecosystems Subprogram have been (1) to document in some detail the extent of convergence in a number of aspects of community structure in regions with similar climates and physical environments and (2) to develop and test predictive models of where convergence is to be expected and why.

The length of time required for the evolution of community structure imposes severe restrictions on the ways in which answers can be obtained to the key questions ecologists wish to ask. With rare exceptions it is not possible to perturb the environment and to measure meaningful evolutionary responses within a period of the creative activity of a single individual, not to mention the probable length of support of any reseach projects by funding agencies. There is ample experience with the effects of introducing species into ecosystems where they have not previously occurred to know that the short-term results are often quite different from those obtained over a longer period. The immediate results of such experiments may provide valuable insights into the nature and strength of present-day interactions in the community, but they tell us little about what to expect over time spans sufficient to allow for evolutionary changes in the component species.

Therefore, studies of ecosystem evolution rely on a number of indirect approaches which take advantage of the "natural experiments" (Cody, 1974) provided by evolutionary processes in different parts of the earth. The hypotheses tested are of the general form "if natural selection had acted in a given manner for a long period of time, then nature should have a given set of characteristics." This type of hypothesis ideally predicts processes of natural selection precisely enough that the appropriate ecosystems for study and the aspects of their components that are most important for testing are clearly specified. G. G. Simpson (1949) suggested that this approach be designated "postdiction" since we are not "predicting" something that will happen in the future but are attempting to decipher events of the past leading to present results.

In our project the physical environment has been treated as the independent variable determining evolutionary processes while the biological interactions are regarded as the dependent variable. The separation of dependent and independent variables is necessary if we are to understand why a system of coevolved species has arrived at one state as opposed to others. The requirement of an independent variable is that it not be affected by feedback from the factors upon which it is acting. In general, the physical environment has this characteristic though there are some exceptions, especially if human activities are considered. Nearly all biological interactions, however, involve strong feedback, and therefore we treat the biotic environment, acting through competition and predation, as the dependent variable. The general hypothesis we are testing is that the properties of communities of plants and animals are ultimately determined by the physical environment provided that there has been sufficient time for the arrival and subsequent evolution of the species in the system. Though the null hypothesis is that initial characteristics of organisms are erased by time, we do not necessarily expect convergence in all details of community structure, and a critical component of the development of theory is to predict those features that will converge and those that will retain the stamp of history no matter how much time has been available for evolution.

The general design of our study has been to select ecosystems that have evolved independently in areas with similar climates and physical environments. The similarity of the physical environments forms the basis for hypotheses about convergences. The independence of the evolutionary histories of biotas permits convergence to be distinguished from parallelism from a common ancestry. In practice a perfect experimental design is impossible because no two sites on the earth are identical in geology, topography, and climate, and no two regions of the earth have been totally isolated evolutionarily. Nevertheless, it is possible to choose study sites in regions that have had relatively little floral and faunal interchange for long time periods.

The choice of sites, however, does not more than provide a place where ideas can be tested. By itself, this process contains no insights nor does it suggest methods. The formulation of hypotheses has been the most critical aspect of this project and our successes and failures have depended in large part on the wisdom and imagination we have employed in their formulation. This depends on general understanding of the theory of natural selection, plus detailed knowledge of the organisms and processes for which detailed models are proposed.

The fundamental process of natural selection is perceived to be very similar to that proposed by Darwin over one hundred years ago. Darwin's version of the theory was purely phenotypic, and he only assumed that the traits he was studying had some heritability. During recent decades a genetical theory of natural selection, which assigns fitnesses to alleles rather than to phenotypes, has also been developed (Fisher, 1958). This version of the theory gains precision in its treatment of inheritance, because genes very accurately determine their progeny, but it loses precision in measuring fitness (which is a property of the phenotype and not the genotype) because genes do not uniquely determine phenotypes. On the other hand, the phenotypic version of the theory is capable of more precision in measuring fitness but loses precision with respect to actual changes in gene frequencies (MacArthur and Connell, 1966). Which of these two versions is more desirable depends upon the goals of the investigation and the extent of knowledge. For most eco-logical traits, information about their inheritance is meager or nonexistent, and for this reason ecologists usually employ phenotypic versions of the theory of natural selection. This is the approach we have, of necessity, used in the present study.

The theory of natural selection as developed by Darwin and subsequently refined by a variety of population biologists is based on the differential fit-ness of individual phenotypes (or genotypes). As first pointed out by R. A. Fisher (1958) the question of the "good of the species" or the "good of the community" has no meaning in terms of the mechanisms now known to be operative though this does not preclude the discovery of presently unknown mechanisms. This problem has been reviewed more recently by Alexander (1974), J. L. Brown (1966), Lewontin (1970), Maynard Smith (1965), and Williams (1966).

These features in the theory of natural selection set the boundaries to the kinds of models we have designed and tested. Most of them are in the class of optimality models (Rosen, 1967; Levins, 1968) in which we attempt to guess what natural selection has actually optimized. The hypotheses have to be stated in a form which leads to "postdictions" about some structures or processes in nature which are open to verification or falsification in the study areas. Failures to obtain confirmation may lead to the rejection or modifica-tion of the original hypotheses and improved insights about evolutionary processes. An hypothesis may be very specific in its focus, such as explaining the adaptive significance of the shapes of leaves, or the role of some specific chemical in anti-herbivore interactions, or it may be more general, dealing with resource acquisition over a life span or means of surviving fluctuations in weather of long periodicity. Normally the narrower the focus of the model the greater is its precision but the less applicable the results are to other evo-lutionary processes.

While employing this approach to ecosystem studies it is vital to distin-guish clearly between strategies and patterns. By *strategies* we mean charac-teristics of individual organisms that are directly determined by natural selection, that is the traits we attempt to predict. By *patterns* we mean characteristics of aggregates of organisms that are the indirect result of natural selection. For example, individual plants may have evolved to maximize the amount of photosynthesis they can carry out per unit of ground space occupied under prevailing conditions of moisture, temperature, light, and nutrients (Horn, 1971). The morphological traits that give this result at the level of individual plants can be predicted and tested. On the other hand, the gross primary productivity of a community of plants is the *result* of the performances of individual plants that are the actual survivors in the community. The only known mechanism by which gross primary productivity could be maximized is group selection, and we therefore treat this community characteristic as a pattern. Our approach, then, is to test a number of individual strategies and from them to attempt to understand patterns at a number of different levels of community organization.

This focus requires different studies than those carried out by investigators directly concerned with, say, patterns of community productivity. In the latter types of studies a compartment model of an ecosystem is developed in which organisms with similar properties with respect to energy utilization are grouped together. Field work is directed toward measurement of flows of energy into and out of each of the compartments, while the modeling efforts are directed toward predicting changes in the flow rates as environmental parameters change. Grouping of organisms is made necessary by the great complexity of most ecosystems, the impossibility of gathering sufficient data for a more detailed analysis, and the real limits of our computational skills in handling and interpreting more complex systems. In these models the properties of the organisms in the different compartments are determined empirically wherever possible, and missing information is inferred on the basis of current knowledge of other organisms. The objectives of the model are to provide a picture of the proximate functioning of the system and to obtain insights about its expected responses to various perturbations, especially those that modern man is prone to impose on such systems. By its very nature, this type of study has a limited capacity to deal with the evolutionary processes which have molded the organisms in the various compartments because evolutionary theory has not been used in assigning species characteristics, nor are species properties permitted to change as a result of their interactions with one another and the external perturbations. Therefore, there is a need for parallel studies of ecosystem processes employing different techniques and asking different types of questions. We believe that our studies will complement the energy-flow models that have dominated ecosystem research for the past two decades.

SELECTION OF STUDY SYSTEMS AND SITES

The most obvious ecosystems for comparative study are those situated in comparable temperate climatic belts in the Northern and Southern hemispheres, separated by broad expanses of tropical and subtropical habitats.

North and South America were separated from one another for most of their geological histories, and the recent land bridges between the two continents have not been favorable for the passage of many arid zone types of organisms. The two continents therefore offer suitable systems for comparative study within the restrictions imposed by the National Science Foundation that the northern study sites must lie within the boundaries of the United States.

The climatic regimes that could be compared between temperate South and North America include cool, temperate maritime (temperate rain forests), Mediterranean climates (chaparral), hot deserts, cool deserts, and grasslands. The selection of Mediterranean and hot desert systems as the focus of two parallel studies was determined by the interests of investigators who were influential in starting the projects. Results of the Mediterranean study of chaparral systems in California and Chile are being published separately. Here we summarize the major results of comparative studies in the hot desert climates of Arizona and northwest Argentina. Details of the many separate investigations will appear as research contributions in appropriate journals and in two companion volumes dealing with a dominant shrub (*Larrea*) of the desert flats (Mabry, Hunziker, and DiFeo, 1977) and a dominant tree (*Prosopis*) of desert washes (Simpson, 1977).

When the project was designed it was already known that the vegetation of the two areas was similar at the level of general plant life forms. We did not know, however, the extent of convergence at other trophic levels in the communities or at finer levels of adaptations and interactions among component plants. Thus, the level of our knowledge was sufficient to indicate that some convergence had occurred but insufficient to bias formulation of hypotheses with respect to most features of the communities.

The two ecosystems we studied are generally known as the Sonoran Desert in North America (Shreve, 1951) and the Monte in Argentina (Morello, 1958), and these two terms will be employed throughout this book to refer to the general vegetation types. Their geographical distributions are shown in Figure 1-1. Extensive descriptions of the flora and vegetation of the two regions are given in Shreve and Wiggins (1964) and Morello (1958). The Sonoran Desert occupies an extensive area in southwestern United States and adjacent Mexico within which the climate changes from predominately winter rains in the west to predominately summer rains in the southeast. To the south the vegetation gradually grades into the thorn scrub of Mexico, while to the north it abuts temperate dry woodland and cold semidesert scrubland.

The Monte of Argentina is oriented as a relatively narrow north-south belt along the eastern base of the Andes Mountains. To the south it broadens and extends to the Atlantic Coast in the provinces of Rio Negro and Chubut, while to the north it narrows and is confined to valleys among the Andean foothills and front ranges. Adjacent vegetation ranges from the cool Patagonian deserts in the south to the dry Chaco and "espinal" vegetation to the east and the cold "Puna" highlands to the north (Cabrera, 1956, 1971). Topographic conditions are such that vegetation gradients are more pronounced to the west where the mountains may rise sharply to heights in excess of 6,000 meters. To the east climatic gradients are gradual except in the northern part of the Monte where high mountains of the Sierras Pampeanas form the east-

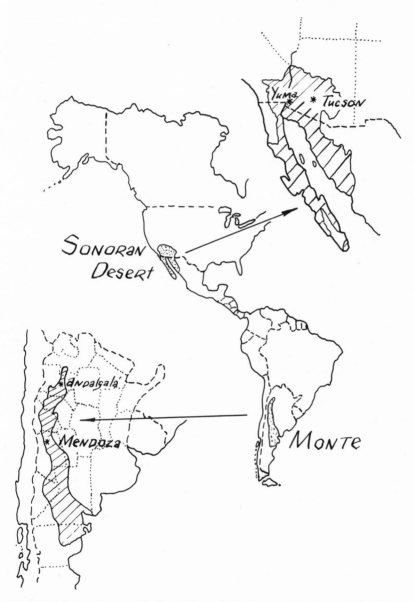

FIGURE 1-1. *Geographical position of the Sonoran Desert and the Monte and of the cities of Tucson, Yuma, Andalgalá, and Mendoza.*

ern boundary and block the flow of moist air from the Atlantic and causing the northward extension of the Monte observed today.

Our initial problem was to obtain the best possible match of the physical environments within these two extensive vegetation types. Exact replication was impossible for two fundamental reasons. First, the small land mass of temperate South America results in a more maritime climate, and all suitable study sites had lesser seasonal fluctuations in temperature than potential sites in Arizona. Second, the Andes are much higher and unbroken than the coastal mountains to the west of the Sonoran Desert in North America, and they more effectively block the eastward movement of Pacific storm systems. Therefore, sites with a total annual precipitation matching the Arizona sites lie at lower latitudes in Argentina and are characterized by receiving most of their rain during the summer. To find sites receiving a significant winter precipitation, it is necessary to go as far south as southern Mendoza province where the total precipitation is lower than in Arizona and where the climate is considerably colder (Capitanelli, 1972).

The presence of the University of Arizona at Tucson and the Desert Biome study site in the Avra Valley made a primary study site in that area the preferred choice in the United States. Accordingly, the climate and topography of the Tucson area were matched with those of an analogous site in the Monte. A decision was made to choose two sites with similar total rainfall and temperature since the rainfall pattern of the Tucson area could not be matched exactly at any of the Argentine sites for which weather records existed.

Argentine Study Area

The general study area for most of the work in Argentina was the Bolsón de Pipanaco, a large basin about 120 km long and 100 km wide, surrounded by high mountains in the Province of Catamarca (Figure 2-1). A map of part of the Bolsón showing the principal study sites is given in Figure 1-2. The primary study transect, designated Joyango, is indicated by 7. The other study sites, used by one or more of the investigators in the project, will be

FIGURE 1-2. *Bolsón de Pipanaco with major sites mentioned in the text. Numbers correspond to the phenological locations mentioned in Table 4-6 (1) Site on the road to Belen where phenological observations were conducted; (2) Site on Rio Amanao where a large number of studies on phenology, pollination, rodent behavior, and plant-insect interactions were conducted; (3) Villavil, site of phenological and plant-insect interaction studies; (4) Site near Cuesta de la Chilca where phenological and cactus studies were undertaken; (5) Km. 6, (6) Km. 34, (8) Km. 66 and (9) Km. 96 of the road to Mazan, where phenological observations were conducted; (7) Site 9, main transect, near Joyango.*

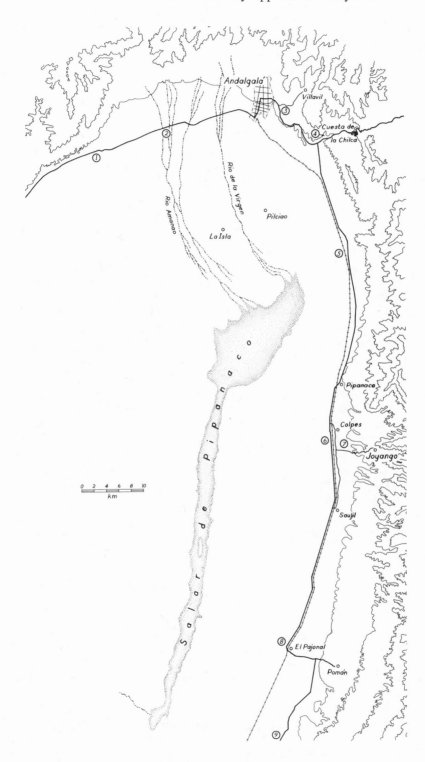

consistently referred to by the designations given in the caption to Figure 1-2.

The Bolsón de Pipanaco has been occupied by Europeans continuously since 1572 when the Adelantado Gerónimo Luis de Cabrera passed through it on his way to founding the city of Córdoba. Prior to that there were an indeterminate number of Indian settlements of tribes belonging to the Diaguita culture, which had developed an irrigation agriculture (Rex Gonzalez, pers. comm. 1970). The Spanish conquistadores at first utilized the Indians in agriculture as field laborers and also introduced goats and sheep. The Indian populations, however, slowly decreased in size, and agriculture in the valley retreated to the mouths of the streams where it persists today.

During the period of independence, the valley played an important role in the many revolts and civil wars that plagued northwestern Argentina, especially the revolts of the Chacho and Varela. After the Argentine Republic was reorganized in 1861, Pipanaco and neighboring areas did not accept the new constitution and civil war raged for another four years.

The greatest period of activity for the Bolsón de Pipanaco came with the opening of a copper mine at Capillitas in the mountains at the northwestern end of the Bolsón, about 1870. Copper ore was brought down from the mountain, first by mule and later by aerial conveyer, and processed in primitive smelters located in the *Prosopis* forest on the valley floor. With the abandonment of the mine about 1920, the area declined economically. When the major railroad network of Argentina was laid in the 1890s, the Bolsón de Pipanaco was bypassed. This, and the shift of the center of economic gravity of the country from the northwest to Buenos Aires (a process slowly taking place for three hundred years but accelerating in the last one hundred and fifty years) further contributed to the economic problems of the area.

Today some fruticulture (grapes, quince, walnuts) in isolated pockets, subsistence goat herding, and limited tourism constitute the principal economic activities. The total population of the valley does not exceed 25,000, and much of the area is free of human disturbance or is barely affected. However, at one time or another, much of the Bolsón was more heavily disturbed. Chemical and industrial pollution is at a minimum, and so is the network of roads.

Arizona Study Area

Field work in Arizona was concentrated in the Avra Valley, roughly 50 kilometers west-northwest of Tucson. The primary study site (Silver Bell Bajada) and secondary sites are indicated in Figure 1-3. Some work was also done at the Saguaro National Monument East, at the foot of the Santa Catalina Mountains.

The Avra Valley was not settled by Europeans until after the Civil War, one hundred years ago. Prior to that the Papago and Pima Indians occupied

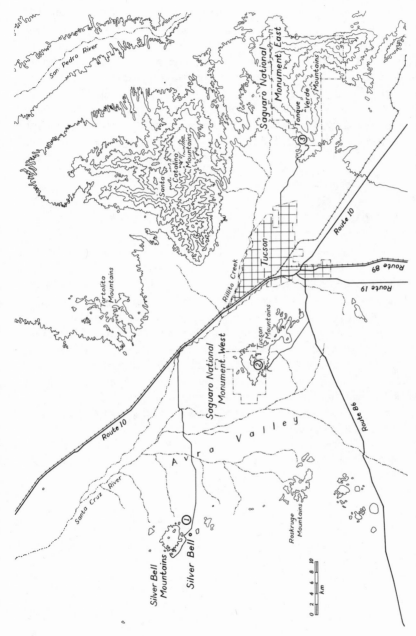

FIGURE 1-3. *Avra Valley and Tucson area with major geographical sites mentioned in text. (1) Site of main transect; (2) Site of phenology locations 5–9; (3) Site of phenology locations 1–4.*

11

the area. Their main settlements were along rivers, especially the Gila, north of our study area. When the region was settled by Europeans, activity was much more intense than at the Argentine site. The middle of the nineteenth century saw the introduction of cattle and a cattle boom which extensively damaged the natural vegetation by overgrazing. Rivers in the area were dammed, further affecting vegetation downstream. The final development was the digging of deep wells and pump irrigation for cotton culture. Mining, particularly for copper, is intensively pursued in southwestern Arizona, including the Avra Valley. The city of Tucson, with about one-half million inhabitants, attracts thousands of tourists annually. An extensive network of roads covers the area. Agriculture is intensive with high use of fertilizers and pesticides. Consequently, air pollution is a serious problem in the area, contrasting strongly with the pristine air in the Bolsón de Pipanaco.

CONCLUSIONS

The hot desert systems of North and South America partially fulfill the general requirements of the research design of the project. They are areas of similar climate and topography and, as will be documented in the following chapter, desert climates have been present in the two areas for long periods of time. Nevertheless, our failure to match physical environments exactly confronts us with continuing interpretational problems. If we fail to find convergence, should we regard the theory as faulty, or do we ascribe the failures to the differences in the physical environment? There is no simple answer to this dilemma, but we can reduce the confusion by specifying as completely as possible the real differences between our major study sites and incorporating these differences into the predictions we make about the evolved traits of the organisms. Therefore, we now turn to a detailed analysis of the geological histories and contemporary physiographic settings of the Bolsón de Pipanaco and the Avra Valley and an analysis of available climatic data to indicate as precisely as possible the similarities and differences.

Chapter 2:
The Physical Environment:
The Independent Variable

· H. P. Bailey, B. B. Simpson, F. Vervoorst

General summaries of the intracontinental geological history of North and South America from Cambrian times to the present can be found in Clark and Stearn (1968) and Harrington (1962). An integration of these résumés with the review of Dietz and Holden (1970) on continental drift provides a picture of the positions of the land masses over the last 600 million years while such internal changes were proceeding. Unlike the situation for most of the continents of the world, the end of the Cretaceous and the beginning of the Tertiary heralded the approach, rather than the separation, of these two continental plates and marked the beginnings of what was to become a physical connection between them. In addition, the Cenozoic was the period during which the modern size, shape, and topography of the land masses developed and most of the extant plant and animal life either arose or underwent most of its diversification. Our emphasis will therefore be on the major paleogeographical developments that occurred after the end of the Mesozoic.

Because of their roughly equivalent positions north and south of the equator, many of the changes in the climate and topography of the two continents during the Tertiary more or less paralleled one another. Both plant and animal fossils indicate that at the end of the Cretaceous, North and South America were warm, relatively mesic, without much climatic zonation, and predominantly covered by humid tropical and temperate forests (Barghoorn, 1951; Schwartzbach, 1963). As the oceans cooled from the Eocene onward (Durham, 1950) and the circulation became more zonal, both continents developed a climatic gradient from the pole toward the equator. In North America, the cooling and drying of the land and the development of the tundra, temperate, and subtropical environments has been summarized by Chaney (1940), Axelrod (1950, 1956), and Gray (1964). In South America, the reviews of the paleobotanical evidence by Gerth (1941) and Just (1952) show how the mesic forests that covered the southern part of the continent in the lower Tertiary became progressively restricted to southeastern Brazil, the eastern slopes of the central Andes, and southern Chile. The central, extra-tropical area of Argentina appears to have been an open, perhaps savanna-like, habitat by the mid-Tertiary (Solbrig, 1976). It is possible, however, that earlier in the Cenozoic, areas of eastern Brazil, particularly those formerly connected with, or close to, Africa, had been semiarid for some time. Although neither eastern Brazil nor Patagonia ever became truly arid, they both served as sources of dry-adapted species for the very arid areas that developed later in central South America.

From the Miocene until recent times, the climate changed rapidly on a global scale. There is evidence of ice formation as early as the Miocene in Antarctica (Flint, 1971) and numerous evidences of glaciations beginning in Pliocene times (Turekian, 1971). The continued cooling of the oceans led to an intensification of the atmospheric pressure system and a corresponding accentuation of mid-latitude aridity. Although initiated in the Cretaceous, the principal Andean geosyncline experienced its greatest movements in the Miocene, followed by various periods of uplifts in localized areas along the western edges of the two continents. These orogenies, varying somewhat in time and magnitude, had the effect of producing rainshadows that augmented the dryness due to the changing circulatory systems in the western parts of North and South America.

At the same time that such parallel changes in topography and climate were occurring, North and South America became first semi-connected and finally completely joined. By the Miocene, Central America was a series of islands stretching between the two continents (Haffer, 1970). Numerous species of animals (and undoubtedly plants) were able to colonize from north to south or vice versa early in the Tertiary by successively hopping from one island to another (G. G. Simpson, 1950; Patterson and Pascual, 1968, 1972).

In the late Pliocene, the remaining submerged portions of Central America were raised and the Panamanian portal closed (Haffer, 1970). Not only were North and South America finally connected, but the main continental land masses were closer to one another than they had ever been in their geological histories. Both paleontological and paleobotanical data reflect the sudden presence of the direct link between the two continents. Swarms of animal taxa formerly found only in North America suddenly appear in the South American fossil record (G. G. Simpson, 1950; Patterson and Pascual, 1968). Several taxa of plants such as *Quercus, Alnus,* and *Juglans* also moved into South America at the end of the Tertiary (Graham, 1973; van der Hammen, 1972).

The Pleistocene ice ages, which affected both continents, seem to have been in phase in the Northern and Southern Hemispheres (Heusser, 1961; van der Hammen, 1972). However, because of the differences in the extent of their surface areas lying within temperate latitude, they were affected somewhat differently by glacial periods. The most important glacial features of North America were the enormous ice sheets covering the northern half of the continent and the tongue of the continental glacier that projected

FIGURE 2-1. *View of the Bolsón de Pipanaco from the Cuesta de Joyango. The white strip in the distance is the Salar de Pipanaco.*

down the Mississippi Valley practically to the Gulf of Mexico (Flint, 1971). In South America, glacial ice was mostly restricted to mountain regions. The primary expression of the Pleistocene climatic changes on the southern continent seems to have been an alternation of humid and arid cycles which affected large areas of Perú, Brazil, Uruguay, Paraguay, and northern Argentina (Vuilleumier, 1971).

All of the large-scale events played a role, some small, some great, in the development of the areas in which the desert scrub study sites are located and should be kept in mind when assessing the local geological history and the significance of the similarities or differences in physiography.

PHYSIOGRAPHIC SETTINGS OF THE STUDY AREAS*

Bolsón de Pipanaco

The South American study site is in the Bolsón de Pipanaco, a large valley in the Province of Catamarca, northwestern Argentina (Figure 2-1). The valley, which physiographically belongs to the Sierras Pampeanas Formation (Caminos, 1972), is about 120 km long by 100 km wide and is almost entirely encircled by high mountain ranges (Figure 2-2). The actual study areas were near the town of Andalgalá at 27.33°S, 66.18°W.

Starting northwest of Andalgalá and proceeding clockwise on Figure 2-2, the mountain ranges are the Sierras de Atajo, Santa Barbara, Capillitas (3,700 m), the Nevados de Aconquija (5,450 m), the Sierra de Ambato (4,515 m), the Sierra de Chazan (1,000 m), and the northern part of the Sierra de Velasco (2,500 m). On the western side of the Bolsón are the Seminaria Valley and an expanse of sand dunes, part of the Campo de Belén, that continue westward until the Sierras de Vinquis (2,800 m), de Zapata (3,000 m), and de Belén (2,180 m). Although bordering the Bolsón in a circumferential fashion, the axes of these ranges are oriented in a north-south direction.

Alluvial cones composed of detritus from the mountains form a coalesced piedmont plain from the Cuesta de Belén northwest of Andalgalá eastward and then south to Mazán. Eroded mountain slopes, a piedmont plain composed of an upper and lower bajada, and a playa are characteristic features of a bolsón. In the case of the Bolsón de Pipanaco, the playa, the bottom of the valley, is occupied by sand dunes and a salt lake (salar). The upper and lower bajadas intergrade into one another although they differ in several physical characteristics. The upper bajada is fairly steep with a grade of 2 to 8 percent and is irregular in shape. The lower bajada has a more gentle slope of about 0.6 to 2 percent. As is typical of mountain erosion

*By B. B. Simpson & F. Vervoorst.

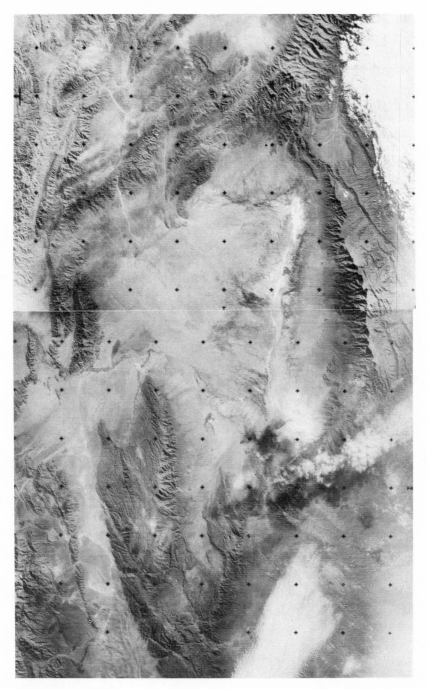

FIGURE 2-2. *Satellite photograph of the Bolsón de Pipanaco. Courtesy of NASA.*

systems, there is a sorting of material as it is washed down the slopes. Consequently, the upper bajada is primarily covered with a succession of boulders, gravel, cobbles, and coarse sand, whereas the lower slopes are composed of pebbles, coarse, medium, and fine sand grading into silt (although the last two often occur in layers). In flat areas dominated by *Larrea* the soil surface is sometimes covered by a clay-like material that resembles loess into which erosion cuts gullies similar to those of the loess of China. Almost all of the studies near Andalgalá were made in areas of upper or lower bajada (Figure 1-2).

The playa at the base of the alluvial fan system is composed primarily of sand and silt and becomes progressively more alkaline and barren as it approaches the salar. Surrounding this usually dry salt lake is a band of low sand dunes that are distinct from the high mounds of Pilciao and Constancia or the expanse of independent dunes at km 1,539 in the Campo de Belén (a secondary study site).

There have been no detailed studies on the soils themselves, but Vervoorst (1954) described some profiles in the *Prosopis* woodland that borders the salar. In this part of the Bolsón, the soils are immature and without edaphic horizons. The soil is colluvial-alluvial, composed predominantly of only slightly cohesive granular sand that can be classified as coarse (0.2 mm) to fine (0.02 mm), and rich in quartz, feldspar, and mica. At lower depths, it becomes more clayey. Evaporation at the soil surface produces a capillary ascent of water laden with salts that are subsequently deposited near or at the surface. The pH is therefore high in the playa with values above 7.5 to over 8.3.

There does not seem to be a true hardpan present in the Bolsón, but there is a layer of thick, somewhat cemented sand at about 1.5 m which appears to impede somewhat the passage of roots but does not prevent downward water movement.

The drainage system of the Bolsón is essentially interior. Rivers and washes converge into the playa from the surrounding mountains (Figure 2-2). Some of these rivers have water along the upper portions all year (i.e., the Ríos Cura, Amanao, Chaquiago, Andalgalá, Villavil, Saujil, Siján, and Pomán) and consequently support small villages where the streams exit onto the bajada. Most of the streams, however, contain water only during the rainy season. Along the western side of the Bolsón are three large rivers, the Ríos del Pasaje (formed by the joining of the Ríos de la Pampa and de la Carpenteria), de Belén, and Londres. These rivers, flowing into the Bolsón from the Campo de Belén, brought down most of the sediment now covering the playa. The salar is displaced to the eastern side of the Bolsón (Figure 1-2) due to the fact that all the major sedimentary streams flow from the west. The largest river of the entire system is the Rio Colorado (Salado) in the southwest sector coming from the Bolsón de Fiambalá. The pattern of this river indicates that it is an ancient river and that the modern course has changed from its former position.

The bottom of the salar is 400 m below the base of the mountains. Rains, heavier along the edges of the Bolsón than in the center, infiltrate the soils of the permeable upper bajadas and percolate down to the level of the water table in the salar. The depth of the subterranean water level therefore decreases toward the center of the playa. Kanter (1948) mentioned that on occasions, sweet water bubbles up into the salar. Drillings some kilometers to the west of Andalgalá reached the water table at 89 and 197 m depths. In Pilciao, the permanent water level is at 35 m, and 15 kilometers farther south in El Carrijal it is at 18 m.

The region of Argentina containing the Bolsón de Pipanaco has been a continental area since Cambrian times. The present relief, however, is due to quite recent events. The Sierras Pampeanas Formation (Caminos, 1972) is part of one of the primary South American "island" shields (Harrington, 1962) and has a Paleophytic base of crystaline material that has undergone regional metamorphic deformation. In pre-Cambrian times the area was covered by sea, but from the Cambrian to the present there are evidences of continental erosion and sedimentation with remains of a period of Triassic volcanism. These deposits indicate that the area has been predominantly dry land for over 500 million years. At the beginning of the Tertiary, the crystalline basement was transformed into a peneplain, signaling the initiation of the Andean orogeny. These early movements consisted of dislocations and uplifts that formed valleys in which coarse deposits accumulated – probably under a warm, dry climatic regime (C. Turner, 1970; Caminos, 1972). More significant movements occurred in the mid-Miocene when block faulting and tilting outlined the present-day structure of the Sierras. The fractures are oriented north-south, and the blocks tilted to both the east and the west. The great period of uplift was in the Pleistocene (Polanski, 1957; Peirano, 1957; Ruiz Huidobro, 1965; C. Turner, 1970; Caminos, 1972) when the vertical faulting brought the mountains to their present altitude. Peirano (1957) emphasizes that prior to the end of the Pliocene there were not separate bolsones in northwestern Argentina but rather one large primitive basin that was fragmented by the Pleistocene uplift of the Sierras Pampeanas. Much of the 40 to 700 m thick alluvial deposits were laid down during the Tertiary Period.

The climate of northwestern Argentina during the late Tertiary was presumably much like that of the present-day Chaco. The comparatively weak Mid-Tertiary uplift of the Sierras Pampeanas undoubtedly brought about some climatic change from early Tertiary mesic conditions by interrupting the flow of moist air into the area from the northeast. Most of the early climatic change to drier conditions was probably due, however, to the same factors, the cooling of the oceans and the increased zonation of climate, that caused continents throughout the world to become more arid at this time. The region became truly xerophytic, however, only after the Sierras Pampeanas were finally uplifted in the last Plio-Pleistocene stage.

Few direct evidences of Pleistocene climatic change have been found in the Sierras Pampeanas per se, but traces of glaciation have been located in the altiplano to the north, the Transpampean Sierras to the west and on higher peaks further south. Estimates of the number of effective glacial episodes vary from one to four (Vuilleumier, 1971). At least one glacial period with several stages and probably at least two glaciations left traces in this area. On the mountains surrounding the Bolsón de Pipanaco, only the Nevados del Aconquija and the Sierra de Ambato were glaciated. In the latter, there are vestiges of glaciers on the summits between Cerro Manchas and Portezuelo de Joyango, both of which are within 100 km of Andalgalá. In ranges with more significant glaciation, such as the Aconquija and Famatina, snowline was lowered from 5,200 m to 3,800 m and from 5,700 m to 5,200 m respectively. Although varying from range to range and from east to west, the snowline was lowered about 1,000 m on the average. Using the standard formula (Flint, 1971) of 0.6° C for each 100 m that snowline is lowered, we can estimate that there was a maximum temperature depression of 6° C. Kessler (1963) estimated 6° C depression for Bolivia and Polanski (1957) postulated a 3.6-4.2° C annual depression for Mendoza, Argentina. A conservative estimate for the area near Andalgalá might therefore be between 4° and 5° C mean annual depression.

Glacial periods appear to have been also times of lake formation in central and southern Argentina. Tapia (1935) reconstructed the extension of lakes in northern Argentina by extrapolating from known lacustrine deposits. According to this reconstruction, all of the low lying areas of the Bolsón de Pipanaco would have been covered by the northwest arm of a lake that reached from the Atlantic Ocean up the Paraguay-Paraná rivers, across both the Salinas Grande of Córdoba and the Salina Antigua, through the Bolsón de Pipanaco up to the Bolsón de Fiambalá. Another large inland lake formed at the same time farther south along the eastern side of the Andes in the provinces of San Juan, San Luis, and Mendoza (Vuilleumier, 1971). The extent and position of these lakes must have had a wide-reaching effect on the biota of central and northern Argentina during glacial periods.

At the end of glacial periods, glacial meltwaters scoured away much of the earlier Tertiary deposits from the valley floors and incised deep channels at the base of mountains and on the valley floor.

Avra Valley and Adjacent Areas

The region of the North American study sites, near Silver Bell, Arizona (Figure 1-3; Figure 2-3, Table 2-1) (32.43°N, 31.0°W), is both physiographically and geologically a part of the Basin and Range Province (Fenneman, 1931). The Province has a relief of more or less parallel mountain ranges separated by broad basins of alluvial fill, and extends from the Colorado

FIGURE 2-3. *View of the Avra Valley from the Tucson Mountains.*

plateau west to the Sierra Nevada and south into Mexico. Climatically and vegetationally, the Province encompasses the Great Basin, the Mojave, and the Sonoran deserts as well as the Mexican Highlands. Silver Bell is in the southwestern portion of the physiographic unit and is in the northeastern part of the Sonoran Desert (Figure 2-4).

The Silver Bell Bajada, extending about 32 km southeastward from the Silver Bell Mountains is loosely surrounded by mountain ranges (Figure 2-4), but only the Santa Catalina Mountains reach significantly high altitudes. Clockwise from the Silver Bell Mountains (1,298 m) are the Tortolita Mountains, the Santa Catalina Mountains (2,799 m) and the Tucson Mountains (1,427 m). To the east are the Rincon Mountains (2,683 m), in the far south the Santa Rita Mountains (2,874 m), and along the western edge the Sierrita, Dobb's Buttes, and Coyote Mountains. None of the ranges within 60 km exceeds 1,500 m. Silver Bell Bajada is a basin, not a bolsón like that of Pipanaco because it has a drainage that eventually reaches the sea *via* the Santa Cruz, Gila, and Colorado rivers. Because of the external drainage, water does not accumulate in the central portion of the area, but runs off toward the Santa Cruz River and ultimately out of the valley. Drillings near Tucson have indicated that the water table was (in 1908) at 13 m in the base of the bajada (MacDougal, 1908). The slopes of the bajada are gentle and range from 2° to 4.5° in the lower bajada to 7° on the upper bajada. The alluvium derived primarily from the Silver Bell Mountains consists of granitic and basaltic rock reaching a depth of 150-540 m near Tucson (Fenneman, 1931). The upper bajadas (including pediments) have coarse grained soils (see Chapter 4) of large stones, coarse sand, and clay. On the lower bajadas, the soil is loam, often with coarse gravel on the surface. The soils of the flats are well developed, show profiles with distinct horizons (Anonymous, 1964), and consequently appear to have been developing over a long period of time. In most of the Sonoran region, there is a calcareous cemented layer (caliche) under-

TABLE 2-1 *Physiography, Geology, and Climate of the Monte and Sonoran Deserts and the Study Sites*

	Sonoran Desert	Monte
Latitudinal extent	22.8°–35.2° N*	24.5°–44.3° S†
Longitudinal extent	109.5°–117° W*	62.9°–69.8° W†
Range of altitudes	0–1050 m	0–5400 m
Range of mean minimum temperatures	1.5–16.5° C (Jan.)*	0.2°–7.5° C
Range of mean maximum temperatures	30–41° C (July)*	16.9°–22.5° C†
Range of mean annual precipitation		
Time of complete land emergence	Cretaceous	Cambrian
First traces of drying	Eocene	Cretaceous
Final formation of arid environment	Plio-Pleistocene	Plio-Pleistocene
Pleistocene effects		
Glaciers within boundaries	No	Yes
Increase in humidity	Yes	Yes
Temperature decrease ca. 3°–6° C	Yes	Yes
Glacial lakes greater than 100 km² within boundary	No	Yes

	Avra Valley	Bolsón de Pipanaco
Latitude	32.4° N	27.3° S
Longitude	61.0° W	66.2° W
Altitude	ca. 580 m	ca. 780 m
Mean annual temperature	19.5° C	18.6° C
Effects of Pleistocene		
Inferred temperature depression	ca. 3° C	less than 5° C
Hydrology	Increased rivers, outwash crossing bajada	Standing large lake covering bolson bottom
Distance to nearest glacial ice	ca. 320 km	less than 100 km
Time since return of arid conditions	ca. 10,000 yrs	ca. 10,000 yrs

*Data from Shreve (1964), p. 19.
†Date from Morello (1958).

lying the surface layers that impedes water infiltration. At a lower depth of about 1-3 m, there is a band of soft soil with stones.

The area which includes the Silver Bell Bajada has a basement of pre-Cambrian granites and schists like the Bolsón de Pipanaco, but deposits indicate that it was basically a continental shelf from Cambrian times to the end of the Mesozoic (E. C. Wilson, 1962). The pattern of shifting marine and fresh water deposits are present up through the Triassic-Jurassic eras when regional movements, uplifts, and faulting began (Wilson and Moore, 1959). About 50 million years ago, in the Cretaceous, the entire region was folded, faulted, and finally raised above sea level. These movements, continu-

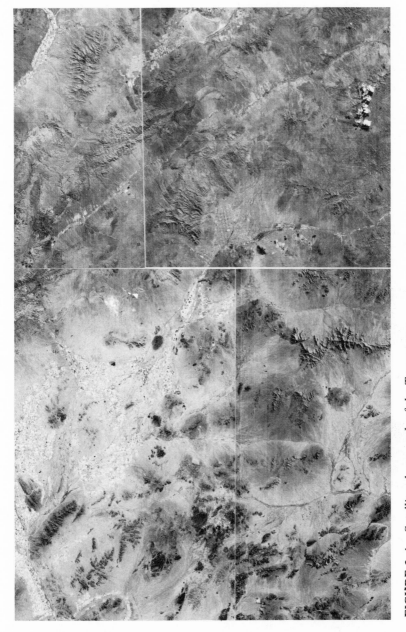

FIGURE 2-4. *Satellite photograph of the Tucson area.*

23

ing until the Miocene, formed local mountain ranges and basins, the features of which were destroyed by later Tertiary erosion (Heindl, 1959). However, the early Cenozoic orogenies did determine the basic north-northwest orientation of the ranges (Wilson and Moore, 1959). From the Miocene to the Pliocene, a rash of volcanism broke out and, combined with substantial high angled faulting formed the backbone of the present topography (Heindl, 1959). Throughout the latter part of the Tertiary, continual erosion accompanied the warping. It is estimated that two-thirds of the original mountain masses were eaten away during this period and now form the thick beds of alluvium on the valley floors. Apparently, no Pleistocene events scoured away these Tertiary deposits.

In surrounding areas also, the Cenozoic was a time of uplift. The Cordillera to the west was outlined and developed. The drying of the American southwest brought about by a combination of the Tertiary cooling of the oceans and the increasing rainshadow effect of the Sierra Nevada brought about by this uplift is well documented by changing paleofloras of the region. Axelrod (1950) has summarized the data from these fossils. They show a progressive change from uniform Cretaceous floras of mild, constantly temperate environments to Miocene floras differentiated into an Arcto-Tertiary flora and a Madro-Tertiary flora (see Chapter 3) to the final development of the modern Sonoran flora in the Pliocene. This final evolution of true desert biotas followed only after the last late Tertiary uplift of the Sierras and the concomitant production of a very strong rainshadow (Axelrod, 1957).

The Pleistocene glacial episodes affected the desert areas although actual glaciation never reached southern Arizona. The nearest glacial ice was over 320 km to the north on the San Francisco Mountains (Kottlowski et al., 1965). Definitive sequences for several glaciations have not been found, but there is no doubt that at least one and probably more period(s) of cooler temperature and/or increased moisture occurred during the Pleistocene. The timing and effect of these changes in climate is confusing and complex (Wells and Jorgensen, 1964; Martin and Mehringer, 1965; Melton, 1965; van Devender, 1974), but reconstructions indicate that during some periods in the Pleistocene, the desert scrub region was displaced to the south and narrowed in an east-west direction (Martin and Meheringer, 1965). The area in which Silver Bell is located was inferred to have been under a cooler and wetter climatic regime that supported a woodland-parkland as recently as 1,700–2,300 years ago. By 1,000 years ago the present climate prevailed and the desert scrub flora had reexpanded its range to its present distribution.

The extensive system of American glacial lakes which has been carefully mapped by Feth (1961), did not develop in southern Arizona. The nearest lake of any size was Lake Bonneville, 1,000 km to the north. Part of the lack of water accumulation is due to the external drainage of the area.

Summary: Physiography and Geology

The available information on physiography and geology reveals that the Bolsón de Pipanaco and the Silver Bell Bajada differ in several structural and historical features. The principal differences in physiography include the fact that Pipanaco is a closed basin without external drainage, completely and closely surrounded by extremely high mountain ranges. The Silver Bell area is part of a system of interconnecting basins among relatively low mountain ranges whose drainage is external. The soils in the Bolsón are immature and show little or no zonation and do not have an underlying layer of caliche. In contrast, the soils of the Silver Bell region are mature with well formed horizons and often are underlain by a hardpan layer.

Geologically, the South American region was a continental land mass for 450 million years longer than the North American counterpart. However, of perhaps more importance, the modern physiography of the Basin and Range Province was fully formed by the end of the Pliocene whereas the Sierras Pampeanas were completely shaped only in the Pleistocene.

During the Quaternary the two areas were affected in distinct ways. The Salar de Pipanaco was flooded by a lake and glaciers formed on nearby peaks. The combination of lowered temperatures, increased humidity, and lack of habitable surface on the floor of the Bolsón during glacial periods would have essentially annihilated a desert scrub biota. Subsequent redevelopment of the modern flora might have been retarded by the presence of large montane barriers. In the Silver Bell area, cool temperatures and increased moisture probably caused the desert scrub flora to shift southwest out of the Tucson region during glacial periods, but reexpansion would have been rapid because of the interconnections of the basins. Moreover, neither glaciers, per se, nor glacial lakes had any direct influence in southern Arizona.

CURRENT CLIMATE*

In an investigation of convergence, analysis of climate furnishes two kinds of information, the first to establish similarities and differences of climate in the areas under examination, the second to furnish specific site information. The latter step establishes particular aspects of climate that enter into life processes of biota at the sites of investigation. The general survey is advisable so that a sense of typicality is given to the site analyses. In our study the essential characteristics of the sites call for a general statement about the cause and location of aridity.

*By H. P. Bailey.

Cause and Location of Arid Regions

Physical Bases of Climatic Similarities in Dispersed Regions

Before launching into the subject of aridity it is appropriate to state the bases of similarity in climate, of any type, in dispersed geographic areas. Those bases can be expressed as the primary controls of climate: circumstances pertaining to the earth's size, shape, orbit, and rotation period.

Solar energy, falling on the outer limits of the earth's atmosphere, represents the primary input of energy to the earth-ocean-atmosphere system. On an annual basis, solar energy is distributed in a zonal pattern, alike in both hemispheres, characterized by a gradient of decrease from equator to pole. In winter the gradient is accentuated, but is much weakened in summer. Solar influences thereby lead to seasonal differences that increase poleward, but the opposite gradient exists for the daily cycle where differences between day and night altitudes of the sun are maximal in low latitudes, not high. Thus, if solar influences alone prevailed, corresponding parallels (latitude lines) in both Northern and Southern hemispheres would display like climates around their perimeters, with due allowance for offset in the timing of the seasons. We would expect, furthermore, that warmth would be nearly uniformly distributed throughout the summer hemisphere, where decrease in solar height is compensated by greater day length, and that warmth in the winter hemisphere would decrease rapidly with latitude as a result of concomitant decrease in solar height and day length. In all seasons temperature differences between day and night would be greatest within the Tropics, and least in polar regions.

Although some resemblance can be discerned between the distribution of air temperature at the surface of the earth with the solar pattern just described, there are many important modifications, among them a significant poleward gradient of temperature decrease in high latitudes in summer, and large differences in the temperature of land and water surfaces. More heat is transferred sensibly to air over land, less is used for evaporation, and much less goes into storage in soil than into the oceans. Daily and seasonal swings of temperature, in consequence, are large over land, and small over water. The distance traveled overland by airstreams after their passage over the coastline thus serves as an important modifier of local climate.

It follows that the climates of windward coasts are oceanic in character but as marine air travels overland continental characteristics develop, a change which prevents uniformity of climate along lines of latitude as promised by insolation. Opportunities for similar climates consequently depend not only upon comparable locations in latitude, but upon comparable circumstances of continental location, land surface, and altitude. In sum, air flow patterns in relation to terrestrial factors alter the location of comparable thermal conditions from a pattern of zones to that of a mosaic.

Planetary distribution of precipitation cannot follow closely the determinants of temperature for the reason that precipitation is much more influenced by air motion. Air columns of similar water vapor content and temperature can differ greatly in raininess, according to the components of motion within them. Ascending columns of moist air are capable of delivering intense rain, but should the air start to sink precipitation ceases. On a planetary scale the Hadley cell characterizes the air circulation of the Tropics, i.e., warm, moist air rises over the equatorial belt with accompanying heavy rain, but descends in subtropical latitudes which are thereby rendered arid (Sutton, 1961).

In middle and high latitudes strong westerly currents prevail at middle and upper tropospheric levels in which storms of sufficient size are embedded to create precipitation by air motions related to their own structures. Thus, although equatorial conditions create the major maximum if global precipitation is arrayed zonally (Haurwitz and Austin, 1944), a secondary maximum is developed in middle latitudes separated by a minimum in the subtropics, a profile quite unlike that for the zonal distribution of air temperature. The subtropical minimum of precipitation is not globe-circling, for the western portions of the oceans and adjacent coastal regions are generally rainy at subtropical latitudes, but aridity is well developed in the eastern parts of the oceans and adjacent land in the latitude range 20 to 30 degrees. The dry sectors concerned may be quite broad, as in the case of the Sahara Desert, or relatively narrow, as in the Americas, but all subtropical arid regions share one characteristic with respect to precipitation: they serve as climatic divides that separate the summer-rain regimes of the Tropics from the winter-rain regimes found along their poleward flanks (Leighly, 1953).

The distribution of precipitation described above complicates a mosaic of climatic regions if thermal and moisture factors are to be combined. The relative weight to be given to each, and the precise definition of terms to be employed remain matters of controversy despite a large amount of effort expended toward resolution of the difficulties involved. The first climatic classification to receive wide attention, as an example in point, was that of Köppen, who devised a scheme in 1900 intended to agree with the distribution of selected vegetation types. Revised three times later, his map in modified form survives in Goode's *World Atlas* (1970) and is still an efficient medium of communication for the purpose intended. Later work has taken one of three lines of emphasis: air stream analysis (Bryson and Hare, 1974), heat balance studies (Budyko, 1956), or moisture balance investigations (Thornthwaite, 1933, 1948; Penman, 1947; Bailey, 1958). All lines of approach have agreed on certain aspects of global climate, among them the fact that a property of symmetry exists in the climatic architecture of the earth. The property of symmetry is seen most strikingly by the mirror images displayed on opposite sides of the Equator when viewing the general circulation, and by many climatic types, including the subtropical deserts. Also, certain climatic types occur on more than one continent in characteristic location, again true of subtropical deserts.

Meteorologically speaking, aridity is the product of descent of air aloft (Leighly, 1953); it has been mentioned earlier that such is the case in the subtropics in their relation to air descent in the Hadley cell. Terrain also contributes to such descent when air is forced to cross mountain ranges. When the mountains are aligned transversely to prevailing flows of air from the sea a standing wave is formed in the lee of the mountains that is persistent enough to impart aridity to regions as extensive as the Intermountain region of the United States, and Patagonia. Although the poleward limit of dry climates so formed lies beyond the reach of the regions to be studied here, it is nevertheless true that both the Sonoran and Monte deserts owe part of their aridity to the mountainous Pacific border separating them from unimpeded access to Pacific air.

Climate of the Southwestern United States and Central Argentina

Arid and semiarid climates affect about one-fourth of the land area of the globe (Meigs, 1953), mainly in subtropical latitudes. The North American arid region is complex owing to the magnitude of the area involved, and varied terrain within it. South of latitude 37° N, and at altitudes lower than 1,500 m, aridity prevails over a broad sweep of the American Southwest. From the basins in contact with the Coast Ranges and Sierra Nevada, where the desert is termed the Mohave, to western and central Arizona where the terms Colorado or Sonoran desert are applied, arid conditions are found in all valleys and basins. The Sonoran Desert also includes much of Baja California, and slopes of Sonora draining into the Gulf of California. High ground of the Sierra Madre Occidental, and its extension into the United States, interposes cooler and wetter ground between the Sonoran Desert and the Chihuahuan Desert. The northern fringe of the latter reaches southern New Mexico, a bit of Arizona, and western Texas.

Fortunately, the genus *Larrea* serves as an indicator of all the desert areas of interest here. As mapped and described by Hunziker et al. (1972) (Figure 2-5), *L. tridentata* in North America occupies an area roughly equal to that in which *L. divaricata* lives in Argentina, about 1 million km² in each case. Although *Larrea* overruns the limits of the Sonoran Desert and those of the Monte, it supplies a common denominator to the characteristics of the arid regions of which those deserts are a part. Furthermore, the geographic ranges of the species concerned offer a spatial frame for selection of climatic data that is free from the bias of typing that later workers may wish to change when considering desert subdivisions.

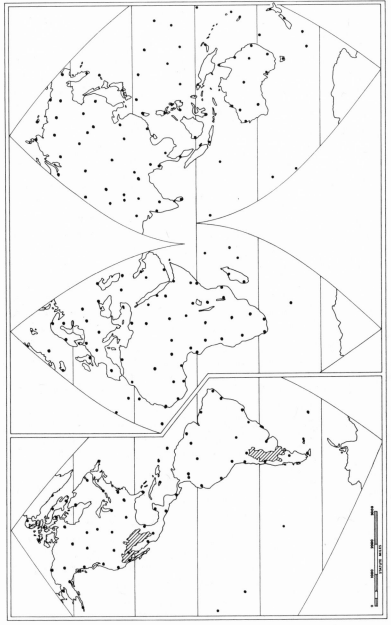

FIGURE 2-5. *Distribution of Larrea tridentata (North America) and L. divaricata (South America) (shaded areas generalized from Hunziker et al. [1972]). Dots show the locations of the global station net utilized in this study.*

To distinguish the climatic characteristics of the *Larrea* regions from those of the global net of stations, also plotted in Figure 2-5, Figure 2-6 has been prepared, where four plots of data are seen to share common axes. The global sample (dots) includes 146 weather records in the Northern Hemisphere, 84 in the Southern, excluding Antarctica. Each point represents an area of 1.25 million km^2, as determined from a grid of 198 quadrilaterals equal in area throughout a hemisphere, after the method described by Bailey (1956) for area-reference grids of the "second" type. Not all grid elements could be presented by climatic data. Antarctica was excluded by choice, and much area in the open sea was not represented by reason of data lacks. The 1931-60 period was adopted as the climatic normal for the world net. *Larrea* localities are identified by symbols given in the legend to Figure 2-5, and are listed in Table 2-2. For them a ten-year mean (1951-1960) was available for all stations except those in Chihuahua, for which the records were more recent (1957-1965).

Quadrant 1: Global Net. This quadrant has the mean annual range of temperature (A) (the mean annual range is the difference between the means of the warmest and coldest months of the year) along its x-axis, and the percentage of mean annual precipitation occurring in the winter half-year (R) as its y-axis (the winter half-year is defined as October-March in the Northern Hemisphere, April-September in the Southern Hemisphere). Thus, the scatter of the data shows global differences in seasonal characteristics of temperature and precipitation, and by density of the scatter an indication is also given of the amount of the earth's surface included.

Accordingly, the densest cluster of dots in the quadrant occurs in middle ranges of R (rain occurs throughout the year) but toward the lower limit of A (slight seasonal difference in temperature), characteristic of the large region contained within the inner Tropics (latitudes less than 15 degrees). Most of the sample, viewed as a whole, lies between R limits of 20 and 60, implying that land areas tend to develop more precipitation in summer than winter. This tendency is more pronounced at places with the highest values of A (all in the Northern Hemisphere), where R falls to the range 10 to 40. However, a thin scatter of data occupies nearly the entire range in R, from 0 to 100 percent.

Quadrant 1: Larrea Localities. *Larrea* localities display little scatter with respect to A, but occupy much of the possible range in R (about 80 percent of the range displayed by the global sample). The Mohave Desert, most easily reached by Pacific air in winter of all the deserts in this group, provides nearly all the places with $R > 50$. However, winter rain in sensible amounts penetrates as far as Arizona, too, thus accounting for the displacement of U.S. stations in Quadrant 1 toward higher R ratings than apply to the Argentine group.

Quadrant 2: Global Net. In this quadrant mean annual precipitation (P) is plotted with reference to its seasonal concentration (R). The rainiest places

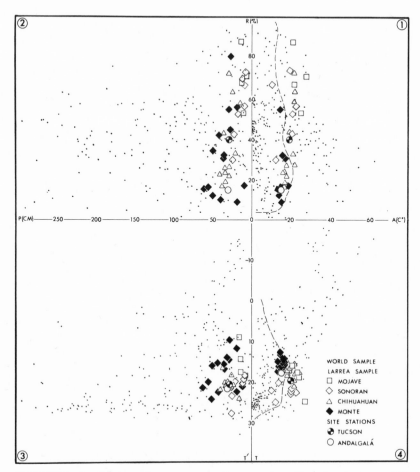

FIGURE 2-6. *Scatter diagrams according to five climatic elements. The global sample of weather stations is shown by dots. Other symbols identify desert components included within the range of* Larrea *as shown in Figure 2-5. Only Northern Hemisphere stations occur to the right of the dashed lines in quadrants 1 and 4, The axes are symbolized and defined as follows: A(C°), mean annual range of temperature (the difference between the means of the warmest and coldest months), R(%), the percentage of the year's precipitation that occurs in the winter half-year (in the Northern Hemisphere the winter half-year is Sept.-Mar.), P (cm), mean annual precipitation, T', the temperature effectively representing the temperature mean of the rainy season (°C), and* T, *mean annual temperature (°C).*

TABLE 2-2 *Location of Weather Stations in* Larrea *Localities*

Country	Desert type	Station name	Lat.	Long.	Alt.	Years of record
United States	Chihuahuan	Clifton, Ariz.	33°03′N	109°17′W	1056m	1951–60
		El Paso, Tex.	31 48	106 24	1194	
		Presidio, Tex.	29 33	104 22	787	
		Roswell, N.M.	33 24	104 32	1102	
	Sonoran	Ajo, Ariz.	32 22	112 52	537	
		Imperial, Cal.	32 51	115 34	−19	
		Parker, Ariz.	34 08	114 17	129	
		Phoenix, AP, Ariz.	33 26	112 02	340	
	Mohave	Barstow, Cal.	34 54	117 01	653	
		Death Valley, Cal.	36 27	116 52	−71	
		Lancaster, Cal.	34 42	118 09	717	
		Las Vegas AP, Nev.	36 05	115 10	659	
Mexico	Chihuahuan	Ciudad Delicias, Ch.	28 11	105 30	1165	1957–65
		El Nopal, Ch.	29 54	105 52	1478	
		Escalón, Ch.	26 44	104 21	1263	
		Estación Las Veras, Ch.	29 49	106 50	1500	
		Maijoma, Ch.	28 54	104 20	1300	
		Nuevo Casas Grandes	30 33	107 56	1473	
		Presa de Chihuahua	29 31	106 12	1595	
		Santa Anita, Ch.	31 14	108 50	1468	
		Villa Ahumada, Ch.	30 37	106 31	1205	
	Sonoran	El Refugio, B.C.	24 46	111 45	9	1951–60
		Guaymas, Son.	27 55	110 54	4	

Argentina	Monte		31°20'S	66°36'W	658m	1951-60
		Chepes	31 20	66 36	658	
		Choele Choel	39 27	65 39	131	
		Chos Malal	37 23	70 17	848	
		Cutral-Co	38 57	69 13	612	
		General Acha	37 22	64 35	238	
		General Conesa	40 06	64 25	60	
		San Antonio Oeste	40 44	64 57	7	
		San Juan	31 36	68 33	630	
		San Luis	33 16	66 21	716	
		San Rafael	35 35	68 24	747	
		Santa Isabel	36 16	66 55	320	
		Santiago del Estero	27 46	64 18	199	
		Tinogasta	28 04	67 34	1201	
		Villa Dolores	31 57	65 08	569	

33

are reasonably the recipients of rain throughout the year (R in middle ranges) but some high annual totals are nevertheless found in monsoon climates where nearly all rain falls in the summer half-year. Annual precipitation as great does not occur with equally high concentrations of rain in the winter half-year.

Quadrant 2: Larrea Localities. The *Larrea* environment is located in a dry pocket of the global matrix. Almost all *Larrea* localities receive less than 50 cm annually, many less than 25 cm. The driest spots in North America are found in the bolsones of the Mohave Desert, where the long-term mean at Death Valley is 4.5 cm. In areas so dry, year-to-year variability is normally high. Coefficients of variation in the Sonoran Desert generally exceed 30 percent, although they mainly lie in the range from 20 to 30 percent in the Monte. At San Juan, however (P is 8.7 cm) the coefficient rises to 60 percent, the highest found so far for the Monte. At Death Valley the figure exceeds 70 percent.

The *Larrea* region of Argentina receives a little more rainfall than is typical of the corresponding region of the United States, but in view of the greater concentration of precipitation in the summer of the southern region it is to be expected that evaporation losses would also be greater there. The implications of that relation will be discussed in Quadrant 3.

Quadrant 3: Global Net. The scatter pattern in Quadrant 3 developed by the global sample is essentially triangular in shape, with a broad base that encompasses the entire precipitation scale, just as its altitude takes in the entire temperature scale. The hypotenuse of the triangle indicates the upper limit of annual precipitation in relation to T' (a temperature term explained in following paragraphs), a limit that shows precipitation to increase with temperature. A few places in middle latitudes with temperatures midway on the scale are very rainy too, proving that the increase of precipitation with temperature is a tendency, but not a strict law. The lower limit of precipitation, in contrast, appears to be indifferent to temperature. The data of both hemispheres are mixed without distinction, except for the fact that only Northern Hemisphere places fall in the sub-zero temperature sector.

Quadrant 3: Larrea Localities. The part of the earth's surface occupied by *Larrea* species under consideration here includes but a small part of the range in P and T' through which the global sample is scattered. *Larrea* localities include only 16 percent of the range in P, and 39 percent of the range in T' applying to the larger sample, and they too show free mixture of the northern and southern stations. That fact, plus the compact scatter of the *Larrea* localities, promises close equivalence in precipitation-evaporation relations in annual terms, insofar as a temperature term can substitute for evaporation. The precipitation-evaporation relation utilized here is an outgrowth of the equation published in 1958 by Bailey. In metric form, that equation is:

$$S = 0.18P/1.045^{T+x}, \tag{2.1}$$

where S is an annual index of moisture,

P is mean annual precipitation in cm,

T is mean annual temperature in °C, and

x is a correction to T taken from a nomogram.

The correction x is positive for summer-rain regimes, and negative for winter-rain regimes. It thus modifies T to become a temperature (T') more representative of the rainy season. Originally segregated to allow the calculation of S from annual data, as in equation 2.1, the correction x is not needed if S is formed from the summation of moisture indices of all twelve months. In that case the monthly moisture index is calculated from this equation:

$$s = 0.18\, p/1.045^t, \tag{2.2}$$

where p and t refer to monthly means of precipitation and temperature.

Calculation of S by summation of monthly indices is easily accomplished by modern calculating equipment, and was carried out for all places included in this study. So that the relations incorporated in equation 2.1 would be preserved in quadrant 3, it was necessary to plot all points with respect to P and T', where T', is calculated from the relation:

$$T' = T{+}x \;\; = \;\; \frac{\log 0.18 + \log P - \log S}{\log 1.045}. \tag{2.3}$$

The greater concentration of precipitation in the Argentine summer, compared to the United States, assigns relatively warm equivalent temperatures (T') to the Argentine rainy season, an upward adjustment lowering the efficiency of rain so that the moisture indices of *Larrea* localities in Argentina are but little greater than those of the United States. Moisture indices of 2.5 and 4.7 plotted in Quadrant 3 of Figure 2-7 have been suggested by Bailey to represent the limits of arid and semiarid moisture provinces, respectively, and it will be noted that all *Larrea* stations are contained within those limits. Taken as a whole more than half the *Larrea* sample lies in overlapping ranges of P and T'.

Quadrant 4: Global Net. Data are much crowded in the lower left corner of this quadrant, where mean annual temperature (T) is warm and the difference between the means of the warmest and coldest months (A) is slight. The data so clustered represent the considerable proportion of the earth's surface lying within the Tropics (within which nearly 40 percent of the total is located). As T decreases the scatter in A increases, implying a general increase in seasonal swings of temperature as climate becomes cooler.

A profound difference exists between the hemispheres on that point, however, a reflection of their difference in the distribution of land area with respect to latitude. At the 55th parallel south, continental area diminishes to the vanishing point, but the width of the Northern Hemisphere continents increases up to the Arctic Circle. Accordingly, mean annual range of temperature (A) reaches its maximum in the Southern Hemisphere, almost 20° C in the plot, at annual means around 20° C, conditions typical of subtropical lowlands. At higher southern latitudes T and A decrease together, their lower limits being reached at the southern tip of South America, where Ushuaia (lat 55 S) records A at 7.6° and T at 5.5°. Only in Antarctica (not represented in the plot) does the opportunity exist in the Southern Hemisphere for continentality to assert itself at high latitudes.

In contrast, the upper limit of A increases fairly regularly in the Northern Hemisphere with decrease of T until the "cold pole" of Siberia is reached, represented in the plot by Verkhoyansk (lat 68 N) where A attains 62.5° at T -15.2°.

To distinguish the important difference just described in the thermal properties of the hemispheres, a dashed line has been introduced in quadrants 1 and 4 that defines the upper limit of A attained by Southern stations. To the right of that line only Northern conditions are presented.

Quadrant 4: Larrea Localities. In Quadrant 4 the scatter of *Larrea* stations is limited in comparison to that of the global net. The range in T of the *Larrea* regions is only 12.2°, a fourth that of the global sample, and their spread in A is 17°, again only a fourth of the global range. Clearly, *Larrea* occupies a relatively small sector of the thermal terrain of the globe. In Figure 2-7 plotting scales have been increased so that the symbols are more clearly separated. Thermal characteristics of the *Larrea* environment appear as follows:

1. Little overlap is apparent in the families of symbols. Localities in Argentina are coolest overall judged by their position relative to T. In the United States *Larrea* endures greater seasonal swings of temperature (A is greater) than in Argentina and most parts of Mexico.

2. By taking advantage of the relation established by Bailey (1966) between the annual range of temperature and the standard deviation of temperatures at all hours of the year, it is possible to distinguish differences in the probable incidence of hours with subfreezing temperatures (assuming a normal Gaussian distribution). A frost frequency of less than 5 percent of annual hours is thereby calculated for all *Larrea* localities; the majority indicate a frost incidence between 0.5 and 3 percent of annual hours. No general difference appears in the frost incidence of the Argentine area compared to the United States, although it is necessary to make allowance for the power of micro-climatic factors to alter frost frequencies at individual sites. It is nevertheless safe to conclude that *Larrea* lives in sites typified by light frost in both the Sonoran Desert and Monte.

3. A more distinctive difference in thermal climate between the two deserts is revealed through calculation of the temperateness index proposed by Bailey in 1964. In that index temperature at all hours of the year is calculated as a variance around a fixed mean, 14° C, which stands as a center of

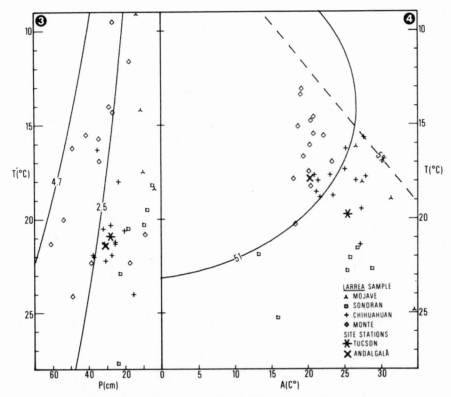

FIGURE 2-7. *Scatter diagrams of selected* Larrea *localities with respect to precipitation and temperature (graph axes defined as in Figure 2-6).*

the terrestrial temperature scale. A closed scale of 100 points is assigned to the index, with temperateness increasing as thermal extremes contract. The upper limit of the index at a scale value of 100 would represent a seasonally constant climate with a daily range of temperature near 4° C.

In terms of the index, Argentina is the most temperate of the *Larrea* regions. All Argentine stations show a temperateness index >51; the majority have indices larger than 55. In contrast, no *Larrea* locality attains an index as high as 51 in the United States although that limit is exceeded slightly in Chihuahua (see the line of index 51 in quadrant 4). In view of the similarity in frost conditions discussed in the previous section in the comparison of Argentina with the United States, extremes of heat rather than cold must account for the lesser temperateness of the Northern continent. That such is the case is indicated by comparison of monthly means for Tucson with those of Andalgalá. (Table 2-3), and other representatives of the Sonoran and Monte desert regions. Annual extremes are also warmer in the United States (Hoffman, 1960).

TABLE 2-3 *Comparative Climatic Data for Andalgalá (AND) and Tucson Airport (TUC)*

Andalgalá 27°35'S, 66°19'W, elev. 1072 meters
Tuscon Airport 32°07'N, 110°56'W, elev. 788 meters

Temperature (deg C)

Months		Mean max.		Mean min.		Highest		Lowest		Rain days	
AND	TUC	AND	TUC	AND	TUC	AND	TUC	AND	TUC	AND	TUC
Jun	Dec	17.5	18.3	2.8	3.3	36.9	28.9	-5.6	-7.8	2	4
Jul	Jan	17.9	17.0	2.2	2.2	33.0	30.6	-6.9	-8.9	2	4
Aug	Feb	21.3	18.9	4.4	3.8	35.5	33.3	-4.8	-6.7	1	4
Sep	Mar	25.2	22.3	7.8	6.0	37.0	33.3	-1.7	-3.3	0.7	4
Oct	Apr	28.3	27.3	11.4	9.8	39.5	38.9	0.8	-2.8	3	2
Nov	May	31.6	31.9	15.1	13.6	40.0	41.7	3.4	3.3	4	1
Dec	Jun	33.2	36.8	17.1	18.9	41.4	43.9	7.9	8.3	5	1
Jan	Jul	33.3	37.2	18.1	22.8	42.4	43.9	6.8	17.2	7	11
Feb	Aug	31.7	35.4	17.4	21.9	40.0	42.8	10.2	16.1	7	9
Mar	Sep	29.1	34.6	15.2	19.7	37.0	41.7	1.8	8.9	6	4
Apr	Oct	25.0	29.0	9.9	13.2	36.5	38.3	2.0	1.7	3	3
May	Nov	21.1	22.2	6.2	6.2	35.4	32.2	-2.4	-4.4	2	3
Year		26.2	27.6	10.6	11.8	42.4	43.9	-6.9	-8.9	43	49
Record*		a	b	a	b	a	a	a	a	a	23 yr

*Key to length of record
a = 1951–1960
b = 1931–1960.

Comparison of the Study Areas

Unfortunately, a climatic approach demands a longer period of observation than the duration of the SES project, and recommends use of nearby stations with established weather records rather than sole reliance on site studies. The figures and table illustrating climatic characteristics (Figures 2-8 and 2-9, Table 2-3), accordingly, have been taken from long-term records. For the Silver Bell site climatic normals for the period 1931-60 were available from Tucson Airport, although shorter records had to be accepted for sunshine measurements, and temperature extremes. For the study site in the Bolsón de Pipanaco, temperature means for the decade 1951-60 at Andalgalá were used, but a thirty-year normal was available for precipitation. So that comparison of thermal extremes would be more representative, the 1951-60 decade was used at both Tucson and Andalgalá. In Figures 2-10, 2-11, and 2-12 the Silver Bell site has been presented in the context of the greater Tucson area (the site shown by the asterisk) together with adjustments of isotherms and isohyets in accordance with terrain, all available surface climatic data, and a radiosonde profile of temperature. Study of those figures has allowed at least a subjective correction to be made of the Tucson Airport data toward conditions more representative of the Silver Bell site. Lack of data prevented a similar analysis of the Bolsón de Pipanaco.

In Figures 2-6 and 2-7 the locations of Tucson and Andalgalá can be found in all quadrants by noting their large, identifying symbols. The two localities are markedly different with respect to only one of the graph axes: R. Only 14.9 percent of the year's rain falls in the winter half-year at Andalgalá, whereas the proportion increases to 39.7 percent at Tucson. It has been noted previously that *Larrea* is tolerant to large differences in the seasonal emplacement of rain, and the differences in R between the two towns is only one-third of the scatter seen in the plot of the *Larrea* sample. To annual plants, however, the difference in precipitation regime between the sites is decisive for winter-blooming species. The index of precipitation effectiveness at the two sites is almost identical (S-2.0 at Tucson compared to S-2.1 at Andalgalá).

Thermal comparisons of Tucson with Andalgalá show differences representative of the regions of which they are a part, and which have been noted previously. In sum, the South American locality is cooler and more temperate, but the differences are a small part of the scatter shown in the entire *Larrea* sample.

Annual courses for four climatic elements are shown as continuous lines in Figures 2-8 and 2-9. The lines were developed from monthly means by six components of harmonic analysis; they display seasonal details with more authority than attends freehand plotting. To maintain equality in light conditions, the plots for Andalgalá are offset six months in time.

The annual march of temperature (curve A) indicates that Andalgalá is only slightly cooler than Tucson in winter, but considerably so in summer.

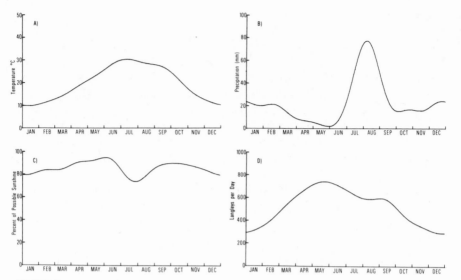

FIGURE 2-8. *Annual march of (A) temperature, (B) precipitation, (C) percentage of possible sunshine, and (D) global insolation at Tucson Airport, Arizona.*

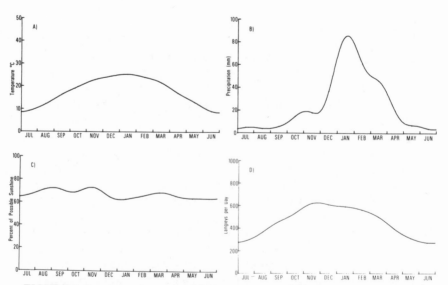

FIGURE 2-9. *Annual march of (A) temperature, (B) precipitation, (C) percentage of possible sunshine, and (D) global insolation (calculated by regression from monthly data on sunshine duration) at Andalgalá, Argentina.*

Daily means progress somewhat differently in summer at the two localities, for the temperature peak at Andalgalá is smooth, whereas that for Tucson dips in midsummer related to a sharp, concurrent increase in cloudiness lacking at Andalgalá. In consequence, the percentage of sunshine possible at Tucson drops markedly in July and August (curve C), whereas sunshine duration remains nearly the same for the three summer months at Andalgalá.

Clouds are not only more consistently present at Andalgalá, but they also cover more of the sky. Thus, whereas the sun shines on 87 percent of possible hours during the summer half-year at Tucson, the corresponding percentage at Andalgalá is but 67 percent. Therein lies the most probable immediate cause of the cooler summer temperature means at the southern site: a greater proportion of solar heat is rejected by reflection from clouds.

Solar energy reaching the surface is measured in the United States by the Eppley pyranometer (as opposed to sunshine recorders that indicate duration of sunshine, but not intensity). Total solar energy received on a horizontal surface (direct plus diffuse radiation) is shown by curve D in the figures under discussion. That for Andalgalá has had to be calculated by a regression equation derived from sunshine duration (Solar Energy Lab, 1966). Pronounced seasonal differences of insolation take place at both localities, in response to changes in height of the sun and day length, changes that are fractionally greater at Tucson in view of its higher latitude.

The lower degree of cloudiness at Tucson allows more solar energy to reach the ground than is probably the case at Andalgalá by the end of a typical year. Tucson received somewhat more than 190 kly/yr, and Andalgalá less than that. Even the summer peak of insolation is likely greater at Tucson than at Andalgalá if the clear skies and warm temperatures of May are counted as summer at Tucson, but July there receives less insolation than falls on Andalgalá in January in time periods averaged over a period as long as a month.

Under clear sky conditions, however, it is quite likely that surface temperatures are elevated at Andalgalá to a level equal to or exceeding those at Tucson. Many pyranometers in the United States have recorded momentary maxima as great as 1.6 ly min on surfaces receiving the solar beam at right angles (Hand, 1937). If all such radiation were absorbed, the equilibrium temperature of the receptor would be close to $373°$ K, the boiling point of water. That ordinary terrestrial surfaces do not attain such a high thermal level attests not only the energy loss through reflection, but the heat transferred through conduction and evaporation processes. The latter in particular is a potent factor in reducing surface temperature, as about 600 calories are required to evaporate a gram of water at terrestrial temperatures. In deserts temperature reduction through evaporation is minimized; at Andalgalá the sun is higher at noon than at Tucson at analogous times of the year and the earth's orbit places the sun closer to the earth in January than July, thereby bringing a 6 percent increase in insolation to the southern summer season. Hence, despite the cooler summer means when expressed in periods as long as a month, the extreme maxima at Andalgalá are close to those measured at Tucson (air temperature is referred to).

It should also be pointed out that the difference in prevailing cloudiness at the two localities leads to different proportions in the contributions of direct versus diffuse radiation. At Andalgalá diffuse radiation (solar radiation scattered from clouds and open sky) may constitute as much as one-third of the total solar input, while one-quarter is a more likely fraction in the case of Tucson for the contribution of diffuse radiation.

The precipitation curves for the two localities (curve B) show the differences that might be expected from prior remarks concerning the seasonal distribution of rain. Although winter rain at both Andalgalá and Tucson is slight, the sum of the three mid-winter months at Andalgalá on the average comes to but 30 mm, whereas at Tucson the total is 66 mm for the corresponding period. At Tucson the combination of that much moisture with other climatic factors allows a period of early spring growth and flowering that is absent at Andalgalá. There, however, temperature and precipitation increase together in spring, while at Tucson the same season brings precipitation decline in the face of rapidly increasing temperatures. Both localities have a rainfall peak in summer, but that at Andalgalá is somewhat more sustained. Four months of summer at Andalgalá attain at least 30 mm each month, while Tucson has only two such months.

The differences just noted concern long-term means, but in any individual year rainfall amounts and the timing of rain periods are subject to much variation. The coefficient of variation for annual rainfall is 29 percent at Tucson, and is similar at Andalgalá. At the heart of the matter are the factors previously described that make for aridity: both localities are relatively remote from sources of moisture and lack dependable mechanisms to bring about the precipitation process.

In view of the importance of water in the life cycle of organisms under desert conditions it is appropriate to consider more closely the gain and loss of water in the soil layer. The analysis provided by Thornwaite and Mather (1957) will be followed here, as it is compatible with the data so far presented. In their scheme the term "actual evaporation" refers to the amount of water in the soil that is lost through evaporation as that loss is limited by the amount brought by precipitation, and as rates of evaporation can be construed to be activated by temperature. Actual evaporation is a promising indicator of biomass production in dry climates. It is also an interesting historical note that Thornthwaite, in his first presentation of his temperature-driven model of evapotranspiration (1945) called upon actual evaporation to supply the index representative of climatic moisture ratings, even though he came to other decisions in later years.

Seasonal variations of actual evaporation at Tucson and Andalgalá are so closely similar to those of precipitation, when based on monthly means, that they can be taken as identical in climates so dry. The evaporation regime at Andalgalá is thus obviously more extreme than that at Tucson. Winter coolness and drought combine at Andalgalá to allow less than 10 mm of water to be transferred to the air each month from May through September, in contrast to January and February, when evaporation exceeds 50 mm in each month. At Tucson, July and August are correspondingly moist, but only in May and June do actual evaporation amounts drop below 10 mm per month (cf., five such months at Andalgalá).

At the end of the year total evaporation is nearly the same at both places. It is known that Thornthwaite's equations for evaporation underestimate its full potential in arid climates (Sellers, 1964), but the error is not important in these cases, where evaporation is limited by precipitation in all months.

Figures 2-10, 2-11, and 2-12 present isotherms and isohyets adjusted to altitude for the greater Tucson area, including the Silver Bell site, by means of a program (Shepard, 1968; Postma, 1973) using an inverse distance gravity model. In original form the program was topographically insensitive, but through a modification developed by David Nichols climatic variables of known but geographically random location respond to the overlay of a topographic surface. The procedure allowed a vertical profile of temperature from radiosondes, and another from ground stations giving rainfall means, to be incorporated in the logic of the isotherms and isohyets.

In Figure 2-10 the rapid decrease of temperature with altitude in the Santa Catalina Mountains first draws attention. During calm nights cold air flowing down the canyons of the mountains envelopes the lowland surface occupied by Tucson in a layer of air sufficiently cold at instrument shelter height to array the isotherms of daily means in patterns displaying mild temperature inversion (the areas closed by the 12° isotherm are cooler than the higher ground surrounding them). Had the daily minima been the subject of analysis the depiction of temperature inversion would have been of greater magnitude. The Silver Bell site, more distant from sources of air drainage so cold as that of the Catalinas, appears on Figure 2-10 to be a degree or so warmer in mean winter temperature.

Summer means are shown in Figure 2-11. Over the lowlands temperature gradients are so flat that little distinction appears. Mean daily temperature close to 29° or 30° prevail throughout the greater Tucson area in valley locations, but daily maxima in July are considerably warmer, 37.2° in July at Tucson Airport (Table 2-3). Warm spells bring still higher temperatures that would affect the Silver Bell site as well as Tucson. Pronounced differences in the temperatures of surfaces exposed to summer sunlight would be expected according to circumstances of ventilation, moisture supply, and opportunity for shade. The factors of micro-climate just mentioned operate in the Bolsón too, of course.

Precipitation shows a pronounced gradient of increase with altitude in the Tucson area. In Figure 2-12 even minor features of relief disturb the isohyets, which indicate a twofold increase in mean annual rainfall on the high ground of the Santa Catalina Mountains (altitudes above 2,500 m). In terms of mean annual precipitation it is not possible to distinguish a

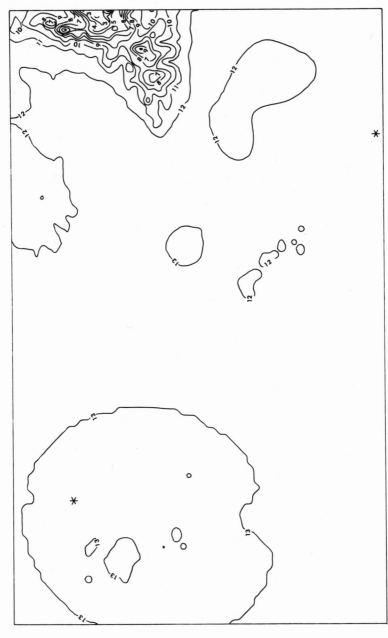

FIGURE 2-10. *Winter temperature isotherms adjusted to terrain in the vicinity of Tucson, Arizona (daily means averaged for the period December-February). The diagram is 75 km in east-west width and 50 km in north-south height. Tucson Municipal Airport (star in lower right corner) is 60 km distant from the Silver Bell Site (star in upper left corner).*

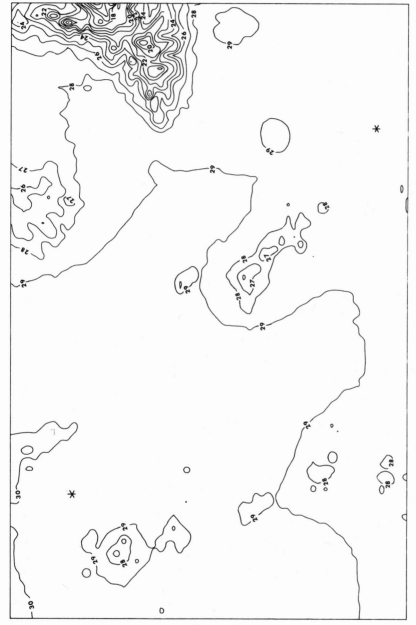

FIGURE 2-11. *Summer isotherms adjusted to terrain in the vicinity of Tucson, Arizona (daily means averaged for the period June-August).*

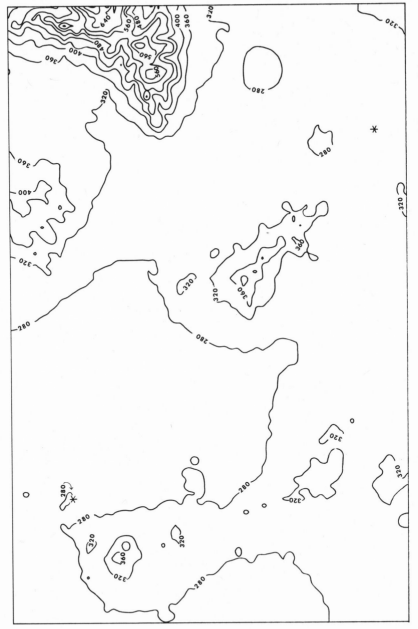

FIGURE 2-12. *Isohyets of mean annual precipitation adjusted to terrain in the vicinity of Tucson, Arizona.*

difference in wetness between Tucson Airport and the Silver Bell site on Figure 2-12, but the greater relief of the immediate surroundings of the Silver Bell site suggests that it might well share some of the increase to be expected on local summits within a few kilometers to the north and west of the site.

Precipitation-altitude relations in the Bolsón de Pipanaco are likely to be quite different from those in Arizona. Although moderate increase of rainfall upward may occur in the first thousand meters above the floor of the Bolsón, at higher elevation the increase may change to decline as moist convective columns from lower layers come into contact and mix with the strong westerlies aloft, air undergoing descent over the Monte and therefore relatively dry. Lacks in instrumental records do not allow definitive statements concerning the properties in depth of the air column over the Bolsón, but the appearance of the high Andes to the west support a thesis of upper-level dryness. This subject will doubtless be illuminated in the extensive work now in preparation as part of the World Survey of Climatology, in which the climatology of Central and South America will be presented as a separate volume (Schwerdtfeger, in press). In the meantime much useful information about air circulation in the Southern Hemisphere is available as a result of the stimulus provided by the International Geophysical Year (1957-58) in the writings of Van Loon (1964, 1965, 1967) and Taljaard (1967).

Their investigations aid in understanding a curious discrepancy in temperature between Andalgalá and Tucson that can be noted by comparing the lowest temperatures of record for the months of July-September (TUC) with January-March (AND), in Table 2-3. In other seasons the lowest temperatures of record are within a few degrees of agreement, but in late summer the difference suddenly increases to more than 10° in the July-January comparison. Summer variability of temperature at Andalgalá is obviously as great or greater than at other times of the year, but such is not the case at Tucson; in fact, it is typical that the entire United States has relatively stable temperature conditions in summer. Analyses of wind and pressure fields have shown that whereas the pace of the westerlies slows down in summer in the Northern Hemisphere, it speeds up in the Southern Hemisphere in its summer period. Pronounced meridional exchange of unlike air masses therefore alters day-to-day temperature much more in the southern summer than is the case in the northern summer. Although the thermal levels are well above the freezing point of water in the localities of concern here, a factor of thermal stress exists at Andalgalá for which there is not a clear counterpart in the Southwest United States.

Summary and Conclusions: Climate

This climatic analysis has presented first the physical principles that lead to similarities in climate of disjunct regions. The analysis then proceeded to examination of the climatic attributes of the territories occupied by two species of *Larrea* in North and South America. Those attributes were presented in four scatter diagrams with common axes. For comparative purposes background data were introduced from a global sample against which the climatic range of *Larrea* could be judged. Similarly, emplacement of data representative of the two study sites of the SES project allowed their differences to be judged relative to the spread of climatic differences encountered in the *Larrea* sample.

The technique just described allows visual comparison to be made on a single sheet of paper that has been drawn in fact from a large body of climatic data. It is a graphical device that has not been used previously in the same form in any previous investigation of convergence phenomena. From it arises a new statistic that could be termed "relative range," which refers to the differences in climatic data of selected sites compared to corresponding differences that exist in the larger biotic unit in which the study sites are located (the range of *Larrea* sp. in this case). By such comparison a basis is established for judging climatic differences in unlike weather elements (Table 2-4).

The entries in column 3 of Table 2-4 show clearly that differences between the northern and southern study sites are minor compared to the full range of conditions occupied by *Larrea tridentata* and *L. divaricata*. Although more rain occurs in the winter of Tucson than at Andalgalá, the dis-

TABLE 2-4 *Comparison of Climates at Tucson and Andalgalá Relative to the Total Climatic Range of* Larrea *Localities*

		Column 1 Limiting values in the *Larrea* sample		Column 2 Corresponding site values*	Column 3 Relative range diff. in col. 2 as a percentage col. 1
Mean annual temp.	High	25.3	TUC	19.8	
(*T*), °C	Low	13.1	AND	17.9	
	Diff.	12.2		1.9	15.6
Mean annual range	High	27.6	TUC	20.3	
of temp. (*A*), °C	Low	10.6	AND	16.2	
	Diff.	17.0		4.1	24.1
Concentration of	High	80.5	TUC	39.7	
precip. in winter	Low	8.7	AND	14.9	
(*R*), percent	Diff.	71.8		24.8	34.5
Mean annual precip.	High	611	AND	308	
(*P*), mm	Low	38	TUC	279	
	Diff.	573		29	5.0

*AND = Andalgalá, TUC = Tucson Airport.

crepancy is not much greater than that seen in the thermal terms analyzed by the relative range statistic.

It could not be expected, of course, that the climates of study sites so far separated could be identical. Reasons for difference start with small individualities of site features and include as well a difference in latitude of four degrees, not to mention the greatly different geometry of the Americas in middle and high latitudes. It is doubtless true that the comparative lack of land area in South America beyond the 40th parallel is more decisive in consideration of evolution and migration of plants and animals than in purely climatic terms. However, even at latitude 28 South there is greater summer thermal stress and the likelihood of vertical gradients of moisture quite different from those observed in Arizona highlands.

Attention to differences should not obscure the high degree of similarity that exists in the climatic data of the two sites seen in Figures 2-6 and 2-7, which indicate that Tucson and Andalgalá represent close homoclimes. The same scatter diagrams also contain examples of even closer agreement (identification of data points is required in such an exercise) and the possibility also exists of adding homologous data points from regions where *Larrea* does *not* exist, as in Australia and Africa. Those suggestions are made to lead other investigators to utilize the versatility of the graphical aids devised for this study in extension of investigations of convergence phenomena.

Chapter 3:
The Biota:
The dependent variable

· O.T. Solbrig, W.F. Blair, F.A. Enders,
A.C. Hulse, J.H. Hunt, M.A. Mares, J. Neff,
D. Otte, B.B. Simpson, C.S. Tomoff.

Testing the primary hypothesis ideally calls for two regions that possess identical physical environments and a phylogenetically unrelated biota. In the previous chapter the similarities and differences of the physical environment were explored. In this chapter we discuss the extent to which the second premise in the research design is met. First we specify criteria by which the phylogenetic similarity of the biota can be assessed and establish the geographical units to be compared. Then we perform an assessment of phylogenetic similarity. Finally we consider how the history of the biota and the actual period of occupancy of the study sites might have influenced the amount of convergence that has occurred or could be expected to occur.

CRITERIA FOR DETERMINING
PHYLOGENETIC SIMILARITY

The best available criterion for assessing the phylogenetic similarity of two biotas is their taxonomic affinity, i.e., number of species, genera, and families common to the two biotas. The taxonomic system is not strictly phylogenetic since it is based largely on the phenotypic resemblance of extant species (Davis and Heywood, 1963; Henning, 1966) but taxonomists weigh more heavily those phenotypic traits that their experience has led them to believe are conservative, that is, those characters that do not provide immediate adaptation. For example, greater taxonomic weight is given to plant reproductive characters which appear to be conservative, than to vegetative characters which are clearly rapidly modified by natural selection. Therefore, since taxonomists try to erect a classification that reflects communality of descent rather than adaptation to similar functions, their classifications are very well suited for our particular purpose.

There are problems in using number of common taxa of different categories as a criterion of phylogenetic similarity. One is that the degree of affinity of taxa of the same rank is not necessarily the same. Thus two genera might be common to both Argentina and the southwestern United States but be represented in one case by two very closely related species and in the other by two distantly related species. A comparison of only the number of common genera will not detect that difference. Another problem is that in certain groups taxa are narrowly defined while in other groups they are defined very broadly; hence what in one family is considered a single genus, in another might be subdivided into several genera. There is no way of resolving these problems, other than by an analysis of each case.

Because taxonomists cannot always detect convergences, use of taxonomic affinity as a criterion of phylogenetic similarity probably errs in the direction of indicating a larger phylogenetic similarity than that which actually exists. The same is true if too inclusive a criterion is used in defining taxa, although too narrow a criterion will give an underestimate. Since erring by overestimating the effect of phylogeny works against the hypothesis of convergence, most of the biases in the taxonomic system are conservative and need not concern us.

GEOGRAPHICAL SCALE OF THE MOST
MEANINGFUL COMPARISON

The relevant space scales for floral and faunal comparisons need to be considered carefully. Three main possibilities exist: (a) to compare the biota of the primary sites; (b) to compare the biota of the general vicinity of the primary and secondary sites; or (c) to make a comparison of the biota of the entire biogeographical regions of the study sites, i.e., the Monte in Argentina and the Sonoran Desert in the United States and Mexico. The best geographical scale depends both on the group of organisms being considered and on the particular type of studies that were undertaken with them. In the case of the flora a comparison restricted to the primary site offers too narrow a frame of reference. Since the detailed plant-ecological studies were done primarily in the area of the Bolsón de Pipanaco in Argentina, and at different places in the area of the Silver Bell and Tucson Mountains, the Avra Valley and the Saguaro National Monument (East and West) in Arizona, a comparison of the floras of these two areas will give the best indication of the extent to which the requirement of phylogenetically unrelated biota has been met.

The same argument applies to the invertebrate fauna, but not to the vertebrate fauna. In the latter case some of our studies were directed at a comparison of species characteristics and community structures of animals ranging over larger areas of the Monte and the Sonoran Desert. Furthermore, because the number of species is fewer, and the mean ranges are larger, a comparison restricted to the Avra Valley area and the Bolsón de Pipanaco would tend to underestimate phylogenetic similarity, an error we wish to avoid. The vertebrate fauna of the entire northern Monte is therefore compared with that of the northern Sonoran Desert.

PHYLOGENETIC SIMILARITY OF THE BIOTAS

In documenting the extent to which the flora and fauna of the South American study sites are related at the family and infrafamily level to the flora and fauna of the North American sites, we shall restrict ourselves to those groups of organisms that were studied as part of the comparative investigation. They are: Tracheophytes among the plants; arachnids and selected groups of insects (Orthoptera, ants, and bees) among the invertebrates; and all groups of vertebrates except fishes.

Plants*

Engler (1876) and Bray (1898) were the first scientists to point out that the semidesert regions of Argentina shared species with the semidesert regions of northern Mexico and the United States, a disjunction of over 5,000 miles. The origin of these disjunctions has been debated repeatedly since that time (I. M. Johnston, 1940; Axelrod, 1941, 1948; Campbell, 1943; Raven, 1963; Solbrig, 1972, 1973). Since we need only to assess the affinities of these two floras we need not be concerned with the controversy over their origin.

From our own collections** the size of the floras of the Bolsón de Pipanaco and the Avra Valley region appears to be very similar. However, the areas over which we collected are not comparable, the Argentine area being considerably larger. At each site approximately 250 species belonging to 115 genera and 50 families were collected. Of this total there are 14 species (5.6 percent), 51 genera (44.3 percent) and 29 families (58 percent) in common between the two areas. On a purely numerical basis, therefore, the two floras show little similarity at the specific level, but a great deal of similarity at the supraspecific level (Appendix A).

Of the fourteen species in common (Appendix B) six are common widespread weeds: *Aristida adscensionis, Eragrostis cilianensis, Erodium cicutarium, Tribulus terrestris, Solanum eleagnifolium,* and *Nicotiana glauca.* The first four are of European origin; the last two come from South America. Of the remaining eight species, five are annual and three are perennial. *Chloris virgata* is common in the lower bajada and along washes at both sites. This species is common in temperate and tropical America, from the United States to Argentina. *Bouteloua aristoides* and *B. barbata* are both very common grasses in *Larrea* flats at both the North and South American sites. *Sporobolus pyramidatus* is a common perennial widespread in tropical America. *Boerhavia coccinea,* a short-lived perennial herb, is widespread in the New World. *Allionia incarnata,* an annual or short-lived herbaceous perennial, widespread at both sites, is found in the southwestern United States and Mexico, and from Venezuela to Chile and Argentina in South America. *Verbesina encelioides,* an annual herb, has a disjunct distribution between North and Central America (southern United States, Mexico, and West Indies) and South America (Bolivia, Paraguay, northern Chile, Argentina, and Uruguay). The final disjunction is a pair of very closely related species, *Larrea tridentata-Larrea divaricata,* the most common, abundant and characteristic species in the Sonoran Desert and over large areas of the Monte. *Larrea divaricata* in the Bolsón de Pipanaco is largely restricted to washes and more humid areas. *Larrea divaricata* is also found in four small pockets

*By O. T. Solbrig and B. B. Simpson.
**Made by C. H. Lowe and J. Cross in Silver Bell and P. Cantino and F. Vervoorst in the Bolsón de Pipanaco.

in Perú and Bolivia. *Larrea tridentata* is abundant throughout the Sonoran, Chihuahuan, and Mohave deserts. *Larrea tridentata* is almost identical to *L. divaricata* in its morphology, but hybrids are only partially fertile (Hunziker et al., in press). In the Bolsón de Pipanaco, *L. divaricata* is a common species and the related *L. cuneifolia* dominates the vegetation.

At the supraspecific level, all genera common to the two sites also extend into intervening areas of tropical America. Most are represented at both sites by distantly related species, but there are at least two cases of pairs of closely related tree species. One is the genus *Prosopis*, where the Arizona species, *P. velutina*, is closely related to three of the four species found in the Bolsón de Pipanaco, *P. nigra, P. chilensis,* and *P. flexuosa*, especially the last. The other is the genus *Cercidium*, represented in the Silver Bell area by *C. microphyllum* and *C. floridum*, and in Argentina by the similar *C. praecox*. Most of the genera shared between the two areas that have no common species are represented by either herbaceous perennials (11) or shrubs or tress (15). Three genera (*Jatropha, Cereus,* and *Opuntia*) are perennial succulents or semisucculents, while only four of the genera are annual taxa (Figures 3-1 and 3-2).

Although the number of species in both sample areas is similar, their distribution among life forms is not. The Silver Bell area has a much greater proportion of annual species (50 percent) than the Andalgalá region (34 percent). The latter has more herbaceous perennials, shrubs, trees, and succulents than the Arizona region. At both sites there are three species of root perennials, a species of hemiparasitic shrub, and a true root parasite (Figures 3-3 and 3-4). The washes and the mountain slopes of Catamarca and Arizona have more genera in common than the desert flats.

The flora of the Monte is closely allied with that of the present-day Chaco. Sarmiento (1972) in a detailed study showed that forty-two out of fifty-eight characteristic genera of the Monte were shared with the dry Chaco and western Chaco woodlands. Vervoorst (1972) showed that species growing along washes and in the moister upper Bajadas were almost entirely Chaco species (Table 3-1) and that along the drier, lower bajadas and *Larrea* flats more characteristic Monte species are found. More than 60 percent of the Monte species and more than 80 percent of the genera are also found in the Chaco. There are, however, important Monte species that range well beyond the limits of the Chaco or the Monte.

The Sonoran Desert flora is derived from the Madro-Tertiary Geoflora which evolved in northern Mexico and the southwestern United States during the Tertiary (Axelrod, 1950, 1958). Thus the Sonoran Desert flora shares elements with other floras derived from the Madro-Tertiary such as the floras of the Mohave and Chihuahuan deserts, the Great Basin flora and the chaparral of California.

In summary then, the flora of the Bolsón de Pipanaco in Catamarca has only six native species, out of more than 250, in common with the area of Silver Bell in Arizona. On the other hand, over 40 percent of the genera and

FIGURE 3-1. Dyckia velazcana *(Bromeliaceae), a succulent common on rocky slopes in the Bolsón de Pipanaco. The genus does occur in the Sonoran Desert in Arizona, but is found on rocky slopes at higher elevations. (Photo by O. T. Solbrig.)*

FIGURE 3-2. Jatropha macrocarpa *(Euphorbiaceae), an Argentine semisucculent. The leaves are not yet fully expanded. (Photo by O. T. Solbrig.)*

FIGURE 3-3. Habranthus *sp. (Amaryllidaceae), a bulbous root perennial common in the Bolsón de Pipanaco. This photograph was taken two days after the first heavy rain of the summer. Prior to the rain, no parts of the plant were visible above the surface. (Photo by P. Cantino.)*

FIGURE 3-4. Prosopanche americana *(Orobanchaceae), a parasite on the roots of* Prosopis *spp. The dark upper portion consisting of the leathery, three-petaled flower is the only part of the plant normally protruding above the ground. The remainder was excavated for this photo. (Photo by P. Cantino.)*

TABLE 3-1   *Percentage of Monte Plant Species Shared with the*
Chaco by Habitat

Community	Number of species	Common Chaco and Monte	Only Monte
Eroding Mountain Slope	12	58%	42%
Upper Bajada	57	63%	37%
Lower Bajada	18	39%	61%
Bottom Land	10	80%	20%
Canyon Forest	11	100%	–
Upper Wash	24	75%	25%
Lower Wash	12	83%	17%
Dunes	10	37%	62%
Halophytes	7	100%	–

nearly 60 percent of the families are present at both sites. In most cases the related species are herbaceous perennials or shrubs which are most commonly found in the more humid environments of the mountain slopes or in the washes. However, the most conspicuous common taxon, the genus *Larrea,* is the dominant element in the flats throughout most of the Monte and the Sonoran Desert.

Invertebrates

Our taxonomic knowledge of the invertebrate fauna of the Monte is still scanty and, although the invertebrate fauna of the Sonoran Desert is better known, it too is in need of more taxonomic research. The present discussion will be restricted to those groups with which we have had direct research experience: grasshoppers, ants, arachnids, and pollinating insects, especially bees. Data are based on our own collections supplemented from the literature (Appendixes D-F).

*Grasshoppers**

The Argentine grasshopper fauna appears to be divisible into the same temporal strata recognized by G. G. Simpson (1950) for mammals, even though a fossil record is lacking. These are: (a) an ancient stock, endemic to South America, which has undergone extensive radiation and is now rich in species (Proscopiidae and Ommexechidae); (b) younger taxa which may have entered South America during late Oligocene to mid-Miocene and which have undergone moderate radiation (Romaleinae, Catantopinae); and (c)

*By D. Otte.

late immigrants, taxa that have recently penetrated South America, perhaps since the Pleistocene, and show little differentiation (Trimerotropis: Oedipodinae).

Ants*

The ant fauna of Arizona includes 209 recorded species (Hunt and Snelling, 1975). Only seventy-seven species are recorded as having been collected in Catamarca Province (Appendix O). The low species total for Catamarca reflects inadequate collecting activity in that region and makes comparison of the complete faunas problematical, but there is general similarity in subfamilial representation and generic composition. Twenty-seven species in seventeen genera were collected at an Avra Valley site (Appendix P); thirty-four species in seventeen genera were collected at a site in the Bolsón de Pipanaco (Appendix O). Though no species are shared between the sites there are ten genera in common (Appendix Q). The greater number of species collected at the Bolsón de Pipanaco site possibly reflects in part the generally favorable weather conditions during the study period there as compared to the generally unfavorable (hot, very dry) weather during the study period in Avra Valley. Despite an overall similarity of the ant faunas there are several conspicuous differences: the greater abundance of species associated with trees and *Prosopis/Acacia* washes in the Bolsón de Pipanaco than in the Avra Valley; the much greater richness of seed-gathering ants in the Avra Valley, and the much greater richness of fungus-growing ants (Myrmicinae, Attini) in the Bolsón de Pipanaco. Also, the Catamarca fauna includes eighteen species of Dolichoderinae, several of which (especially species of *Dorymyrmex* and *Forelius*) are much larger, more conspicuous, and more abundant than any of the eight Arizona species. The Arizona fauna, on the other hand, has a total of forty-two species of Formicinae in the genera *Lasius, Acanthomyops, Myremcocystus,* and *Formica,* genera that do not occur in the Neotropical Realm. The contrasting diversities in these two groups may represent a pattern of parallel radiation under constraints of biogeographic separation. No other units of the ant fauna show such biogeographic difference in distribution of important genera, and in no other groups are such disparate species abundances seen.

Bees†

Both areas are rich in bee species with 116 at the Monte site and 188 from Silver Bell in the Sonoran Desert. With the exception of the recently

*By J. H. Hunt.
†By J. Neff.

introduced honeybee, *Apis mellifera,* no bee species are shared by the two sites and only twelve of the ninety-five total genera have representatives at each area. Total number of shared genera for the two deserts is probably in excess of twenty, but sparse knowledge of the Monte faunas hinders broad comparisons. At the family level, the faunas of the two deserts are quite similar with the minor exception of the absence of the relictually-distributed Melittidae from South America, although the distribution of species among the families at the two sites is rather distinctive (Appendix E). As noted by Michener (1940) the Sonoran bee fauna is a complex mixture of groups of northern and southern affinities. Cosmopolitan groups and groups of northern affinities such as *Andrena* and *Dufourea* are best represented in the spring while groups of southern or Neotropical affinities predominate during the summer bloom. The latter group includes many members of the Exomalopsini, Eucerini and Centridini of the Anthophoridae; most of the Panurginae (with the very important exception of *Perdita*) and the Oxaeidae. The Monte bee fauna has a number of obvious similarities to the Sonoran fauna, due both to the presence of virtually cosmopolitan genera such as *Anthidium* and *Colletes* as well as many of the widespread Neotropical elements which are at or near their northern extension in the Sonoran Desert. While many of the Neotropical elements are widespread throughout South and Central America (such as *Exomalopsis* and the Augochlorini) a number of groups such as *Protoxaea, Caupolicana,* and *Centris* (*Paracentris*) are essentially limited to temperate and/or semiarid regions and are absent in intervening wet tropical areas. Distinctive features of the Monte include the diversity and abundance of colletid bees, particularly among the Paracolletini and Xeromellisinae, as well as a number of distinctive groups of Eucerine and Exomalopsine genera and the unique *Canephorula.* An unusual disjunct distribution is found in the Eucerine genus *Martinapis,* which contains only two species, one in the Monte and the other in the Sonoran and Chihauhuan deserts of North America.

*Arachnids**

Both deserts have approximately the same richness of genera of spiders, scorpions, and solpugids (Appendix F), but since the fauna of the Monte has not been studied as extensively, the slightly higher number of genera from the Sonoran Desert may be spurious. Approximately 30 percent of the genera and subgenera of spiders which live on the plants are shared between deserts, but these spiders represent roughly 70 percent of the number of individuals taken by quantitative sampling of the bushes. Similarly, predatory insects such as bugs (*Nabis* sp., *Geogoris* sp., in particular) and neuropterans (*Chrysops* sp.) share genera in the two continents. This taxonomic simi-

*By F. A. Enders.

larity between the faunas of predatory arthropods contrasts with the lack of relation found in comparisons of herbivorous arthropods (Appendix D). Also the arachnids which live on the ground are less closely related taxonomically, between continents, than are those which live on the bushes. The scorpions represent two distinct families, and solpugids are primarily Eremobatidae in North America, but Ammotrechidae in the Monte. On the other hand, some of the ground-dwelling spiders (genus *Lycosa,* for example) are more closely related probably because of the long distance dispersal by ballooning, not possible among solpugids and scorpions. This method of dispersal is reduced or lacking in spider species which show less taxonomic similarity between the two continents: e.g., Homalonychidae-Sicariidae.

Vertebrates*

The Monte and the Sonoran Desert share very few species of vertebrates. Only ten out of ninety-eight bird and six out of eighty-four mammal species are common to both regions (Appendix G). All are widespread species, not restricted to the desert region. There are no common species of anurans or reptiles. The situation is not very different at the generic level. The only shared anuran genus, among eleven, is the nearly cosmopolitan *Bufo.* Only one of nineteen lizard genera (*Cnemidophorus*) is shared. Two of twenty-eight genera of snakes, the primitive pantropical *Leptotyphlops,* and the predominantly North American genus *Crotalus,* are represented in both deserts.

One family of anurans out of seven, three of five lizard families, and four of five snake families are represented in both deserts. Sixteen of thirty-five families of birds are present in both deserts. Finally, there are seven families of mammals shared by the Monte and the Sonoran Desert of a total of twenty-four present in either one or the other region. However, two of these are bats and three are wide-ranging carnivores. The overall phylogenetic similarity of the Monte and the Sonoran Desert vertebrate faunas, like the invertebrate faunas, is therefore much less than the similarity of the plants of these areas.

The amphibian and reptilian faunas of the Monte are largely shared with the Chaco (Table 3-2). Twenty-two (44 percent) of the fifty species of amphibians and reptiles that have been recorded for the Monte have Monte-Chaco distributions. Birds and mammals do not fit this pattern, for the largest element in both is one of widely distributed species, while only nine (15 percent) of the sixty-one bird species and none of the thirty-two mammal species have a Monte-Chaco distribution.

*By W. F. Blair, A. C. Hulse, M. A. Mares, and C. S. Tomoff.

TABLE 3-2 *General Distributions of the Species of Terrestrial Vertebrates that Comprise the Monte and the Sonoran Desert Faunas*

A. SONORAN DESERT

Class	Endemic	Sonoran Chih.	Son. + adjacent	Sonoran Chih. grasslands	W. Mex. lowlands	Widespread	Totals
Anurans	2		1	6	2	1	12
Lizards	8		7	4			19
Snakes	10	3	3	5		3	24
Turtles	1			1			2
Birds	6		14	3		34	57
Mammals	1	2	6	4	2	68	83

B. MONTE

Class	Endemic	Monte-Chaco	Monte-Pat.	Monte-Chaco-Pat.	Monte-Chaco-Cord.	Widespread	Totals
Anurans		10			2	2	14
Lizards	11	4					15
Snakes	2	6	1	1		4	14
Turtles		1					1
Birds	2	9	5		2	43	61
Mammals	3(4)			4	1	23	32

BRIEF HISTORY OF THE BIOTA OF THE SONORAN
DESERT AND THE MONTE*

The most important historical difference between the Bolsón de Pipanaco and the Silver Bell area is the greater impact that Pleistocene glaciations had on the South American site. Also severe arid conditions may have existed for different periods of time in North America and South America (Chapter 2). It is important to assess the significance of this difference for the potential time available for convergence on the two sites. The papers of Axelrod (1950) and Solbrig (1976) dealing with the origin of flora of the Sonoran Desert and the Monte respectively and those of Patterson and Pascual (1968, 1972) on the evolution of mammals may be consulted for further details.

Monte

Very little factual evidence exists regarding the history of the flora and the fauna of the Monte during the Tertiary. Extrapolating from the fossil evidence that points to a subtropical forest in Patagonia at the end of the Cretaceous and early Tertiary, and the absence of any appreciable mountain barrier to the west of the region at that time, it can be assumed that the climate of the area must have been more mesic. However, the expected presence of subtropical high pressure zones and some geomorphological evidence of local aridity in the Cretaceous deposits of central Argentina (Gordillo and Lencinas, 1972) imply that there may have been a pronounced dry season at mid-latitudes (approximately 30° S). Also, the South Atlantic had a very limited surface at that time (Dietz and Holden, 1970). This has led Solbrig (1976) to postulate that the region that today is the Monte and dry Chaco had a savanna or deciduous forest type of vegetation, rather than a rain forest, at the beginning of the Tertiary. Phylogenetically this flora is supposed to be related to the present Chaco flora, and has been termed the "Tertiary-Chaco Paleoflora." This is the presumed parent stock for much of the flora of the present-day Monte and Chaco.

From the biogeographical standpoint the most important aspect of the Tertiary history of South America is its isolation from the biotas of other continents. The island nature of South America allowed the evolution of several distinctive groups of vertebrates, most notably notoungulates and marsupials. Prior to the Pliocene connection of North and South America only platyrrhine primates, caviomorph rodents, and procyonid carnivores had invaded the continent. It is still a matter of debate whether the first two came from the north (Wood and Patterson, 1971) or from Africa (Hoffstetter, 1972).

The fossil record of mammalian life in southern South America is very good. All but a few of the known fossil localities are in Argentina, but out-

*By. O. T. Solbrig.

side the present Monte area. The early Tertiary mammalian faunas from the Paleocene and Eocene of Patagonia consist of marsupials, edentates, and a variety of ungulates. In early Oligocene the first records of caviomorph rodents and platyrrhine primates are found. The forms from that early period appear to be adapted to a subtropical, forested region.

The Tertiary in South America is categorized by the slow lifting of the Cordillera de los Andes, particularly from the Miocene to the present (see Chapter 2). After a warm beginning, the climate began to cool and became drier starting in the Eocene. This climatic trend, and the increasing barrier to moisture laden winds from the west, led to a gradual replacement of the forests of the late Cretaceous and early Paleocene by grasslands and, eventually, more dry-adapted vegetation in Patagonia, the Pampa region, and probably the Monte region as well. Unfortunately the evidence is scanty and at times indirect. In Patagonia there is direct evidence of the deterioration of the climate (Menendez, 1972; Petriella, 1972), as well as indirect evidence from paleosoils (Volkheimer, 1971). One of the strongest bits of indirect evidence for the existence of extensive grasslands comes from the presence, from the Eocene on, of two well-developed and predominantly grazing lines of ungulates, the *Proterotheriidae* and the *Macraucheniidae*.

The Pliocene provides the first unmistakable evidence for the existence of more or less extensive areas of semidesert (Vuilleumier, 1971; van der Hammen, 1972). With the rising of the Bolivar geosyncline in late Pliocene, South America ceased to be an island continent and became connected to North America. This had a very marked influence on the fauna of the continent (G. G. Simpson, 1950; Patterson and Pascual, 1968, 1972). Extensive faunistic interchanges took place during the Pliocene and Pleistocene between the two continents with eventual extinction of several of the South American mammalian lines such as marsupial carnivores, ground sloths, and notoungulates.

By the end of the Pliocene the landscape of South America was essentially identical to its present form (Chapter 2). However, the flora and fauna of the Pliocene was yet to be affected profoundly by the events of the Pleistocene. Vuilleumier (1971), and van der Hammen (1961, 1972) have reviewed the Pleistocene events in South America. In northern South America (Venezuela, Colombia, and Ecuador) one to three glaciations took place corresponding to the last three events in the northern hemisphere (Würm, Riss, and Mindel). In Perú, Bolivia, and northern Chile and Argentina, there were at least three, and in some areas possibly four glaciation events. All of these glaciations, with the exception of the Patagonian glaciation (Auer, 1960; Czajka, 1966) were montane rather than continental. Semidesert areas probably persisted in the Monte region during the Pleistocene, but the extent and the area must have fluctuated considerably (Chapter 2).

In late Pleistocene many areas of what is today the Monte became available for colonization by desert plants and animals. Given the broken nature of the topography in its northern part, there is the possibility that not all species were able to surmount the physical barriers of the large mountains that surround some of the valleys such as the Bolsón de Pipanaco. This would be particularly true for small, flightless forms of animals.

Sonoran Desert

The climatic changes that took place in the Sonoran Desert since Cretaceous time parallel largely what we know from the Monte area (Chapter 2). The evolution of the vegetation of the area is tied to the development of the Madro-Tertiary Geoflora at the beginning of the Cenozoic (Axelrod, 1950, 1958), its subsequent expansion during the Tertiary, and the evolution of a desert vegetation from some Madro-Tertiary elements since the early Pliocene.

The climate of the Sonoran Desert during the Cretaceous was warm and fairly humid, and the region was apparently covered by a subtropical forest which persisted into the Paleocene. The middle and late Cretaceous era of the western United States reflects a cooler climate than that indicated by succeeding Paleocene floras of the same areas. Geological evidence also indicates a seasonally-dry continental environment. Axelrod (1958) attributes this in part to the ridge of high pressure at mid-latitude that causes the western parts of continents at intermediate latitudes always to be the driest. However, these dry environments at this time were not severe and were restricted in area.

By the Eocene and Oligocene, conditions had apparently become drier since the first records of the Madro-Tertiary Geoflora are found at this time (R. W. Brown, 1934; Chaney, 1944; MacGinitie, 1953; Axelrod, 1958). The early examples of the Madro-Tertiary Geoflora from the Green River of Utah and the Florrisant beds of Colorado, consist of genera that today are found in woodland, savanna, chaparral, and thorn shrub vegetation. Among them genera such as *Celtis, Platanus, Bursera, Prosopis,* and *Zizyphus* are found in the Sonoran Desert today. From the structure of the known fossil floras and from paleoclimatic considerations, Axelrod (1950, 1958) feels that the vegetation of the area at the time is best described as a subtropical savanna. Zweifel (1956) has suggested that *Scaphiopus couchi,* the most desert-adapted anuran in North America, may have evolved in the southwestern United States in mid-Oligocene. From the Oligocene there are also records of ancestors of two genera of Sonoran Desert lizard genera (Estes, 1970); *Paradipsaurus* from the early Cenozoic of Mexico (probably Oligocene) which resembles *Dipsosaurus,* and *Heloderma,* a Sonoran Desert endemic genus, which is known from Oligocene beds of Colorado. The first records of Heteromyidae, which contains the most desert-adapted genera of rodents in North America, come also from the Middle Oligocene (Estes, 1970). Consequently, it appears that by the end of the Oligocene aridity was shaping the evolution of the biota in the southwestern United States.

From the Eocene on there was a worldwide drying trend, the underlying causes of which are not entirely understood (Chapter 2). This was paralleled by an expansion of the area occupied by the Madro-Tertiary Geoflora, and the development of numerous adaptive types within it. According to Axelrod (1958) these types include plants with swollen bases for water storage (*Idria, Bursera*); winter deciduous habit (*Acacia, Populus*); drought deciduousness (*Bursera, Cercidium*); and different types of succulent Cactaceae. By early Miocene the Madro-Tertiary Geoflora was already the dominant vegetation in southeastern California (Axelrod, 1939), and by late Miocene it extended into the Central Great Basin. Although we do not have any record from southcentral Arizona, it is reasonable to assume that the Madro-Tertiary vegetation was present there at least by the end of the Miocene, if not earlier. This was not a desert vegetation as we know it today but a combination of woodland, chaparral, and subtropical shrub that occupied areas with different degrees of moisture and temperature, similar to the zonation that is found today in central California.

By the early Pliocene the region of the Mohave and Sonoran deserts was still characterized by oak woodland, chaparral, and thorn scrub vegetation. Some small areas of true desert on the lee of mountain ranges could have existed that did not enter the fossil record (Axelrod, 1958). The late Pliocene and Quaternary elevations of the Sierra Nevada-Cascade ranges and of the mountains of southern California created the semidesert conditions that exist today in the Sonoran Desert. The fossil evidence suggests that adaptations leading towards desert-adapted vertebrate taxa in North America were occurring over a wide part of the western half of the continent through much of the Cenzoic, particularly after the Miocene, corroborating the climate and plant data.

The Pleistocene did not have as drastic an effect on the Sonoran Desert as it had on the Monte because the absence of large neighboring mountain ranges precluded mountain glaciers. However, there were climatic changes in temperature and humidity (Chapter 2). As a result there were probably changes in the ranges of species, but the lack of closed valley systems surrounded by high mountains made reinvasion of the area a relatively easy matter.

In summary, the biogeographical events in the Cenozoic of the Sonoran Desert parallel largely those documented for the Monte. There is clearer and much firmer evidence for the gradual drying and the vegetational changes in the Sonoran Desert than there is in the Monte. The drying trend appears to have occurred somewhat earlier in the north, but this could possibly be due to incomplete evidence from South America. Pleistocene and post-Pleistocene events are, however, more dissimilar at the two localities. Since these late events determine the present-day distribution of the biota, this difference is significant in terms of the present research objectives.

SUMMARY AND CONCLUSIONS

The flora of the Monte is derived from elements of a more tropical and mesic flora that at one time extended throughout South America from Venezuela to central Patagonia. The flora of the Sonoran Desert is equally derived from a more tropical, southern flora, the ancestor of the Madro-Tertiary flora, which at one time extended through Central America from the Panamanian gap to the present southern United States. Whether the ancestral floras of the Monte in South America and of the Madro-Tertiary in Central America are the same cannot be stated with certainty. The present-day similarity of the flora of Brazil and Central America suggests that at the beginning of the Tertiary the South American and Central American floras were probably more similar than today. In each of these floras there were elements better adapted to drought conditions from which most of the present-day Monte and Sonoran Desert floras are derived. We feel that the great similarity of the flora at the family and generic levels between the Monte and the Sonoran Desert had its origin in this process of parallel or convergent evolution towards arid adaptation from common or closely related, more mesic ancestors. Some elements, particularly those few species of ephemerals that are common to the two areas, probably got there through long-range dispersal from one region to the other in recent times, and some, most notably the ancestral *Larrea divaricata-L. tridentata* probably had a more extensive range in tropical regions at one time (Pleistocene?) affording a kind of bridge for moving from one semidesert to the other (Raven and Axelrod, 1974). However, a very large number of genera and a fair number of the families are found only at one of the two areas, emphasizing the substantial independence of the evolution of the two floras.

The phylogenetic similarity of the flora of the Monte with that of the Sonoran Desert complicates, but does not invalidate, the research design for the following reasons. (1) All but fourteen of the species in the region where the intensive comparisons took place are different. (2) Although many genera are represented in both areas, the species at the two sites are usually not closely related and are often ecologically distinct. (3) A majority of the genera and many of the families are represented at only one of the two sites. Nevertheless, there is sufficient similarity that caution is required in distinguishing parallel evolution from convergence.

The fauna of the Monte and the Sonoran Desert are much less related phylogenetically than the flora. South America was an island continent during most of the Tertiary, which had a very profound influence on animals which as a rule are much less adept than plants at crossing water barriers. The species that are shared by both areas are invariably widespread species that occur in a variety of habitats such as the grasshopper *Trimerotropis palidipennis,* the kestral (*Falco sparverius*), or the cougar (*Felis concolor*). In spite of some phylogenetic similarities at the generic and familial level, the faunas are sufficiently unrelated to allow easy recognition of convergences.

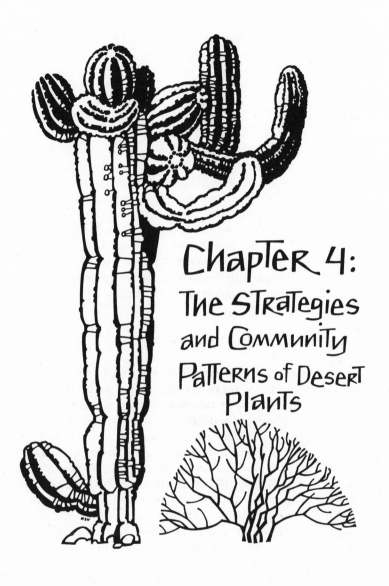

Chapter 4:
The Strategies and Community Patterns of Desert Plants

· O.T. Solbrig, M.A. Barbour, J. Cross,
G. Goldstein, C.H. Lowe,
J. Morello, T.W. Yang.

The phenotypic characteristics of plants are molded by features of the physical environment, especially climate, by competitive interactions with other plant species, and by interactions with organisms belonging to different trophic levels. That the correlation of plant physiognomy with climate is independent of phylogeny, was pointed out last century by Humboldt (1849) and Grisebach (1845), and led botanists to emphasize the physical environment in plant evolution to the neglect of interactions with other species (Schimper, 1903).

Though the structural similarity of plants from desert environments regardless of phylogenetic relationship or geographical distribution is a well-established fact, the reasons for this apparent convergence are less well understood. In this chapter we examine how the physical environment acts as a selective agent on plant form and function, and predict the possible outcomes. These predictions are tested against our observations in Andalgalá and Silver Bell. In the second part of the chapter we explore some patterns of desert plant communities and attempt to predict them from knowledge of the characteristics of individuals. Interactions of plants with other kinds of organisms are considered in Chapter 6.

DROUGHT RESISTANCE IN DESERT PLANTS*

Light, water, minerals, and carbon dioxide are the principal resources required by photosynthetic organisms. Subtropical warm deserts are characterized by high levels of solar radiation, low rainfall, and immature soils with varying levels of mineral nutrients (Chapter 2). Carbon dioxide availability in desert atmospheres is comparable to that in mesic environments. Consequently, photosynthesis in subtropical warm deserts is normally limited by water availability, rather than by light or CO_2. Mineral deficiencies in the soil exert a modifying effect in certain cases. We therefore expect to find precise and unique adaptations in desert plants for water economy. Uneven distribution of moisture availability also restricts the time when conditions are favorable for seed germination. Therefore we also expect timing of flowering and seed maturation among desert plants to be strongly influenced by rainfall patterns.

It has long been recognized that many desert plants have characteristics which distinguish them from plants in mesic areas. These characteristics, called xeromorphic by Schimper (1903), include reduction of surface to volume ratio of leaves, reduction of intercellular spaces, increase in conducting elements and in sclerenchyma, increase in chlorenchyma, and a number of changes in the form and size of leaves (Table 4-1). In addition, the leaves of many desert plants show characteristic physiological traits, such as either increased stomatal resistances and low tissue hydrature or succulence and

*By O. T. Solbrig.

TABLE 4-1 *Some General Characteristics of Desert Plant Life-Forms*

a. *Ephemerals*
   Prolongued seed viability
   Stagered germination
   Fast shoot and root growth rates
   Roots in superficial soil layers
   Minimum of xerophytic characteristics
   Mesic canopy strategy
   Length of active period controlled by water stress
   Regulation of body size in function of available soil water
b. *Phreatophytes*
   Large seeds
   Root growth much faster than shoot growth in seedlings
   Roots in deep layers of soil
   Xerophytic characters depending on permanency of water source
   Blooming in dry season and dropping seeds before the onset of rains
   Mostly C3 photosynthesis
c. *Evergreen shrubs*
   Medium to large seeds
   Capacity to tolerate prolongued drought
   Extensive root systems
   Large number of xerophytic characteristics: small leaves, thick cuticles, sunken
      stomata, small cells.
   Capacity to withstand high water stresses and still be photosynthetically active
   "Xeric" canopy strategy
   Supression of flowering in years of great water stress
   C3 type photosynthesis
   Herbivore defenses based on digestion reducing substances
d. *Succulents*
   Special germination requirements (i.e., "nurse plants")
   Roots in superficial soil layers
   Ephemeral roots, and fast growth of new roots in response to rain
   Water storage capacity
   Incapacity to tolerate low tissue water potential
   CAM photosynthesis.

high osmotic pressures. The regular appearance of some of these traits in unrelated plants from different deserts, such as in *Larrea cuneifolia* (Zygophyllaceae) from South America; *Simmondsia chinensis* (Buxaceae) from the United States, and *Artemisia herba-alba* (Compositae) in the Middle East, suggest strong selection and provides a basis for predicting convergence in these and other traits of desert plants.

However, plants with these xerophytic characteristics are not confined to deserts. They occur in habitats in which low soil water availability is accompanied by atmospheric conditions that promote rapid water loss. Such conditions are given in extremely salty soils (salt marshes), in extremely cold soils (arctic and high mountain environments), in extremely shallow soils with a great deal of runoff (table lands, rocky slopes) and under special edaphic conditions (serpentine soils, limestone outcrops, gypsum soils).

Another characteristic of deserts is the coexistence of plants with very different morphologies and life forms in the same or adjacent habitats. For example all warm desert areas have a flora containing perennial evergreen and deciduous shrubs, succulents of various shapes (cylindrical unbranched, cylindrical branched, roseatte, etc.), a large number of annuals and geophytes, and small trees along washes and depressions. This variety of life forms indicates that there are several competitively viable solutions to the problems of survival and reproduction in deserts. Therefore, we must explain why, though certain constellations of morphological features regularly appear in taxonomically unrelated desert plants, there is not convergence on one life form.

Natural selection maximizes fitness over entire life cycles, and not necessarily short-term photosynthesis or decreased water loss. However, a plant capable of maximizing photosynthesis within the constraints of its available resources and the physical environment should have advantages in competition with other plants, defenses against herbivores, and should have more energy available for reproduction. Consequently it is reasonable to expect natural selection to maximize net yearly photosynthate production. However, convergence will occur only if there are few solutions to the problems of maximizing photosynthesis under severely limited moisture conditions with high temperatures.

A land plant lives in two different media: air and soil. The plant extracts water from the soil and transpires it through the leaves. Drought resistance therefore consists of (1) the ability of the leaf to photosynthesize under conditions of low water potential, and (2) soil water extraction by roots. Because the leaf is the organ of greatest photosynthetic activity and of greatest exposure to the drying power of the air, modifications of the characteristics of leaves are more striking than modifications in other structures of desert plants. The stems of desert plants are similar to those of plants in other environments except that a larger proportion of them are photosynthetic. In roots, modifications occur mostly in position within the soil and total biomass. The traits of leaves and roots are, however, intimately coevolved. Canopy characteristics influence the effectiveness of different types of roots, and vice versa.

Canopy

Photosynthesis requires carbon dioxide which diffuses into the leaf through the stomata, the opening of which is dependent on leaf hydrature and/or atmospheric humidity. Stomata close when the leaf tissue water potential approaches some variable, species-specific critical level. Stomatal closing is not necessarily simultaneous or total and the plant can regulate water loss by controlling the number of stomata closed and the degree of closure (Meidner and Mansfield, 1968). Plants also lose water through the epidermis and adaptations such as sunken stomata, layers of trichomes lining the stomatal cavity, resin layers on the epidermis, etc., reduce transpirational losses, especially when the stomata are partially or entirely closed. These same structures also reduce the rate of CO_2 diffusion into the leaf when the stomata are open, thereby setting a limit to the maximum rate of photosynthesis attainable under conditions of maximum water availability. Consequently leaves cannot simultaneously have high stomatal resistances to regulate water loss under moisture stress and the low stomatal resistances which permit high photosynthetic rates per unit leaf area under conditions of high moisture availability. Increase in number of stomata per unit area can compensate for high individual stomatal resistance, but only partially (Table 4-2).

Most plant species close their stomata before leaf water potential reaches –15 Bars. Severe and often irreversible damage results if the cells continue to lose water after the stomata have closed. Nevertheless, some desert plants can withstand very high levels of dessication before total stomatal closure (Table 4-3).

The ability to endure relatively high levels of dessication (high negative leaf water potential) is enhanced by small cells, thick cell walls, and biochemical changes (Stocker, 1956; Boyer, 1973). However, these characteristics reduce the potential rates of photosynthesis when soil water is plentiful. The negative effects can be somewhat compensated by the positions of chloroplasts and the number of stomata per unit surface area, but their effects are not sufficient to completely counteract the general inverse relationships between high maximum rate of photosynthesis and the ability to continue to photosynthesize under conditions of low water availability (Orians and Solbrig, 1977).

No systematic measurements of tissue water potential or photosynthetic rates were made by us. However, a number of studies on Sonoran Desert

TABLE 4-2 *Stomatal Density ($\#/mm^2$) for Various Species of Sonoran and Monte Plants*

| Species | Reference | Mean stomatal density | | Distribution |
		Upper	Lower	
Larrea cuneifolia	Morello, 1955a	90	120	Chaco
Larrea cuneifolia	Morello, 1955a	145	165	Monte
Larrea cuneifolia	Barbour et al., 1974	162	162	Monte
Larrea divaricata	Morello, 1955a	104	130	Monte
Larrea divaricata	Barbour et al., 1974	305	305	Monte
Larrea tridentata	Barbour et al., 1974	208	208	Sonoran Desert
Larrea nitida	Morello, 1955a	100	150	Patagonia
Zuccagnia punctata	Morello, 1955a	110	140	Monte
Prosopis alba	Morello, 1955a	48	25	Monte & Espinal
Encelia farinosa	Barbour, 1967	280	362	Sonoran Desert

TABLE 4-3 *Leaf Water Potentials of Five Desert Shrubs, at Two Localities and Five Different Dates**

| Date | Species | Leaf water potential (bars) | |
		Max.	Min.
	Tummamoc Hill, Arizona		
March 1	*Encelia farinosa*	–16.0	–21.9
July 24	*Encelia farinosa*	–14.8	–29.4
	Cercidium microphyllum	–16.9	–22.4
	Acacia greggii	–16.3	–24.7
Nov. 9	*Encelia farinosa*	–31.8	–36.9
	Cercidium microphyllum (leafless)	–31.6	–36.3
	Acacia greggii	–32.0	–47.6
Dec. 26	*Encelia farinosa*	–8.7	–20.1
	Cercidium microphyllum	–17.3	–27.6
	Acacia greggii	–19.0	–35.0
	El Rincon, Baja California Sur, Mexico		
Nov. 3	*Encelia farinosa* ssp. *radians*	–10.8	–33.8
	Viguiera tomentosa	–29.8	–45.6
	Acacia sp.	–11.8	–32.2

*Data kindly submitted by Dr. J. Ehrelinger.

plants are available (Table 4-3) and data obtained by us (Barbour et al., 1974; Morello, 1955a) exist for *Larrea divaricata* and *L. cuneifolia* (Table 4-4).

Plants rely on evaporative cooling to keep their leaves close to air temperature. The efficiency of this mechanism depends on a number of factors, primarily heat load, wind, and leaf shape (Gates, 1968). The greater the heat load, the less wind, and the larger the leaves, the greater the rate of transpiration required to keep the leaf within the optimal temperature range of photosynthesis. In warm deserts plants experience great heat loads, but are usually unable to evaporate great amounts of water. Therefore natural selection can act only on the remaining parameter, physical structure, especially leaf shape, to minimize heat load. Thus, desert shrubs possess very small leaves or none at all. Other adaptations include leaf and branch orientations which reduce high noon heat loads, thick layers of trichomes and light-colored surface that increase light reflectance, etc. Although these adaptations reduce evaporation and heat load, they also reduce photosynthetic rate by increasing stomatal resistance and/or reducing light interception and absorption. Parkhurst and Loucks (1972) present models which relate leaf size to water-use efficiency which give reasonable predictions of leaf sizes in desert habitats.

In the Bolsón de Pipanaco and the Avra Valley, evergreen perennial shrubs tend to have the smallest leaves of all types of plants. This group includes all species of *Larrea, Tricomaria usillo, Cercidium praecox, Bul-*

TABLE 4-4. *Shootwater Potential (ψ), Transpiration and Net Photosynthesis of 6-8 Month Old Greenhouse Seedlings at 38° C, 19% Relative Humidity, 48000 lux*

Species	ψ	Transp. mg. dm^{-2} hr^{-1}	Photosynthesis mg. g^{-1} hr^{-1}
A. Watered every 2 days			
Larrea tridentata	−16.1	4680	3.52
Larrea divaricata	−14.9	7560	4.93
Larrea cuneifolia	−15.0	5040	3.87
B. Watered every 8 days			
Larrea tridentata	−44.5	180	0.51
Larrea divaricata	−46.5	684	0.17
Larrea cuneifolia	−41.6	1368	0.93

Source: From Barbour et al., 1974.

nesia retamo, and *Zuccagnia punctata* in the Andalgalá area, and *Larrea tridentata, Simmondsia chinensis, Cercidium microphyllum,* and *C. floridum* from the Avra Valley area. Also in the Argentine site there is a totally aphyllous shrub, *Cassia aphylla.* Trees along washes (various species of *Prosopis* and *Acacia* in Catamarca, *Olneya tesota* and *Acacia* spp. in Arizona) often have divided leaves with small leaflets, although some wash species (*Bulnesia retamo, Cercidium microphyllum*) are almost aphyllous. Plants that are active only during the wet season tend to have larger leaves. Some species are polymorphic, producing larger leaves, with fewer stomata per unit surface, and a lower density of trichomes during the wet season, and smaller leaves when under drought stress. Examples are *Ambrosia dumosa* and *Encelia farinosa* from Silver Bell. Species of *Jatropha* at both sites adjust the size and surface characteristics of their leaves by delaying full expansion of the leaf blade until the onset of the rains (Table 4-5). The sizes and characteristics of leaves of annuals and geophytes are very variable, but in general they tend to have larger leaves than the perennial species. These leaf size patterns are similar to those observed in other desert areas such as the Sinai in Israel (Evenari et al., 1971).

Photosynthesis involves an energy flux and a flux of CO_2. Photons are used to split water and produce both ATP and a reductant, $ADPH_2$, which are used in the subsequent step of fixing CO_2 from the air and converting it into carbohydrate molecules. The photochemical steps involving the absorption of light energy and the splitting of water are, as far as is known, identical in all green plants with chlorophyll. However there are three different photosynthetic biochemical pathways known by which plants fix CO_2. They are: (1) the Calvin cycle or C3 plants; (2) the dicarboxylic acid cycle or C4 plants; and (3) crassulacean acid metabolism or CAM plants (Mooney, 1972). C3 plants have the greatest range of optimal temperatures, 10° to 35° C (Larcher, 1969; Mooney, 1972), but the lowest water use efficiency per gram

TABLE 4-5 *Average Leaf Biomass of Individual* Jatropha macrocarpa
Plants in a Population at Joyango Transect * *(in gm dry weight)*

Date	Dry weight (gm)	St. dev. (s)
10-30-72	0.019	0.007
11-30	0.024	0.014
12-11	0.043	0.021
12-24	0.086	0.050
1-8-73	0.220	0.154
1-22	2.375	1.511
2-5	3.016	1.804
2-19	5.099	2.403
3-5	4.440	2.108
3-19	4.729	3.026
4-2	2.316	2.326
4-30	0.179	0.129

*Each sample consisted of the leaves of twelve plants. Plants started leafing in October, but leaves did not expand until after the first big rainfall in the second week of January.

of carbon fixed of the three types. C4 plants expend less water per gram of carbon fixed than C3 plants, have higher photosynthetic temperature optima and the highest photosynthetic rates among the three types. CAM plants lose the least amount of water per gram of carbon fixed because a decoupling of the carbon fixation path from the light reaction of photosynthesis allows them to fix carbon in the dark. However, CAM plants have very low photosynthetic rates and a strict requirement of high day temperatures and low night temperatures (Ting, 1971; Mooney, 1972). The path of carbon fixation of about 100 nonsucculent Monte plants was checked (W. Brown, Mabry and Di Feo, unpublished, Appendix R), including some of the most common perennial species such as *Larrea cuneifolia, L. divaricata, Ximenia americana, Atamisquea emarginata, Nicotiana glauca, Jatropha peiranoi, J. macrocarpa, J. excisa, Geoffrea decorticans, Zuccagnia punctata, Tricomaria usillo, Bulnesia retamo,* and *Acacia aroma.* Only seventeen of the plants tested had a C4 carbon fixing system. Plants in this category were mostly annual or summer active perennial herbs, including the dominant summer annual grass, *Bouteloua barbata.*

The same situation applies to the Sonoran desert.* The majority of species are C3 including all the dominant shrubs tested to date: *Larrea tridentata, Encelia farinosa, Fouquieria splendens, Ambrosia dumosa, Olneya tesota,* and *Acacia greggii.* C4 plants are mostly annuals or perennial herbs, but not exclusively. CAM plants include the Cactaceae, most Agavaceae, and *Dickya tuberosa* in the Bromeliaceae.

Ability to withstand high negative water potentials requires mechanisms that prevent embolism of the conducting system. The normal evolutionary

*Data kindly supplied by Dr. Joe Berry of the Carnegie Institution of Washington.

result is a large number of small diameter vessels. However, although such morphology safeguards the plant against embolism, by increasing the resistance to flow of the xylem, it lowers the maximum rate of flow that can be attained.

Xerophytic characteristics not only reduce the maximum attainable rate of photosynthesis, but they are also energetically costlier (Orians and Solbrig, 1977). In the absence of precise quantitative data regarding the costs of producing different types of leaves, only general predictions can be made.

In summary, the morphological features that are characteristic of many desert plants (and other xerophytes) such as small leaves, thick cuticles, sunken stomata, high stomatal density, leaf surface hairs, small cells, thick cell walls, and narrow conducting elements are all adaptations to function under conditions of low and intermittent soil water availability and high evaporative demand. However, because of the tight linking of the flux of water vapor with the flux of carbon dioxide through the stomata, plants cannot decrease H_2O vapor loss in relation to increases in CO_2 flux without trade-offs that reduce photosynthesis in some other way. CO_2 flux per unit H_2O flux is higher in C4 than in C3 plants, since PEP carboxylase has a greater affinity of CO_2 than RuDP carboxylase and is not oxygen inhibited. However, C4 type photosynthesis appears to create temperature and hence temporal constraints, and has evolved primarily in herbaceous, summer active desert plants. A reduction in H_2O vapor loss without affecting CO_2 flux can be achieved by opening the stomata only during that time of day when relative ambient humidity is high. However, because such leaves cannot cool by evaporation during the hottest part of the day (when relative ambient humidity is lowest), adopting this strategy requires morphological adjustments (small leaves, orientation changes, reduction of cuticular transpiration, etc.) that reduce the efficiency of light interception and increase stomatal resistance. Consequently all possible canopy adaptations that improve water conservation reduce the rate of photosynthesis when there is abundant water.

Roots and Soil Water Extraction

Plant soil water relationships have been reviewed recently by Slatyer (1967), Kozlowsky (1968), Kramer (1969), and Buckman and Brady (1974) and mechanisms of drought resistance in higher plants by Stocker (1956), Walter (1963), Parker (1968), and Walter and Stadelman (1974). These relationships appear to be complex, and soil texture and chemical composition play a major role in movement of water from soil to plant. Generally, energy needed to remove water from soil increases exponentially with decreasing soil moisture. The ability of cells to withstand great negative potentials before plasmolysis begins determines the limiting energy levels at which a plant ceases to remove soil water. In warm deserts, the soil is well below field capacity most of the year. Furthermore, in much of the upper soil profile, water is held with such strong forces that very high negative plant water potentials are required to extract *any* soil water. Low soil moisture is especially pronounced in flats with fine-textured soils. When a hard desert summer rain falls onto a fine-textured soil, the upper layers become quickly saturated, but percolation to lower layers is slow. Consequently, there may be a great deal of runoff or ponding at the surface from which water is lost by evaporation. Light but persistent winter rains result in less runoff and more percolation. A confounding effect of fine soil texture is low available oxygen in the root zone, which in turn affects both nutrients and water uptake. Lunt et al. (1973) concluded that absence of *Larrea* and *Artemisia* species from fine-textured soils was primarily due to the high oxygen demands of these species. These types of soils are found in the Avra Valley and Bolsón de Pipanaco mostly in the Bajadas and in the flats (Chapter 2; Table 4–8). Coarser soils of middle and upper-Bajadas, on the other hand, permit greater infiltration of water, particularly during hard summer rains. If the soil is rocky enough, special microhabitats are formed below buried rocks where pockets of moisture persist for a long time. Rocks on the surface affect exposure, topography, and runoff patterns, creating additional microhabitats. It is in such areas that the greatest richness of plant forms is found (Whittaker and Niering, 1963). Coarser textured soils allow more percolation and saturate to lower depths. Furthermore, since rains in desert areas (particularly summer rains) are often intense but of short duration, a fair amount of runoff can take place, especially if there is a variable topography as in the Avra Valley and the Bolsón de Pipanaco. As a result, water tends to accumulate in depressions and along and below washes.

Water is lost from the soil solution through evaporation and through transpiration by plants. Evaporation takes place only from the upper layers of the soil, but such evaporative losses can be sizable. However, once the capillary column is broken, no more water is lost from deeper soil layers (unless it moves in the vapor phase, a controversial and not well-understood subject).

The availability of water in the soil should determine the distribution of plant roots. Basically three sources of soil water can be identified: (1) water in the upper 20 cm of the soil. This zone saturates most often, but also dries out most quickly. Harvest of this water favors roots with the ability to remove water from the soil solution at a fast rate. (2) Water at intermediate depths. The total amount that percolates to this zone during the season is less than that reaching the upper layers, but because of reduced evaporative loss, this water potentially can be harvested over a longer period of time. (3) Water in the depressions and under washes. This source of water is both plentiful and often relatively permanent. Because it is found at lower depths, however, it can only be reached by an extensive system of tap roots. These three types of water can be regarded as distinct resources because efficient exploitation of one of them cannot eliminate either of the others. Therefore stable coexistence of species utilizing these different water sources is possible.

A study of root distributions in flats and adjacent washes was conducted in the area of the Rio Amanao (Le Claire and Solbrig, unpublished), paralleling a similar study done by Cannon (1911) at Tummamoc Hill, near Tucson. Morello (1955a,b) also studied distribution of roots in *Larrea divaricata* and *Zuccagnia punctata* in the Monte. The patterns of root distributions in the Andalgalá area are similar to that in the Tucson area. The upper 20 cm of the soil in flats and bajadas are occupied almost exclusively by roots of ephemeral plants or succulents. Live roots are found in this area of the soil only during the wet season. Only very occasionally are roots of perennial shrubs found in this superficial layer. At intermediate depths (40-50 cm, occasionally to 100 cm) in flats and bajadas, the roots of perennial shrubs are found. These plants have an extensive network of roots, extending in a radius of 5-10 m from the base of the stem. Topography and soil texture affect the extension and depth of the roots of shrubs, which show very plastic responses to soil humidity. Although some of these roots are alive even in the driest part of the year, there is evidence that part of the root network dies back during the dry season. In washes, trees and shrubs (even those that are also found in the flats such as *Larrea* spp.) have deeper roots. A *Prosopis flexuosa* tree had a sizable tap root at 8 m of depth. However, wash plants also have a well developed system of roots at upper and intermediate levels (Figure 4-1).

LIFE FORM STRATEGIES IN RESPONSE TO
WATER RESOURCES*

In the preceding sections we have shown that the canopy characteristics associated with drought resistance inevitably reduce the maximum rate of photosynthesis the plant can attain under conditions of high water availability. It was also shown that soil water in deserts is more than one resource for plants and that soil texture, topography, and runoff patterns determine the distribution of and availability of these different water resources. From these considerations we can predict the canopy and root strategies that yield the highest net annual photosynthate, and also suggest why the number of desert plant life forms is limited.

At least four basic growth form types have evolved in desert regions: drought-escaping plants, deep rooted phreatophytes, drought-enduring evergreens, and succulents (Cannon, 1911; Shantz, 1927).

A drought-escaping plant completes the active part of its life cycle during that portion of the year when water stress is at a minimum, and escape the drought by going dormant. Annuals adapted to a short growing season so that they can complete their life cycle from germination to seed production during the wet season are preadapted to desert conditions, since in general most seeds are capable of enduring drought. In warm deserts with both sum-

*By O. T. Solbrig.

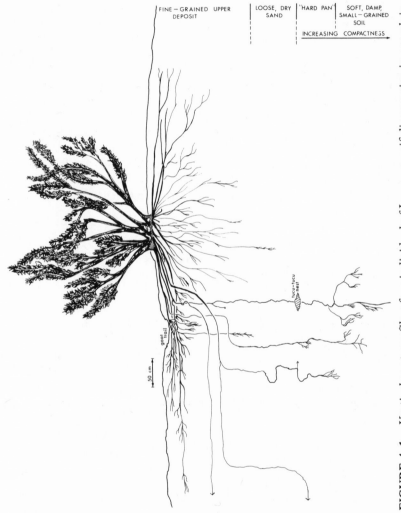

FINE – GRAINED UPPER DEPOSIT

LOOSE, DRY SAND

"HARD PAN"

SOFT, DAMP, SMALL – GRAINED SOIL

INCREASING COMPACTNESS

tucu-tucu nest

goat trail

50 cm

FIGURE 4-1. *Vertical root profile of an individual of* Larrea cuneifolia *growing in a wash in Andalgalá. Drawn to scale. Only roots larger than approximately 1 mm are indicated.*

mer and winter rainy seasons, two sets of ephemerals may evolve (Figures 4-2 and 4-3), each adapted to different temperature regimes (Went, 1949). Because of the unpredictability of the rainy season, their germination requirements have evolved to relate to soil moisture, and they have the ability to remain dormant for long periods, up to ten or more years (Cohen, 1967, 1968; MacArthur, 1972). Perennials which lose their leaves during seasons of high water stress are similar to ephemerals in that they live through stress in a state of dormancy, but they differ in supporting more tissue during the drought periods, and in their ability to respond with faster growth rates when moisture appears. Root perennials (Figure 3-3) are somewhat intermediate between annuals and deciduous perennial shrubs. However perenneting organs other than seeds (corms, bulbs, stems) have a lower survival probability than seeds. They are especially vulnerable in extremely dry years. Consequently in harsh and unpredictable environments, annuals and perennials coexist (Charnov and Schaffer, 1973). In the southwestern United States deserts, the annual flora increases with increasing aridity and year-to-year variability, from 1 percent of total cover in areas with 20 percent coefficient of variation in annual rainfall to 94 percent of total cover in Death Valley, where the coefficient of variation in rainfall is larger than 50 percent (Schaffer and Gadgil, 1975).

Since ephemerals and drought-deciduous perennials are active only during the wet season, they should be under strong selection to evolve morphological and physiological characteristics that result in high productivity and high seed production when water is available. Consequently we expect to find a minimum of xerophytic characteristics in these plants. We also expect a pre-

FIGURE 4-2. *Summer annuals at Andalgalá. The most common species shown is* Verbesina encelioides. *(Photo by P. Cantino.)*

FIGURE 4-3. *Winter annuals at Silver Bell Bajada. (Photo by M. A. Mares.)*

dominance of C4 species among summer active drought-evading plants. Finally we expect drought-evaders to have their roots in the upper soil layers where wet season water is plentiful. Our observations confirm these expectations.

Deep rooted phreatophytes tap permanent or semipermanent underground water which must be translocated from great depths, sometimes more than 10 m. Therefore a great negative water potential may exist even if water is plentiful and hence the leaves often show some xerophytic characteristics. The establishment of seedlings of phreatophytes depends on sufficient rain to moisten the upper soil layers until the roots reach more permanent water (Birand, 1961). This requirement should favor such traits as large seeds to provide the energy for the large root, allocation of cotyledon reserves mostly to root growth, a tap root system, and ripening of fruits at the onset of the rainy season. Establishment of new plants may occur only during exceptionally wet years when the entire soil column is moistened for a prolonged period.

We expect the canopy characteristics of phreatophytes to vary according to the predictability of the water their roots are tapping. If the underground water being tapped is plentiful throughout the year, plants with mesophytic canopy characteristics will be favored. However, if the water is available only seasonally, selection will favor either species with more xerophytic leaves or deciduousness. For example, species of *Prosopis* by closing their stomata during the hot and dry midday hours, markedly increase their water utilization efficiency per gram of carbon fixed (Mooney et al., 1977).

Drought-enduring evergreen shrubs often known as "true xerophytes" photosynthesize throughout the year, by tapping the water that percolates to intermediate depths in flats and bajadas. Since this water is limited, we expect these plants to have characteristics that permit soil water extraction and photosynthesis under high soil water potentials. As predicted they usually possess a number of stereotyped, xeromorphic characters such as microphylls, sunken stomata, thick cuticles, generalized root system, associated with water economy, but there are exceptions. For reasons still not understood, cells of true xerophytes are able to withstand a very low degree of hydrature. They also appear to have wide tolerance limits for moisture and other physical characteristics of soil. Plants such as *Larrea* are able to maintain small, but positive growth under extreme water stress levels leading to plant water potentials below -50 Bars (Woodell et al., 1969; Strain, 1970; Oechel et al., 1972; Barbour et al., 1974). Under more mesic conditions, photosynthetic rates are moderately high and transpiration can be very high. Overall production on a leaf or shoot dry-weight basis may even be comparable to that for shrubs of the eastern deciduous forest (Barbour, 1973).

According to Ludwig (in press), the generalized root system of these plants gives them the potential for either extensive tap root or lateral root development. This appears to be an adaptation to exploit the highly varied desert soil moisture environments. However, this adaptation is probably not unique to desert shrubs. Other xeric-adapted traits may be similarly nonspecific since they can be induced by high light, low moisture, or mineral deficiencies in the soil (Daubenmire, 1974).

Because the light and dark reaction of photosynthesis has been decoupled, succulents can exist for long periods without any external source of water, and without opening the stomata. Energy for maintenance is obtained by reutilizing respiratory carbon. This mechanism allows succulents to photosynthesize during the entire year but results in very low rates of carbon gain compared to other desert plants even under the most favorable conditions (Mooney, 1972). These plants can, however, persist in environments too dry for any other perennial plant (Mooney and Dunn, 1970).

Succulents have very low negative tissue water potentials (in the order of -1 to -5 Bars) and apparently cannot withstand the internal water stresses to which other desert plants are normally subjected (Kluge and Fisher, 1967; Szarek and Ting, 1974). Consequently if they maintained permanent root systems they would lose water to the soil during the dry season. Instead they obtain their water from the superficial soil layers after heavy rains swelling up as they store it in their tissues (Table 4-6). During dry periods the permeable roots hairs are shed, reducing water loss to the soil. However, they must be regrown if more water is to be taken in.

Of the four life forms characteristic of the vegetation of the Bolsón de Pipanaco and the Avra Valley, only the drought-enduring evergreen shrubs

TABLE 4-6 *Growth of Plants of the South American Giant Cactus* Trichocereus terscheckii

Date	Plant number and size in meters											Mean	Mean monthly increment	
	1	2	3	4	5	6	7	8	9	10	11		Absolute (m)	%
9/11/72	0.261	0.581	1.203	1.470	3.450	3.980	4.370	4.537	4.706	5.282	5.801	3.240	—	—
10/9/72	0.262	0.574	1.215	1.472	3.451	3.980	4.386	4.542	4.708	5.296	5.809	3.245	0.005	0.15
11/6/72	0.260	0.582	1.210	1.483	3.455	3.987	4.390	4.539	4.711	5.296	5.816	3.248	0.003	0.09
12/3/72	0.255	0.584	1.201	1.480	3.456	3.987	4.394	4.541	4.714	5.300	5.815	3.247	-0.001	-0.03
1/1/73	0.255	0.584	1.198	1.474	3.454	3.987	4.385	4.552	4.709	5.298	5.810	3.245	-0.002	-0.06
1/29/73*	0.277	0.588	1.221	1.515	3.450	3.987	4.412	4.559	4.717	5.315	5.836	3.261	0.016	0.49
2/26/73	0.280	0.590	1.235	1.535	3.469	3.988	4.398	4.565	4.732	5.326	5.837	3.269	0.009	0.28
3/24/73	0.283	0.600	1.246	1.582	3.483	4.000	4.410	4.589	4.733	5.349	5.848	3.284	0.015	0.49
4/23/73	0.284	0.601	1.252	1.575	3.478	3.997	4.403	4.582	4.737	5.336	5.846	3.281	-0.003	-0.09
5/21/73	0.283	0.600	1.250	1.579	3.471	3.995	4.403	4.585	4.736	5.333	5.844	3.280	-0.001	-0.03
7/16/73	0.282	0.599	1.245	1.582	3.477	4.001	4.403	4.592	4.742	5.345	5.845	3.283	0.003	0.09
10 month														
Increment	0.021	0.018	0.042	0.112	0.027	0.021	0.033	0.055	0.036	0.063	0.044	0.043	0.004	—
% Increase	8.05	3.10	3.49	7.62	0.78	0.53	0.76	1.21	0.76	1.19	0.76	1.33	—	—

*The rainy season extends from approximately the middle of January to the middle of March

are restricted to desert areas. Ephemerals are found in a variety of temporary habitats, for example, early spring annuals in the Eastern Deciduous Forest, winter annuals in California grasslands, or more commonly fugitive species occupying disturbed habitats. However, desert annuals show greater germination specialization than nondesert ephemerals. Succulents are found outside of desert areas in islands of local dry environments, such as rocky outcrops. Phreatophytes are found along permanent and semipermanent bodies of water, and in areas where the water table is not too deep. On the other hand, many of the life forms characteristic of mesic areas with closed canopies such as vines, and large leaved, monolayer trees and shrubs, are absent in warm deserts.

The variety of life forms in warm deserts is the consequence of insufficient soil water to allow the production of a continuous vegetation canopy, but sufficient soil water to allow some storage in intermediate and deep layers. In areas with higher rainfall density of plants is increased, and a continuous canopy is formed. Under conditions of a continuous canopy and competition for light, the ephemeral and succulent are not competitively viable. Also, in those circumstances, xerophytic shrubs are replaced by shrubs or trees with more mesic leaves. On the other hand, in areas of low rainfall, there is insufficient percolation and runoff for enough water to reach lower soil layers where it can be utilized by xerophytic shrubs and phreatophytes during the dry season. In such environments xerophytic shrubs and phreatophytes cannot compete with drought evading plants and succulents (Mooney and Dunn, 1970).

Since the overall rainfall and topography are similar in the Bolsón de Pipanaco and the Avra Valley (Chapter 2) convergences in plant life forms and their distributions are expected. This is verified by our observations. Three species of xerophytic shrubs dominate the flats at each site: *Larrea cuneifolia, Tricomaria usillo,* and *Cassia aphylla* in Catamarca; *Larrea divaricata, Krameria grayi,* and *Simmondsia chinensis* in Arizona. A number of tree species and large shrubs dominate the washes: *Prosopis flexuosa, P. chilensis, P. torquata,* and *Acacia aroma* in the Bolsón de Pipanaco; *Prosopis velutina, Olneya tessota, Acacia constricta,* and *A. greggii* in the Tucson area. (See section on plant communities, below, for details).

STRATEGIES IN RELATION TO TIMING OF BLOOMING AND FRUITING*

The phenological behavior of desert plants is determined principally by water availability and not by photoperiod because moisture availability is not strongly correlated with calendar dates. This discussion is concerned

*By O. T. Solbrig and T. W. Yang.

primarily with the temporal patterns of flowering, fruiting, and germination of perennials. We first identify and analyze the main selective forces and the constraints operating on germination, flowering, and fruiting.

Germination and Establishment

Seedlings are the most vulnerable stage in the life cycle of a xerophyte. A seedling has a limited energy reserve, a low water absorption capacity, and the cotyledons and young leaves are exposed to the great temperature fluctuations encountered near the ground. Since no seedling can survive long without a supply of water, germination can only take place during the rainy season.

Establishment also involves surviving the dry season, either in an active or dormant state. In both cases special morphologies are needed (deep roots, ability to withstand high negative water potentials, adaptations to withstand water loss, withstanding overheating, etc.). Since these physiological and morphological characteristics require a greater energetic expenditure than tissues without them, seedlings of desert perennials cannot grow as fast as ephemerals which lack these features. The probability of establishment should be a function of the reserves in the seed, and we therefore expect desert perennials to have larger seeds than desert ephemerals.

The probability of establishment of perennials should be proportional to the length of the rainy season and inversely proportional to the length of the dry season. Establishment should take place preferentially in years with unusually long wet seasons, and may be especially enhanced by two or more consecutive years of long wet/short dry seasons. Since the occurrence of these special conditions is correlated with average yearly rainfall, establishment should be more frequent in wetter deserts, leading to a more even age distribution in the latter.

Finally, microtopography should play an important role. Rocks, depressions, and different exposures produce pockets of humidity and shade. Establishment should consequently be uneven over space. Finally, seeds should show adaptations to germinate only under special conditions of temperature and humidity.

Blooming and Fruiting

Flowering, fruiting, and seed maturation are energy and water consuming events. From a strictly energetic point of view it would be advantageous to bloom and fruit during the rainy season, when photosynthetic rates are at their maximum and soil water is plentiful. However, this will result in seed dispersal at the end of the rainy season which is an unfavorable time for seed germination. The alternatives are as follows: (1) to bloom and fruit during the rainy season, producing seeds that will not germinate until the following year, or (2) to bloom and fruit during the dry season producing seeds capable of immediate germination at the beginning of the rainy season. Which of these alternatives is competitively superior depends on their costs and benefits under specific environmental conditions. The first alternative may result in more flowers and seeds but because seeds are exposed to predation in the soil for an entire year, there is greater pregermination mortality. In addition there is a cost associated with seed dormancy such as thick seed coats, tissues that can withstand extreme dehydration, ability to cut down respiration, etc. There is also an inverse correlation between seed size and ability to survive in soil (Salisbury, 1942).

The reverse is true for the second alternative. The seeds need not have the adaptations for survival during the dry season, but the plants bloom and fruit when water is most scarce. This may limit the number of flowers and fruits produced. Since phreatophytes and succulents have water available to them during the dry season they should adopt the second alternative. All other plants may be forced to adopt the first alternative. Furthermore, the drier the environment the greater the relative cost of producing flowers and fruits during the dry season.

From these arguments we make the following predictions. Ephemerals should ripen their seeds at the end of the rainy season. Xerophytic shrubs should bloom in response to rain and fruit during the rainy season. Blooming in phreatophytes and succulents should be photoperiodically controlled and should occur in advance of the rainy season. All plants can be expected to require a certain soil moisture threshold before flowering is triggered. The drier the desert the fewer the plants that bloom during the dry season. All desert plants should possess narrow germination requirements.

Results

From June 1972 to August 1974 qualitative phenological observations were performed on a number of perennial species in the Bolsón de Pipanaco and the Avra Valley and in the Tucson area (Yang and Abbe, 1974; LeClaire et al., in prep.). The species selected (Table 4-7) were those with more than 1 percent coverture in the permanent transect plots plus a few additions. At least two stations for each species were selected (Figure 1-2) and weekly (or biweekly, in times of dormancy) observations of (1) leaf initiation and leaf drop, (2) stem elongation, (3) various aspects of flowering, and (4) fruit production were recorded. Each population consisted of ten marked plants selected at random. The objectives were to assess the phenological behavior and its correlation with the temperature, precipitation and photoperiod regimes of each region, and to test whether the bimodal rainfall pattern of the Tucson area resulted in a significantly different phenological behavior in that area compared with plants growing under unimodal rainfall pattern in Andalgalá. The presence in our sample of two sibling species (*Larrea divaricata* and

TABLE 4-7 *Species Studied Phenologically and Localities*

A. Bolsón de Pipanaco	#1	#2	#3	#4	Locations* #7	km6	km34	km66	km96
Acacia aroma	–	+	+	–	–	–	–	–	–
Acacia furcatispina	–	–	+	–	–	–	–	–	–
Bulnesia retamo	+	+	–	–	–	–	–	–	–
Cassia aphylla	–	+	+	–	–	–	–	–	–
Cercidium praecox	+	+	+	–	–	–	–	–	–
Jatropha macrocarpa	–	–	–	–	–	–	–	–	–
Larrea divaricata	+	–	+	+	+	+	+	–	–
Larrea cuneifolia	+	+	+	+	+	+	+	+	+
Mimosa ephedroides	–	–	–	–	+	–	–	–	–
Prosopis chilensis	+	+	–	–	–	+	+	+	+
Prosopis torquata	–	+	+	–	–	–	–	–	–
Trichomeria usillo	+	+	–	–	–	–	–	–	–
Ximenia americana	–	+	+	–	+	–	–	–	–
Zuccagnia punctata	–	–	–	–	+	–	–	–	–

B. Avra Valley and Tucson Area	#1	#2	#3	#4	#5	#6	#7	#8	#9
Acacia constricta	+	–	–	–	–	–	+	–	–
Acacia greggii	+	–	–	–	–	–	+	–	–
Ambrosia deltoidea	–	–	–	–	–	+	–	–	–
Calliandra eriophylla	–	–	+	–	–	–	–	–	+
Cercidium floridum	–	–	–	–	–	–	–	–	–
Cercidium microphyllum	–	+	–	–	–	+	–	–	–
Encelia farinosa	–	–	+	–	–	–	–	–	–
Fouquieria splendens	–	+	–	–	–	+	–	–	–
Jatropha cardiophylla	–	–	+	–	–	+	–	–	–
Krameria grayi	–	–	–	–	–	–	–	+	–
Larrea tridentata	–	+	–	–	–	+	–	–	–
Olneya tessota	–	–	+	–	+	–	–	–	–
Simmondsia chinensis	–	+	–	+	–	+	–	–	–

*Locations in South America are indicated in the map of the Bolsón de Pipanaco (Figure 1–2). Locations in the Avra Valley are in the Saguaro National Monument East (1–4) or West (5–9).

L. tridentata), one in each area, of several genera (*Prosopis, Cercidium, Jatropha,* and *Acacia*) with at least one species in each area, as well as several unrelated species (*Olneya tesota, Fouquiera splendens, Simmondsia chinensis* in Tucson; *Cassia aphylla, Tricomaria usillo, Bulnesia retamo* in Andalgalá) also permits an assessment of the role of phylogeny in the evolution of phenological behavior.

Comparative phenological observations over a short two-year period are insufficient to establish with any degree of certainty whether species are convergent in their phenological response to environmental variables, because of the great annual variation in rainfall in desert regions. We therefore describe the general patterns observed, pointing out the differences and similarities between species, and the correlation with rainfall and photoperiod, withholding final judgment as to the exact causes.

Vegetative Behavior

Three main variables affecting vegetative behavior were recorded: leaf initiation, shoot initiation, and leaf drop. Within a species shoot initiation and leaf initiation are usually correlated the latter preceding the former.

Two poorly defined groups of species can be recognized in relation to the pattern of leaf and shoot initiation in the Bolsón de Pipanaco. One group is formed by species where vegetative growth starts as soon as temperature increases in the spring (September). The majority of species studied are in this group: *Acacia aroma, Cassia aphylla, Jatropha macrocarpa, Larrea divaricata, L. cuneifolia, Prosopis chilensis, P. torquata, Tricomaria usillo,* and *Zuccagnia punctata.* The other group is formed by species that delay the onset of vegetative growth until November, December, or even January, depending on the beginning of the rainy season. Of the species studied, *Acacia furcatispina, Bulnesia retamo, Cercidium praecox,* and *Mimosa ephedroides* are in this category. However, *Bulnesia* and *Cercidium* have photosynthetic bark and presumably are photosynthesizing prior to the onset of leaf growth. Leaf fall begins in the autumn after the rains have ceased. The exact date depends on the length of the rainy season, the plants apparently retaining the leaves as long as there is sufficient moisture in the ground.

As mentioned above, this is a crude separation since there is a fair degree of interspecific and yearly variation in the exact time of leaf initiation. *Larrea cuneifolia, Cassia aphylla,* and *Tricomaria usillo* tend to have the longest growing season. Our observations indicate that they do best on the flats of the dry lower Bajada. Presumably they represent the extreme xerophytic shrub strategy. *Cassia* has photosynthetic bark and no leaves, and young stems of *Tricomaria* are also photosynthetic. *Larrea* keeps some leaves throughout the winter.

In Arizona we also can distinguish two modes. One is species that are vegetatively active throughout the year, the other is species that show winter dormancy. *Larrea tridentata, Simmondsia chinensis, Krameria grayi,* and *Ambrosia deltoidea* belong in the first group. *Cercidium microphyllum* and *Calliandra eriophylla,* although not active all winter, had only a very short inactive period in the winter during the time of our observations. Species with a winter dormant period that lasted three to five months were: *Olneya tesota, Prosopis velutina, Cercidium floridum, Acacia greggii,* and *A. constricta.* Three other species studied proved to have unique patterns of vegetative growth. *Jatropha cardiophylla* showed leaf and stem growth only during the short summer rainy season, between June and August. *Encelia farinosa* had the opposite behavior, being vegetatively active from the end of the summer rainy season throughout the winter until the beginning of the warm summer period in June. Finally, the ocotillo, *Fouquieria splendens,* had a pattern of leaf production and stem elongation that is uniquely opportunistic in response to soil moisture. A burst of leaves is produced whenever strong rain falls, be it in the summer (July), late fall (October), or spring (March).

At both sites the xerophytic shrubs (*Larrea cuneifolia, L. tridentata, Cassia aphylla, Krameria grayi,* and *Simmondsia chinensis*) are active throughout all or most of the year. The phreatophytes (*Prosopis* spp., *Acacia* spp., *Cercidium floridum, Cercidium praecox*) were mostly summer active, even in Arizona with its winter rains. Finally, it is noteworthy that only two species in our sample, *Encelia farinosa,* and *Ambrosia deltoidea* showed an adaptation to the winter rain pattern of Arizona.

Blooming and Fruiting

Table 4-8 shows the dates of blooming and fruit dispersal of all the species studied. The date given are general approximations indicating the time at which the majority of the plants in the populations studied were blooming or had mature fruits. There were small differences from site to site and occasional blooming of one or two plants took place out of season. For detailed data the reader is referred to Yang and Abbe (1974) and LeClaire et al. (in prep.).

Blooming at both the North and South American sites took place in the spring or early summer. There was a notable greater variability in blooming in September and some were blooming in March. At Arizona, with one exception, all species bloomed between April and June, the exception being *Simmondsia chinensis* which bloomed in March. The more synchronized blooming in Arizona is probably the result of the bimodal pattern of precipitation which allows all species to bloom in spring when there is still moisture in the soil resulting from the winter rains, and to disperse their seeds at the beginning of the summer rainy season in July. Such behavior is not possible in the Bolsón de Pipanaco where winter rains are very limited. Consequently we observe a different blooming behavior at the Argentine site. One group of species (*Cercidium praecox, Jatropha macrocarpa,* and *Prosopis chilensis*)

TABLE 4-8 *Times of Blooming and Fruiting of Assorted Species*

A. Bolsón de Pipanaco	Blooming		Fruiting	
	1972-73	1973-74	1972-73	1973-74
Acacia aroma	Nov.-Dec.	Nov.-Dec.	April	May
Acacia furcatispina	Feb.	Jan.	April	Feb.-Mar.
Bulnesia retamo	Sept.-Jan.	Sept.-Jan.	Nov.-Mar.	Dec.-Jan.-Mar.
Cassia aphylla	Jan.	Jan.	Mar.	Mar.
Cercidium praecox	Nov.-Jan.	Nov.-Jan.	Dec.-Jan.	Jan.-Mar.
Jatropha macrocarpa	Oct.-Jan.	Oct.-Jan.	Jan.-Mar.	Jan.-Mar.
Larrea divaricata	Sept.-Mar.	Sept.-Feb.	Dec.-Mar.	Dec.-Mar.
Larrea cuneifolia	Jan.	Jan.	Feb.-Mar.	Jan.-Mar.
Mimosa ephedroides	Jan.-Mar.	Dec.-Jan.	April	Feb.-Mar.
Prosopis chilensis	Oct.	Oct.	Dec.-Jan.	Dec.-Jan.
Prosopis torquata	Jan.-Feb.	Dec.-Jan.	Apr.-May	Mar.
Tricomaria usillo	Oct.-Jan.	Oct.-Jan.	Dec.-Feb.	Nov.-Feb.
Ximenia americana	Nov.-Jan.	Nov.-Jan.	Jan.-Mar.	Jan.
Zuccagnia punctata	Oct.-Feb.	Dec.-Jan.		
B. Avra Valley & Tucson Area	1973		1973	
Acacia constricta	May-Jun.-Jul.		Sept.	
Acacia greggii	May.-Jun.		Jul.-Aug.	
Ambrosia deltoidea	Apr.		May.-Jul.	
Calliandra eriophylla	Apr.-May		Jun.	
Cercidium floridum	May		Jun.-Jul.	
Cercidium microphyllum	May		Jul.	
Encelia farinosa	Apr.-May		Jun.	
Fouquieria splendens	May		Jun.-Jul.	
Jatropha cardiophylla	Jul.		Aug.	
Krameria grayi	May		Jun.	
Larrea divaricata	May		Jul.	
Olneya tessota	Jun.		Jul.	
Prosopis velutina	May-Jun.		Jul.-Aug.	
Simmondsia chinensis	Mar.		Jun.-Jul.	

bloom during the dry spring and drop their seeds in January at the beginning of the rainy season. *Acacia aroma* also blooms during the dry season, but its fruits do not ripen until the onset of winter. Another group of species (*Acacia furcatispina, Mimosa ephedroides, Prosopis torquata,* and *Zuccagnia punctata*) do not bloom until the onset of the summer rains, dropping their seeds at the end of the rainy season. Finally, five species have what is best described as a "mixed" blooming pattern. These species, *Bulnesia retamo, Ximenia americana, Cassia aphylla, Larrea divaricata, L. cuneifolia,* and *Tricomaria usillo* (particularly the last four) bloom in response to soil moisture increases. They bloom heavily with the onset of summer rains but also bloom occasionally during the dry season if there are off season rains. Many of these flowers do not produce fruits and seeds, but some do. The last four species mentioned are producing flowering buds during the dry spring season and continuing until the big flowering takes place. Excepting *L. divaricata,* which behaves as a phreatophyte in the Bolsón de Pipanaco, the other three species are the extreme xerophytic evergreen shrubs in the sample. The xerophytic evergreen shrubs in the North American sample — *Larrea tridentata, Simmondsia chinensis,* and *Krameria grayi* — also produce a few flowers throughout the dry fall and spring, which can be interpreted as an "opportunistic" strategy to maximize the probability of early fruiting if an unseasonable rain falls.

Summary and Conclusions on Phenology

As was stated at the beginning of the presentation on phenology, the time length of the observations is too short to arrive at any definite conclusion. However, some apparent trends can be pointed out.

We predicted in the introduction that a selective advantage would accrue to a species that could disperse its seeds at the beginning of the rainy season. We also pointed out, however, that there was a heavy cost in loss of water for a species adopting this strategy. In Arizona, where as a result of the bimodal pattern of precipitation the springs are wet, most species have a spring blooming pattern and a summer seed drop. At the Argentina site, on the other hand, where springs are dry, only four species in our sample, three phreatophytes and a succulent, have this strategy. Blooming in all these species is presumably photoperiodically controlled (Turner, 1963). The extreme xerophytic shrubs on the other hand, both in the North and in South America, although primarily summer bloomers, respond to increased soil moisture by blooming aseasonally (Oechel et al., 1972). They are presumably photoperiodically neutral.

PATTERNS OF PLANT COMMUNITIES IN DESERTS*

Some properties of communities such as species diversity, cover, and abundance occur in regular patterns. These properties are molded by interactions among species and by physical properties of the environment and should also be predictable from an understanding of how individual attributes are molded. Two characteristics of warm deserts, obvious even to the casual observer, are the sparseness of plant cover and the diversity of life forms. Less obvious but equally characteristic are (1) a high species richness in certain areas but a very low richness in others, and (2) the great importance of soil texture characteristics, and of slope exposure as determinants of vegetation distribution. All of these traits can be explained in principle by the effect of soil texture on water absorption and retention, the uneven precipitation, and the trade-offs between drought resistance and photosynthetic efficiency of different life forms. The more even the precipitation and the finer the soil texture, the lower the species richness; the more uneven the available soil water, because of soil texture, topography or exposure, the

*By O. T. Solbrig.

larger the number of species and life forms able to coexist. Finally, since photosynthesis is limited by available CO_2, which depends on leaf hydrature, the drier the environment, the less the total yearly productivity leading to less aggregate cover and standing biomass.

Another apparent characteristic is a regular spacing of individual plants (Went, 1955), but evidence for this presumed pattern is ambiguous (Barbour, 1969; Woodell et al., 1969; Anderson, 1971; King and Woodell, 1973). Since little water is available in desert soils much of the time, a dense enough canopy for light competition cannot be supported. However, upper and intermediate soil layers, especially in the 10-100 cm area, should be completely occupied by roots. This could lead to a regular spacing of shrubs, especially if they are of the same size, but such a regular spacing is seldom observed. Also desert soils may not always be completely occupied by roots although the data are still few (Abdel Rahman, 1953; Abdel Rahman and Batanouny, 1965; Migahid and Abdel Rahman, 1953).

These results have led to doubts about the basic premise that competition for water is an important determinant of plant community structure in desert environments (Walter, 1963; Barbour, 1973). However, regular spacing of plants and complete soil occupancy by roots are expected only if the amount of water in the soil is uniform. Under conditions of heterogeneous water supply in space and time, even if the soil volume is occupied by roots and competition for water does take place, spacing patterns may be complex. If the distribution of water in time allows ephemeral plants as well as ephemeral roots in perennial plants to develop at times of high water availability, they may preempt the soil space, preventing invasion of these sites by the roots of woody perennials. Furthermore, differences of rainfall levels from year to year may cause patchy germination and establishment of new plants. Even if their spacing tends to become more regular with time, patchy spacing patterns may persist many years. Finally, if water distribution is patchy because of soil characteristics and irregular rainfall, regular spacing patterns are unlikely to be encountered, irrespective of the intensity of competition for water.

Since the principal difference in the physical environment between the Avra Valley region and the Bolsón de Pipanaco is the pattern of rainfall, especially the scarcity of winter rains at the latter site, major differences in the plant communities should be observed in relation to those elements that depend largely or exclusively on winter precipitation. The most obvious group is the winter-spring ephemerals, which are, as expected, completely absent from the Bolsón de Pipanaco. Winter active perennial shrubs (e.g. *Ambrosia* spp., *Encelia farinosa*) are also absent in Catamarca.

Other groups of plants are also affected by the difference in the rainfall pattern. Because 80 to 90 percent of the rain falls in the summer in the Bolsón de Pipanaco, the summers are wetter in the South American sites with comparable soil texture and yearly average rainfall to the North American sites. The summer annual flora should therefore be richer and of greater biomass in South America. On the other hand, for those plants that are partially active throughout the year — namely succulents and xerophytic shrubs — the dry season is more severe since it is not interrupted by winter rains. The effect of this more prolonged drought should be most evident in plants of desert flats. This may account for the more xerophytic characteristics of *Larrea cuneifolia* when compared with *L. tridentata* (Barbour et al., 1974) and for the higher proportion of aphyllous shrubs and succulents in South America.

To assess the correlation of the pattern of plant communities in the Avra Valley and the Bolsón de Pipanaco with soil texture characteristics and with soil moisture, three studies were undertaken: (a) a comparison of the structure of the woody vegetation along a soil gradient where rainfall patterns were relatively uniform; (b) a study of the structure of *Larrea* dominated communities along the same gradient, and (c) a study of *Larrea* communities along moisture gradients where soil characteristics are similar. Three principal characteristics of the vegetation were studied: species richness and diversity, percentage of ground cover, and spacing pattern of shrubs.

Gradient Analysis of Bajada Communities*

Two, 10 Km long transects were established at Bajada sites with similar physical characteristics in each of the two areas, extending through an elevational distance of 150 m in Arizona and 300 m in Catamarca. The North American transect, near the town of Silver Bell in Arizona (Figure 1-3) faces east and has a mean slope of about 1.5°. The South American transect, near the village of Joyango in Catamarca (Figure 1-2) faces west and has a mean slope of 4.5° (Figures 4-4 to 4-7). Furthermore, the Sierra de Ambato rises almost 5,000 m above the Joyango transect while the North American transect is subtended by the Silver Bell Mountains that are less than 1,500 m in height. The size of the mountains and the difference in slope result in a much greater degree of dissection of the South American site, small washes being more prevalent there than on the Silver Bell Bajada. Consequently the riparian element is more extensively developed at Joyango. In both areas soil texture becomes coarser with increasing elevation (Table 4-9). At both transects the yearly march of temperature is similar. Annual precipitation at the base of the Arizona transect is estimated to be 245 mm, 60 percent of which falls in summer, while that at the base of the Catamarca transect is estimated to be 165 mm, 90 percent of which falls in summer (Chapter 2). At both sites there is indirect evidence (Chapter 2) that rainfall increases slightly with elevation.

On each transect, 20 X 50 m (1/10 Ha) permanent quadrats were established (thirty-seven in Arizona, and eleven in Catamarca), as far from the

*By J. Cross, G. Goldstein, C. H. Lowe, and J. Morello.

FIGURE 4-4. *Upper portion of the transect at Silver Bell. The large tree to the left is* Olneya tesota. *Also on the picture is a* Cereus giganteus, *several* Opuntia fulgida, *many* Larrea tridentata *and* Ambrosia deltoides. *(Photo by O. T. Solbrig, March, 1974.)*

FIGURE 4-5. *Lower portion of the transect at Silver Bell. The larger shrubs are* Larrea tridentata *and the smaller ones are* Ambrosia dumosa. *(Photo by O. T. Solbrig, March 1974.)*

direct influences of drainageways as possible. At each quadrat soil trenches were dug and soil samples were taken at surface, 2 cm 5 cm, and thence at 10 cm intervals down to 1 meter. Mechanical analysis for texture in these samples are reported in Table 4-9.

Community attributes measured were: presence of all perennial plants; ground cover estimated by the line intercept method; and mean distance between bushes (base to base) (Table 4-10). It was hoped that these measures would summarize community structure in a way suitable to permit comparison of one region with another. A discussion of methodology and an extended presentation of results can be found in Morello (1972) and Lowe, Morello, Cross, and Goldstein (in prep.).

FIGURE 4-6. *Upper portion of the transect at Joyango look-ing downslope toward the Salar de Pipanaco which is visible in the distance. Common shrubs in the photo are* Larrea cuneifolia *and* Zuccagnia punctata. *Several* Opuntia glomerata *are also visible. (Photo O. T. Solbrig, December 1972.)*

FIGURE 4-7. *Lower portion of the transect at Joyango look-ing upslope to the Sierra de Ambato. The transect extended from the foreground of the photo (at the marker visible to the lower right) to the small hill at the right center of the photo. All of the shrubs in the foreground are* Larrea cunei-folia. *(Photo by M. A. Mares.)*

TABLE 4-9 *Summary of Site and Soil Data for Quadrats on Silver Bell (AZ) and Joyango (ARG) Transects*

Plot #	Elevation (m)	Slope angle (%)	Rock and gravel (%)	Sand (%)	Silt and clay (%)
AZ-30	593	2.1°E	7.77	65.85	26.38
-18	617	0.7°E	16.18	34.02	49.80
-15	628	0.8°E	28.34	29.72	41.94
-01	631	0.7°E	31.04	36.46	32.50
-02	634	0.5°E	59.02	21.41	19.57
-03	637	1.2°E	39.53	32.12	28.35
-04	639	1.0°E	36.52	36.72	26.76
-05	664	1.1°E	44.17	23.54	32.29
-06	672	1.2°E	53.92	23.12	22.96
-07	677	1.2°E	21.91	46.21	31.88
-08	681	1.9°E	54.97	25.13	19.90
-09	692	4.2°E	38.55	28.92	32.53
-11	698	1.2°E	20.18	43.72	36.10
-12	706	1.9°E	50.43	28.55	21.02
-13	708	2.8°E	14.98	34.74	50.28
-27	783	2.1°E	54.84	28.09	17.07
ARG-03	838	1.3°W	13.00	75.94	11.06
-11	878	1.2°W	5.94	58.35	35.71
-01	895	1.0°W	7.90	65.14	26.96
-04	907	2.2°W	19.67	49.18	31.13
-05	930	–	47.21	38.34	14.45
-06	945	5.0°W	36.63	50.53	12.82
-07	981	5.0°W	28.80	49.28	21.92
-09	1030	9.5°W	–	–	–
-08	1061	5.5°W	24.93	45.06	30.01
-10	1103	10.0°W	–	–	–
-02	1120	26.5°W	49.12	27.57	23.31

Results and Discussion

Species composition of the vegetation sampled on the Arizona and Argentina transects is given in Appendix C. *Nicotiana glauca,* an introduced riparian species, is the only perennial common to the two gradients. *Larrea tridentata* is a major dominant on the Arizona transect and the only *Larrea* species present there, while on Bajada Joyango in Argentina its counterpart is *Larrea cuneifolia; L. divaricata* is a minor riparian species in that area. No perennial plant species of the 177 in the non-riparian desert scrub is found on both sites, but 17 (15.3 percent) of the 111 represented genera are shared in the 13 (32.5 percent) families in common in the total of forty families represented (Appendix C).

Plant density, species diversity, and ground cover increase upslope with increase in soil particle size. The curvilinear correlation between alpha diversity and soil particle size (Figure 4-8) is highly significant ($r = 0.721$),

TABLE 4-10 *Summary of Vegetation Parameters for Quadrats on Silver Bell (AZ) and Joyango (ARG) Transects*

Plot #	No. of species	Density	% Total cover	Mean distance (m)	Diversity (H)	Diversity (alpha)
AZ –30	3	118	26.22	0.986	0.354125	0.560197
–18	5	133	24.73	1.159	0.772615	1.026239
–15	8	495	15.50	0.550	1.002187	1.355049
–01	6	287	12.13	0.960	0.948372	1.072783
–02	5	396	17.55	0.790	0.744425	0.806708
–03	5	203	15.83	1.002	0.817891	0.927052
–04	5	440	19.54	1.047	1.278535	0.790779
–05	16	749	29.54	0.516	0.657423	2.874416
–06	15	1222	26.91	0.367	0.498155	2.407185
–07	15	430	21.74	0.898	1.129613	3.021189
–08	14	502	35.39	0.736	1.251121	2.671225
–09	18	1319	23.57	0.426	1.205361	2.947944
–11	26	1079	32.53	0.447	0.971849	4.796885
–10	19	1023	50.17	0.456	1.768605	3.311909
–12	17	723	25.75	0.548	0.929147	3.119409
–13	18	836	36.78	0.499	1.360925	3.238622
–27	31	2882	46.16	0.209	1.786951	4.852800
ARG –03	12	872	12.92	2.158	1.103864	1.968176
–11	8	624	26.79	–	1.025072	1.294986
–01	3	117	9.07	2.358	0.135568	0.561335
–04	14	2259	28.90	–	1.120937	1.989671
–05	24	1123	43.25	–	2.107586	4.311968
–06	13	1246	41.99	–	1.235675	2.023045
–07	9	1413	24.45	–	0.627538	1.285586
–09	17	1382	41.85	–	1.947586	2.729391
–08	10	1684	34.41	–	1.154693	1.410689
–10	19	1854	50.52	–	1.741641	2.946975
–02	18	349	26.40	–	2.049801	4.022694

as is the curvilinear relationship between cover and soil texture (Figure 4-9). For Bajada Joyango, slight but not significant differences were found when total community cover was plotted on soil texture as sampled at ten soil levels to 1 meter (Figure 4-9) or when only the primary root zone was included (Figure 4-10). Mean distance between plants decreases upslope, and is inversely correlated with soil particle size (Figure 4-11).

While the measure of alpha diversity (see Williams, 1964) is highly correlated with several other parameters (Figure 4-8, and 4-12, and others), the same analyses using the information theory (Shannon-Weiner) diversity index H′ are not. This is of interest because H′ was highly significantly correlated with soil texture (semi-log) in a preliminary investigation in the Tucson Mountains, the desert range next east of the Silver Bell Mountains in southern Arizona (Yang and Lowe, 1956). The meaning of this difference is not clear.

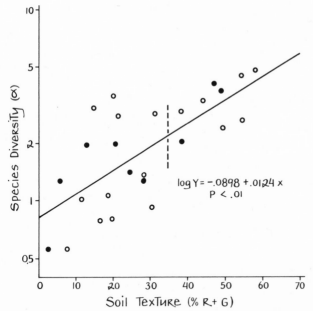

FIGURE 4-8. *Correlation between species diversity and soil texture (% rock plus gravel, root zone only). Open circles Silver Bell, black Joyango.*

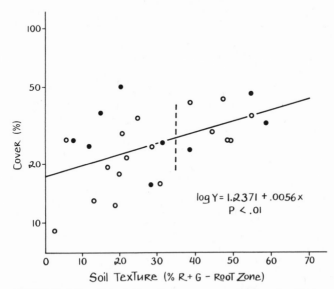

FIGURE 4-9. *Correlation between cover (%) and soil texture (% rock and gravel, root zone only). Open circles Silver Bell, black Joyango.*

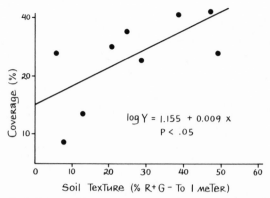

FIGURE 4-10. *Correlation between cover (%) and soil texture (% rock and gravel to 1 meter for Joyango.*

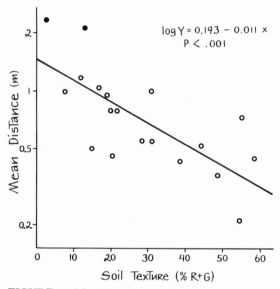

FIGURE 4-11. *Correlation between mean distance in meters and soil texture (% rock and gravel, root zone only). Open circle, Silver Bell, black Joyango.*

The combined data for the Joyango and Silver Bell bajadas show a highly significant positive correlation between log community cover and log species diversity (Figure 4-12). If taken separately, the correlation coefficient (+0.685) for the Arizona sample is significant at the 1 percent level with 15 d.f.; the Argentina correlation coefficient (+0.638), while not significant because of only 7 d.f., does not differ significantly from that of the Arizona co-

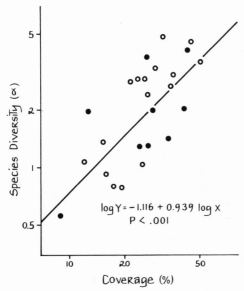

FIGURE 4-12. *Correlation between species diversity and % cover. Open circle, Arizona, black Joyango.*

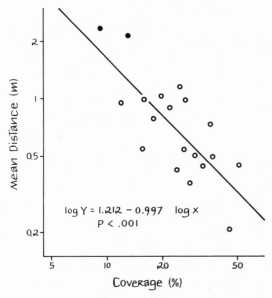

FIGURE 4-13. *Correlation between mean distance and % cover. Open circle, Arizona, black Joyango.*

efficient. Percentage plant cover is inversely correlated with mean distance (Figure 4-13).

In addition, it is of further interest to note that heterogeneous variance seems to occur in both Argentina and Arizona desert shrub communities. For example, compare the lower and upper halves of the curves and their break near the midpoint of the gradient variation in soil texture (see vertical dotted line in Figure 4-9 and also Figure 4-8). The small sample size of these initial data preclude the demonstration of statistically significant differences in variance between subsets separated by the dotted lines, but the trends are definitely there (in both the graphs and the statistics) and invite further investigation of the problem. While we do not presently have an explanation for heterogeneous variance we observe (1) that it is remarkable in its precise position of occurrence in both the Monte and Sonoran Desert vegetation data, and (2) that it indicates greater variation in diversity in desert shrub communities characterized by lower levels of community species diversity on each of the two continents.

Larrea Communities Along Bajada Gradients*

Larrea-dominated plant communities along the bajada transects were analyzed separately. In Arizona, *L. tridentata* was the important species. In Catamarca, *L. cuneifolia* was the dominant, *L. divaricata* being restricted to relatively narrow strips near watercourses. Community attributes measured were: ground cover and presence of all perennial plants, density of *Larrea* shrubs, patterns of *Larrea* shrub distribution, and frequency distribution of *Larrea* shrub heights. The approach is similar to that utilized by Barbour (1968, 1969) in comparing *Larrea* populations of the three warm deserts of North America. A discussion of methodology and an extended presentation of results can be found in Barbour and Diaz (1973).

Seven of the permanent 20 X 50 m plots in the Silver Bell Bajada and five in Joyango Bajada were chosen for sampling (Table 4-11). The methodology used was slightly different from that of the previous study, accounting for the slight differences between the values of the same parameters in Tables 4-11 and 4-10.

Considering the physical differences, it is not surprising that the plant communities did not change with elevation along both transects in exactly the same way. In both cases, total ground cover and species diversity tended to increase with increasing elevation. The lower quadrats contain three or four perennial species, but with *Larrea* contributing more than two-thirds of the cover (Table 4-11), while the higher communities usually contain more than ten species of great morphological diversity (arborescent cacti, trees,

*By M. Barbour.

TABLE 4-11 *Community Data for Silver Bell and Joyango Transects*

Plot #	Gravel (%)	Total cover (%)	*Larrea* Cover	(Rel)	No. spp.	*Larrea* den. (shrubs/ha)	Pattern
ARIZ 001	1.3	19.9	19.5	(97.0)	4	1,086	Clumped*
002	20.6	14.0	11.3	(80.7)	4	611	Clumped*
003	19.7	41.8	6.2	(15.1)	8	247	Clumped
022	22.3	25.8	15.2	(60.8)	3	910	Clumped
021	39.8	26.6	13.7	(52.1)	17	572	Random
006	56.7	50.9	29.3	(57.6)	14	507	Random*
005	48.3	56.0	0.4	(0.1)	16	13	–
ARG 004	2.9	6.2	6.2	(100.0)	3	816	Clumped*
007	14.2	12.4	8.6	(68.7)	4	533	Clumped*
005	30.1	27.4	16.0	(58.4)	10	1,027	Clumped*
006	36.6	30.8	25.0	(76.0)	5	2,280	Random
008	14.8	36.6	10.9	(28.0)	14	780	Clumped

The asterisk (*) indicates a nonhomogeneous stand for which pattern data may not be accurate.

tall shrubs, short shrubs, small cacti), and few or no *Larrea* shrubs. An abrupt upper end of *Larrea* dominance was especially noticeable on the Arizona bajada, a 50 m difference in elevation resulting in a drop of density from 507 to 13 shrubs per hectare (Table 4-11).

Density of *Larrea* shrubs generally drops with increasing elevation along the Arizona transect, but it peaks in the middle of the Catamarca transect. We do not know the reason for this difference, but a similar mid-bajada density peak for *Larrea* also has been reported near Death Valley, California, in the Mohave Desert (Barbour, 1968).

The *Larrea* height frequency diagrams did not appear to change with elevation, but they were different from one bajada to the other. Arizona sites had a few shrubs of height less than 50 cm, and there was a strong single peak tendency in shrub heights, with only a moderate spread in height from smallest to tallest. Catamarca sites showed many more small (young?) shrubs, a wider range of heights, and less of a tendency to peak at any one height (age?) (Figure 4-14).

Individual *Larrea* shrubs in both cases were usually clumped, with some tendency to become random with increasing elevation. No site showed a regular shrub distribution.

Moisture Gradients*

The objective of this research was to compare the structure of *Larrea*-dominated plant communities along moisture gradients radiating from the primary sites. Community attributes measured were: ground cover and

*By M. Barbour.

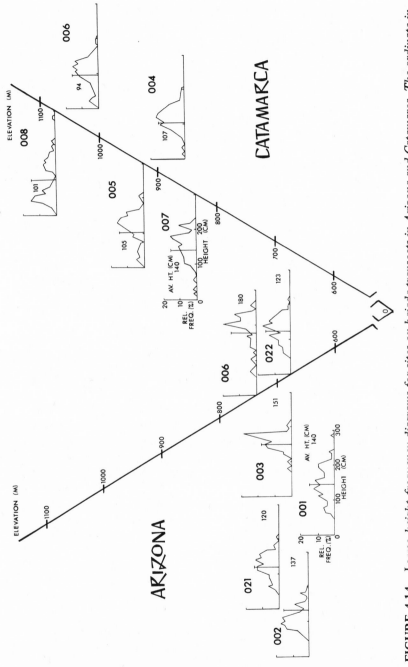

FIGURE 4-14. *Larrea* height frequency diagrams for sites on bajada transects in Arizona and Catamarca. The ordinate intersects the elevation scale at the correct point. Large number indicates population number, smaller sized number corresponds to the average height of the population. See Table 4-11 for additional data. Adapted from Barbour and Diaz, 1973.

presence of all perennial plants, density of *Larrea* shrubs, patterns of *Larrea* shrub distribution, and frequency distribution of *Larrea* shrub heights. A discussion of methodology and an extended presentation of results can be found in Barbour and Diaz (1973).

The Arizona moisture gradient stretched some 240 km from Yuma in the drier west to Tucson in the moister east (Figure 1-1). Sample points were selected roughly every 30 km. In Argentina rainfall increases in the Bolsón de Pipanaco from south to north. Sample points were selected approximately every 20 km along the route from Mazán to Andalgalá (Figure 1-2). Some additional sites are located on the west side of the Bolsón de Pipanaco. The sample size for the moisture gradient studies was 32 × 48 m.

As mentioned, the pattern of rainfall in the two areas is different. The absolute limits on the rainfall gradients sampled were also somewhat different. Minimum precipitation on the Arizona gradient was estimated to be 77 mm, maximum 275 mm in the Tucson area; for Catamarca the minimum was estimated to be at or below 77 mm, maximum 370 mm. In Arizona, increase in rainfall was generally accompanied by increase in elevation: nearly 1,000 m separated the sites with highest and lowest rainfall. In Argentina, however, differences in rainfall could be obtained with very slight change in elevation: only 200 m separated the sites with highest and lowest rainfall.

Despite these physical differences, community patterns were similar. Generally for both areas, as moisture increased so did total cover, absolute *Larrea* cover, and *Larrea* shrub density (Table 4-12). Major exceptions to this trend were associated with sites not dominated by *Larrea*, sites where the relative cover of *Larrea* was below 40 percent. Comparing sites of equivalent rainfall in both regions, the absolute values of total cover, *Larrea* cover, and *Larrea* density were often similar.

Species diversity did not correlate with rainfall in either area. Sites with both low and high precipitation could exhibit low diversity, and sites with similar precipitation could exhibit greatly different diversity. Generally, coarseness of soil texture affected diversity much more than did precipitation, diversity increasing with increasing percentage of gravel and rock (Table 4-12) as it did on the Joyango and Silver Bell transects.

Pattern of *Larrea* shrub distribution in Arizona was predominantly random at sites with 70-103 mm rainfall, and it was clumped at all sites with higher rainfall. In Argentina, pattern was regular at one site with low rainfall, but was either random or clumped at sites with higher rainfall. The rarity of regular shrub distribution, even at sites with low precipitation, has been documented for other deserts as well in reviews by Anderson (1971) and Barbour (1973).

The height frequency diagrams of *Larrea* populations in both regions showed the same changes with increasing moisture (Figure 4-15). In dry sites the distributions tended to have one pronounced peak and a relatively narrow to moderate range of heights overall. In wetter sites they tended to

TABLE 4-12 *Community and Site Data for Arizona and Catamarca Moisture Gradient*

Code	Est. ppt. (mm)	Elev. (m)	Slope and aspect	Gravel (%)	Total cover (%)	Cover	Larrea (Rel)	No. spp.	Larrea den. (shrubs/ha)	Pattern
ARIZ 010	70	94	1/2°SW	27.5	6.6	0.4	(6.1)	4	215	Random
011	85	94	0°	2.8	8.2	4.7	(57.3)	3	189	Random
012	95	125	2°N	7.3	4.7	4.3	(91.5)	3	338	Clumped
013	103	141	1°SW	0.9	9.4	5.9	(62.8)	2	266	Random
014	113	234	1°E	4.8	14.9	7.0	(47.0)	8	403	Clumped
015	185	375	0°	7.4	14.5	8.6	(59.3)	7	670	Random
016	198	390	1°E	32.2	11.4	8.6	(76.0)	8	787	Clumped
017	218	563	2-1/2°NW	5.4	22.6	19.5	(86.3)	5	1,131	Clumped
018	218	500	1/2°NE	17.8	9.2	8.8	(95.6)	2	1,118	Clumped
019	218	500	2°W	31.1	16.7	8.2	(48.8)	6	953	Clumped*
020	225	531	0°	0.1	19.9	19.9	(100.0)	2	1,066	Clumped*
001	245	607	1°E	1.3	19.9	19.5	(97.0)	4	1,086	Clumped*
007	275	953	0°	25.7	34.1	29.3	(83.0)	7	1,378	Random*
004	275	1063	8°N	52.0	50.6	32.0	(57.1)	19	3,770	Clumped*
008	275	750	1-1/2°NW	32.6	36.0	7.0	(19.2)	11	462	Clumped
009	275	719	1/2°W	37.7	41.0	17.0	(41.5)	8	579	Clumped*
017	75	1067	1°N	45.7	12.2	3.5	(28.7)	8	288	Random*
021	75	840	3°W	5.4	31.2	9.3	(29.8)	10	1,177	Regular
019	100	818	2°NW	3.6	14.5	14.5	(100.0)	1	787	Clumped*
020	115	880?	2°SW	8.2	12.9	11.7	(90.7)	6	1,300	Random
018	140	885	2°W	1.7	12.5	12.5	(100.0)	2	1,320	Clumped*
009	155	885	1°W	1.5	14.8	14.8	(100.0)	4	953	Clumped
004	165	861	1°W	2.9	6.2	6.2	(100.0)	3	816	Clumped
002	215	788	1°W	2.8	42.0	13.0	(31.0)	9	469	Clumped*
010	220	825	2°W	7.4	23.3	21.1	(90.6)	6	527	Random
011	250	748	0°	4.2	25.4	23.8	(98.4)	4	1,853	Clumped
001	260	1015	2°W	18.5	34.0	33.0	(97.1)	6	2,541	Random*
012	280	1015	2°NW	9.0	49.6	5.2	(10.5)	16	351	Clumped
003	280+	1100?	0°	16.1	46.0	23.0	(50.0)	14	2,058	Random*
014	320	1140	0°	0.4	18.8	18.4	(97.9)	5	2,505	Clumped*
016	330	1170	2°NW	1.8	34.8	34.8	(100.0)	2	3,003	Clumped*
015	370	1279	2°NE	0.4	79.7	77.3	(97.0)	7	5,722	Random

The asterisk (*) indicates a nonhomogeneous stand for which pattern data may not be accurate.

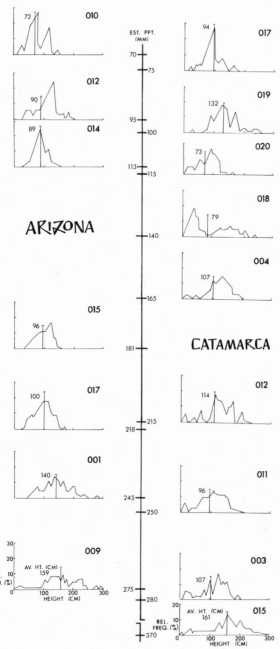

FIGURE 4-15. Larrea *height frequency diagrams for sites on the Arizona (left) and Catamarca (right) moisture gradient. The sites are arranged in the order of decreasing rainfall from bottom to top. Estimated average rainfall for each site is indicated on the central scale. Large number indicates population number. Smaller sized number corresponds to the average height of the population. See Table 4-12 for additional data. Adapted from Barbour and Diaz, 1973.*

have many peaks or in some cases no recognizable peak at all, and a very wide range of heights. This is a trend one would expect, if indeed height does correlate with age, for with increasing moisture the probability of seedling establishment every year should become greater, and the standing population of shrubs should exhibit many age categories. Nevertheless, establishment appears to be of more frequent occurrence in the Catamarca area than in the Arizona area, whatever the rainfall. With few exceptions, Arizona sites with rainfall below 218 mm showed few, if any, shrubs of height less than 50 cm, indicating that periods of establishment in that range of aridity probably do not occur often. In contrast, every Catamarca site showed many shrubs of 10–50 cm height — even in the most arid sites. Possibly the difference in establishment is due to seasonal differences in rainfall, differences in the genetic potential of the two *Larrea* species, or to other ecosystem differences not immediately apparent at this time.

SUMMARY AND CONCLUSIONS

In both the Bajada gradient and the moisture gradient species richness and life form diversity were strongly correlated with soil texture and only weekly with total rainfall. However, cover and plant density were directly correlated with moisture availability and with soil texture. These results accord with expectations from knowledge of the life form strategies of plants discussed in the first part of the chapter, since each life form is presumably exploiting a different water resource. Increase in soil texture (larger percentage of rock and gravel) allow more percolation and soil-water storage and create soil-water microhabitats. Furthermore, in North and South American sites with comparable soil texture and yearly rainfall, community parameters were very similar. The only observed difference was in the *Larrea* height frequency diagrams, the Arizona sites having fewer peaks than comparable Catamarca sites, indicating possible differences in the frequency of successful establishment of *Larrea* seedlings. This could be due to the difference in rainfall pattern between the two areas, or it may be due to different predation regimes (Chapter 6).

Chapter 5:
The Strategies and Community Patterns of Desert Animals

·M.A. Mares, W.F. Blair, F.A. Enders,
D. Greegor, A.C. Hulse, J.H. Hunt,
D. Otte, R.D. Sage, C.S. Tomoff.

INTRODUCTION

Characteristics of animals living in deserts are molded both by the physical environment and by other living organisms with which they interact. Here we emphasize relationships with the physical environment; biological interactions are stressed in the next chapter.

Desert climates are characterized by long periods without rain, lack of available surface water most of the year, great diurnal variations in temperature, and extremely high midday temperatures in the summer. For some types of organisms these conditions pose serious physiological problems while for others they do not. For example, maintenance of a favorable internal water balance under hot, dry conditions is difficult for amphibians and most mammals, but relatively trivial for insects, reptiles, and birds. Water stress is a problem for adult amphibians, but breeding, which depends on available surface water, is particularly vulnerable to drought. On the other hand, desert ponds may be especially favorable environments for amphibians because of their high primary productivity and/or large amounts of allochthonous material, and the absence of fishes which are often major predators on, and competitors with, amphibian larvae.

We expect convergent evolution at the species level to be most striking in those groups where adaptation to desert conditions requires the greatest changes in morphology, physiology, and behavior. In these cases selective pressures exerted by the physical environment are likely to override differential selection caused by initial differences in colonizing species, potential problem of invading species, and order of arrival of the species and, hence, the competitive environment faced by an invading species. Among animal groups in which only minor changes in morphology, physiology, and behavior are required for desert life, species attributes and community structures are more likely to reflect biological interactions. Therefore, in the latter groups convergence may be less striking and niche boundaries less predictable, even though patterns of within-habitat and between-habitat richness might be very similar.

The stressful nature of desert climates may have been overemphasized because scientists belong to a taxonomic group that has greater water conservation problems than most. For example, Hamilton (1973) has suggested that the high incidence of black coloration in desert insects is actually adaptive because it enables them to reach higher body temperatures early in the morning by direct absorption of solar radiation. He points out that normal operating temperatures of most animals are remarkably close to the lethal maximum and suggests that a high body temperature confers advantages in a highly competitive world. These include faster growth rates, more rapid access to resources, faster escape reactions, and longer operating hours.

Nevertheless, heat that *is* excessive for all living organisms does occur regularly during summer days in the Sonoran Desert and the Monte and can be avoided by living in shaded areas (usually of limited extent in deserts), by fossorial activity, or by being active when temperatures are lower, such as at night, dawn, and dusk. However, as an animal evolves adaptations for nocturnal activity, certain other traits are usually lost. Since a nocturnal, burrow-inhabiting rodent may be seldom exposed to very high ambient temperatures, selection for energy-consuming physiological mechanisms involved in dissipating excess body heat may be weak. Therefore, loss of these abilities may result. Similarly, adaptations for digging may make rapid locomotion above ground impossible or the best colors for thermoregulation may preclude cryptic matching of background, etc.

Mechanisms for conserving water involve increasing intake, reducing loss, or both. Water can be obtained from succulent food (green vegetation or animal matter), from dew deposited on vegetation at night, and from free surface water when available. Limited amounts of water can be obtained from dry foods as breakdown products of carbohydrate metabolism. Water losses can be reduced behaviorally (time of activity, amount of activity, resting in moist microhabitats such as burrows or crevices in bark) and by changes in the means of eliminating nitrogenous wastes. For aquatic organisms, nitrogen is eliminated as toxic ammonia. In situations where water is limited, however, a less toxic and less soluble nitrogenous waste product may be advantageous. Most desert frogs and all mammals are ureotelic, eliminating wastes as urea. Desert insects, all birds, desert reptiles, and at least two frogs are uricotelic, with insoluble uric acid as the primary nitrogen-elimination product.

ADAPTATIONS OF ANIMALS TO HEAT AND WATER STRESS

Anurans*

Anurans, by virtue of their highly permeable skins, probably face a more difficult evolutionary problem in adapting to aridity and high temperatures than any other vertebrate group. Most desert anurans are limited to pools, streams, or rivers with permanent water, but some species live in places with only temporary availability of free surface water (see Mayhew, 1968, for a review). Species of the genus *Bufo*, which constitute a major segment (58.3 percent) of the Sonoran Desert anuran fauna and a minor segment (6.7 percent) of the Monte anuran fauna, possess a thickened dry outer skin layer (the stratum corneum) that reduces cutaneous water loss and permits activity away from free water, but no other anurans possess a comparable trait. In all temperate environments anurans are primarily nocturnal organisms, and desert species do not differ from others in their daily cycles.

*By W. F. Blair and A. C. Hulse.

Both the Sonoran Desert and the Monte have highly xeric-adapted frogs with the following adaptive characteristics which are typical of such frogs (Mayhew, 1968):

1. No definite breeding season
2. Reproductive activity limited to temporary water
3. Breeding activity initiated by rainfall
4. Males possess loud voices
5. Rapid egg and larval development
6. Tadpoles utilize both plant and animal food
7. Tadpoles are cannibalistic
8. Tadpoles produce a growth inhibitor that affects other tadpoles
9. Tadpoles are heat tolerant
10. Adults possess metatarsal tubercles for digging
11. Adults capable of withstanding severe desiccation
12. Nocturnal activity of adults.

The length of this list testifies to the difficulty anurans have in handling heat and water stress and is an example of strong convergence in a group that must make substantial morphological, physiological, and behavioral changes to live in hot deserts. In the Sonoran Desert these species are members of the genus *Scaphiopus*, and in the Monte they include members of the genera *Pleurodema, Odontophrynus, Leptodactylus, Lepidobatrachus,* and *Ceratophrys*.

Tadpoles of many desert amphibians can withstand very high temperatures. The Critical Thermal Maximum (CTM), the temperature at which locomotor activity becomes so impaired that an animal loses the ability to escape from conditions which will lead to its death (Lowe and Vance, 1955), is about 45° C for both *Scaphiopus couchi* and *Pleurodema nebulosa,* the highest of all desert frogs thus far studied. Larval *Scaphiopus hammondi* are more sensitive to high temperatures in early embryonic stages than at later stages (H. A. Brown, 1967), and we have found the same for *Pleurodema nebulosa*. The explanation may be that very high water temperatures early in development are nearly always associated with drying of the pond before development can be completed.

Adaptations to water loss are more varied than adaptation to elevated temperatures. They include various mechanisms to retard water loss, high tolerance to desiccation, and the ability for very rapid uptake when water is available. The most intensive studies of adaptive responses to water loss by desert anurans have been conducted on members of the North American genus *Scaphiopus* (McClanahan, 1967, 1972; Ruibal et al., 1969; Shoemaker et al., 1969). Cei (1959) has investigated intraspecific differences in desiccation tolerance in *Bufo arenarum,* and Shoemaker et al. (1972) have worked on physiological responses to water loss in *Phyllomedusa sauvagei,* a Chacoan species that may enter the Monte.

Mechanisms to retard water loss include the relatively impermeable skins of adult *Bufo,* and the habit of encysting in a tough cocoon of keratinized skin used by hibernating *Scaphiopus couchi* (Mayhew, 1965) and *Lepidobatrachus llanensis* (Shoemaker and McClanahan, 1973). Water loss rates are also reduced by retention of urea during hibernation which increases the osmotic pressure of body fluids (McClanahan, 1972). As indicated previously, at least two frogs are uricotelic, including *Phyllomedusa sauvagei* of the western Chaco. In addition, *P. sauvagei* is capable of encysting on tree branches by spreading a thin, cutaneous ester-lipid secretion over the entire body surface forming a tough flexible watertight cocoon (Shoemaker et al., 1972, and McClanahan, pers. comm.).

Tolerance of water loss in many desert species of anurans is remarkable. Many species can lose up to 50 percent of their body weight and still survive. These same species also can take up water rapidly after dehydration, probably through a highly vascularized region of skin located on the ventral surface of the inguinal region (seat patch). Water absorbed through the ventral pectoral skin and the dorsal skin in *Bufo punctatus* is insignificant compared with that absorbed by the seat patch (Ruibal et al., 1969). Cei (1959) has shown that *Bufo arenarum* from dry regions are more resistant to desiccation than individuals from more mesic regions even though this species is seldom encountered away from permanent water in desert areas.

Many adaptive characteristics of desert frogs listed above relate to breeding in temporary ponds that form after heavy rains. Rapid growth rates, generalized diets, cannibalistic tendencies, heat tolerance of tadpoles, and adult breeding cycles triggered by rainfall are all part of this coadapted set of characteristics. Most anurans in the Sonoran Desert and the Monte breed in such temporary ponds following heavy summer rains (Table 5-1), but the duration of these ponds differs in the two deserts. Parts of the Sonoran Desert are underlain by an impermeable caliche (calcium carbonate) layer that strongly retards or prevents penetration of water through the soil column. In these areas ponds have a long life span and are utilized by several species of anurans. The Andalgalá area lacks a hard-pan layer in the soil and, even though summer rainfall is heavier than around Tucson, water is lost more rapidly through percolation and the same ponds form and dry up three or four times during a summer. This difference in pond persistence probably accounts for differences in activity patterns of adult frogs which are on the surface for only short periods (less than one week) in the Sonoran Desert but for much longer periods (more than a month) in the Monte. Apparently pond persistence is so reliable in the Sonoran Desert that adults do not have to lay additional batches of eggs. In contrast, *Pleurodema* adults lay multiple clutches in the Monte and many larvae fail to complete development because of drying up of ponds. Only *Pleurodema nebulosa* normally breeds in temporary ponds near Andalgalá, and it is restricted primarily to ponds greater than 25 cm in depth. *Pleurodema nebulosa* is replaced by *Odontophrynus occidentalis,* and *Pleurodema cinerea* in temporary ponds along permanent

TABLE 5-1 *Time to Metamorphosis (days) for Monte (M) and Sonoran (S) Desert-inhabiting Anurans. Habitats Are Permanent Water Areas (P), and Temporary Ponds (T).*

Species	Habitat	Days to Metamorphosis				Source
		<10	10–30	30–60	>60	
Scaphiopus couchi	(S) T	X	X			This study; Mayhew (1965)
Scaphiopus hammondi	(S) T	X	X			This study; Sloan (1964)
Hyla arenicolor	(S) P			X	X	Wright and Wright (1949)
Hyla pulchella	(M) P				X	This study
Rana sp.	(S) P				X	This study
Bufo arenarum	(M) P,T			X		This study
Bufo woodhousei	(S) P,T			X		Bragg (1940a)
Bufo cognatus	(S) P,T			X		Bragg (1940b)
Lepidobatrachus sp.	(M) T		X			Ruibal (1962)
Pleurodema nebulosa	(M) T	X				This study
Pleurodema cinerea	(M) T			X		This study
Pleurodema guayapi	(M) T	X				This study
Leptodactylus bufonius	(M) T			X		This study
Leptodactylus ocellatus	(M) P				X	This study

streams. Around Tucson, most temporary pond breeders use ponds formed on desert flats and up to seven species may breed in the same pond.

Rapid larval development is advantageous to all species of anurans breeding in temporary waters. In general, anurans breeding in permanent water tend to have the longest hatching and development times while temporary pond species have the shortest (Table 5-1). *Pleurodema nebulosa* hatches in about twelve hours under typical field conditions and metamorphosis may be complete in seven days. *Scaphiopus hammondi* can undergo complete metamorphosis in less than nine days (Zweifel, 1968) and *S. couchi* in less than six days (Hulse, unpubl.).

Convergence among individual species may relate to general morphology, distributional patterns, reproductive biology, physiological and behavioral adaptations, and so forth. Convergence is the most logical explanation for similarities when species pairs are widely separated phylogenetically. Many analogous species pairs of amphibians and reptiles occur in the two deserts (Table 5-2) among which *Scaphiopus* and *Pleurodema,* which belong to very dissimilar families, provide one of the most thoroughly studied cases (Table 5-3).

Morphologically, *Scaphiopus hammondi* and *Pleurodema nebulosa* are very similar (Figure 5-1). Both are small stocky, squat, toad-like frogs with smooth moist skin. Both have well-developed metatarsal spades for digging and a seat patch. Although these are two of the most xeric-adapted frogs, both have wide ecological tolerances and range from low deserts into high mountain areas. In all habitats breeding is restricted to temporary ponds and surface activity is stimulated by summer rains. Frogs of both species appear on the surface within hours of the first heavy rains, breeding choruses of males are formed, and mating occurs almost immediately. Both egg and larval development are rapid. Eggs hatch within twelve hours and metamorphosis occurs in less than nine days. Under stress conditions larvae of both species become cannibalistic and at all times are carnivorous. The spadefoot *Scaphiopus couchi,* the most thoroughly studied and seemingly the most xeric-adapted of North American desert anurans, is very similar to *Lepidobatrachus* (*L. llanensis* and *L. asper*) (Figure 5-1) insofar as the adaptations of these Chaco ceratophrynids are known (Blair, 1976). Known characteristics in common include: (1) approximately similar body size, (2) smooth moist skin, (3) fossorial habit, (4) metatarsal spade for digging, (5) development of a body covering of dead stratum corneum cells while buried, (6) opportunistic breeding in temporary rainpools, (7) absence of foam nesting. One known difference is that *Lepidobatrachus* are cannibalistic as larvae, while there is no evidence of such behavior in *Scaphiopus couchi.* Other poorly known Monte species which seem to approximate adaptations of these analogs are the cannibalistic *Ceratophrys ornata* and *C. pierotti* and the noncannibalistic leptodactylids *Odontophrynus americanus* and *O. occidentalis.*

TABLE 5-2 *Probable Convergent* Pairs of Amphibians and Reptiles in the Monte and Sonoran Deserts*

	Monte	Sonoran Desert
Anura	*Pleurodema nebulosa*	*Scaphiopus hammondi*
	Lepidobatrachus (2 spp) *Ceratophrys* (2 spp)	*Scaphiopus couchi*
	Leptodactylus ocellatus	*Rana* sp.
	Bufo arenarum*	*Bufo woodhousei**
Lizards	*Hyla pulchella* †	*Hyla arenicolor* †
	Homonota underwoodi & Homonota horrida	*Coleonyx variegatus*
	Liolaemus goetschi	*Dipsosaurus dorsalis*
	Liolaemus darwini	*Uta stansburiana*
	Liolaemus marmoratus	*Phrynosoma platyrhinos & Phrynosoma solare*
	Chemidophorus longicaudus Teius teyou	*Cnemidophorus tigris*
Snakes	*Pseudotomodon trigonatus*	*Hypsiglena ochrorhyncha*
	Leptotyphlops borrichianus & Amphisbaena angustifrons	*Leptotyphlops humilis*
	Philodryas burmeisteri	*Masticophis flagellum*
	Crotalius durissus	*Crotalus atrox*
	Bothrops neuwiedi	*Crotalus scutulatus*

*Congeneric pairs could indicate parallelism instead of convergence.
†In canyons of adjacent mountains.

A striking pair of ecological analogs in the two deserts is presented by a ranid, an apparently unnamed parapatric member of the *Rana pipiens* complex, of the Sonoran Desert and the leptodactylid *Leptodactylus ocellatus* of the Monte. Both live along the interface between land and permanent water and divide their time between the two. Similarities in body size, proportions, and pattern are remarkable. They differ in that *L. ocellatus* is a foam breeder, the *Rana* is not.

Among the seven species of *Bufo* in the Sonoran Desert, *B. woodhousei* shares the most adaptations to xeric habitats shown by *B. arenarum* of the Monte. Although congeneric, the southern species is related to the tropically distributed *B. marinus* species group, while the northern species is a member of the *B. americanus* group, a North American species assemblage. Thus, they

TABLE 5-3 *Comparison of Various Traits for Two Closely Convergent Desert Anurans,* Scaphiopus hammondi *and* Pleurodema nebulosa

S. hammondi	P. nebulosa
Skin moist	X*
Skin smooth	X
Background coloration gray	X
Pattern of discrete black spots	X
Seat patch present	X
Metatarsal tubercles present	X
Elliptical pupil	Pupil round
Size 30 to 60 mm.	X
Males call floating in water	Males call from bank
Call mostly at night	X
Calling rain initiated	X
Breeding restricted to temporary ponds	X
Calling activity of short duration (1 to 4 days)	X
Axillary amplexus	X
Eggs encased in gelatinous sheath	Foam nest
Eggs dark pigmented	X
Eggs attached to submergent or emergent vegetation	X
Eggs submerged but near surface	Eggs floating
Hatching time about 12 hours	X
Time till metamorphosis less than 9 days	X
Larvae heat tolerant	X
Larvae carnivorous	X
Larvae cannibalistic under stress	X
Maximum size of larvae 30 mm	X
Size at metamorphosis 8 to 10 mm	X
Hatch at stage 19	X
Egg masses vary from 25 to 250 eggs	More than 250 eggs
Females probably only lay once a year	More than once
Metamorphosed tadpoles initially active during the day	X
Adults insectivorous	X
Adults on surface for short period of time	Surface activity varies
Spend resting period in ground	X
During resting period adults store urea	–
Form cocoon while buried	–
Vocal sac slightly discolored	Vocal sac dark
Venter immaculate	X
Ranges from low desert into high mountains	X
Apparently no tolerance to salinity	Tolerance to salinity
When disturbed jumps into water	X
Tympanum distinct	X
No cranial crests	X
Interorbital boss present	Boss absent
Hindfeet completely webbed	Hindfeet lack webbing

*X's indicate that a particular characteristic is shared.

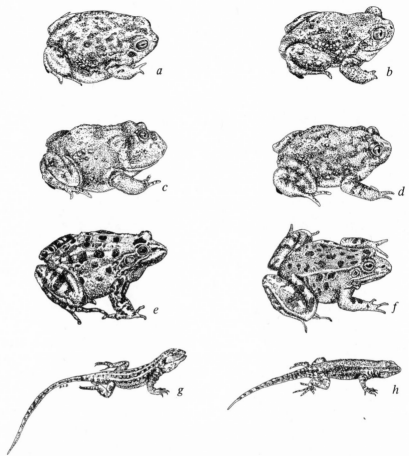

FIGURE 5-1. *Some convergent species pairs of amphibian and reptiles. (a)* Pleurodema nebulosa, *(b)* Scaphiopus hammondi, *(c)* Lepidobatrachus llanensis, *(d)* Scaphiopus couchi, *(e)* Leptodactylus ocellatus, *(f)* Rana *sp.*, *(g)* Liolaemus darwini, *and (h)* Uta stansburiana. *(Illustrations by Dean Rocky Barrick.)*

are not as closely related as might be supposed from their placement in the same genus (Blair, 1972). Both are large, widely distributed toads found in habitats ranging from xeric to mesic that have apparently invaded deserts by means of river systems. Both breed in permanent water independently of rainfall but occasionally breed in temporary ponds as well. Time to hatching and metamorphosis is not exceptionally rapid (Table 5-1).

Several species in both deserts do not fit into ecologically equivalent pairs. The large, smooth-skinned, partially aquatic *Bufo alvarius* and the small ant-eating microhylid *Gastrophryne olivacea* clearly have no counterparts in the Monte. Information about the biologies of the other species is inadequate to assess their similarities.

Mammals*

As ureotelic homeotherms, mammals must lose a certain amount of water to excrete nitrogenous waste products, since urea is more soluble than uric acid. Thermoregulation is accomplished by energy expenditure for increased metabolic rates at low ambient temperatures, or by evaporative cooling at higher environmental temperatures (from either skin or respiratory tract surfaces). Desert mammals range in size from shrews, bats, rodents, and mouse opossums weighing only few grams, to camels which may exceed 500 kilograms. Since body temperature is generally uniformly high in mammals, they have some advantages over heterotherms in hot environments because of their increased ability to lose heat. Desert cottontails and hares in North America (*Sylvilagus audubonii* and *Lepus californicus*) maintain high body temperatures at times and can reduce heat load by radiation, convection and conduction to the environment (Schmidt-Nielsen et al., 1965; Hinds, 1973), but because of homeothermy, mammal energy expenditures are high, respiration is high, and much water is needed for either body cooling or to replace water evaporated from respiratory surfaces. Therefore, the number of physiological problems posed to mammals by deserts is intermediate between those for amphibians and those for birds, reptiles, and insects.

Body size greatly influences adaptive strategies to a xeric environment. Large animals are not readily able to avoid desert heat and require large amounts of water to maintain osmotic balance. Schmidt-Nielsen (1964) has shown that camels use a complex of behavioral, morphological, and physiological traits to maintain water balance. Camels withstand very high body temperatures before evaporative cooling is employed, and the excess heat load accumulated during the day is radiated away at night. Their thick fur minimizes water loss due to perspiration, and during the day postures are selected such that heat gain is minimized and heat loss is maximized.

Small mammals can more readily avoid desert heat by spending days in burrows, but they face other difficult problems in adapting to heat and aridity. Small body size precludes evaporative cooling as a homeostatic mechanism because of the relationship between surface area, heat load, and transpiration. For example, a ten-gram rodent would have to evaporate water at a rate of about 30 percent of its body weight per hour on a hot summer day in the Sonoran Desert to remain in thermal balance (Schmidt-Nielsen, 1964). Desert rodents generally minimize heat gain by being nocturnal or crepuscular (as are most desert mammals); by living in cool burrows during daylight hours; or by being diurnal but concentrating activity in shaded, cool microclimates, such as forested arroyos. Lowe and Hinds (1971) have shown that such shaded spots are subject to temperatures ranging to 42° C even in winter. Various physiological and morphological characteristics of desert mammals are listed in Table 5–4.

*By M. A. Mares and D. Greegor.

TABLE 5-4 *Some Physiological and Morphological Adaptations*
of Small Mammals to Arid Environments

1. Ability to exist on metabolic water from carbohydrate metabolism
2. Ability to hibernate or aestivate
3. Countercurrent nasal vascular system (retrieves water otherwise lost in exhalation)
4. Greatly lengthened Henle's loop in kidney
5. Bipedality (hopping on hind feet)
6. Granivory (seed eating)
7. Bullar hypertrophy (inflated auditory bullae)
8. Pale-colored pelage
9. Strongly countershaded (darker dorsally than ventrally)
10. Produce dry feces
11. Possess lower overall metabolic rates
12. Possess higher maximum lethal temperatures
13. Frequent cool microhabitats
14. Nocturnal
15. Fossorial

Sources: Schmidt-Nielsen, 1964; MacMillen, 1972; Hudson and Deavers, 1973; Mares,
    1973a.

Adaptations of mammals are similar in unrelated species of different deserts. For example, kangaroo rats (*Dipodomys,* Heteromyidae) of North American deserts are quite similar in overall biology to some African gerbils (*Gerbillus,* Muridae; cf. Schmidt-Nielsen, 1964; Walker, 1964). These are, in turn, reminiscent of Australian hopping mice (*Notomys,* Muridae; MacMillen and Lee, 1967, 1969), or jerboas (Dipodidae) of African and Asian deserts (Walker, 1964). Apparently mammals, particularly small mammals, are quite restricted in their evolutionary options for adapting to xeric environments. Accordingly, it might be expected that mammals of the Monte and Sonoran deserts would share many morphological, behavioral, physiological, and ecological characteristics. It is not the occasional convergent pair that is of interest, but the extent to which measurable convergent evolution has occurred among species composing the mammalian community, and between the communities themselves. In the following discussion, a number of characteristics of mammals of both desert systems are compared. Since these communities are strongly distinct phylogenetically, possession of similar desert adaptations should be due to convergent evolution.

Time of Activity

Both deserts possess largely nocturnal mammal faunas (Table 5-5 and Appendix N). We have compared the desert faunas with mammals of a non-desert area (eastern deciduous mixed forest near Pymatuning Lake, Linesville, Pennsylvania (from Doutt et al., 1966; Burt and Grossenheider, 1964; field

TABLE 5-5 *Activity Periods, Food, and Nest Placement
for the Mammals (Excluding Bats) of the Monte
and Sonoran Desert Study Sites, Compared with
Those of the Eastern Deciduous Forest in Pennsylvania.*

| | Time of activity | | | | | |
	Sonoran		Monte		Pennsylvania	
Nocturnal	72.7*	(32)†	73.7	(14)	37.5	(12)
Diurnal	6.8	(3)	10.5	(2)	25.0	(8)
Crepuscular	15.9	(7)	5.3	(1)	9.4	(3)
Day & Night	4.5	(2)	5.3	(1)	31.3	(8)
Seasonal	0		5.3	(1)	0	

| | Food | | | | | |
	Sonoran		Monte		Pennsylvania	
Granivory	18.2	(8)	0		0	
Herbivory	22.7	(10)	21.1	(4)	25.0	(8)
Omnivory	11.4	(5)	21.1	(4)	18.8	(6)
Micro-omnivory	18.2	(8)	21.1	(4)	25.0	(8)
Insectivory	4.5	(2)	5.3	(1)	21.9	(7)
Carnivory	25.0	(11)	31.6	(6)	12.5	(4)

| | Nest placement†† | | | | | |
	Sonoran		Monte		Pennsylvania	
Above Ground	0		0		14.8	(4)
Ground Surface	21.2	(7)	0		22.2	(6)
Below Ground	75.8	(25)	92.9	(13)	59.3	(16)
Catholic	3.0	(1)	7.1	(1)	3.7	(1)

*Numbers are percentage of the fauna comprising each category.

†Numbers in parentheses are actual numbers of species in each category.

††Nest placement has not been included for larger species (see Appendix N).

work of MAM) so that some indication of degree of similarity between both deserts and an outside reference system can be gained. Both northern faunas are more closely related, taxonomically, than are the desert faunas. The most notable points in Table 5-5 are the dearth of strictly nocturnal mammals and the preponderance of either diurnal species, or species which are active both day and night in the eastern deciduous forest. The crepuscular habit does not seem to be particularly favored in deserts, although it is more common among North Temperate mammals than among those in South Temperate areas. The crepuscular species in both northern areas are primarily lagomorphs and deer. Both groups are absent from the Monte indicating that while being crepuscular could be useful in a desert, it is not necessarily strongly favored. Indeed, only one Monte mammal is essentially crepuscular (*Dolichotis patagonum*, the Patagonian "Hare"), and it is much more common in Patagonia and in South Temperate grasslands than it is in the Monte.

Food Habits

Although a detailed food study was beyond the scope of our investigation, some data are available on the foods of most Sonoran and Monte mammals. Both the Monte Desert and eastern deciduous forest area lack specialized granivorous mammals, while this group comprises almost one-fifth of the Sonoran Desert fauna (Table 5-5 and Appendix N). Most Sonoran granivores are members of the family Heteromyidae, each species of which is practically a synopsis of specialized traits for a dry environment. Granivory is probably one of their major adaptations. Seeds are one of the most abundant and predictable resources in deserts. Since many desert plants are ephemerals, passing the bulk of their life cycle as high energy seeds awaiting infrequent summer or winter showers for germination, they form small, easily-stored food packets for seed-eating specialists. Ephemerals also shunt the bulk of their energy into reproduction so that a large seed supply following the rainy season is practically assured. Even with several consecutive years of drought during which no annual plant growth occurs, there are still large numbers of seeds in desert soils (Tevis, 1958).

Moles and shrews (Talpidae and Soricidae) form a large segment of the eastern deciduous forest fauna, indicating that insects and other forest floor and soil invertebrates are common there. Such an extensive invertebrate ground fauna is not available in the desert, and only two insectivorous species, a rodent (*Onychomys torridus*), and a shrew (*Notiosorex crawfordi*), are found in the Tucson area, while a single species of mouse opossum (*Marmosa pusilla*) occurs in the northern Monte.

The number of herbivores and micro-omnivores (small, euryphagic species) is about the same in all three areas, while carnivores form the predominant trophic assemblage in both deserts and the smallest trophic group in the eastern forest. Carnivory may be selected over omnivory in a desert because few alternative food choices are available. Desert seeds are generally not fleshy and are adapted for withstanding long droughts; the lack of an invertebrate soil fauna has been noted. Thus, for the nonherbivore (or non-granivore), the largest, most predictably available food packets in deserts are other vertebrates.

Nest Placement

Nest placement by desert mammals is mainly underground (Table 5-5 and Appendix N), while in the eastern forest many nests are placed in trees or shrubs. Lagomorphs nest on the ground but almost all desert rodents nest underground, pack rats (*Neotoma*) being a notable exception (J. H. Brown, 1968; Olsen, 1973). Numerous rodents, primarily squirrels (Sciuridae) nest above ground in the deciduous forest. Trees in the desert are not as large, are seldom hollow, and are neither as branched nor as leafy as those of forests. Given the absence of dense ground vegetation, it is not surprising to find that very few smaller mammals nest on the ground in deserts.

The armadillo, *Chaetophractus vellerosus,* is one of the most common Monte mammals. Although members of the family Dasypodidae are not found in the Sonoran Desert, the nine-banded armadillo, *Dasypus novemcinctus,* is found from the central United States to northern Argentina, primarily in forested areas (A. Cabrera, 1957; Hall and Kelson, 1959; Walker, 1964). We compared aspects of the ecology of *D. novemcinctus* with that of *C. vellerosus* to determine which adaptations of the latter have arisen in response to its arid environment (Greegor, 1975). Armadillos, as a group, possess a low resting body temperature and show large daily fluctuations in body temperature (Johansen, 1961; Roig, 1971, 1973). Both traits are useful in desert climates (Schmidt-Nielsen, 1964). In addition, armadillos are burrowing animals of relatively low vagility and do not use respiration for evaporative cooling (Clark, 1951; Fitch et al., 1952; Johansen, 1961). Individual *C. vellerosus* moved up to 1.4 kilometers in an evening, and covered a 4.7 hectare area in a three-day period, but such movements are insufficient to reach the few, widely scattered waterholes in the Monte. Free water is thus essentially unavailable for this species. *Dasypus* subsists chiefly on ground insects (Kalmbach, 1943) while *Chaetophractus* is an omnivore and eats insects and other invertebrates, plant matter, carrion, and even small vertebrates (Figure 5-2). Its food habits greatly resemble those of skunks (*Spilogale* and *Mephitis*) of the Sonoran Desert.

Kidney morphology of *D. novemcinctus* and *C. vellerosus* also demonstrates the latter's adaptation to desiccation. *Chaetophractus* possesses an elongate renal papilla which facilitates water uptake in the kidney, while renal papillae of *Dasypus* are not decidedly elongate (Figure 5-3). Relative medullary thickness (RMT) correlates positively with ability to concentrate electrolytes in urine (B. Schmidt-Nielsen and O'Dell, 1961) and the RMT of *Chaetophractus* is within the range of highly desert-adapted kangaroo rats, while those of *Dasypus novemcinctus* and *D. mazzai* (a tropical forest armadillo from near the northern boundary of the Monte) are more allied with white rats, *Rattus norvegicus,* which are not desert adapted. When both *C. vellerosus* and *D. novemcinctus* were placed on reduced water diets with fresh ground horsemeat as food (66.7 percent water), both species maintained weight, but when the meat was boiled to reduce water content (40.6 percent water) *Chaetophractus* lost weight at a slower rate than *Dasypus* (2.09 percent vs 15.28 percent over an eleven-day period (Figure 5-4)).

All Argentine desert armadillos (*Chaetophractus, Zaedyus, Burmeisteria,* and *Chlamyphorus*) are hirsute, while more tropical genera (*Dasypus, Cabossus,* and *Priodontes*) are naked. Hair may function as an insulation layer against environmental heat.

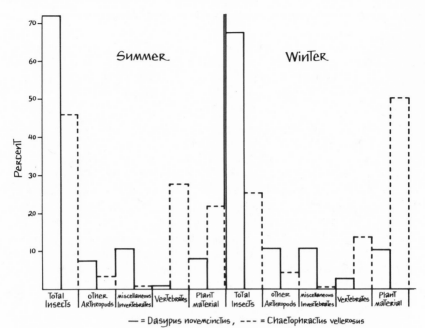

FIGURE 5-2. *Summer and winter food of* Dasypus novemcinctus *in North America (data from Kalmbach, 1943) and* Chaetophractus vellerosus *in the Monte. Percentages based on a volumetric analysis of stomach contents.*

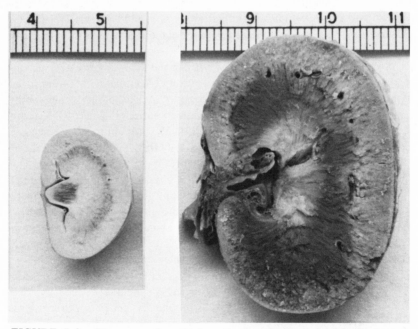

FIGURE 5-3. *Diagrams of sagittal sections of kidneys of desert-adapted* Chaetophractus vellerosus *(left) and nondesert adapted* Dasypus novemcinctus *(right). Note the elongate renal papilla on* Chaetophractus, *a structure correlated with water retention ability.*

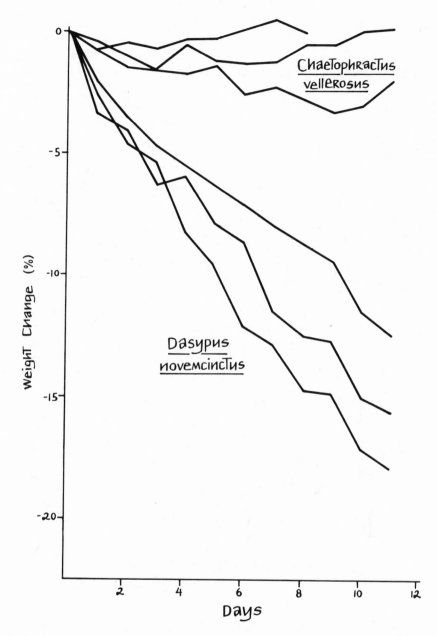

FIGURE 5-4. *Weight change, expressed as percentage of original body weight, of three* Dasypus novemcinctus *and three* Chaetophractus vellerosus *maintained on boiled horsemeat (containing 40.6% water) under identical laboratory conditions in Tucson, Arizona.* Chaetophractus *lost an average of 0.19% body weight/day, while* Dasypus *lost 1.48% body weight/day on the average.*

Rodents

Physiological adaptations were studied in three species of Monte Desert rodents, *Eligmodontia typus, Phyllotis darwini,* and *P. griseoflavus* (Mares, 1973a, 1975a, b, unpubl.) and comparative studies were done on a number of nondesert Argentine species.

None of the Monte rodents is able to exist indefinitely using only metabolic water and/or water contained in air-dried seeds (Figure 5-5). North American heteromyids and murids (cricetines) can exist without free water on essentially dry foods (see Mares, 1973a). *Phyllotis griseoflavus* is probably more adapted to live without water than either *E. typus* or *P. darwini,* although microhabitats frequented by it are not as arid as those preferred by *E. typus. Phyllotis griseoflavus* inhabits dry rocky hillsides (Figure 5-6) and the vicinity of permanent streams (as does *P. darwini*), and in the lowland desert is essentially limited to dry forested gullies. *Eligmodontia typus* is found in arid creosotebush flats (*Larrea*), or in low shrubby, sandy areas supporting cacti or halophytic plants. *Phyllotis darwini* probably inhabits more mesic habitats than either of the other two species.

Since *E. typus* cannot live on dry food alone, further studies were conducted to determine possible water sources in food items (Mares, 1973a, 1975b; unpubl.). Cacti (*Trichocereus*) were offered to water-stressed gerbil

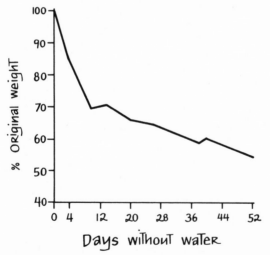

FIGURE 5-5. *Weight changes, expressed as percent of original body weight, for* Eligmodontia typus *during water deprivation while being fed air-dried seeds containing about 8% water (by weight). Seventeen animals were tested. Four survived for 52 days. (Adapted from Mares, 1975a.)*

FIGURE 5-6. *Vegetation on a dry, rocky wash near Villavil. Bolsón de Pipanaco.* Acacia aroma *and* Trichocereus terschekii *are conspicuous in the foreground. (Photo by O. T. Solbrig.)*

mice (*E. typus*) as a water source and they were able to maintain weight on the cacti when other water was unavailable (Figure 5-7). Gerbil mice also have a marked ability to utilize saline solutions, being able to consume up to 2.0 Molar sodium chloride solutions (about 4X the concentration of sea water) and still obtain usable water (Figure 5-8). No other known mammal can survive while drinking such extremely concentrated salt water, although the Australian *Notomys cervinus* is able to drink sodium chloride solutions of up to 1.0 Molar (MacMillen and Lee, 1969). *Eligmodontia typus* may thus obtain both food and water from succulent halophytic plants that are common in many areas where the rodent is found, much like *Dipodomys microps* of the Great Basin Desert in North America, and the Australian *N. cervinus* (Kenagy, 1972, 1973; MacMillen and Lee, 1969).

Although possessing some tolerance to aridity, when such parameters as ability to withstand desiccation before death or urine-concentrating ability are considered, Argentine desert rodents rank below many rodents of the North American deserts (Table 5-6). Generally Monte rodents do not seem to be as highly adapted physiologically for a desert existence as numerous species from other deserts. They have not evolved the ability to exist without free water and depend upon succulent vegetation for their water requirements. Some South American cricetine rodents apparently can live without free water, indicating that genetic plasticity for evolution of this ability exists

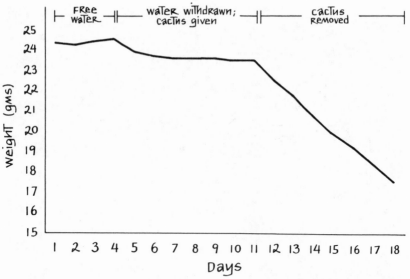

FIGURE 5-7. *Average weight in grams for a sample of* Eligmodontia typus *with unrestricted access to free water, with cactus* (Trichocereus) *as a water source, and with no free water. Air-dried seeds were available without restriction during all experiments. (Adapted from Mares, 1975a.)*

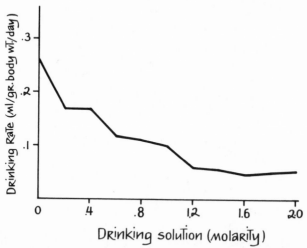

FIGURE 5-8. *Drinking rate, expressed as ml/gram body weight/day, of ten* Eligmodontia typus *with distilled water and various saline solutions. An unusual ability to tolerate salinity is evident. Solutions of up to 2.0 m sodium chloride (four times the concentration of sea water!) were accepted. (Adapted from Mares, 1973a.)*

TABLE 5-6 *Maximal Urine Concentration Values (Milliosmols) for Various Rodent Species from Different Deserts*

Species	Maximal urine values (m. osmols/l)	Locality	Source
Notomys alexis	9370	Australia	MacMillen & Lee (1969)
Leggadina hermansburgensis	9000	Australia	MacMillen et al. (1972)
Peromyscus truei	8150	North America	Andersen (1973)
Peromyscus difficilus	7500	North America	Andersen (1973)
Eligmodontia typus	5763	Argentina	This study
Dipodomys merriami	5540	North America	Schmidt-Nielsen et al. (1948)
Peromyscus leucopus	5500	North America	Andersen (1973)
Peromyscus maniculatus	5500	North America	Andersen (1973)
Peromyscus boylei	5350	North America	Andersen (1973)
Calomys musculinus	5183	Argentina	This study
Notomys cervinus	4920	Australia	MacMillen & Lee (1969)
Dipodomys agilis	4100	North America	Carpenter (1966) MacMillen (1964)
Phyllotis darwini	3619	Argentina	This Study
Peromyscus crinitis	3430	North America	Abbott (1971)

within the group. *Phyllotis gerbillus* of the Sechura Desert of Perú and *Calomys musculinus,* a species limited to mesic parts of the northern Monte and which occurs in the high Cordillera, can exist fairly well without free water, although their ability to maintain weight under strict water deprivation is not as pronounced as in some heteromyids (cf. Koford, 1968; Mares, unpubl.)

Insects, Reptiles, and Birds*

These animals are all uricotelic and lose very small amounts of water in voiding nitrogenous waste products. Both insects and reptiles are exothermic (Schmidt-Nielsen, 1964), that is, their metabolic rate is variable and body temperature is regulated using external heat sources such as sunlight. This form of regulation is usually effective in arid situations because of the high incidence of sunny days and because small animals can readily move into and out of shaded spots to maintain a stable, high body temperature without having to rely on evaporative cooling.

All three groups possess relatively impermeable body surfaces, those of insects being covered by a chitinous exoskeleton, those of reptiles by a horny or scaly, keratinized skin, and those of birds by feathers. Individuals of many

*By W. F. Blair, A. C. Hulse, R. D. Sage, and C. S. Tomoff

species of all three groups drink water if it is available but nearly all can maintain water balance through the water content of their food. A few desert granivorous birds, such as doves and parrots, make long flights to obtain free surface water, but most species do not. In all groups there are few marked physiological adaptations to desert conditions, the desert species being generally indistinguishable from their mesic environment relatives in their heat tolerances and mechanisms for retardation of water loss.

Most obvious adaptations of these animals to desert physical environments are behavioral. For example, nocturnal activity, at least during hot summer months, is common among desert snakes (Table 5-7), insects, and spiders. Those snakes that do remain diurnal during summer are either fast-moving and semiarboreal species (*Masticophus flagellum* in the Sonoran Desert and *Philodryas burmeisteri* in the northern Monte) or are found in close association with permanent water. Nocturnal feeding activity is especially pronounced among desert arthropods during summer.

Many morphological adaptations of desert insects, birds, and reptiles are related to living in or on specific soil types since soil conditions are so little modified by vegetation in desert areas. Sand dunes, for example, tend to be inhabited by species with special adaptations for moving across sand and/or

TABLE 5-7 *Comparison of the Two Desert Snake Faunas with a Nondesert Fauna for Four Ecological and Morphological Characteristics*

	<50 cm.	50–150 cm.	Body size >150 cm.		
Sonoran	41.7 (10)*	37.5 (9)	20.8 (5)		
Monte	29.4 (5)	47.0 (8)	23.6 (4)		
Ozark	23.3 (7)	50.0 (15)	26.7 (8)		

	Diurnal	Nocturnal	Activity		
Sonoran	54.1 (13)	83.3 (20)			
Monte	47.0 (8)	82.3 (15)			
Ozark	76.7 (23)	36.6 (11)			

	Arboreal	Fossorial	Habitat Terrestrial	Semi-aquatic	
Sonoran	4.2 (1)	25.0 (6)	58.3 (14)	8.4 (2)	
Monte	5.9 (1)	29.4 (6)	64.7 (11)	0.0	
Ozark	3.3 (1)	23.3 (7)	46.7 (14)	26.7 (8)	

	Arthropods	Amphibians	Food Lizards	Snakes	Birds & mammals
Sonoran	20.8 (5)	8.3 (2)	50.0 (12)	16.6 (4)	54.2 (13)
Monte	11.8 (3)	11.8 (2)	35.3 (6)	11.8 (2)	23.5 (4)
Ozark	33.3 (10)	40.0 (12)	10.0 (3)	6.7 (2)	46.3 (14)

*Numbers in parentheses are actual numbers of species in each category.

for burrowing in it. Convergence in sand-adapted characteristics is found between the lizard genus *Uma* in the Sonoran Desert and two species of *Liolaemus* in the Monte, all of which have fringed toes, countersunk jaws, nasal valves, specially reinforced skulls, and streamlined, shovel-shaped heads and smooth scales to facilitate burrowing.

Several species pairs of snakes from the disjunct deserts are convergent in morphology, diet, and place exploitation, but these pairs are tentative since little is known about the life histories of many species in either desert region. *Hypsiglena ochrorhyncha* and *Pseudotomodon trigonatus* are similar in size, general body shape and coloration. Both are rear fanged oviparous, nocturnal species that feed mainly on lizards. The blind snake, *Leptotyphlops humilis*, of the Sonoran Desert has four counterparts in the Monte, *L. borrichianus*, *L. unguirostris*, *L. melanotermus,* and *Amphisbaena angustifrons.* All are small, fossorial, basically sightless reptiles. In each case the main diet of these reptiles is composed of ants, although termites are eaten occasionally. *Masticophis flagellum* and *Philodryas burmeisteri* are both large, nonconstricting snakes, active diurnally, and semiarboreal. In both cases food consists mainly of lizards, birds, and some small mammals.

Several species pairs of lizards from disjunct deserts show convergence in various aspects of their biology. Suggestions for convergent pairs are often tentative since little information is available for life histories of the Monte fauna and at times is scanty for Sonoran Desert species.

Both deserts possess subfamilially distinct representatives of the Gekkonidae. In the Sonoran Desert it is the eublepharine *Coleonyx variegatus* (Figure 5-9 and in the Monte the gekkonines *Homonota horrida* and *H. underwoodi* (Figure 5-10). Both genera have elliptical pupils (an adaptation for nocturnal existence), but *C. variegatus* has eyelids while *Homonota* does not. Scales in *Coleonyx* and *H. underwoodi* are smooth but *H. horrida* possesses keeled scales. *Coleonyx variegatus* has a thick tail that is used for fat storage and is also readily autotomized and functions as a caudal lure to attract predators away from the head. In *Homonota* the tail is thinner than in *Coleonyx* and the lizards do not exhibit the marked functioning as a caudal lure behavior characteristic of *Coleonyx,* and the tails break off less easily. Ecologically the species are similar. Although *H. horrida* in Córdoba climbs readily over rocks neither *Homonota* nor *Coleonyx* are commonly found on even the lowest branches of desert shrubs, indicating that they are not good climbers. Both genera are nocturnal and both have clutch sizes of one or two eggs, as do all geckos.

Teiid lizards of the genus *Cnemidophorus* are found in both deserts. *Cnemidophorus tigris* (a large species) is present in the Sonoran and *C. longicaudus* (an intermediate-sized species) inhabits the Monte. Both are active, terrestrial, diurnal foragers found in open and closed microhabitats. During hot summer months activity patterns are bimodal with a peak in both early morning and late afternoon.

FIGURE 5-9. Coleonyx variegatus *(Gekkonidae). (Photo by M. L. Erckmann.)*

FIGURE 5-10. Homonota underwoodi *(Gekkonidae). (Photo by M. L. Erckmann.)*

A notable example of convergence between desert lizards is seen in the pair *Liolaemus darwini* (Monte) and *Uta stansburiana* (Sonoran) (Figure 5-1). Table 5-8 compares these lizards for several morphological, behavioral, reproductive, and demographic characteristics. The two species are similar in reproduction, behavior, and morphology, but differ in all demographic characteristics and some reproductive ones. These differences could be due to the fact that data for *Uta* are from a population in xeric Texas grassland (Tinkle, 1967). Climatic conditions in west Texas differ considerably from those encountered in the Monte of Argentina and may account for the ecological differences of the lizards.

TABLE 5-8 *Comparison of Various Characteristics of* Uta stansburiana *and* Liolaemus darwini, *two closely convergent desert lizards*

Uta	Liolaemus
	Basically restricted to desert
Small, less than 70 mm. SVL	X*
Strong sexual dimorphism	X
Males often spotted with blue	X
Antehumeral spot present in both males and females	X
Wide ranging in desert and grassland	Basically restricted to desert
Terrestrial	X
Diurnal	X
Follicles 7–8 mm at time of ovulation	X
Rapid corpora lutea degeneration	X
Vitallogenesis stops in late summer	X
Spermatogensis begins in fall	X
Spermatozoa produced in spring	X
Testes regress until late summer	X
Fat 3 to 4% of body weight in fall	–
Fat bodies cyclic	X
Vitellogenesis begins at time of emergence	Begins during hibernation
Average clutch 3.9 eggs	Average clutch 5.7 eggs
Length of season about 120–150 days	Four months
2–3 clutches per season	At least two clutches
Hatching time from 59–79 days	–
Hatching size about 22 mm.	25 mm
100 days for males to reach maturity	150–180 days
105 days for females to reach maturity	150–180 days
Females mature at 40 mm.	50 mm
Four weeks between clutches	X
Opportunistic feeding	X
Little time spent foraging	X
No seasonal change in diet	Seasonal shift in amount of plant material eaten
19 adults per acre	74 adults
Male home range 3 times greater than female	Six times greater

*X's indicate that a particular trait is shared.

PATTERNS IN COMMUNITY STRUCTURE
IN SELECTED ANIMAL TAXA

Some patterns in community structure in animal groups are more readily explained by the food resources provided by desert plants and the organisms that feed directly on them. They will be dealt with in the following chapter. Other patterns, however, are of a taxonomic nature and are appropriately considered here. We have data useful for comparing two aspects of community patterns in some animal groups we have studied. They are within-habitat number of species (*alpha* species richness) and between-habitat changes in the kinds and number of species (*beta* species-richness). Within-habitat richness is often less sensitive to historical considerations since habitats tend to fill up to the maximum number of species they are capable of supporting even if the total species pool is somewhat impoverished (Cody, 1974). Changes in species composition across environmental gradients, however, are much more sensitive to the total species pool and, perhaps, their order of invasion of the environment.

Anuran Communities*

Sonoran and Monte anurans are listed in Appendix H. In addition, both deserts have one tree frog (*Hyla*) that enters the desert along streams originating in nearby mountains. The anuran fauna of the Monte is composed of slightly more species and genera than that of the Sonoran desert but more species can be found in a single area in the Sonoran Desert. To compare species turnover and overall distributional patterns in the two deserts, collections were made along a transect from Tucson to Yuma in Arizona, and from Andalgalá to the city of Mendoza in Argentina. The northern transect was along an east-west moisture gradient with Tucson the mesic endpoint and Yuma the most xeric locality (with about 268 mm and 86 mm, respectively). In Argentina, Andalgalá was the most mesic southern desert site (approximately 300 mm rainfall annually) and precipitation decreased southward through the province of San Juan (about 85 mm annually), but again increased toward Mendoza (about 190 mm annually) where winter rains become heavier. Cei (1956) was used to supplement distribution ranges for Argentine species.

In the Sonoran Desert, greatest species richness of amphibians was found in the vicinity of Ajo, Pima County (Appendix H), an area of intermediate rainfall. The increased number of amphibians in the region is due partly to the fact that two species (*Bufo retiformis* and *Pternohyla fodiens*) with southern affinities reach their northern limits there, though why their ranges stop there is not known. The driest locality examined (Yuma) has only four

*By A. C. Hulse and W. F. Blair.

amphibians, all of which are found throughout the length of the transect. Tucson has seven species, two of which reach the southwestern limit of their range in that vicinity. In Argentina, Andalgalá and Mendoza have approximately the same number of species, although turnover in species composition is great and only four species are shared by the two localities.

The extent of convergence in the two anuran communities can be seen more clearly by comparing them with a nondesert fauna from the Ozark Plateau (Dowling, 1956) which is taxonomically closely related to the Sonoran Desert fauna. Body size, time of activity, conditions that initiate breeding, site of egg deposit, tadpole diet, and rate of development are compared in Table 5-9. Some general convergent trends in community structure in the deserts are evident in the reliance of anurans on temporary water, greater proportion of species with carnivorous tadpoles, and short larval development times. However, the Sonoran Desert fauna is more like the Ozark fauna in time of activity.

Reptiles*

The reptile faunas of both deserts are rich and diverse (see Appendix G). More species appear to inhabit the Sonoran Desert than the Monte, but this may be an artifact of more intensive collecting. To determine overall distributional patterns of lizards (not enough detailed data were collected on Monte snakes to estimate patterns of species turnover) in the two deserts, the same transects were used as for anurans. Little species turnover of lizards occurred along either the Monte or Sonoran transects (Appendix J). Of fifteen species of lizards present along the Monte transect, nine were found around Andalgalá and twelve near Mendoza, with seven species shared. San Juan, the mid-point of the transect, has eleven species and shares seven with Andalgalá and eight with Mendoza. Species turnover is similar in the northern desert. Of fifteen species of lizards found on the transect, eleven occur around Tucson and thirteen near Yuma, with nine species shared. Ajo, the mid-point of the transect, has ten species: all are shared with Tucson and eight with Yuma.

In both deserts the majority of lizards are terrestrial in open microhabitats (Table 5-10), but many of these species sporadically enter closed habitats and some, such as *Cnemidophorus tigris* and *C. longicaudus,* are almost as common in closed microhabitats as in open ones. The Sonoran Desert lacks truly fossorial lizards. The Monte lacks totally arboreal lizards, although *Leiosaurus catamarcensis* may be quite arboreal, whereas the Sonoran Desert has three species that are almost entirely arboreal.

Lizards of the two deserts appear convergent in several characteristics when compared with a nondesert lizard fauna from the Ozark Plateau (Table

*By A. C. Hulse, R. D. Sage, and W. F. Blair.

TABLE 5-9 *Comparison of the Two Desert Anuran Faunas with a Nondesert Fauna for Six Ecological and Morphological Characteristics*

	Body size		
	<6 cm % N	6–10 cm % N	>10 cm % N
Sonoran	33.0 (4)*	41.6 (5)	25.4 (3)
Monte	40.0 (6)	33.3 (5)	26.7 (4)
Ozark	35.7 (5)	28.6 (4)	35.7 (5)

	Activity†	
	Diurnal	Nocturnal
Sonoran	25.0 (3)	100.0 (12)
Monte	13.3 (2)	100.0 (14)
Ozark	28.5 (4)	100.0 (14)

	Initiation of breeding activity	
	Rain	Other
Sonoran	75.0 (9)	25.0 (3)
Monte	86.7 (13)	13.3 (2)
Ozark	100.0 (14)	00.0

	Breeding site†	
	Temporary water	Permanent water
Sonoran	75.0 (9)	41.6 (5)
Monte	86.7 (13)	13.3 (2)
Ozark	42.8 (6)	85.7 (12)

	Diet in tadpoles	
	Carnivorous	Herbivorous
Sonoran	16.6 (2)	83.4 (10)
Monte	40.0 (6)	60.0 (9)
Ozark	7.1 (1)	92.9 (12)

	Rate of development		
	<30 days	30–60 days	>60 days
Sonoran	16.6 (2)	75.0 (9)	8.4 (1)
Monte	33.3 (5)	60.0 (9)	6.7 (1)
Ozark	7.1 (1)	28.5 (4)	64.4 (9)

*Numbers in parentheses are actual numbers of species in each category.

†Totals do not necessarily equal 100% since some species are found in more than one category.

TABLE 5-10 *Habitat Utilization by Lizards of the Monte and Sonoran Deserts*

Argentina	Place	Arizona
Liolaemus robertmertensi Teius teyou cyanogaster Tupinambis rufescens Cnemidophorus longicaudus	Terrestrial (in closed microhabitats)	Heloderma suspectum Coleonyx variegatus
Homonota horrida Homonota underwoodi Liolaemus darwini Liolaemus goetschi Liolaemus lentus Liolaemus sp. 1 Liolaemus sp. 2 Liolaemus sp. 3 Leiosaurus bardensis	Terrestrial (in open microhabitats)	Callisurus draconoides Crotaphytus collaris Crotaphytus wislizeni Dipsosaurus dorsalis Sauromalus obesus Phrynosoma platyrhinos Phrynosoma solare Phrynosoma m'calli Uta stansburiana Uma notata Uma inornata Cnemidophorus tigris
Leiosaurus catamarcensis	Arboreal	Sceloporus magister Urosaurus graciosus Urosaurus ornatus
Amphisbaena angustifrons Amphisbaena sp	Fossorial	None

5-11). Most lizards of the Ozark fauna are insectivorous whereas herbivores and carnivores are present in the deserts. The Monte also has an omnivorous species. The Plateau lizard fauna is depauperate and composed primarily of scincids. Large species (> 20 cm) snout-vent length are found only in the desert areas (two in the Monte and three in the Sonoran Desert), but this is related to heat rather than aridity since large lizards are found in most hot climates whether they are wet or dry. Diurnal activity predominates in all three areas, but the Ozark Plateau fauna has no nocturnal species while both deserts do. For unknown reasons there are arboreal lizards in both North American areas but none in the Monte.

Habitat utilization patterns for snakes in the two deserts are shown in Table 5-12. Only those species whose distribution in the desert is restricted to wash areas are considered to occupy closed habitats. Many snakes listed in open microhabitats are often encountered in washes, but are also regular on desert flats. Habitat utilization in both deserts is very similar for all but fossorial species. In both areas, the majority of species are found in open microhabitats with only two species in each desert being restricted to wash areas. Both deserts have one semiarboreal snake, and the Sonoran Desert has twice as many fossorial species as the Monte. Sandy areas in the Monte are widespread but scattered, while dunes are more extensive and continuous in

TABLE 5-11 *Comparison of Four Characteristics of the Lizard Faunas of the Two Deserts with a Nondesert Fauna*

	<10 cm	Body size 10–20	>20 cm
Sonoran	41.2 (8)*	47.0 (8)	11.8 (2)
Monte	73.3 (11)	20.0 (3)	6.7 (1)
Ozark	57.2 (4)	42.8 (3)	0.0

	Diurnal	Activity	Nocturnal
Sonoran	88.2 (16)		11.8 (2)
Monte	86.7 (13)		13.3 (2)
Ozark	100.0 (7)		0.0

	Terrestrial	Habitat	Arboreal
Sonoran	82.3 (14)		17.7 (3)
Monte	100.0 (15)		0.0
Ozark	85.7 (6)		14.3 (1)

	Herbivorous	Feeding Omnivorous	Carnivorous	Insectivorous
Sonoran	11.8 (2)	0.0	17.6 (3)	70.6 (12)
Monte	6.6 (1)	6.6 (1)	6.6 (1)	80.0 (12)
Ozark	0.0	0.0	14.2 (1)	85.8 (6)

*Numbers in parentheses are actual numbers of species in each category.

the Sonoran Desert. Dunes near Andalgalá were carefully surveyed for small fossorial snakes, but none was found nor were any tracks observed in the soft sand.

Due to the lack of data for the Monte, we can compare food of snakes only superficially. Arthropods constitute a greater percentage of the diet of the Ozark community than that of either of the desert faunas, even though the two deserts have a greater percentage of small fossorial snakes which might be expected to feed on small invertebrates. The food of snakes from the Ozark Plateau and those of the deserts reflects differential availability of prey items. Anurans, common in the deciduous forest but scarce and season-ally active in deserts, are eaten by about 30 percent of Ozark snakes, but only by 10 percent of snakes from either desert. Lizards, scarce in the Ozarks but common in deserts, are a common food for many desert snakes, preyed upon by few Ozark snakes. Birds and mammals comprise the bulk of dietary items for both North American snake communities, while they are taken by less than 30 percent of Monte snakes.

TABLE 5-12 *Habitat Utilization by Snakes in the Monte of Catamarca and the Sonoran Desert of Arizona*

Argentina	Place	Arizona
Clelia occipitolutea Leimadophis sagittifer Lystrophis semicinctus Philodryas psammophideus Oxyrhopus rhombifer Pseudotomodon trigonatus Phimophis vittatus Bothrops neuwiedi Crotalus durissus Micrurus frontalis	Terrestrial (in open microhabitats)	Lichanura trivirgata Salvadora hexalepis Arizona elegans Pituophis melanoleucus Lampropeltis getulus Rhinocheilus leconti Sonora semiannulata Trimorphodon lambda Hypsiglena ochrorhynchus Crotalus atrox Crotalus scutulatus Crotalus mitchelli Crotalus cerastes Crotalus tigris
Philodryas patagonensis Lygophis lineatus	Terrestrial (in closed microhabitats)	Thamnophis cyrtopsis Thamnophis marcianus
Philodryas burmeisteri	Semiarboreal	Masticophis flagellum
Leptotyphlops borrichianus Leptotyphlops anguirostris Leptotyphlops melanotermus Elapomorphus tricolor Elapomorphus bilineatus	Fossorial	Leptotyphlops humilis Phyllorhynchus decurtatus Phyllorhynchus browni Sonora semiannulata Chionactis occipitalis Chionactis palarostris Chilomeniscus cinctus Micruroides euryxanthus

Mammals*

The mammalian fauna of the Sonoran Desert near Tucson is more than twice as rich as that of the Andalgalá area. Twenty-eight species of mammals are found at the southern site, while sixty-four occur in arid areas near Tucson (Appendix K). The northern site has twice as many genera (40 vs. 21), more families (17 vs. 11), and more orders (7 vs. 5). Many families (Tayassuidae, Leporidae, Cervidae, Erithizontidae) which are found in Arizona occur within relatively short distances of the Monte (some only a few miles away) but apparently have never evolved desert species. The major differences in the two faunas are (Mares, 1973a):

1. Three orders (Artiodactyla, Lagomorpha, and Insectivora) found in the north do not occur in the south.
2. The order Edentata is not present in the Sonoran Desert.

*By M. A. Mares.

3. Bat species at the northern site outnumber those of the southern by more than two to one (20:9).
4. Rodent species in the north outnumber those in the south by about two to one (14:8).

The overall impression after studying mammals in the Monte is one of faunal scarcity. Along dry, forested gullies (Figure 5-11) caviomorphs, particularly *Microcavia australis* (cavies), are locally abundant. Fossorial gopher-like tuco-tucos (*Ctenomys*) are also locally abundant and conspicuous because of their habit of vocalizing with a deep thumping call. Nevertheless, there is a paucity of small nocturnal rodents. If carrying capacities of the two deserts are equal, one might logically suppose that Monte species would be more common than those found in the Sonoran, but this is not true (Figure 5-12). Small mammals are about fifteen times as common (or easy to trap) in xeric localities in the Sonoran Desert as in analogous sites in the Monte. Biomass data were, unfortunately, not obtained in the Monte and it is possible, though unlikely, that total biomass of mammal tissue supported by a given area of Monte Desert is comparable to values obtained for Arizona. Patagonian "Hares" are large herbivores and weigh up to 15 kilograms; cavies weigh up to 300 grams; and tuco-tucos weigh about 90 grams. Uncontrolled hunting in the Monte also complicates our estimates.

Rodent species occurring along the Argentine transect are shown in Appendix L, while rodent and lagomorph species along the North American

FIGURE 5-11. *View of the Río Amanao, Bolsón de Pipanaco. The large trees are* Prosopis flexuosa. *(Photo by M. A. Mares.)*

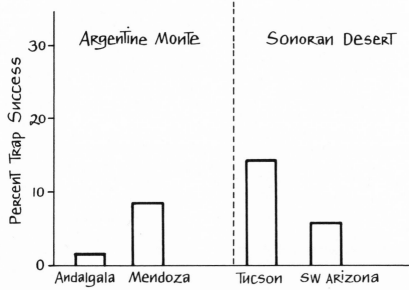

FIGURE 5-12. *Percentage trap success expressed as number of captures/100 trap nights, where one trap-night = one trap placed for one night of Monte and Sonoran desert rodents. The Andalgalá-Tucson sites differ by about a factor of 10. Southwestern Arizona localities have the lowest abundances in the northern Sonoran Desert, but capture success is still greater than in the Andalgalá area. Trap success increases in the Monte near Mendoza as one moves out of the lowland desert toward the Andes and elevation increases. Mendoza captures were almost all* Eligmodontia typus. *North American data are based on early spring field work, March and April, when desert rodent populations are lower, and thus represent minimal values. Monte data are year-round averages. (Adapted from Mares, 1973a.)*

transect are in Appendix M. Coefficients of community similarity demonstrate that while species found along transects overlap broadly, some species turnover nonetheless occurs between sites. The rodents at Tucson are more similar to those of Yuma than to those of Gila Bend (near the midpoint of the transect), while the latter two drier sites are most similar in faunal composition. Few species not present in Tucson occur in the other two Arizona areas, while seven species found in Tucson are absent from the other sites. Four of these latter species (*Spermophilus spilosoma, Perognathus flavus, Dipodomys spectabilis, Dipodomys ordii*) are essentially from eastern arid or semi-arid areas and reach their western limits in the vicinity of Tucson. *Sylvilagus floridanus,* the cottontail rabbit, occurs north, east and south of Tucson, but reaches the western limit of its distribution at 32° North latitude near the Tucson area. *Leptus alleni,* the jackrabbit, is essentially a Mexican species which reaches its northern limit near Tucson, while *Peromyscus merriami*, a field mouse, has an extremely small geographic range in New Mexico and southern Arizona, including Tucson.

Vegetation around Tucson is quite complex in diversity and physiognomy compared to either Gila Bend or Yuma, probably helping to account for the area's high mammal species richness (Rosenzweig and Winakur, 1969; Rosenzweig et al., 1975). Increased aridity could be the primary factor preventing these six species from ranging westward. Four species found at Gila Bend and Yuma (*Perognathus longimembris, Dipodomys deserti, Peromyscus crinitus, Neotoma lepida*) are elements of the western Sonoran Desert fauna which do not range eastward as far as Tucson.

No real reduction in species richness occurs along the Andalgalá-Valle de la Luna transect. More extensive field work will probably yield *Ctenomys fulvus* in the area of Valle de la Luna. Were this species to be taken there, the coefficient of community would be 0.875, showing very little species turnover along the transect. Therefore, both turnover of species (between-habitat richness) and within-habitat richness is higher in the Sonoran Desert than in the Monte.

Birds*

In their within-habitat species richness, between-habitat species richness, and niche patterns, birds are the best known of all animal groups. In both temperate and tropical habitats, the diversity of bird species breeding in an area can generally be predicted from a knowledge of the foliage height structure of the vegetation, though tropical habitats support more species than temperate habitats of equivalent foliage height complexity (MacArthur et al., 1966; Karr, 1971; Cody, 1970). The reason for this relationship is presumably that greater foliage height complexity allows for a greater variety of efficient means of exploiting prey than are possible in structurally simpler environments, probably due to complex vertical gradients in light intensity and foliage and branch structure and density (Orians, 1969).

Hot-desert vegetation is extremely interesting to students of bird community structure because the diversity of plant life forms is not adequately reflected in the standard foliage height profiles. Previous work indicated that the correlation between bird species diversity and foliage height diversity is poor in Sonoran Desert vegetation (MacArthur, 1964; Tomoff, 1974). Those results indicated that birds selected their breeding habitats on the basis of particular plant species which provided critical nest sites and/or food resources but which contribute little to the vegetation profiles.

Since Avra Valley and Bolsón de Pipanaco have similar numbers of bird species (thirty-seven and forty-two respectively), comparisons of patterns of species richness and turnover along habitat gradients are especially interesting.

*By C. S. Tomoff

In both deserts bird species richness increases from *Larrea* flats through mixed shrub and cactus communities to riparian habitats. The most significant regressions are obtained between bird species diversity and plant cover diversity, a measure of the proportion of total plant cover found in each of the following groups of perennial plants: herbs; small, non-spinescent shrubs; spinescent shrubs; cacti; and small trees of washes (Figure 5-13). Both foraging substrates and nest site diversity are involved in this correlation.

Nest site selection is highly specific to plant forms in both deserts. Most bird species nest in only few species of plants, even though they may be rare. For example, though tree trunks with woodpecker holes and natural cavities are sparse in desert habitats, 25-33 percent of species require such sites. Similarly, spinescent trees and shrubs provide the most frequently used life form in the Monte, while in some habitats in the Sonoran Desert over 75 percent of nests are built in cacti. Holes and spiny sites probably provide the greatest protection against nest predators and weather extremes. Birds with the most specialized nest-site requirements have the patchiest distributions and are often associated with particular microsites. Hole-nesting species are often limited to riparian or giant cactus communities even though they regularly forage over desert flats. Species with more varied nest site requirements are more widely distributed throughout interwash flats and riparian habitats. Also, densities of breeding birds are positively correlated with densities of

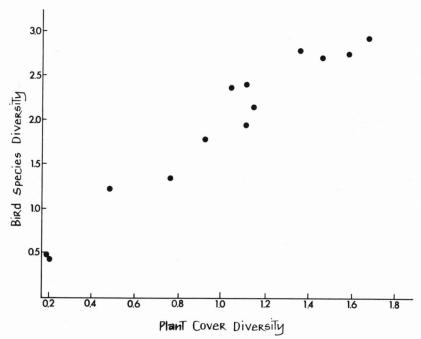

FIGURE 5-13. *Relationship between bird species diversity and plant life form diversity.*

prime nest plants more than they are with overall plant densities (and, presumably, total food availability).

Thus, birds select similar nest sites in the two deserts. The use of mostly cacti in the Sonoran Desert, but mostly spinescent shrubs in the Monte, is presumably related to the comparatively greater abundance of cacti in the Sonoran Desert. This convergence reflects strong predation pressure on nesting desert birds and the poor protection provided by the dominant sclerophyll desert shrubs.

Birds also have similar diets at the two areas (Table 5-13). Proportions of insectivorous and frugivorous (and granivorous) species are similar in both areas. Within frugivorous and insectivorous groups, considerably fewer ground-feeding species occur in the Monte. The rich winter annual flora in Arizona may provide a source of food (seeds and insects) absent in Monte.

Arthropods

Arthropod community structure cannot be analyzed like vertebrate groups due to large numbers of unknown species in most taxa. Therefore, many comparisons appear later where we analyze arthropod feeding guilds.

Grasshoppers*

An intensive effort was made to explain differences in the number of grasshopper species in Sonoran and Monte deserts. In particular, data were assembled on the association between the richness of grasshopper species and richness of flora by counting the number of grasshopper and plant species in

TABLE 5-13 *Diets of the Non-Raptorial Birds of the Monte and Sonoran Deserts*

	Monte (41 spp.) percent of species	Sonoran (37 spp.) percent of species
Frugivores		
Ground foraging	11	30
On-plant-feeding	18	2
	29%	32%
Insectivores		
Ground-foraging	14	26
Bark-foraging	14	7
Foliage-gleaning	20	17
Flycatching	23	17
	71%	68%

*Summarized from Otte, 1977, in press.

50 × 50 m plots throughout both deserts as well as in the Chihuahuan and Baja California deserts (see Figure 5-14). The following general patterns emerged:

As the number of plant species (*P*) increases, number of grasshopper species (*G*) increases. However, *G* may eventually level out as *P* continues to increase. At Silver Bell there is a steady increase in *G* as one ascends the floristically more diverse slopes, but rocky hillsides, very rich in plant species, contain few grasshopper species, perhaps because suitable oviposition sites are scarce in rocky soil.

In the Sonoran Desert about one grasshopper species is added for every two plant species added (G:P ≈ 1:2). This relationship is most noticeable in lower altitude communities which contain few plant species. In the Chihuahuan Desert the G:P ratio is about 1:3. In Baja California and Argentine Monte it is about 1:4.

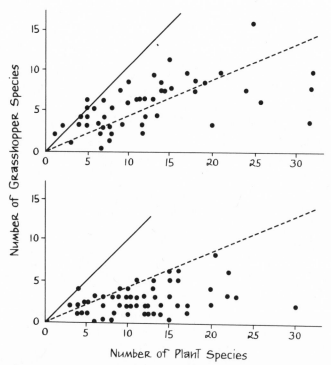

FIGURE 5-14. *Relationship between grasshopper species richness and plant richness. Upper graph plots data from the Sonoran and Chihuahuan deserts. The lower graph plots data from the Monte. The solid line represents the expected relationship if the number of grasshopper and plant species were equal. The dashed line is the actual regression for the Northern Hemisphere.*

The number of grasshopper species per site in Chihuahuan and Sonoran deserts was not different, but the number of plant species in Chihuahuan sites was higher than in Sonoran sites, causing the Chihuahuan G:P ratio to be lower.

Although Sonoran and Monte deserts contained similar numbers of plant species per plot, the Monte contained significantly fewer numbers of grasshopper species. For example, twenty-seven species were collected in the desert around Silver Bell, but only seven species were collected in the entire Bolsón de Pipanaco, a much larger area.

Differences in numbers of species in North America and South America could be influenced by differences in area or by differences in length of borders shared with rich source areas, but including or excluding the Andean border affects the number of species per border mile only minimally. On an area basis the Monte desert also is poor in species.

No clear latitudinal gradients in species richness are apparent in Argentina between 20° and 40° S latitude. In general, sites close to the Andean range are drier and have roughly half as many grasshopper species as eastern Monte sites.

A comparison of temperate grasslands bordering on the deserts revealed a higher per locality species density in North American grasslands. Total number of temperate grassland species is also much higher in North America than in South America, suggesting that North American deserts are supplied with species from much richer source areas.

It is improbable that differences in Sonoran-Monte species richness are due to differences in dietary breadths. Diets are quite similar in the two areas, but a component of the environment for which grasshoppers might indirectly compete is what Ricklefs and O'Rourke (1975) have termed the escape space, the background against which prey species seek refuge through camouflage or hiding. Creosote bushes (*Larrea*) furnish several kinds of hiding places. In North American deserts, these bushes are subdivided among as many as three grasshopper species. In the Sonoran Desert, for example, *Bootettix argentatus* resembles and occupies the foliage, *Ligurotettix coquilletti* resembles and occupies the stems (feeding on the foliage at night), and *Cibolacris parviceps* resembles the ground where it remains during the day (it also feeds on the foliage at night) (Otte and Joern, 1977). Thus, food requirements of these species are very similar, but they hide in very different places.

In the Monte the subdivision of *Larrea* as a resource is not as pronounced. Three stick-like acridoid species (family Prosocopiidae) each feed principally on two *Larrea* species (*L. cuneifolia* and *L. divaricata*). Initial surveys suggest that the grasshoppers are largely allopatric, displacing one another from north to south (*Astroma riojanum* → *Anchocoema subalata* → *Astroma compactum*). In each species sexes are strongly dimorphic in size and color. Males resemble small, live terminal twigs and females resemble larger, more basal branches and dead twigs. Females are also color polymorphic, especially in the nymphal stages. During the day males remain closer to the bush periphery and on foliage, and females are found on thicker stems where they either lie flat (stem mimicry) or mimic small dead twigs by facing downwards and protruding their abdomens outwards at an angle. As a class, females are much more color polymorphic than males.

Measures of diet breadth (as measured by the number of plants found in the stomachs of a sample of individuals collected at any given site, as well as across a larger portion of a species' range) indicate that North and South American desert species are not significantly different. However, mean diet breadth values for desert species are significantly lower than mean values for grassland species. A part of this difference is due to the larger number of plant species available to grassland species. In fact, there is probably no fundamental difference in potential diet breadth among polyphagous species of deserts and grasslands. But the proportion of specialized feeders is significantly higher in deserts.

If grasshopper species compete for food, diet breadths should decrease as number of coexisting species increases. However, we detected no significant differences in these parameters between North and South American desert species.

Some species specializing on annual plants are occasionally forced under conditions of severe shortage to feed on plants they normally avoid. *Trimerotropis pallidipennis* and *Psoloessa texana* are two Sonoran species which normally feed largely on annual grasses (*Bouteloua*); but when *Bouteloua* and other annuals fail to emerge, they may feed on such perennials as *Larrea*, a genus high in resin concentrations (Rhoades, 1977a), and *Ambrosia*, a genus rich in alkaloids.

Desert-inhabiting species may be divided into drought-enduring (true desert) species and drought-evading (marginal or opportunistic desert) species. These represent ends of a continuum, comprised at one end of species capable of enduring harsh conditions, and at the other end of species which opportunistically exploit water holes, washes, or other moist areas. The latter may display large-scale population fluctuations within the desert and have distributions which lie mainly outside the arid regions. *Bootettix, Ligurotettix, Cibolacris,* and *Trimerotropis pallidipennis* are species at the drought-enduring end of the spectrum, while *Melanoplus lakinus, Schistocerca americana, Syrbula fuscovittata,* and *Mermeria* species are at the other end.

A degree of host-specificity similar to that of *Astroma* is observed in the North American genera *Anconia* and *Aeoloplides*. Species in the former genus feed principally on *Atriplex,* while members of the latter feed mainly on various Chenopodiaceae. *Aeoloplides* may also feed on other plants when chenopods become scarce. Like *Bootettix,* these species are also foliage mimics, but, as is the case in *Astroma,* oligophagy seems to be permitted because the species are well camouflaged on several related plant species. A similar loose bond with host plants exists in the North American *Larrea* specialist, *Ligurotettix coguilletti*. This stem-mimic from the Sonoran Desert resembles South American *Larrea* specialists in that it is most commonly found on *Larrea* but sometimes feeds on quite unrelated plant species (*Atriplex*, Chenopodiaceae; *Simmondsia*, Buxacaceae; and *Ambrosia*, Asteraceae). A close relative of *Ligurotettix, Goniatron planum* from the Chihuahuan Desert is a stem-mimic which also lives on a few structurally similar but unrelated plant species. We found it to be abundant on large stands of *Flourensia cernua* (Asteraceae), *Cordia parvifolia* (Boraginaceae), and *Sericodes greggii* (Zygophyllaceae).

In North American deserts the rare stem-mimicking grasshopper *Clematodes larrae* has, so far as we are aware, been found only on *Larrea* bushes. The Romaliine grasshopper, *Tytthotyle maculata* is also frequently found on *Larrea*, but little is known about its feeding habits.

In Arizona, species which may be classified as oligophagous are *Hesperotettix viridis*, which feeds mainly on species of *Haplopappus* and *Gutierrezia* (*Asteraceae*): *Campylacantha olivacea vivax*, feeding on *Flourensia* (Asteraceae); *Aztecacris gloriosus, Poecilotettix pantherina*, and *P. longipennis*, all of which feed on *Baccharis* (Asteraceae). In Argentina, *Clarazella patagona* is also oligophagous. At Villa Unión in the northern Monte this species was found living on two related plant species on a river bank, *Tessaria absinthiodes* and *Baccharis salicifolia*. Nymphs of *Clarazella* were trimorphic, the grey brown and the pale green morph were both taken from *Tessaria*, on which they match the stems and leaves respectively, while the bright green morph was found only on *Baccharis* which it matched in color. Quite possibly these colors are developmentally flexible as they are in other acridids (Otte, 1972).

Several desert species are highly polyphagous, and each of them spends most of its time on or near the ground. (a) *Trimerotropis pallidipennis* is the only species common to both North and South American deserts. It is a ubiquitous dryland, ground-mimicking species occurring in deserts and grasslands from Canada to Patagonia (with gaps in its range in Central America). In North America it is a highly vagile species, with large numbers occasionally flying about at night. Adults of this species can be found during most months of the year.

Trimerotropis pallidipennis is also the most ubiquitous species in western Argentina, both temporally and spatially, but there it seems to inhabit an even wider variety of habitats than in North America, extending from mountain grasslands at 3000 m or more down to low altitudes arid salt flats, and through the length of the monte from the Bolivian highlands well into Patagonia. It is possible that its greater ecological amplitude in South America is due to the absence of congeners there. In western North America, *pallidipennis* interacts with numerous other *Trimerotropis* species. (b) *Melanoplus lakinus* (Catantopinae) is widely distributed in grasslands but its distribution in deserts is marginal. In some portions of the Great Plains (North Platte, Nebraska)

94 percent of the individuals examined had fed on the forb *Kochia scoparia* and only 1 percent had fed on each of three other plants (Mulkern et al., 1969). In the desert we found *lakinus* feeding on a wide variety of plant species and having one of the broadest diets. (c) *Dichroplus vittatus* (Catantopinae) of Argentina is similar to *Melanoplus lakinus* in several respects. Both sexes are generally nonflying; it appears to be an opportunist in deserts, inhabiting principally the denser vegetation in swales and washes; and it feeds on a wide variety of forb plants. Both species feed on *Allionia incarnata* (Nyctaginaceae), a plant species shared by North American and South American deserts. (d) Species of *Schistocerca* have broad diets in both deserts. *S. americana cancellata* of Argentina is more abundant in thorn scrub regions of Argentina and may be more of an opportunist in desert regions, thriving when conditions are favorable and disappearing during dry years. It feeds on many plant species at or near the ground.

In Argentina, grasshoppers were found to be associated mainly with *L. divaricata* and *L. cuneifolia,* the two most widespread species of the genus. No grasshoppers were found on *L. nitida,* even though thorough searches were made at numerous localities. In South America only the *Astroma-Anchocoema* lineage has come to specialize on *Larrea;* but in North America five different lineages (*Bootettix, Ligurotettix, Clematodes, Tythotyle,* and *Cibolacris*) have independently developed the ability to specialize on *Larrea.* It must be emphasized, though, that the South American fauna has been less extensively studied and other specialists may yet be revealed.

This initial survey indicates that the number of species specializing on *Larrea* bushes at any one locality is roughly similar in three deserts. At Andalgalá (Arg.) 12 percent (1/8) of the species were *Larrea* specialists. At Tucson (Ariz.) 12 percent (3/24) and at Cuatrocienagas (Chihuahuan Desert) 14 percent (2/14) were specialists.

Ants*

Ants were studied intensively at one site on each continent. Five hectares, including several habitat types, were surveyed (Appendix P) in the Avra Valley near Silver Bell, Arizona (site 002; Barbour and Diaz, 1973) during August 1973. The site near Andalgalá, Catamarca, Argentina, north of Route 62 at km 1512, was surveyed (Appendix O) in December 1973 and January 1974. The ant fauna of these two sites are remarkably similar at the generic level (Appendix Q).

The total ant fauna of Catamarca, Argentina, is incompletely known (Appendix O) but it is almost certainly less than the 209 species recorded for Arizona (Hunt and Snelling, 1973). Despite this, species richness at the

*By J. H. Hunt.

Catamarca study site is greater than at the Arizona study site. Figures 5-15 and 5-16 illustrate habitat distributions for species collected and/or observed along line transects at the two sites. From these figures estimates may be made of within-habitat species richness for two habitats, *Larrea* flat and *Prosopis/Acacia* wash. The Catamarca values are greater: 10 vs. 7 and 21 vs. 16.

Data illustrated in Figures 5-15 and 5-16 are for foraging ants. Nest site selection is frequently more circumscribed. Desert ants have only a narrow range of nest sites available; most species excavate nests in the soil. Seed-gathering ants (*Pogonomyrmex, Aphaenogaster, Veromessor,* and some *Pheidole* species) nest in soil, usually in *Larrea* flats and frequently in fully exposed sites. Fungus-growing ants (*Cyphomyrmex, Trachymyrmex, Acromyrmex*) nest in soil, almost always in *Prosopis/Acacia* washes and usually

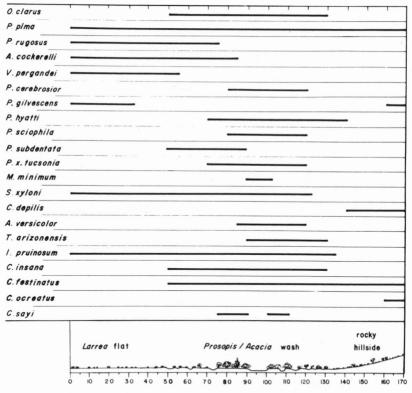

FIGURE 5-15. *Habitat distribution of foraging ants collected or seen along a 170 m line transect at a 5 hectare study site (site 002, Barbour and Diaz, 1973) in the Avra Valley near Silver Bell, Arizona. Collections and observations were made in August 1973. The listing of genera and species follows the sequence of Appendix P. Note that three species are found only in one habitat (rocky hillside) that has no analogue at the Catamarca study site.*

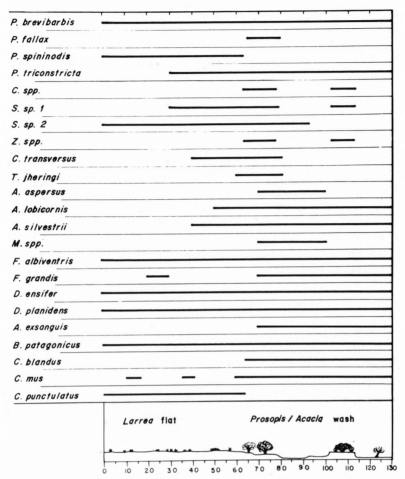

FIGURE 5-16. *Habitat distribution of foraging ants collected or seen along a 130 m line transect at a 5 hectare study site located north of the highway at km. 1512 near Andalgalá, Catamarca. Collections and observations were made in December 1973 and January 1974. The listing of genera and species follows the sequence of Appendix O.*

in the shade of overhanging vegetation. A few species nest in plant cavities (especially in boles of trees). Only one species (*Camponotus sayi*) at the Avra Valley site nests exclusively in trees; another (*Caematogaster depilis*) probably nests in plant cavities. Seven species (*Crematogaster* spp., *Zacryptocerus* spp., *Camponotus blandus*, and *Camponotus mus*) at the Catamarca site nest in boles of trees in *Prosopis/Acacia* washes. The *Pseudomyrmex* species collected at the Catamarca site also nests in plant cavities, though no nest was found.

Desert ant species range from generalized to very specialized foragers. Some seed-gathering species are food specialists, as are all fungus-growing species, though all of them utilize a variety of plant species as food. Some seed-gatherers plus many other species are generalist scavengers, taking dead arthropods and other organic detritus. Some generalist scavengers (notably *Myrmecocystus* spp., *Crematogaster* spp., some *Camponotus* species, and most species of Dolichoderinae) gather nectar from flowers or honeydew from Homoptera when these foods are available. Nectarivory, however, seems much less common in deserts than in more mesic habitats. Each of the study sites has an abundant, aggressive, generalist scavenger fire ant species: *Solenopsis xyloni* in Arizona and *Solenopsis* sp. in Catamarca.

No desert ant is an active forager twenty-four hours a day. Most ground-foraging species are not active during midday and they usually have a peak of foraging activity at and following dusk. Some remain active throughout the night, usually with a second peak of foraging activity shortly following sunrise. The few midday ground foragers include *Dorymyrmex planidens, Camponotus mus,* and *Acromyrmex striatus* in Catamarca. Several arboreal species in Catamarca (*Zacryptocerus* spp., *Crematogaster* spp.) are active during midday, but the arboreal *Camponotus sayi* in Arizona was active only at night. These ants probably show different times of foraging at other seasons of the year. Reproductive flights of most species come soon after periods of heavy rain.

Most terrestrially foraging species, especially nocturnal ones, have rather diffuse foraging patterns with solitary foragers radiating out from the nest. Conscpicuous "trunk trails" occur in some diurnally foraging terrestrial species, notably *Pogonomyrmex rugosus* and *Veromessor pergandei* in Arizona and *Acromyrmex lobicornis* and *A. silvestrii* in Catamarca. "Trunk trails" are columns of ants that follow semipermanent, often cleared, trails to foraging areas at some distance from the nest. Columns are chemically marked and are formed on what were originally recruitment trails laid by scout ants to new food sources (B. Hölldobler, pers. comm.). The evolution of these "trunk trails" is probably ultimately related to predator resistance (Hunt, unpubl.).

Morphological characteristics of ants in arid habitats include a psammophore, a structure located on the ventral surface of the head posterior to the mouth opening used to transport sand (Figure 5-17). In some species of *Pogonomyrmex* the psammophore is a ring of inward-facing hairs. In species of *Myrmecocystus* the long fringed maxillary and labial palpi form a basket. The psammophore of several *Dorymyrmex* species in Argentina is composed of both hairs and palpi. Another feature of some desert ants is a specialized caste of workers, "honeypot" repletes, with greatly distended gasters that serve as reservoirs for liquid food. The repletes of species of *Myrmecocystus* in North America are well known (E. O. Wilson, 1971). Other arid land ant species with similar repletes are *Camponotus inflatus* in Australia and the tiny *Brachymyrmex giardii* in Chile. While similar repletes occur in *Prenolepis imparis* of woodland habitats in Ohio (Talbot, 1943), repletes

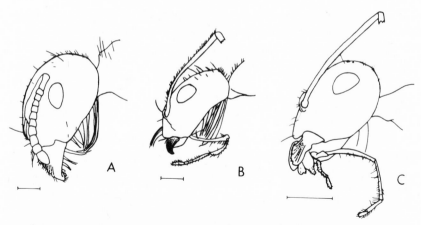

FIGURE 5-17. *Psammophores (sand-carrying devices) on three ant species. A* = Pogonomyrmex rugosus *(Myrmicinae); B* = Dorymyrmex planidens *(Dolichoderinae); C* = Myrmecocystus flaviceps *(Formicinae).*

are more often found in arid areas. Other species also characteristic of arid areas (especially of the subfamily Dolichoderinae) have workers with slightly distensible gasters that may temporarily store liquid food. The psammophores are truly convergent, because dissimilar structures in unrelated species provide a similar solution to the common problem of sand transport. To the extent that repletes appear primarily in deserts, this trait might represent convergence, but all Western Hemisphere ants with true, large repletes are in the subfamily Formicinae, suggesting parallel evolution rather than convergence. Truly convergent repletes in species of Dolichoderinae are found in Australia (R. R. Snelling, pers. comm.). Study site ants have no obvious morphological or behavioral convergences other than psammophores. Their many visible similarities appear largely to be components of the basic biologies of the higher taxa (genera, tribes, and subfamilies) which the study site species represent.

In summary, the ants of the study sites in Catamarca and Argentina have a strong taxonomic similarity. Because of this taxonomic similarity there are conspicuous similarities in habitat preference, nest site selection, foraging behavior, food habits, and morphology. Only psammophores show recognizable convergent evolution. Despite the striking overall similarity of the ant faunas there are several significant ecological differences: (1) more arboreally nesting species are associated with *Prosopis/Acacia* washes in Catamarca than in Arizona; (2) granivorous ants are represented by more species and greater biomass in Arizona than in Catamarca; (3) fungus growers (Myrmicinae, Attini) are represented by more species and greater biomass in Catamarca than in Arizona; and (4) Catamarca has a richness and abundance of species in the subfamily Dolichoderinae unparalleled in Arizona, but the presence in Arizona of many species of Formicinae (especially *Myrmecocystus* spp.) may represent an ecological analogue for food habits and foraging strategies. Only the fourth of these differences seems to have its foundation in the biogeography of the ant taxa themselves. The relative rarity of granivorous ants in Catamarca will be discussed again in Chapter 6.

Non-Insect Arthropods*

Studies of arachnids were conducted by beating animals from plants onto sheets or capturing them directly with a beating net. Sets of liter tin cans were also placed in the ground as pitfall traps (using ethylene glycol as the preserving fluid). In addition ground and plants were searched at all times of day and night. Field work in Argentina covered two field seasons (thirteen months) and in Arizona parts of three years (seven months). Study sites included bajada slopes and flatlands as well as sites with low and high rainfall. Data to contrast grasslands with deserts were obtained by pitfall samples and nocturnal observations (with both blacklight and headlamps) in higher elevation grasslands near Oracle (some sites of Beatty, 1961) and Elgin (some sites of Pulliam, 1975), Arizona, and near El Pucará and Minas Capillitas, Catamarca, in the mountains surrounding the Bolsón de Pipanaco.

Mites were regularly taken from *Larrea* in both deserts, but not as commonly from other plant species, and were especially common after summer rains. Mites are not a significant part of either arthropod community. The larger velvet mites were much less common in the Monte than in the Sonoran Desert but did occur in grasslands at El Pucará.

Centipedes, millipedes, and isopods were taken commonly in the Sonoran Desert, particularly on upper bajada slopes. In Argentina, some centipedes, millipedes, and isopods were found in higher elevation grassland, or in washes where rivers enter the Bolsón, but these litter-inhabiting species could not be found in interwash areas. Millipedes and isopods are abundant in several study sites in the Sonoran Desert (Tucson to Yuma, Arizona), constituting a significant difference between the two deserts. Similarly, pseudoscorpions occurred in pitfall interwash samples from upper bajadas near Tucson, but in Catamarca only rarely *in a wash* near Londres (maximum rainfall site).

Spiders on comparable plants of the two deserts are generally similar in types present and their abundances. Gross similarities seem best attributed to the basic biological requirements of the spider subfamilies (such as type of food or escape strategies) satisfied by particular microhabitats (Enders, 1975, 1976, in prep.). Spiders have highly variable hunting techniques but similar diets, all eating living animals (Knost and Rovner, 1975). Turnbull (1973) reviews spider ecology, and more complete details of spider biology are available (McCook, 1890; Bristowe, 1929; Kaston, 1948; Gertsch, 1949).

*By F. A. Enders.

Since spiders can balloon great distances through the air (Bristowe, 1929), most families are very widespread, and there are few cases of marked convergence of species from different taxa in North and South America, except among non-ballooning terrestrial species.

In ground-dwelling spiders which probably do not balloon, there are definite indications of convergence: *Sicarius* (Aguilar and Mendez, 1971) and *Homalonychus* (different families, Sicariidae and Homalonychidae), *Grammostola* and *Aphonopelma* (different subfamilies of the Theraphosidae), and *Xenoctenus* and *Syspira* (Clubionidae and Ctenidae) (all cases with Argentina first, United States second). The Argentine desert species is always larger than its U.S. equivalent. While these three types of spiders can be grouped in a series of "guilds," ranging from less to more active, all three types occurred commonly together only in Argentina. In the United States, the less active type (*Homalonychus*) is most abundant in winter-rain deserts, while the most active type is most abundant in the summer-rain Chihuahuan Desert.

In contrast, scorpions and solpugids do not spread long distances (except by rafting; Newlands, 1973), and different families in those groups show species convergence (Table 5-14). Monte species of scorpions in the Bothriuridae are analogous to species of Vejovidae of North America. Because of the

TABLE 5-14. *Probable Equivalent Species in the Scorpion Faunas of Silver Bell and the Bolsón de Pipanaco*

Habitat	Size	Abundance*	Species
Dry sandy areas	Medium	1	*Brachistosternus* (Monte)
Dry sandy areas			
Dry sandy areas	Small to Medium	1	*Parauroctonus mesaensis* (Sonoran)
Wet sandy areas	Very small	5	*Vachonia* (*martinezi?*) (Monte)
Dry winter-rain sandy areas	Small to Medium	6	*P. weygenberghi* (Sonoran)
Wetter rocky desert to grassland	Small	2.5	*Bothriurus burmeisteri* (Monte)
Wetter rocky desert to grassland	Small	3	*Vejovis spinigerus* (Sonoran)
Desert	Small	2.5	*Timogenes* small (Monte)
Desert	Small	2	*V. confusus* (Sonoran)
Desert, uses burrow	Large	4	*Timogenes* large (Monte)
Desert, uses burrow	Large	4	*Hadrurus hirsutus* (Sonoran)
Jungle (?)	Medium	(6)	*Tityus* (reported near Monte†)
Riparian woodlands	Medium	5	*Centruroides sculpturatis* (Sonoran)

*Abundance is on an ordinal scale from 1 for the commonest species in a desert to 6 for the rare species.

†*Tityus* was not collected by Enders, but is reported in Catamarca and Tucumán, in wetter habitats than desert. Similarly, *Centruroides* was never taken from actual desert habitats.

variety of methods used to collect arachnids in deserts, it is difficult to compare absolute densities. Collections taken from measured portions of various desert shrubs indicate that spiders were more abundant (per volume of plant) in bushes after rainfall (or watering the bushes). In the Monte, there were greater spider densities at the wet end of the moisture gradient (near Andalgalá and Londres) than at the dry end (Aimogasta and Mazán), whereas, surprisingly, the greatest abundance of spiders on bushes in the Sonoran Desert occurred on bushes at the drier end of the moisture gradient (less than 100 mm annual precipitation; Dateland, Yuma) after rainfall.

No diurnal terrestrial species occur in the Sonoran Desert except the abundant long-legged *Oxyopes* (Oxyopidae) species which climb on bushes (especially *Ambrosia* and herbs) at midday. The *Oxyopes* species in the Monte occurs only in the wettest areas (upper bajada and high annual rainfall) and is less abundant, perhaps because of the absence of easily-climbed semishrubs. Flushing spiders by use of insecticide did reveal a considerable population actively foraging on the ground during midday in the wet season in the Monte, but most terrestrial species are nocturnal there as in Arizona.

The Sonoran Desert has two foraging "generalists," a lycosid (*Lycosa carolinensis*) and much larger theraphosid (*Aphonopelma* sp.). More individuals of the two generalists forage under bushes than between them, and they place their burrows under *Larrea* bushes. Prey density is probably higher directly under bushes. Actual measurements indicate that flying insects are most abundant during the dry season at the top edge of *Larrea*, which is where webs are built during the dry season (of *Metepeira* sp., Araneidae, in both deserts). Vertical distribution of flying insects is more diffuse after rains, when webs (of other araneid species, as *Mecynogea tucumana*) are found throughout the bushes.

Spiders that are foraging specialists usually prey on abundant prey. Examples include ant specialists (*Euryopis* and *Steatoda*, an errant and web theridiid species, respectively) in the United States which live on bushes, and also the specialist on spiders in bushes in the United States (*Mimetus* sp., *Mimetidae*). Another interesting example may be a terrestrial specialist (*Hiltoniella birabeni*) on fungus ants (*Acromyrmex* sp.) in Argentina. This spider punctures fungus ants with a battering ram of "teeth" on its cephalothorax. There appears to be greater specialization for prey type among terrestrial spiders in the Monte, but among arboreal ones in the Sonoran Desert.

A prime characteristic of spiders on foliage is their dispersibility. Most of the original density (5–15 cu. m.$^{-1}$), and the same species, returned within a week to *Acacias* from which spiders had been removed by organophosphate pesticides. Thus, greater abundance of spiders on *Acacia* (and other wash shrubs) compared to *Larrea* (and other interwash shrubs) may be due to spiders responding to abundance of prey on wash plants.

Most species of desert spiders breed in spring or early summer, as is true for most temperate zone spiders (Tretzel, 1955). Some species of lycosid spiders present their egg sacs to the sun's rays, but no such behavior was observed in desert forms. In fact, eggs of desert lycosids are apparently placed in underground burrows, since adult females were found in burrows, while immatures were on the surface, and no egg cases were taken on the surface. Recently emerged young were noted in burrows of both lycosids and the ecologically similar tarantulas.

Solpugids

These animals are found in scrublands and grasslands (Goetsch and Lawatsch, 1944; Muma, 1966b). Probably due to their ground-nesting habit, their populations are reduced by flooding (Muma, in prep.) and by irrigation (Goetsch and Lawatsch, 1944). Gertsch (1949) describes the general biology of solpugids, but there is no general account of the biology of New World species other than information in Muma's many papers (1966a, 1966b).

Solpugids are nocturnal insectivores which lack poison. Their ability to exploit very low prey densities may depend on their active manner of foraging (Schmoller, 1970; Cloudsley-Thompson, 1975). Solpugids were taken both in grassland and desert in both continents in approximately the same abundance, but they were common only in dry areas. In wet areas spiders were more abundant, and scorpions were at least as abundant as solpugids at the dry end of the moisture gradient. Limited field work in sand dunes suggests that solpugids may outnumber scorpions there.

More species of solpugids were taken in the Sonoran Desert because of the greater number of closely-related replacement species (especially of the genus *Eremobates*) in different parts of the desert. A similar situation apparently occurs in the genus *Pseudocleobis* (Ammotrechidae) in higher altitudes near the Monte (in prepuna and puna). Considering only solpugids in a single locality, the two deserts have about the same richness of species. Despite the similarity of numbers of individuals and species in the two deserts, species of solpugids which seem to be equivalents in habitats used (species which search mainly ground vs. those which search mainly vegetation) are of different sizes in the two continents. Large solpugids in Arizona search the ground, and a slightly smaller species is regularly found on foliage. In Catamarca there is a very large solpugid which searches foliage (*Oltacola*, Ammotrechidae), but a very small solpugid (*Mummucia*) searches on the ground. This is the opposite of the situation found in ground-dwelling spiders, in which Sonoran Desert ground inhabitants are smaller, but those on bushes include larger species (especially *Phidippus*, Salticidae). Possibly the smaller solpugid in the United States is replacing the clubionid-like guild which is virtually absent there, while the larger solpugid in the Monte only represents a larger member of the "clubionid-like guild," separated from the small *Anyphaena* species and the larger *Clubiona* species of the clubionid-like guild by prey size. In this view, the very small ground solpugid coexists in Argentina with the larger *Xenoctenus* spider, but the very large ground *Eremorhax* solpugid in the United States coexists with the smaller *Syspira* spider (or may replace it). If solpugids are better adapted to dry environments than clubionid spiders, the ground fauna of the Monte can be considered to be less xeric-adapted, with spiders instead of solpugids acting as ground carnivores.

North American solpugids feed on soft prey when very young and are usually associated with termites (M. H. Muma, pers. comm.). Since the Monte virtually lacks termites, differences in the solpugid faunas might eventually be ascribed to differences in availability of preferred prey. For example, the very small *Uspallata pulchra* of the Monte occurs only in washes, the only place we found termites in Argentina. Even the large foliage-hunter seems to prefer washes. Like ground-dwelling spiders, solpugids which appear as equivalent species in the two deserts are of different families or subfamilies. They have very low probabilities of dispersal over great distances, because immatures do not balloon.

Scorpions

While Scorpions are typical of deserts (Schmoller, 1970; S. C. Williams, 1970), numerous species of mesic-adapted scorpions occur abundantly in wetter sites (Savory, 1964). In our studies (using pitfall traps and black-light technique) scorpions were abundant in desert but represented by only one rare species in each continent in high altitude grassland. The scorpions found in the two deserts are sit-and-wait predators, most of which live for more than a year. Adaptations of scorpions to deserts are superficially well known (Cloudsley-Thompson, 1962, 1975) but little studied. The lethal upper temperature for the Monte *Brachistosternus* species was high, like that reported for a few scorpions in other deserts, but well below that for web spiders (which are subjected to higher temperatures in their exposed micro-habitat than the burrowing scorpions). A hairy burrowing species which can build a new burrow in about fifteen minutes at dawn (Aguilar, 1968), its prey is mainly caterpillars and beetle larvae. Even at the end of the long dry season, individuals collected were well nourished and survived many weeks in captivity without food (as other arachnids, J. F. Anderson, 1974). Farther south, the same scorpion was found on the top of the *Larrea* bushes (E. Maury, pers. comm.). No such observations were made in the Bolsón de Pipanaco. During the rainy season these scorpions sit and run on top of the matted grasses, as also did *Vejovis confusus* and *V. spinigerus* of the Sonoran Desert.

Species in the Monte are apparently nearly equivalent to those in the Sonoran Desert (Table 5-14) in abundance, size, and habitat use (Beatty, 1961; S. C. Williams, 1970). While most scorpions use some daytime retreat, the largest ones are more often associated with burrows into which they retreat when disturbed. Species listed from sandy areas all have elongate shapes and considerable hairiness and spination supposedly useful when burrowing in sand.

The main difference between the faunas of the two deserts is that the two species of burrowing scorpions in the Monte differ in size, while the two in the sandy areas of the Sonoran Desert differ in seasons of activity, one coming out in winter, the other in summer. The concentration of rain in summer in the Monte precludes temporal isolation so that size differences rather than differences in times of activity might be favored. Since prey abundance is probably related to rainfall, peak rainfall in the western part of the Sonoran Desert, where the two *Parauroctonus* species coexist, is probably never great enough for coexistence on the basis of prey size alone, but the occurrence of two peaks of rainfall allows the evolution of two species, one active mainly in winter, the other mainly in summer.

O. Francke (pers. comm.) has found that *Parauroctonus* individuals remain in their burrows most of the time, spending only two to three days in surface activity per month. Observations indicate that *Brachistosternus* spends more time on the ground surface and probably occurs at similar surface densities at night as *Parauroctonus*. One of the two Monte sand desert scorpions, particularly *Vachonia,* only two specimens of which were taken (despite repeated searches of the surface near the original collecting locale), may regularly be missed during counts of surface-active scorpions by use of a black light. Moonlight did not seem to have the strong negative effect on surface activity noted by Hadley and Williams (1968) for Sonoran Desert species.

Published works indicate that tolerance to heat stress by arachnids of similar microhabitats does not differ more than about 2° C in different hot deserts. Enders tested groups of spiders and scorpions in individual vials by half-hour exposures in a heated constant-temperature bath. Argentine *non-web* spiders *and* scorpions died at lower temperatures (50 percent mortality below 43° C), while Monte *web* spiders had the highest upper lethal temperatures reported for any spider; 50 percent mortality occurred at 43.8, 44.0, 44.5, 45.8, and 47.8° C for five different species. The *Diguetia* (Diguetidae) species, which showed the highest heat tolerance, is of a monotypic family endemic to American hot deserts. Spiders which do not leave their webs during the heat of the day should have the highest heat resistance. Study of temperature tolerances of *Argiope* species (Araneidae), using slightly different methods (Enders, unpubl.), suggests that those orb-web spiders of more temperate, mesic areas may have even greater tolerance to high temperature than do the desert *Diguetia.* Greater temperature tolerance in *Argiope* would probably be related, proximally, to the fact that they are exposed on a web all day long, rather than using the shade of retreats. When the temperature inside a spider's diurnal retreat comes close to the spider's upper lethal temperature, other web spider species in cooler regions, which live in retreats near the ground (like *Diguetia*), also leave the retreat (Norgaard, 1956). From the present limited knowiedge of desert spiders, it appears that retreat-using spiders are more abundant and typical in desert regions than are the spiders which do not use retreats.

ASSESSMENT OF CONVERGENT EVOLUTION
OF DESERT MAMMALS:
MULTIVARIATE ANALYSIS*

Mares (1973a, 1975a,b, 1976) analyzed possible convergence of the rodent communities of the Tucson, Sonoran Desert area, and the Andalgalá, Monte Desert site, using multivariate techniques. Analyses were limited to morphological characteristics which reflected ecologically significant attributes of the rodents. For example, a bipedal mouse has large hind feet and a long tail which is used for balancing. Thus the bipedal, richochetal locomotive pattern of many desert rodents can be potentially described by measuring the relative length of the tail. Food habits can also be inferred from morphological traits. Many desert rodents are seed eaters, and this dietary specialization is accompanied by a number of dental modifications. Incisors are opisthondont (inflected). Molariform teeth of such species are not crested and have simple cusp patterns (Hershkovitz, 1962). The resultant basin-like tooth surface is an efficient crushing apparatus for seeds. A grazing rodent, such as a vole (*Microtus*), has a complex molariform enamel pattern of many ridges which forms a tough cutting, grinding surface for the often silicaceous foods preferred. Morphology can thus reflect ecology to a strong degree, and by using such characters and the cluster analysis techniques of numerical taxonomy, Mares (1973a, 1975a,b, 1976) was able to arrive at phenograms of shared ecologies. He compared the rodents of both desert areas with those of the Ponderosa Pine community of the Sandia Mountains of central New Mexico. This allowed for a nondesert fauna closely related phylogenetically with the Sonoran fauna to act as an indicator of how closely the unrelated desert faunas had converged. Species of desert rodents that are closely clustered indicate analogous ecologies, insofar as these were reflected in the morphological measurements included in analyses, and such species are considered equivalents.

The twenty-eight-character distance phenogram comparing all rodents in the three faunas is shown in Figure 5-18. In constructing the phenogram, characters strongly correlated with size were deleted from consideration. The pocket mice (perognathines) are closely clustered together, and are grouped with a second close cluster composed of kangaroo rats (*Dipodomys*). Since these are ecological clusterings, the groupings indicate very similar ecologies for these granivorous heteromyid rodents (Rosenzweig and Winakur, 1969;

*By M. A. Mares.

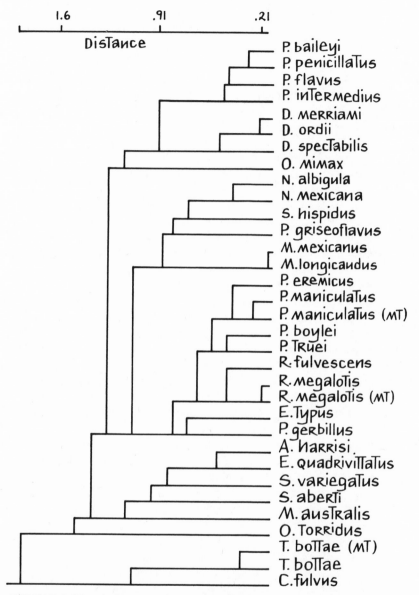

FIGURE 5-18. *A distance phenogram of rodent species of three communities (Tucson desert region, Andalgalá desert region, and a coniferous forest area in central New Mexico). Unweighted arithmetic pair-group method with averages was used in clustering. Twenty-eight morphological traits were utilized. Cophenetic correlation coefficient = 0.834. (Mares, 1973a).*

Rosenzweig and Sterner, 1970). *Dipodomys* and the perognathines are the most highly evolved desert rodents in North America, and the only Monte species that is even distantly assigned to the heteromyid cluster is *Octomys mimax*, a packrat-like rodent from the most arid parts of the Monte. Examination of Euclidian distances (Sokal and Sneath, 1973) reveals that *O. mimax* is actually closest to *Perognathus baileyi* (1.104 units) and quite close to *Perognathus penicillatus* (1.162 units), *Dipodomys ordii* (1.189 units), and *Dipodomys merriami* (1.188 units). Distances to true packrats *Neotoma* (which are more ecologically allied with *Octomys* in overall ecology) average 1.154 units (Figure 5-18). Undoubtedly similarity to *P. baileyi* is the reason for *Octomys* being clustered with the heteromyids rather than the neotomyines. *Octomys* is neither small, bipedal, nor granivorous (as is *Perognathus*); however, since many of the traits utilized are ratios, size differences between species disappear. *Octomys* does possess numerous highly evolved desert traits (fairly light coloration, tufted tail, simple planar moliform teeth, inflated tympanic bullae, and so forth) and it is these traits which cause it to be linked with the heteromyids. Correlation phenograms (Mares, 1973a, 1976) clustered *Octomys* with the more ecologically similar *Neotoma* (Figure 5-19).

Other clusters of interest include the grouping of packrats (*Neotoma*) with *Phyllotis griseoflavus,* a Monte leaf-eared mouse that resembles packrats in many aspects of its ecology (Mares, 1973a). The two small South American phyllotines (*Eligmodontia typus* from the Monte and *Phyllotis gerbillus* from the Sechura Desert in Perú) are grouped together, and both species are clustered with the small North American cricetines, *Reithrodontomys* and *Peromyscus.*

South American cavies (*Microcavia*), which seem to fill a niche analogous to Sonoran Desert ground squirrels, are loosely clustered with that group. *Onychomys torridus* is not closely clustered with any North or South American species, reflecting the uniqueness of this insectivorous rodent and the lack of a Monte analogue. The gopher-like tuco-tucos (*Ctenomys*) are clustered with northern pocket gophers (*Thomomys*), indicating the similar niche filled by these species in either hemisphere (Figure 5-19). Thus, considering the natural history and physiology of the animals, the clustering techniques yielded analog pairs (i.e., ecological equivalents) that were quite logical. Cluster analysis offers a somewhat objective method of assessing convergence if morphological traits which strongly reflect ecological attributes are utilized.

Canonical and Discriminant Function Analysis allow similar groups of organisms to be clustered together, and these groups are separated from other clusters. The more differences found between groups (i.e., the fewer the shared characteristics), the further apart each group is plotted on canonical axes. Each character that contributes to the separation of groups is utilized in the stepwise discriminant function analysis, such that those traits which are most different between groups are entered first. Thus the program allows one to show which traits are important in separating two or more groups (a forest

FIGURE 5-19. *Some convergent species pairs of mammals. Upper row, left:* Ctenomys tulvus; *right:* Thomomys boyyae. *Center row, left:* Octomys mimax; *right:* Neotoma albigula. *Bottom row, left;* Dolichotus patagonum, *right:* Lepus alleni. (Illustrations by Dean Rocky Barrick.)

from a desert group, for example, or two desert groups from each other). For the rodents of the Monte and Sonoran areas and the Sandia Mountain fauna, since the two northern faunas were closely related taxonomically, it might be expected that the two northern faunas would be plotted closely to one another. But, if convergence has occurred between the desert faunas, the two unrelated desert groups of rodents would be plotted closer together, in *n*-dimensional space (twenty-seven-dimensional, since twenty-eight traits were used, see Dixon, 1970). Figure 5-20 illustrates the positioning of the three rodent faunas on the first two canonical axes. The first canonical axis accounts for about 99 percent of the dispersion (i.e., the x axis reflects most of the differences). The similarity between the two desert faunas is evident. Convergence of the rodent faunas of the two desert areas has occurred.

Because heteromyids (pocket mice and kangaroo rats) can be considered

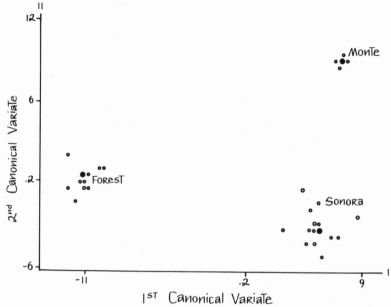

FIGURE 5-20. *Distribution of three rodent faunas along the first two canonical axes. The first canonical axis accounts for 99 percent of the dispersion. Individual species values denoted by open circles; faunal means indicated by larger closed circles. The clumping of the two desert faunas indicates that community convergence has occurred (Mares, 1973a).*

the most highly desert-adapted rodents in North America, it was decided to compare the degree of desert adaptation of this group with that of the non-heteromyid desert rodents of both the Sonoran and Monte deserts. This was accomplished by using canonical analysis and discriminant function analysis. The non-heteromyid desert rodents were compared to two groups; a non-desert rodent assemblage (forest) and the desert heteromyid group (K-rat). Only the most convergent species would be expected to be allied with the K-rat group; such an association would indicate a high degree of desert adaptation. For comparative purposes, the Sechura Desert mouse (*Phyllotis gerbillus*), and an Old World gerbil (*Meriones hurrianae*) were also assigned as being of unknown affinity, along with the non-heteromyid species of the two deserts. Theoretically, only the most highly evolved desert species would be assigned to the heteromyid category. The computer program assigned each unknown species to either the forest or heteromyid group on the basis of shared characteristics. Only the Old World gerbil and the Monte Desert gerbil mouse, *Eligmondontia typus,* were assigned to the K-rat group (Figure 5-21). *Octomys mimax* was clustered with the K-rats until the last character (dorsal color) was included. Since it was a darker color than most heteromyids, it was excluded from the K-rat assemblage. Nevertheless, if only

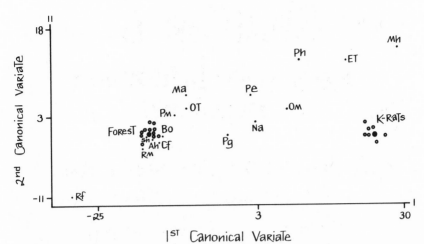

FIGURE 5-21. *Distribution of two designated groups (New Mexico Forest rodents and kangaroo rat assemblage) and other North and South American desert rodents along the first two canonical axes. Non-heteromyid (i.e., non-K-rat) species were assigned to either the highly desert-adapted K-rat group or the nondesert forest fauna. Only the most highly desert-adapted species would be expected to be grouped with the K-rats. With the exception of* Phyllotis griseoflavus *(Ph),* Thomomys bottae *(Bo) and* Meriones hurrianae *(Mh), all species abbreviations are composed of the first letters of the generic and specific names and are from species listed in Appendix N.*

other morphological traits had been considered, *O. mimax* would have been grouped with the most highly desert-adapted rodents.

The natural history investigations of the biology of Monte rodents, the physiological studies of selected species, and the multivariate analyses of morphoecological traits all indicate that measurable convergent evolution has occurred between the mammals (particularly rodents) of the Sonoran and Monte deserts. This convergence has been shown particularly in phenotypic characteristics which evidently are highly evolved toward meeting the rigors of life imposed by the xeric environment. Although the Sonoran Desert supports a much richer fauna and there are few one-to-one analogue pairs in either desert, most of the niches evident in one hemisphere are filled either wholly or in part by various species in the other hemisphere. The greater species richness evident in the Sonoran Desert is due to a finer subdivision of the overall mammal niche space, and/or a different, richer, and more diverse resource base in the northern desert. Evidence from our study of seed plants and arthropods suggests the latter.

Chapter 6:
Resource Utilization Systems

·g. H. Orians, R.g. Cates, M.A. Mares, A. Moldenke,
J. Neff, D. F. Rhoades, M.L. Rosenzweig,
B.B. Simpson, J.C. Schultz, C.S. Tomoff.

In the previous two chapters we examined possible convergences among plants and animals of the Monte and Sonoran deserts in a variety of taxa. This analysis provided an overview of species richness in different taxa, patterns of convergence or nonconvergence in individual traits among those species, and information on the ways in which species in those taxa exploit desert environments in the two regions. It is also instructive to examine community structure by concentrating on a set of resources and how they are utilized. This perspective is not entirely different from the previous one since there is considerable trophic uniformity within some taxa. But since many taxa (i.e., mammals, birds, ants) include species with, for example, very different diets, a resource focus brings together data in a usefully different manner.

Since virtually all solar energy enters ecosystems by means of photosynthesis, all animals depend directly or indirectly on plants for energy and most mineral resources. Previous chapters have demonstrated strong convergences among photosynthetic plants of the two deserts in general morphology, distribution of life form types along environmental gradients, and overall density of individuals. On the other hand, there are differences in phenology, largely correlated with the paucity of winter rains in the Monte, which cause significant differences in patterns of availability of resources provided by plants. These differences must be combined with direct effects of climate on animals to develop an understanding of how communities of animals exploiting these different resources evolved. We begin with a brief discussion of the direct influence of the physical environment on resource acquisition and allocation by plants and then consider kinds of resources provided by these tissues and how their characteristics are affected by feedback from animals.

Plants produce a variety of structures and substances that are food for one or more species of animals. These include vegetative and floral tissues, sap, pollen and nectar, fruits, seeds, and detritus. These different tissue types are physically and chemically distinct and evolved under different selective pressures. Some, such as nectar and fleshy fruits and, in some cases, pollen, have evolved to attract animals to the plant and are the cost the plant pays for pollen transfer and seed dispersal. In all other cases, a plant should benefit if its tissues are not consumed by animals. These other tissues, accordingly, are defended by physical and chemical means. Detritus, which is not directly defended, nevertheless reflects to a diminishing degree with time, the defenses of the tissues from which it was derived.

These different tissues and substances also have varied distributions in space and time and range from being abundant to relatively scarce. The amount of consumption may also influence the budgeting of energy resources by the plants and thereby affect production of new tissues. For example, grazing may stimulate new leaf production (Feeny, 1970).

These characteristics of tissues produced by plants mean that the morphology, physiology, and behavior required for their efficient exploitation may be very different. For example, exploitation of nectar is enhanced by high mobility for all but the smallest of animals, while leaves are easily found and eaten by an animal of low mobility. Feeding on the different resources exposes animals to different amounts and kinds of predation. Varied and often complicated capacities may be required to detoxify or otherwise overcome defenses of plant tissues. For these reasons, animals utilizing these different resources are often distinct, and they can be grouped into feeding guilds (Root, 1967). We gave special attention to three plant resources: foliage, seeds, and pollen plus nectar. Their characteristics, summarized in Table 6-1, differ sufficiently that animal species utilizing them overlap little in most communities and especially in the deserts we have studied. Two of these sources offer substantial water to animals while the third (seeds) does not, so that the seed-eating guild faces more severe water-acquisition problems than the others.

Since there is so little overlap in species composition between these three guilds, and since differences in the resources generate very different predictions about patterns of convergence in the three systems, we treat them separately. However, among predators on these three groups of consumers of plant tissues, there is much more overlap.

We treat eaters of foliage and seeds before considering flower visitors since the latter are involved in more complex mutualistic foraging systems. For each case we attempt to predict the resource pattern from the action of natural selection on it and then predict how natural selection has determined patterns among animals eating the resources.

THE PLANT-FOLIAGE EATER-PREDATOR SYSTEM*

Vegetative tissues of plants constitute the largest single block of food in all terrestrial communities. Their annual production is determined primarily by availability of water, light, and minerals and is correlated with actual evapotranspiration (Rosenzweig, 1968b).

The Action of Natural Selection on Plant Foliage

Allocation of energy to different tissues by plants is molded evolutionarily by several factors. One is consumption of their tissues by animals. Because terrestrial plants are relatively large in relation to many of their herbivores and consist of a complex mixture of tissue types, nearly all individual plants receive some grazing, but this grazing, though usually damaging, is not often directly lethal. All conceivable defenses against herbivores have costs, which include energetic costs of producing and maintaining chemicals and structures of no other use to the plant, and the direct and indirect negative impacts of

*By R. G. Cates, G. H. Orians, D. F. Rhoades, J. C. Schultz, and C. S. Tomoff.

the diversion of resources to defenses rather than to other structures and processes that contribute to fitness. Investment in vegetative tissue defenses should be proportional to the level of grazing by herbivores, the time over which the tissue would contribute to the fitness of the plant if it were not eaten, and the significance to the plant of a loss of a unit of that tissue. In general, the longer the potential income period from photosynthetic tissues the greater the optimal investment in their defense. Also, the longer a tissue is present, the greater the probability that it will be found by herbivores.

A general hypothesis based on the above premises was developed as part of the project (Rhoades and Cates, 1976). It postulates that ephemeral plants

TABLE 6-1 *Comparison of the Major Characteristics of the Principal Resources Produced by Plants of Desert Scrub Habitats in Arizona and Catamarca*

	Foliage	Seeds	Nectar and pollen
Background characteristics	May be mimicked by utilizers *and* predators	Never mimicked	May be mimicked or matched by predators but not by utilizers
Package sizes relative to sizes of utilizers	Variable, often large	Generally small	Small
Distribution in time	Wet season or all year	Seasonal production	Highly seasonal production
Distribution in space	Widespread and abundant	Widespread and abundant in season; initially patchy but becomes more widely dispersed	Widespread but very patchy
Depletability	Normally depressed relatively slowly (days-months) not easily stored by utilizers	Overall resource has slow extinction rate, easily stored by utilizers	Individual units instantly depleteable; overall resource has high extinction rate; readily stored by utilizers
Recovery characteristics	Slow to moderately rapid	No recruitment until next season	Pollen not replaced once consumed; nectar sometimes replaced, recovery rapid
Nutritional	Usually heavily defended chemically and/ or physically; low in proteins; high in cellulose	Highly concentrated and nutritious but variably defended physically and chemically	Nutritionally attractive, but not necessarily a balanced diet

and tissues (flowers, young leaves, etc.) if defended at all should be defended primarily by toxins or specific enzyme inhibitors that are effective at low concentrations and have as their target tissue cell types or metabolic systems such as muscles and nerves present in the herbivores but not in plants. These tissues have the shortest existence, and hence the shortest potential income time, though some, like flowers, may be very important to the plant. For the same reason they are most likely to escape from herbivores in space and time, thus reducing the level of grazing.

Escape in space and time should be more effective against monophagous than against polyphagous herbivores, since the former group have no alternative food sources. If so, defenses of ephemeral plants and tissues should evolve to provide protection, especially against generalist herbivores. Chemical divergence of these defenses by apostatic selection is to be expected since selective forces acting on the herbivores should render them most capable of dealing with the commonest type of chemical defense, conferring higher fitness on plant species and/or individual plants with deviant chemical types.

Since perennial plants and long-lived plant tissues are more consistently available, dietary specialization by herbivores, leading in turn to the evolution of convergent plant defenses that are particularly effective against specialist herbivores, is expected. Plants and tissues whose occurrence in space and time is predictable have converged toward defense by nonspecific protein-complexing and digestibility-reducing systems which are costly to produce and maintain but are more difficult for herbivores to circumvent than toxins and specific enzyme inhibitors. For example, the tannin systems that are so common among woody perennials (Bate-Smith and Metcalf, 1957) function by combining with proteins of plant cells, rendering them less available to herbivores. They must be isolated from other constituents of the cell(s), which requires investment in intracellular structures that may also interfere with cell physiology and division.

Selection to maximize carbon fixation and minimize losses to herbivores in deserts is affected by the short period of availability of water which favors combining responses to herbivores and the physical environment. For example, resinous coatings on leaves discourage grazing and also lower the rate of water loss from leaves (Rhoades, 1976a).

Plants of different life forms in deserts present an array of tissue types of various characteristics and temporal and spatial patterns of availability (Table 6-2). Structural features associated with these traits influence the kinds and number of hiding places available on plants. This potential richness of hiding places may be a major factor influencing kinds and numbers of species of herbivores utilizing the plants (Table 6-2). These characteristics constitute bases for predicting patterns of herbivore diets. Based on the hypothesis outlined above, we have predicted the chemical defenses of ephemeral and longer-lived tissues of the major plant life forms of hot deserts (Table 6-3). Chemical defenses of different tissue types can presumably

TABLE 6-2 *Temporal and Physical Traits that Generally Characterize Life Forms of Desert Plants as Resources for Herbivores*

Life form	Leaf structure and functioning	Temporal and spatial pattern of availability of photosynthetic tissues	Hiding-place characteristics	Physical defenses against herbivores
Ephemerals and Root Perennials	High transpiration rates; low stomatal resistance; high surface to volume ratios; C_3 or C_4 photosynthesis	Present for short periods only; positions usually predictable; leaves close to ground	Few backgrounds to match; small absolute scale of plant	Photosynthetic tissues easily chewed; no spines
Deciduous Shrubs and Small Trees	High photosynthetic rates; low stomatal resistance; high surface to volume ratios; C_3 photosynthesis	Present for relatively short time periods; positions very stable; leaves distributed over broad height range	Great diversity of hiding places; large absolute scale of plant	Leaves easily chewed; may or may not have spines
Evergreen Sclerophyllous Shrubs and Small Trees	Low net photosynthesis; high stomatal resistance; low surface to volume ratios; very tough	Permanently available; positions highly stable; leaves distributed over broad height range	Great diversity of hiding places; large absolute scale of plant	Leaves tough; usually not spinescent
Succulents	Thick cuticles; sunken stomata (leaves often entirely lacking); CAM photosynthesis; low surface to volume ratios of photosynthetic tissues; tough	Permanently available; positions highly stable; photosynthetic surfaces distributed over broad height range	Relatively uniform surface but protection afforded by spines	Photosynthetic tissues very tough; many spines

169

TABLE 6-3 *Predicted Chemical Characteristics of Desert Plants as Resources for Herbivores*

Life form	Chemical defenses	
	Short-lived tissues	Long-lived tissues
Ephemerals*	toxins	–
Root perennials	toxins	digestion-reducing substances
Woody perennials	toxins, digestion-reducing substances	toxins, digestion-reducing substances, low intrinsic digestibility and nutrient content
Stem-photosynthesizing succulents†	–	toxins, digestion-reducing substances, low intrinsic digestibility and nutrient content

*All tissues considered to be short-lived.
† All tissues except flowers considered to be long-lived.

evolve independently of their physical characteristics, but there is likely to be strong evolutionary feedback between the two since the extent to which physical defenses affects grazing pressure in the absence of chemical defenses influences the probability that a tissue will be found by herbivores.

Patterns of Resource Availability and Defenses

As shown in Chapter 4, the physiognomy of the vegetation around Andalgalá and Tucson is strikingly similar. Both deserts are rich in annuals (though Catamarca lacks winter annuals), have few species of root perennials (more in Arizona than in Catamarca), and many shrubby, woody perennials. In Arizona the latter very from tiny, matted plants to small trees. In Catamarca, however, the low shrub layer at most study sites in the Bolsón is missing. Major differences in patterns of availability of leafy tissues for herbivores in the two deserts are caused by the low, unpredictable winter rainfall in the Monte. At Andalgalá, there is no flora of winter annuals, and tissues of ephemeral plants are available only during summer (December-March), while in Arizona there is both a summer (July-September) and a late winter-early spring (February-April) period of regular availability of these tissues. Similarly, at Andalgalá there is no consistent early spring leafing of deciduous shrubs. Initiation of growth of new leaves does not normally begin until December or January. At Silver Bell, leaf initiation by deciduous trees and shrubs begins in late March and continues through the summer. Therefore, young leaves are available on these plants in Arizona for a longer time (six months) than at Andalgalá (three months).

Patterns of Defense of Desert Plants

The richness of desert plant life forms and seasonality of tissue production results in an extremely variable set of anti-herbivore adaptations, both chemical and physical. Desert plants contain a variety of toxins. Approximately 2.6 percent of the annuals and 1.7 percent of the perennial Sonoran vegetation are listed as poisonous to livestock (Kingsbury, 1964), and the actual number with toxins is probably much higher, since livestock are presumably not adversely affected by all insect-oriented toxins. When toxins are present in perennials they tend to be concentrated in the youngest, most ephemeral tissues. For instance, poisonous amines and nonprotein amino acids of *Prosopis velutina, P. chilensis, P. flexuosa,* and *P. torquata* display such a distribution (Cates and Rhoades, 1977). Similarly, cyanogenic glycosides of *Acacia* species are concentrated in young leaves (Rehr et al., 1973). Distribution of digestion-reducing substances among desert plants of various growth forms and among different tissues of these plants is presently under study. Leaves of species of both *Larrea* and *Prosopis* contain high concentrations of digestion-reducing substances (Rhoades, 1977b; Cates and Rhoades, unpub.) The phenol-oxidase system of *Larrea* also appears to function as a digestion-reducing system (Rhoades, 1977b). A survey of oxidase activities among nine annuals and eighteen perennials from the Bolsón de Pipanaco showed that three species have oxidase activities significantly higher than the average value for all desert plants studied (0.0908 mls O_2 g dry wt^{-1}min^{-1}). Significantly, these species (*Larrea cuneifolia,* 0.4210; *Prosopis torquata,* 0.4130; and *Bulnesia retamo,* 0.2344 mls O_2 g dry wt^{-1}min^{-1}) are all perennials.

Tannins are digestion-reducing substances (Feeny, 1970), and the association between tannin content and woody perennials has been noted by Bate-Smith and Metcalf (1957). Desert species so far known to contain tannins in their leaves (*Olneya tesota, Prosopis chilensis,* and *P. torquata*) are all perennials.

Predictions contained in Table 6-3 are not specific to desert conditions. However, deserts have larger numbers of annuals and stem-photosynthesizing succulents than most other environments. The occurrence of desert annuals is unpredictable in time and some species may appear only in years of very heavy rains, but they are probably more predictable in space than annuals in more humid regions that depend on occasional short-lived disturbances for their existence. Therefore, we have not made specific desert-related predictions concerning the action of selection of the defenses of plant tissue.

Though more complete data may show otherwise, there is as yet no evidence that basic chemical defenses of various plant life forms differ in the two deserts. This similarity suggests that these attributes are predictable from a knowledge of the physical environment and that real convergence and/or parallelism has occurred between plants in the two deserts. Therefore, the differences between plant resources available to herbivores in Arizona and Catamarca primarily involve their temporal and spatial distribution rather than their pattern of defenses. The most important of these differences is related to the light and unpredictable winter rains at Andalgalá, which causes the absence of summer deciduous semi-shrubs and winter active annuals and root perennials in Catamarca.

The Action of Natural Selection on Predators of Herbivores

Natural selection should favor foraging behavior that maximizes energy intake per unit foraging time if the foraging process precludes other simultaneous activities. If there is an absolute food shortage or there are competing uses of time, and/or if there is a risk associated with foraging, selection should favor foraging when risks are lower and competing uses of time are less valuable. Once a decision to forage has been made, foraging behaviors that are under direct control of a predator and which can therefore influence energy intake per unit time are (a) choice of foraging habitat, (b) choice of foraging patch, (c) choice of foraging mode, and (d) choice of individual prey items. These decisions are listed in general order of increasing frequency but decreasing significance per individual decision. The way in which these decisions should be made to maximize energy intake per unit time foraging has been the subject of considerable recent attention (Charnov, 1976; Holling, 1959, 1965, 1966; MacArthur, 1972; MacArthur and Pianka, 1966; Pulliam, 1974; Rapport, 1971; Schoener, 1971). The general result is that if prey types are ranked by the expected net energy from one item of type i per mean handling time for an item of prey type i, then whether or not prey type i should be eaten is independent of the rate of encounter of prey type i and dependent only on the rate of encounter with prey with rank higher than i; that is prey yielding more energy per unit time. Thus, the first ranked prey is always taken and prey are added to and dropped out of the diet in order of rank. Detailed proof of this assertion is given by Charnov (1976), and special cases are given by Schoener (1971), MacArthur (1972), and Pulliam (1974).

A similar result applies to the use of patches within an environment. If the rate of energy capture within a patch declines as a result of the activities of the predator, the predator should leave the patch when the availability of prey has dropped sufficiently that its energy intake rate equals the average value in all patches that should be included in the itinerary given the existing overall prey availability in the habitat.

These formulations hold if there is no risk during foraging or if the risk is equal in all habitat and patch types. However, if risk is unequal in space and time, predators should deviate from the foraging behavior predicted for equal risk. Also, if the prey itself is dangerous, the predator should carefully assess the capabilities of individual prey and the details of the encounter and probable pursuit situation before making a pursuit decision.

The preceding discussion has assumed that individuals of all prey types are equally susceptible to capture. However, all real environments are structured, providing, for example, variation in quality of hiding places. A predator foraging in these environments increases the proportion of prey in better hiding places even if prey do not respond to activity of the predators and even if prey abundances remain unaltered (F. E. Smith, 1972). Consider two prey species similar enough that a predator encounters them randomly with equal ease. Those individuals that differ in hiding places and/or appearances that reduce their chances of being found by a predator employing a single search mode should survive better. Individuals that differ most from the associated species are least likely to be found. The evolutionary result of many generations of predation is a divergence of the prey so that they are no longer readily encountered by a predator using a single search mode. This should be most important for small herbivores whose risk from predation is strongly influenced by the structure of the plants on which they forage and rest.

Interactions between plants and herbivores are influenced by several factors related to the nature of the food resources provided by plants. Food resource predictability should affect both the total level of utilization of the resource and the proportions of dietary generalist and specialists. Unpredictable (more difficult to find) resources are partially protected by escape in space and time from grazing, especially by specialists. Other things being equal they should experience lower total grazing levels and a higher proportion of grazing by dietary generalists than experienced by predictable resources. Convergence of chemical defenses of different plants should favor herbivore dietary generalization whereas divergence should favor specialization because one detoxification or neutralization mechanism may work on all plants with similar defenses.

Each individual plant is effectively an island in space and time (Janzen, 1968, 1973). Herbivores may have difficulty in locating isolated plants, and even within the plant an herbivore may devote considerable time and effort searching for individual leaves of better than average nutritional qualities. For many herbivores, rate of ingestion of food is potentially so rapid that the gut can be filled in a relatively short time. Hence, much or most food processing can be carried out in a suitable hiding place.

There is little variation in the energy content of vegetative tissues (calories gram dry wt^{-1}). Slight differences that do exist may influence herbivore grazing behavior (Paine and Vadas, 1969), but in general other chemical and nutritional components of plant tissues are more important than calories. These include levels of usable carbohydrates (Oelberg, 1956), proteins (Bell, 1970; Klein, 1970), toxic compounds, and digestion-reducing substances.

Many herbivores often occur on a single plant, and they may mutually affect their survivorships by altering the chemical state of the plant and by attracting predators. Consequently, determination of host suitability may include assessment of kinds and density of herbivores already on the plant.

Herbivore Foraging Patterns

Perennial plants and long-lived plant tissues should receive higher total grazing pressure than ephemeral plants and plant tissues, if all are equally well (or poorly) defended. In addition, the proportion of grazing by dietary specialists should be higher for the former group than for the latter. However, plants and tissues whose occurrence in space and time is predictable should receive higher grazing pressures and evolve more effective defenses, which, in turn, lowers grazing levels. Dietary specialization for herbivores utilizing perennial plants and tissues should be favored by resource predictability. However, convergence to the digestibility-reduction mode of defense by these plants should, in turn, select for dietary generalism in the herbivores. Similarly, the dietary generalization expected for herbivores utilizing ephemeral plants and tissues will be countered by the diversity of toxic defensive substances in these resources, each of which requires a separate detoxification or neutralization mechanism. Herbivores utilizing predictable resources are, in addition, more predictable resources to their predators and parasites than are herbivores utilizing unpredictable resources, and may be more readily found and eaten. For these reasons the actual levels of grazing and extent of dietary specialization on the tissues of different kinds of plants may be similar despite differences in selective pressures.

Foraging Patterns Related to Herbivore Size

An important variable in plant-herbivore interactions is the enormous range in size between individual plants and individual herbivores. Large herbivores have a less favorable gut surface/body weight and, if they are large with respect to their host plants, they must eat parts of many plants to complete their life cycle. Therefore, they encounter individual plants approximately in accordance with their abundances in the foraging area. By contrast, herbivores that are small relative to the size of their host plants may spend their entire life cycle on or within a single plant or part of one. The search for a plant may be confined to a single, mobile stage in the life cycle, such as the ovipositing female.

These size relations strongly influence the evolution of dietary choices, efficiencies of utilization of tissues of different species of plants, and evolution of predator avoidance characteristics, because they determine the amount of time the herbivores spend in different patches and how often they must move between them. Herbivores larger than the plants (or parts of them) they consume, must daily eat from a number of different plant individuals (Freeland and Janzen, 1974). A small herbivore can live most or all of its life within the confines of a single plant individual, even though it may have to move within that individual to find additional leaves or leaves of better quality than those immediately available to it. Large herbivores should be more generalized with respect to plant species they eat than small herbivores.

For a small herbivore that spends, or can spend, its entire feeding life on a single tissue or plant, natural selection should favor physiological traits that improve its efficiency of digestion of that tissue even if the herbivore loses efficiency in its ability to utilize other tissues. The major constraint on evolution of such specialization imposed by the plant resource itself is its temporal and spatial availability. Though herbivores may normally be limited by rates of assimilation rather than rates of encountering host plants, a specialist on a rare plant may not find its host. Also, there is mortality during the search, and if the host plant is short-lived, finding the plant soon enough to permit completion of the life cycle prior to leaf senescence may be difficult. Similarly, longer-lived plants produce tissues, e.g., flowers and new leaves, that are present for only short times. We therefore expect that small herbivores utilizing annual plants and ephemeral tissues should, on the average, be more generalized in their choice of host plant than small herbivores that eat primarily more permanent tissues and plants. Table 6-4 presents available data for small herbivores on the two major study sites. Unfortunately, only fragmentary comparative data are available for large herbivores.

Molding of Herbivore Characteristics by Predators

Food plants are also the habitats of herbivores and, especially for small herbivores, interactions between predation and host plant characteristics should be strong (Rand, 1967; Clarke, 1968; Kettlewell, 1958). Ricklefs and O'Rourke (1975) term the constellation of morphological traits that allows prey to match their background an "escape space" and treat this space as a

TABLE 6-4 *Dietary Patterns Among Small Herbivores at Silver Bell and Bolsón de Pipanaco, Determined by Field Data Gathered 1972-1975*

| Herbivores | N of herbivore species | Plant taxa fed upon by herbivores | | | | | |
| | | Family | | Genera | | Species | |
		n	$\bar{x}$	n	$\bar{x}$	n	$\bar{x}$
Lepidoptera	20	28	1.4	41	2.0	53	2.65
Coleoptera	10	12	1.2	14	1.4	18	1.8
Orthoptera	7	14	2.0	16	2.29	15	2.14

potentially limiting resource for which prey compete. The number of available backgrounds may bound the escape space of cryptic prey, while physiological, phylogenetic, and ecological parameters limit the diversity of characteristics available to prey for developing predator-avoidance strategies other than crypsis. Constraints of energy limitations and mutual interference among behavioral and morphological traits make many possible escape patterns evolutionarily unlikely. We develop this argument by assuming that prey have a fixed total energetic investment and that traits "compete" for their share of a budget within this limit.

An insect herbivore that devotes a significant amount of energy to digesting toxic plant material gains less net energy per unit time and can be highly motile only at the price of growing more slowly. This should favor reduced locomotion and remaining close to its food source, which in turn favors primary crypsis, i.e., mimicry of one substrate, which the cryptic individual matches in color and/or form. The high risk of capture for a cryptic herbivore away from its normal substrate results in close association with a single substrate and food, favoring dietary specialization. Such species may eventually sequester toxins and become unpalatable to predators; evolution of warning coloration may follow.

If different plant species possess very different hiding substrates then host plant-specific feeding by cryptic herbivores may be favored, even if chemical defenses of other associated plants are similar. On the other hand, if substrate differences are minor, then dietary choices ought to be related to chemical characteristics of the food tissues. Structurally complex plants should support more cryptic insect species than simpler plants.

Another characteristic of host plant tissues which may influence the evolution of crypticity and substrate-specificity is the predictability in space and time of hiding substrates. It is more difficult to evolve both mimicry of and dietary specialization to ephemeral and/or unpredictable substrates. Therefore, generalist feeding is expected among herbivores utilizing ephemeral or unpredictable tissues. However, such tissues may be defended primarily by toxins, which are usually species-specific and require specific detoxification mechanisms. The balance between these opposing selective forces is difficult to predict, but evolution of primary crypsis on annual plants and short-lived tissues of perennials ought to be difficult. Other predator-avoidance syndromes should predominate among utilizers of these tissues. However, if many ephemeral plant tissues are sufficiently similar in appearance (e.g., young growing leaves and stems of woody legumes) then a cryptic, dietary generalist may exploit the young tissues of several plant species, provided it can handle their chemical defenses.

An herbivore exploiting diverse resources cannot match all of the substrate types it utilizes and, in addition, the selective advantage of specialized mimicry of any one of them is reduced. Therefore, lack of close association with one substrate and use of noncryptic predator-avoidance techniques should be commonly associated with dietary generalization.

Any activity increasing the conspicuousness of a cryptic prey on its substrate will be selected against. For this reason, a combination of primary crypsis with other, more mobile predator-avoidance behavior such as defense (threat displays, active resistance, etc.), escape, use of refugia, etc., is unlikely, since these responses enhance conspicuousness and, hence, the probability of being detected. Because activities of prey may include association with several substrates, a more generalized background matching, *secondary crypsis,* may be mixed with active predator-avoidance patterns. Secondary crypsis may take the form of polymorphism within populations, or just a general resemblance to background colors, and is expected among mobile, generalized prey.

Different herbivore types are differentially susceptible to desiccation, both because of their abilities to control water loss and because of differences in the moisture content of the tissues they consume. Mature leaves of sclerophyllous desert shrubs have a lower moisture content than young leaves of the same plants or wet season leaves of deciduous shrubs and annuals and root perennials. Plant sap is high in water content at all times (A. F. G. Dixon, 1970). Therefore, desiccation-sensitive insect larvae, such as Lepidoptera and sawflies (Hymenoptera) should be especially active in spring in Arizona when there are many young leaves and cooler temperatures. Summer species should be restricted to plants with high leaf moisture content. Dominant utilizers of mature tissues of sclerophyllous shrubs should be members of the Orthoptera and adult Coleoptera, which can control water loss better than larval lepidopterans and sawflies. Sap-sucking insects should be relatively independent of direct heat and drought stress, but they depend on fluid movement within the phloem which ceases when stomata are closed (Zimmerman and Brown 1971). Therefore, they should be most abundant during wet periods when plants are actively transpiring.

Eventually it should be possible to develop a more comprehensive theory combining interactions between plants and small herbivores and between herbivores and their predators to predict life history characteristics of insects utilizing tissues of desert plants. Such a theory would relate hemimetabolism and holometabolism to dietary generalization, substrate mimicry, and times of activity. At present, however, we can only test parts of simpler aspects of our theories.

Tests of Predictions Concerning Grazing Patterns and Characteristics of Grazers on Desert Plants

Unpredictable resources may experience reduced grazing because they escape from herbivores in both space and time. This basic postulate in our theory formed the basis for a number of predictions. Detailed studies to test this postulate were carried out during summer (January-March) of 1974 in Argentina with several species of annuals and one invasive perennial. The most detailed study was made on *Ibicella parodii* (Martyniaceae), a species with large, readily countable leaves, common enough to yield large numbers, but rare enough to provide many well-isolated individuals. About 180 plants were individually tagged and visited every five to seven days during the growing season. At each visit counts were made of the number of damaged and undamaged leaves, flowers, fruits, and the number of all herbivores present. The distance to the nearest conspecific neighbor was measured for each plant. These data provide an accurate picture of the seasonal patterns of attack by herbivores and the total reproductive output of each plant (Table 6-5).

Grazing pressure was the chief source of death among individuals of *Ibicella*. Only eighty-one marked plants survived, while eighty-three were killed by grazing insects, two by grazing mammals, and eleven apparently by competition with annuals of other species, as judged by the fact that they did not grow despite being grazed only very lightly. Deaths from grazing by insects were caused entirely by one species of noctuid larva so far found only on *Ibicella* in the Andalgalá area. One hundred and twenty-eight plants survived long enough to start to produce fruits, but probably only fifty-six were able to ripen at least one fruit. The rest were killed by insects before fruits could mature, and in many cases fruits were actually consumed by caterpillars after they had demolished the leaves. Nevertheless, some protection was afforded by isolation. These data suggest that escape in space and time from specialized herbivores may occur over relatively short distances among annuals. However, grazing patterns of generalized insects may be more influenced by the overall plant density and may be relatively insensitive to the density of any one species.

Extensive studies were also carried out to determine the temporal patterns of activity of insect herbivores and extent of dietary generalization and specialization of insects utilizing ephemeral versus long-lived plants and tissues. Predictions concerning seasonal patterns of activity can be examined with data from sampling *Larrea cuneifolia* shrubs near Andalgalá. Beginning in December prior to the first summer rains and continuing through the entire summer rainy period, insects were removed from individual shrubs with a D-Vac vacuum sampler. As predicted, the prerain fauna is dominated by desiccation and resistant forms such as Hemiptera, Homoptera, Orthoptera, and Coleoptera (Table 6-6). Lepidopteran larvae on *Larrea* were never abundant and did not occur in any of our samples, but some were observed in March. Comparable quantitative data are not available for other plant species, but our general observations indicate that peak caterpillar abundance closely follows water availability, while other leaf-feeding taxa reflect this trend less strongly.

Quantitative data are available for the herbivore fauna on *Larrea tridentata* in Arizona in April and August (Table 6-7). Homoptera are much more abundant on *Larrea* in Arizona than in Argentina, but the most striking seasonal change is the virtual restriction of Hemiptera to the early spring, a

TABLE 6-5. *Effect of Distance of Nearest Conspecific Neighbor (nn) on Intensity of Grazing on* Ibicella parodii

	Clumped (nn < 2.5 m)		Intermediate (nn 2.5 - 10 m)		Isolated (nn > 10 m)	
	proportion	n	proportion	n	proportion	n
Plants killed by grazing	0.63	56	0.38	23	0.32	12
Plants killed by grazing that were found by catepillars from neighboring plants	0.49	24	0.41	9	0	0
Plants that started to produce fruit	0.60	53	0.85	52	0.97	37
Plants that ripened at least one fruit	0.18	16	0.44	27	0.47	18
Total number of plants	89		61		38	

pattern parallel to the restriction of this group to the prerain and early rainy season in Catamarca. In Arizona, the absolute abundances of herbivorous insects is much higher in the late winter and spring than in the summer. Caterpillars on *Larrea* in Arizona are dominated by a geometrid, *Semiothisa colorata,* which occurs in both spring and summer, but the spring hatch is much larger than the summer one.

Extensive studies were made of the feeding patterns of insect herbivores in the two deserts. Data were gathered on plant species eaten in the field, plants which insects could be induced to eat in the laboratory, tissue preferences of insects, and efficiency of extraction of nitrogen from those tissues.

The lepidopteran herbivorous community was more extensively studied than the other groups listed in Table 6-8. Of the twenty-eight species for which we obtained feeding data, thirteen are found on annuals and fifteen on woody perennials. None of the larvae feeding on annuals feed on perennials and *vice versa*. Of the fifteen species on perennials, 73 percent are specialized (feeding on a single plant species or at most two species in a genus), and 27 percent are generalized in their feeding habits. This contrasts sharply with the species on annuals, where 77 percent feed on more than one plant species, while only 23 percent are restricted to a single plant species.

Food preferences among orthopterans were estimated by comparing the proportion of guts containing each plant species with the relative frequency of the plants in the general area, determined by identifying the plant nearest the right toe at intervals of 3-5 meters. Rare plants not recorded in those samples were noted and given an arbitrary frequency of 1. The proportion of food specialists (species feeding on one or a few closely related plant species) is about 25 percent at both study sites in contrast to about 3 percent in a variety of North American grassland sites (Table 6-9). This suggests strong convergence, probably related to the greater diversity of plant life forms and, hence, hiding places in the desert than in grasslands, where the dominant

TABLE 6-6. *Distribution of Insects (excluding Bees) on* Larrea cuneifolia *near Andalgalá during Summer 1971–1972. Based on Sampling 1455 Plants with a D-Vac Vacuum Sampler*

Taxon	December N	% of sample total	% of taxon total	January N	% of sample total	% of taxon total	February N	% of sample total	% of taxon total	March N	% of sample total	% of taxon total
Number bushes sampled	492			487			238			238		
Homoptera	41	5.5	24.0	19	3.4	11.1	70	20.2	40.9	41	10.0	24.0
Hemiptera	49	6.5	62.0	30	5.4	38.0	0	0	0	0	0	0
Hymenoptera	99	13.2	19.3	122	22.1	23.6	38	11.0	7.4	258	62.8	49.9
Orthoptera	492	65.4	45.3	335	60.6	30.9	163	47.1	15.0	95	23.1	8.8
Coleoptera	71	9.4	33.8	47	8.5	22.4	75	21.7	35.7	17	4.1	8.1
		100.0			100.0			100.0			100.0	
Total Insects	752			553			346			411		
Insects/Bush	1.53			1.14			1.45			1.73		

180

TABLE 6-7 *Distribution of Insects (Excluding Bees) on* Larrea tridentata *in the Sonoran Desert during Spring and Summer, 1972–1973, Based on Sampling 832 Plants with a D-Vac Vacuum Sampler*

Taxon	N	April % of taxon total	% of sample total	N	August % of taxon total	% of sample total
Number Bushes Sampled	539	539			293	
Homoptera	1,050	69	42.9	464	31	75.3
Hemiptera	1,017	97	41.5	28	3	4.6
Coleoptera	220	73	9.0	83	27	13.5
Orthoptera	42	62	1.7	26	38	4.2
Lepidoptera	121	89	4.9	15	11	2.4
			100.0			100.0
Total Insects	2,450			616		
Insects/Bush	4.55			2.10		

TABLE 6-8 *Dietary Characteristics of Species of Herbivorous Insects from Arizona and Argentina*

	Herbivores							
	Lepidoptera		Coleoptera*		Orthoptera		Hemiptera	
Foraging Characteristics	N	%	N	%	N	%	N	%
A. *Species feeding on woody perenials*								
generalists	4	27	17	52	7	54	5	45
specialists	11	73	16	48	6	46	6	55
	15	100	33	100	13	100	11	100
B. *Species feeding on annuals*								
generalists	10	77	6	66	+	+	+	+
specialists	3	23	3	33	+	+	+	+
	13	100	9	100				

*Argentina only
+Insufficient data

plants are structurally very similar. Similarly no grass-eating grasshopper in either desert is obligately monophagous, though *Opeia obscura* is locally monophagous on *Bouteloua gracilis* (Mulkern et al., 1969; Joern, in prep.). On both continents a number of grasshoppers feed on several grasses that are similar in overall appearances, further indicating the importance of matching backgrounds as an evolutionary factor determining dietary preferences.

The pattern of utilization of *Larrea* among Acridide (short-horned grasshoppers) is similar in the two deserts, about 12 percent of species being specialists on *Larrea* (1/8 at Andalgalá and 3/24 at Tucson). A similar value

TABLE 6-9 *Degree of Polyphagy (log* B = $-\Sigma p_i$ *log* $_e p_i$) *and Number of Species Eaten by Desert and Grassland Grasshoppers.* B=*Diversity Index,* N_p = *Number of Plant Species Eaten,* M=*Monophagous Species,* O=*Oligophagous Species.*

	Catamarca	Arizona	Mean of five North American grassland localities
Mean N_p	9.4	8.8	12.8
Range N_p	1–27	1–24	1–30
B	2.5	2.5	5.1
% M + 0	25	25	3

Source: Grassland Data from Mulkern et al. (1960) and Veckert and Hansen (1971).

was obtained at Cuatrocienagas in the Chihuahuan Desert (2/14 species). Thus, though *Larrea* arrived more recently in North America, the same fraction of the orthopteran fauna eats it as in Argentina (Figures 6-1 and 6-2). Even more surprisingly, three *Larrea* specialists occur in Arizona as compared to only one in Catamarca. Not including mantids, six species of Orthoptera regularly use some portion of *L. tridentata* as food while only three species are associated with *L. cuneifolia* with any regularity. Of the three Argentine species, one, *Dichroplus vittatus,* only occasionally feeds on *Larrea* fruits, and the other two species are oligophagous. Four of the six Arizona orthopterans studied eat no other plant (or very nearly so). One species, *Melanoplus lakinus,* is only rarely found on *L. tridentata.* Thus, none of eight Catamarca insect species feeding exclusively on *Larrea* are orthopterans, while four of eighteen monophagous insect species found on *L. tridentata* at Silver Bell are orthopterans. Relationships between *Larrea* and orthopteran herbivores are more specialized in the North American desert despite the apparent recency of *Larrea* there.

In both deserts the food niche width of vegetation-inhabiting orthopterans is roughly half that of ground-inhabiting forms (Table 6-10). More ground-inhabiting species occasionally feed on *Larrea* than do species living on other species of shrubs in the area (Figures 6-3 and 6-4).

Among Coleoptera feeding patterns seem more strongly influenced by secondary biological interactions. Food preferences were estimated for more common phytophagous species, mostly members of the Scarabaeidae (lamellicorn beetles), Meloidae (flower beetles), Curculionidae (weevils), Chrysomelidae (leaf beetles), and Buprestidae (wood-borers), by a combination of field observations and laboratory preference trials (choice tests). About two-thirds of the species on annual or herbaceous perennial plants were found feeding on two or more genera or would accept readily two or more genera in the laboratory. Beetle species associated with woody perennials were more evenly divided between generalist and specialist feeders (Table 6-8).

FIGURE 6-1. Bootettix punctatus *(Acrididae) a specialist on* Larrea tridentata *in the Sonoran Desert. (Photo by J. C. Schultz.)*

FIGURE 6-2. Astroma quadrilobatum *(Proscopiidae), the dominant orthopteran on* Larrea cuneifolia *in the Monte. It also occurs on* Bulnesia *and* Zuccagnia. *Note the damage to the leaves of the* Larrea. *(Photo by M. L. Erckmann.)*

FIGURE 6-3. Taeniopoda eques *(Acrididae), a ground inhabiting grass-hopper of the Sonoran Desert that rests in bushes at night. (Photo by M. L. Paulson.)*

FIGURE 6-4. Trimerotropis pallidipennis *(Acrididae), a widespread grasshopper found in both the Monte and Sonoran Desert. It feeds on leaves of forbs at night, but rests on the bare soil surface during the day. (Photo by M. L. Paulson.)*

TABLE 6-10 *Comparisons of Food Niches of Ground-Inhabiting and
Vegetation-Inhabiting Grasshoppers. All Figures
Are Mean Values. (*$B = -\Sigma p_i \log_e P_i$*)*

	Arizona		Catamarca	
	ground-inhabiting species	vegetation-inhabiting species	ground-inhabiting species	vegetation-inhabiting species
Total no. of plant species eaten	12.3	6.4	15.0	6.1
No. of plant species eaten/locality	4.1	2.4	6.2	2.8
Niche breadth (*B*)	3.0	1.7	3.6	2.1
No. of species of grasshoppers	8	11	4	7

Of the thirteen species of Coleoptera feeding on woody perennials, ten fed primarily or exclusively on flowers. We expected a low degree of taxonomic specialization on these tissues which are not likely to be well defended. However, just over half of the flower-feeding beetles are family specific, and 38 percent are species specific (Table 6-11). In the case of meloids, the flower is both adult food and the site at which the parasitic larva attaches itself to a host bee. This relationship may be species specific and hence influences the adult beetle's feeding site, but we did not study host/parasite relationships.

Many scarabaeids feed while copulating (Richter, 1958). These beetles spend daylight hours in the soil, emerging for nuptial flights and associated feeding by night. The probability of finding a mate might be enhanced by visiting specific copulatory sites. Many insects (e.g., Lepidoptera) produce chemical signals that can be sensed over long distances and which identify meeting places for copulation. Host specificity by flower-feeding beetles may have evolved through use of an externally-produced (flower-produced) signal identifying flowers as places for mating.

Coleoptera are more prominent users of *Larrea cuneifolia* in Catamarca than of *L. tridentata* at Silver Bell. Only seven of twenty-two species commonly associated with *L. tridentata* are beetles, while fourteen of twenty species utilizing *L. cuneifolia* are coleopterans. Two buprestid species feed and oviposit on *L. cuneifolia* in Catamarca, while only one species is suspected of ovipositing on *Larrea* in Arizona and may be collected at flowers near Silver Bell. The curculionid faunae of the two plants appear similar, but fewer scarabs and darkling beetles (Tenebrionidae) are associated with North American *Larrea* than with Catamarca's *L. cuneifolia*. Five of seven beetle species feeding on *L. tridentata* are monophagous while eight of fourteen species on *L. cuneifolia* eat nothing else. Feeding specialization appears some-

TABLE 6-11   *Diets of Beetles at Andalgalá*

Tissues fed upon	N of species	Number of beetle species feeding only on:					
		One plant family		One plant genus		One plant species	
		N	%	N	%	N	%
Flowers	13	7	54	5	38	5	38
Leaves, stems	19	12	63	11	58	9	47
Total	32	19	59	16	50	14	44

what greater among the few *Larrea*-feeding beetles of Arizona, a trend similar to that among Orthoptera.

Observations on Hemiptera feeding give a less clear picture of differences in feeding specialization. All seven species feeding on *Larrea tridentata* are relatively specialized (six monophagous, one oligophagous), and the same is true of the *L. cuneifolia* Hemiptera (three monophagous, two oligophagous). The greatest difference between these faunas and perhaps the explanation for the different species numbers is the seasonality of their occurrence. Five species at Silver Bell have either exclusively winter distributions or obvious winter abundance peaks. Most notable among these are three species in the Membracidae (treehoppers; Homoptera). This group is absent from *Larrea* in the Catamarca desert, which receives primarily summer rains. Although several *L. cuneifolia* Hemiptera tend to appear early in the season, there really is no opportunity for a "winter" fauna at Catamarca, which may explain the difference in species numbers between the two *Larrea* communities.

Tissue preferences of nocturnally-feeding generalists and specialists (twenty-eight Lepidopteran species) on annuals are much less variable than that of generalists and specialists on perennials (Table 6-12). Leaf tissues were observed being eaten in the field. We also estimated the amount of each leaf tissue type available to the herbivores on those plants. From those we calculated the ratio:

$$\frac{\text{Number of insect feeding observations per tissue}}{\text{Proportion of the tissue type available}}$$

Relative tissue preference (RTP) was determined by assigning a value of 100 to the most highly preferred tissue and scaling other values as follows:

$$\text{RTP} = \frac{\text{No. of feeding observations}}{\substack{\text{proportion of that tissue} \\ \text{available}}} \times \frac{\substack{\text{proportion of most preferred} \\ \text{tissue available}}}{\substack{\text{No. feeding observations of} \\ \text{most highly preferred tissue}}} \times 100$$

In both Arizona and Argentina, generalist Lepidoptera (with one exception) feeding on woody perennials prefer mature leaves whereas specialists

TABLE 6-12 *Leaf Tissue Preference of Lepidopteran Larvae on Plant*
Species at the Bolsón and Silver Bell Sites*

| | Young | | Intermediate | | Mature | | Number of |
	Pref.†	Number of obs.	Pref.†	Number of obs.	Pref.†	Number of obs.	herbivore species
Perennials							
Specialists	100	(787)	12	(268)	3	(140)	10
Generalists	41	(292)	13	(414)	100	(856)	3
Annuals							
Specialists	100	(447)	36	(107)	11	(88)	3
Generalists	17	(103)	60	(219)	100	(345)	4

*All comparisons are significant ($p < 0.05$) except for specialists and generalists on intermediate leaves of perennials.
†The most frequently used tissue has been assigned a value of 100.

prefer young leaf tissues. The exception is *Melipotis* sp. (Noctuidae; owlet moths, an oligophagous species which feeds on young tissues of *Prosopis chilensis, P. flexuousa,* and *Acacia aroma*).

These patterns of feeding behavior are also correlated with the ability of these two types of herbivores to assimilate nitrogen from leaf tissues of plants. Efficiency of nitrogen assimilation was determined by collecting bulk samples of leaves from three randomly selected plants. In each experiment a known mass of leaf material was presented to caterpillars (1.36–1.50 g fresh wt) for a thirteen-hour nighttime period. Then frass and leftover leaf material were collected, dried, weighed, and analyzed for total nitrogen by Kjeldahl techniques. From the same bulk sample an identical amount of leaf material was taken as a control, dried to determine water content, and analyzed for nitrogen. The difference between total leaf nitrogen consumed and total fecal nitrogen is an estimate of the amount of nitrogen assimilated during the thirteen-hour period. Specialist lepidopterans on woody perennials are more efficient on their preferred tissue than generalists on woody plants are on their preferred tissue (Table 6-13). Beetles (two species only) appear to follow the same trend, but they extract less leaf nitrogen than caterpillars. This may be misleading, however, because we are comparing larval lepidopterans with adult beetles. Larvae are probably more strongly influenced by the anti-herbivore chemistry of their foods because they are under strong selection to grow rapidly and because they are also accumulating energy reserves to complete metamorphosis and to form gametes. Adult beetles are not growing, are more mobile, and hence at less risk while eating and resting, and will not metamorphose again.

Since close background matching results in increased risk for cryptic prey when not on the substrate they mimic, hiding close to food, nocturnal activity, and feeding specialization should be common among cryptic herbivore species. Cryptic insects on shrubs in the Argentine desert and on *Larrea*

TABLE 6-13 *Assimilation of Nitrogen from Preferred Leaves by Herbivores on Plant Species from the Bolsón and Silver Bell Sites*

	Lepidoptera			Coleoptera		
	N herbivore species	N trials	% assimilation ($\bar{X}$)	N herbivore species	N trials	% assimilation ($\bar{X}$)
Perennials						
Specialists	9	29	36*	1	5	14
Generalists	3	21	24	–	–	–
			$\bar{X} = 30*$			
Annuals						
Specialists	3	15	69*	–	–	–
Generalists	10	50	52	1	15	22
			$\bar{X} = 61$			

*Significant differences ($p < 0.05$).

tridentata in North America tend to be monophagous (Table 6-14). All the species feed mostly at night, and the few for which we have observations (primarily *Larrea* herbivores) also copulate and oviposit at night. On cool, overcast mornings some Lepidoptera were observed feeding during daylight hours, suggesting that selection by physical factors (temperatures, humidity) may also favor nocturnal feeding. Moreover, feeding activities of some of these herbivores (notably *Astroma quadrilobatum*-Orthoptera: Proscopidae-on *Larrea*) appeared to be reduced on nights with full moons. This pattern suggests that light cues may directly influence feeding activity. Cool, wet nights could interfere with feeding and/or food processing, favoring early morning feeding.

Less close background matching or the evolution of alternate defensive strategies should occur in animals which must cross several substrates to perform various life functions, such as reproduction or feeding (Figure 6-5). For example, predatory arthropods may have to hunt on a variety of substrates though certain sites which attract large numbers of prey, such as flowers, may be favored waiting places. Predators cryptic on flowers include a number of insects (Hemiptera: Reduviidae-assassin bugs, Phymatidae-ambush bugs; Neuroptera: Mantispidae-mantis-like Neuroptera), and spiders (Thomisidae-crab spiders) are specialists of this sort. The largest predatory arthropods, however, utilize other means of predator avoidance. All mantids observed in both deserts (three species in each) fall into one of two basic categories. Two species in Arizona (*Stagmomantis californica* and *Litaneutra minor*) and one in Argentina (probably *Stagmomantis* sp.) actively escape when a predator approaches, usually by running down stems or flying from one shrub to another. The remaining species (*Stagatoptera* sp. in Catamarca and *S. limbata* in Arizona) depend primarily on threat or startle displays,

TABLE 6-14 *Diet Breadth of Cryptic Insects* on Woody Perennials*

Plant species	Monophagous species	Proportion	Oligophagous species	Proportion	Polyphagous species	Proportion
Cassia aphylla	5/6	.833	0/6	0	1/6	.167
Larrea cuneifolia	10/15	.667	2/15	.133	3/15	.200
Larrea tridentata	15/22	.682	0/22	0	7/22	.318
Other shrubs/trees	9/12	.750	3/12	.250	0/12	0

*Primary and secondary crypsis

which are well-documented in the family (Varley, 1939; Balderrama and Maldonada, 1973). In all cases, a primary predator avoidance technique is found in combination with nonspecific secondary crypsis. This general background resemblance probably reduces mean distance at which predators detect these insects, thereby increasing the probability that the prey becomes aware of the predator before the predator detects the prey. This would allow prey to initiate either escape or display when the time and predator-prey distance are optimal for successful avoidance.

Such escape- or threat-based predator-avoidance techniques are also common among insect herbivores that feed on a variety of backgrounds. Escape with secondary crypsis characterizes many grasshoppers (Acrididae) encountered during this study, most of which exhibit at least oligophagous feeding patterns (Otte, in press). Some species, (e.g., *Trimerotropis pallidipennis*) possess colored hindwings used in reproductive display. The sudden appearance and then disappearance of these colorful structures during flight from predators may make tracking of the grasshopper difficult, lending a dual function to wing color (Cott, 1940; Robinson, 1969). This effect is enhanced by grasshoppers' general background resemblance and their comparative invisibility on the ground before and after a flight. Specific background resemblance among ground-dwelling grasshoppers would be difficult, since they must traverse many backgrounds to feed on scattered grasses and forbs of the desert floor. The more sessile, wingless nymphs of generalist species such as *Trimerotropis* are often polymorphic, resembling the range of colors found among sand and pebbles.

Two common generalist Lepidoptera species were encountered foraging on the desert floor in Arizona. Larvae of *Hyles lineata* (Sphingidae-hawk moths) were conspicuous members of the ground-dwelling herbivore fauna (Figure 6-6) and their brightly colored integuments suggest that they are distasteful. We have no direct evidence of this, but cactus wrens (*Campylorhynchus brunneicapillus*) and curve-billed thrashers (*Toxostoma curvirostris*) spend up to fifteen minutes killing each larva and removing its gut.

Vanessa cardui (Nymphalidae-brushfooted butterflies), a black spiny caterpillar that occurred on several plant species, spins tough webbing over its

FIGURE 6-5. Eacles imperialis *(Citheroniidae) on* Ximenia american *at Andalgalá. This species is cryptic when small but has a conspicuous threat display when larger. (Photo by M. L. Erckmann.)*

FIGURE 6-6. Hyles lineata *(Sphingidae), a common generalist of the Sonoran Desert. (Photo by M. L. Erckmann.)*

feeding site. Other species in the genus advertise their presumed low value by grouping together (Tinbergen et al., 1942).

Other insects in each desert which fed on a variety of woody perennial host plant species did not employ primary crypsis either. Notable among these are species in several families of Coleoptera, especially Scarabaeidae, Curculionidae, and Meloidae. The majority of scarab species for which we have dietary information (six species in Catamarca, five in Arizona) hide in soil by day and fly to feeding substrates at night. Four Catamarca species are monophagous. One hides in host plant flowers by day. In Arizona, one scarab species flies and feeds by day and utilizes rapid escape with secondary crypsis techniques. The other species studied remain in soil by day. Monophagy by these beetles is linked with their reproductive behavior, in that in most cases the female must feed while copulating. Hence certain substrates, especially those emitting chemical signals (such as flowers) may serve as mating sites, making it difficult to separate the selective agents for host specificity.

One weevil in Arizona (*Eupagoderes marmoratus*) and two in Catamarca (*Naupactus sulfureosignathus* and *N.* sp.) feed on leaves of from three to many plant species. *Eupagoderes marmoratus* in Arizona has a very hard integument and when disturbed clings very tightly to the substrate or drops to the ground. This species combines elements of resistance and escape in its predator-avoidance technique. The two *Naupactus* species are both brightly colored or marked and may be distasteful. Each clings tightly to the substrate or drops to the ground when disturbed.

The Meloidae are a group of beetles well known for their chemical defenses (Werner et al., 1966). Three of six species studied in Catamarca are flower feeders. Two are oligophagous, feeding on three species in two genera of the Zygophyllaceae, while the third specializes on flowers of *Cassia aphylla*, a legume. All are brightly marked or colorful; two drop when disturbed, and the third shows no disturbance response; all three exude hemolymph. The three leaf-feeding meloid species are less brightly colored but exude orange hemolymph when disturbed. One species is monophagous while the other two feed on a variety of short plants. The monphagous species, *Epicauta centralis*, specializes on the annual *Kallstroemia tribuloides*. This beetle is quite obscure in the light/shadow environment under *Kallstroemia*'s pinnately-compound leaves. The other two species, *Epicauta punctata* and *E. pluvialis*, demonstrate running or dropping behavior when disturbed on their more erect host plants.

Primary crypsis on or near the food tissue is prevalent among insect herbivores feeding on predictable tissues of woody perennial plants (Table 6-15), particularly on long-lived and well-defended tissues such as old leaves and stems. Primary crypsis is not common among insect herbivores feeding on annual plants since their tissues are comparatively ephemeral and generally unpredictable in space and time. Furthermore, they are usually structurally rather simple, not affording a variety of hiding substrates.

TABLE 6-15   *Distribution of Cryptic Insect Species on*
Desert Plants at Andalgalá and Silver Bell

	Herbivore species cryptic/non-cryptic	Proportion cryptic
Annual plants	3/24	.13
Perennial plants	21/38	.55
On perennial plants:		
Leaves	5/21	.24
Young stem	4/21	.19
Old stem	12/21	.57

Flowers are generally more ephemeral than most vegetative tissues, and crypsis is not common among flower feeders. A comparison of the flower faunas of *Larrea cuneifolia* and *Cassia aphylla* illustrates this point. *Cassia* flowers are longer lasting as a group than those of *Larrea*. A greater proportion of flower-feeding insects of *Cassia* show cryptic adaptation than do those of either *Larrea* (Table 6-16). In fact, *Cassia* has one of the longest flowering periods of any of the Catamarcan shrubs, with the possible exception of *Nicotiana noctiflora*. These two species host the only flower-cryptic herbivore species found during this study.

To test whether plant species which offer more backgrounds host more cryptic prey species or morphs, morphological complexity of the dominant woody perennials at Andalgalá was estimated from the number of different surface textures and colors found on each individual. As expected the more morphologically complex species support more cryptic herbivore species (Figure 6-7). Measurements for *Larrea tridentata* at Silver Bell are included.

Evolution of specialized adaptations such as those involved in substrate mimicry may be influenced by historical factors and host plant abundance. Herbivore species may accumulate on plant species over evolutionary time and more common species may accumulate on plant species over evolutionary time and more common species may accumulate herbivores more rapidly than less common ones (Southwood, 1972, Strong, 1974). Certainly the position of the two *Larrea* species near the upper end of Figure 6-7 might be explained in part in this way. The two *Larrea* species are numerical dominants over much of their ranges. If specialized crypsis evolves slowly, then the patterns of adaptation within the two *Larrea* insect faunas suggest historical differences between the two deserts. However, resident insects on *L. tridentata* at Silver Bell show a greater proportion of cryptic species specialized for feeding, hiding, and ovipositing on the shrub than do the insects associated with *L. cuneifolia* in Catamarca (Table 6-17), despite the more recent arrival of *L. tridentata* in North America (Wells, 1966, 1975).

Though these tests have yielded some interesting results, some of which support the predictions, there are many unexplained differences between the two deserts. In addition our knowledge of plant chemistry, herbivore feeding patterns, and herbivore escape behavior is so incomplete that all current con-

TABLE 6-16 *Dietary and Cryptic Characteristics of Insects Feeding and Hiding on Flowers of Three Desert Shrubs*

	Hiding Cryptic morphs	Propor- tion	Monopha- gous species	Propor- tion	Feeding Oligopha- gous species	Propor- tion	Polypha- gous species	Propor- tion
Cassia aphylla	4/9	.44	8/8	1.00	0/8	0	0/8	0
Larrea cuneifolia	0/4	0	0/9	0	5/9	.56	3/9	.33
Larrea tridentata	0/8	0	3/17	.18	1/17	.06	2/17	.12

clusions are likely to be modified as more complete data become available. A comprehensive theory of plant-herbivore-predator interactions will require far more data and insight than were available to us for this project.

Patterns of Resource Utilization by Predators on Herbivores

Viewed as foraging substrates for predators on herbivores, desert plants are highly structured, providing a variety of types of backgrounds such as foliage, twigs and small branches, and larger, furrowed stems. These differ in color, spatial distribution, and kinds of perches they provide. As shown previously, each substrate has different kinds of herbivorous insects, especially during the day when most insects are inactive and hiding. At night, when the bulk of herbivores are feeding, the distribution of prey is different and most individuals are concentrated on the foliage of the plants.

At night, prey cannot be detected at a distance on foliage and nocturnal predators rely on contact with prey for perception. Their hunting techniques involve rapid movement over the branches and foliage of the plants, and the most common response of the prey upon perceiving the approach of such a predator, typically via vibrations of the substrate, is to drop off the plant. In both deserts this predator community is dominated by solpugids and hunting spiders (Lycosidae, Clubionidae) with poor eyesight. As pointed out in Chapter 5, spiders and solpugids may replace one another within their guild in the two deserts. These predators do not select for divergent visual characteristics of their prey and do not appear to influence the choice of foraging sites by herbivores.

During the day, the major visual predators on herbivorous insects on desert shrubs are birds, and in our study particular attention was paid to the insectivorous bird community associated with *Larrea* flats. The bird species regularly utilizing *Larrea* bushes in the two deserts and their modes of foraging are shown in Table 6-18. Additional species occasionally utilize *Larrea*, especially during periods of peak availability of insect prey, typically in late summer. Both deserts have two common foliage gleaners, one a very active forager that typically perceives prey at a distance, and the other a slower-

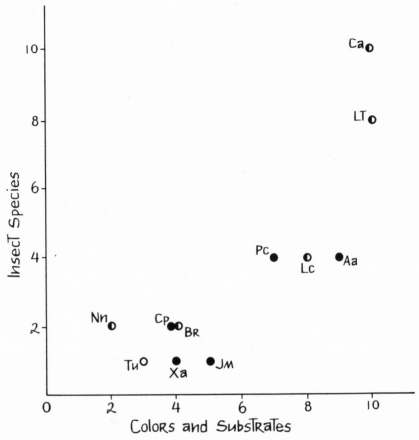

FIGURE 6-7. *The relationship between the complexity of shrubs, in terms of the variety of colors and substrates they contain, and the number of species of herbivorous insects that regularly feed on them. The proportions of species that are monophagous primary cryptics and secondary cryptics are shown by the shading patterns of the circles.*

Aa. = Acacia aroma	*Lt.* = Larrea tridentata *(USA)*
Br. = Bulnesia retamo	*Nn.* = Nicotiana noctiflora
Ca. = Cassia aphylla	*Pc.* = Prosopis chilensis
Cp. = Cercidium praecox	*Tu.* = Trichomeria usillo
Jm. = Jatropha macrocarpa	*Xa.* = Ximenia americana
Lc. = Larrea cuneifolia	

moving predator that perceives its prey at close ranges. Additional species in both deserts locate insects on the lower branches by scanning a bush from the ground and moving up only when a suitable prey item has been located. These different birds capture various insects on *Larrea* with different ease and tend to capture prey on the bushes in very different order (Schultz, in prep.). *Larrea* bark is normally simple and with few furrows. Consequently the branch-exploiting avifauna is poor in species and numbers of individuals compared to that found on some of the larger shrubs of the washes which support

TABLE 6-17   *Predator-Avoidance Relationships of Herbivorous Insects on Three Desert Shrubs*

			Number of prey morphs per guild				
	Primary Crypsis	Escape	Defense	Aposematic	Refuge	Total morphs	Within-bush specificity
Cassia aphylla	9	2	1	3	2	17	H = .6891
Proportion	.53	.12	.06	.18	.12		N = 21
Larrea cuneifolia	4	6	7	4	2	21	H = .8858
Proportion	.19	.29	.33	.19	.10		N = 44
Larrea tridentata (U.S.)	11	17	4	2	1	23	H = .7941
Proportion	.48	.30	.17	.09	.04		N = 31

TABLE 6-18   *Foraging Modes of Insectivorous Birds on* Larrea

		Species of bird in:	
Substrate	Foraging mode	Monte	Sonoran Desert
Foliage	Snatch and glean; distance perception	Lesser Wagtail-tyrant (*Stigmatura budytoides*)	Black-tailed Gnats hatcher (*Polioptila melanura*)
Foliage	Snatch and glean; close perception	Tufted Tit-spinetail (*Leptasthenura plantensis*)	Verdin (*Auriparus flaviceps*)
Foliage	Glean and probe	Short-billed Canastero (*Asthenes baeri*)	Cactus Wren (*Campylorhynchus brunneicapillus*)
Bark	Probe and dig	Checkered Woodpecker (*Dendrocopus mixtus*)	Ladder-backed Woodpecker (*Dendrocopus scalaris*)
Ground and lower branches	Hops from ground up to branches	Sandy Gallito (*Teledromus fuscus*)	Bendire's Thrasher (*Toxostoma bendiri*)

three or four species of bark-gleaning, probing, and digging species. Also birds that capture insects by snatching them from the foliage while in flight seldom forage in *Larrea*. Again, the larger shrubs and trees of the washes support such flycatchers, and their absence from *Larrea* is probably due to the generally small size of the shrubs and the short inter-branch and inter-spray distances that greatly limit maneuverability for flying birds within the confines of the bushes.

Thus, birds, the prime visual selective agents on herbivorous insects on *Larrea* and other desert shrubs, have been evolutionarily molded by their prey to adopt foraging modes that result in efficient foraging on different parts of the complex structural mosaic provided by the shrubs themselves. We would expect similar patterns of utilization on insects on desert shrubs throughout the warm deserts of the world.

A number of life history traits enhance a bird's ability to utilize prey that are seasonally predictable but vary from year to year in abundance and precise location. Included among these traits are strong dispersal abilities and tendencies, semi-social or social breeding behavior, and variable clutch sizes. The summer peak of insects on the shrubs and herbs also provides opportunities for migrant species that enter the desert and breed during these periods of high resource availability. The proportion of residents, breeding migrants, nonbreeding migrants, breeding nomads, and transients depends on the resource patterns in the desert and in the surrounding areas from which some species are drawn. For example, in Arizona a conspicuous element of the avifauna consists of winter visitors derived from the large expanses of deserts, grasslands, and woodlands lying to the north. In South America, on the other hand, there is only a small land mass to the south, and this area is characterized by a maritime climate with relatively mild winters as compared with severe winters of interior North America. Accordingly, at Andalgalá, there is no winter influx of species that breed at higher latitudes.

In both deserts there is an influx of birds utilizing *Larrea* in late summer. At Andalgalá, in late spring when the ground is dry, few grasses and forbs are present, and *Larrea* has few leaves on it, only three species of birds regularly foraged on *Larrea* (*Stigmatura, Leptasthenura,* and *Teledromus;* Figures 6-8 and 6-9). During early summer when there is new leaf growth and flowering begins, four to eight species of birds regularly forage on *Larrea,* some of them catching flying insects associated with flowering. By late summer when invertebrates on *Larrea* are most diverse and abundant, the number of species of birds regularly foraging on *Larrea* rises to ten or more. Similarly, in Arizona, the few species regularly foraging on *Larrea* in late winter and spring are supplemented in summer by species moving out from the washes and later by summer transients.

SEEDS-SEED EATER SYSTEM*

Often, granivores are the most conspicuous faunal element in deserts. This is not surprising since annuals produce large numbers of seeds and even though they may mature during a brief period, they are readily stored and can be eaten during times of the year when other resources are scarce (J. H. Brown, 1973). However, though we expected the Monte fauna to show a prevalence of granivores similar to that of the Sonoran Desert, this is not the case. These are fewer species and genera in seed-eating guilds in the Monte, and rate of disappearance of canary seed (*Phalaris canariensis*) from different types of feeding trays is also lower there.

Seeds were placed in clear glass ashtrays or petri dishes distributed in pairs along line transects in either dry washes or fairly uniform stands of *Larrea.* One of each pair was covered with 1/4 inch mesh hardware cloth to make it inaccessible to vertebrates. This tray had strips of masking tape placed in it and up and down its sides to facilitate entry by arthropods. The maximum slope was 90°. The other tray was open but required an arthropod to negotiate a smooth glass overhang much steeper than 90°. This effectively eliminated most ants, the only arthropods seen taking seeds during our

*By M. A. Mares and M. L. Rosenzweig.

FIGURE 6-8. Teledromus fuscus *(Rhinocriptidae), a primary ground inhabiting species that hops up into the lower branches of* Larrea cuneifolia *to capture insects. (Photo by M. L. Erckmann.)*

FIGURE 6-9. Stigmatura budytoides *(Tyrannidae), a common insect gleaning bird of Larrea flats in the Monte. (Photo by M. L. Erckmann.)*

experiments. Trays with 15 g each of canary seed were placed in the desert at various times throughout the year within a few days of a new moon. They remained in place for eighteen to thirty-six hours and were visited at daybreak and nightfall to discriminate bird impact from that of mammals. Seeds were counted and replenished at each visit. More detailed description of this technique appears elsewhere (Mares and Rosenzweig, in prep.). The technique was conceived independently of a similar one designed by Brown et al. (1975), but then was made to conform as nearly as possible to theirs.

Mammals

Monte mammals are strikingly dissimilar from those of the Sonoran Desert. Most prominent among the differences is the fact that not a single granivorous mammalian taxon lives in the Monte, whereas the North American deserts contain an abundant and rich endemic granivorous rodent family, the Heteromyidae. In Arizona, rodents in other families also rely heavily upon seeds (e.g., *Reithrodontomys*). Moreover, in Arizona one almost always catches ten or more heteromyids for every specimen of less obligately granivorous rodent.

Our feeding tray trials clearly reinforce the conclusion that Argentina's desert rodent fauna is poor compared to North America's and that a seed in Argentina is much less likely to be consumed by a rodent. Trays in fairly uniform *Larrea* stands were relieved of 584 g of a possible 2,025 g of canary seed in Arizona but only 11 g of a possible 3,150 g in Catamarca (Table 6-19). Along desert washes the situation was even more disparate. Mammals in Arizona took 1,387 g of 1,980 g offered, but in Catamarca only 28 g of 2,830 g.

Ants

The ant situation is not clear. Leaf cutting ants are a richer and more important group in Catamarca while seedeaters are a richer and more important group in Arizona (see Chapter 5). This taxonomic picture is supported by our impressions of abundance: the ants one usually sees in Catamarca are leaf-cutters, whereas in Arizona they are granivores. Although leaf-cutters did carry off rolled oats when it was used as bait in Catamarca, they showed no interest in whole canary seeds. Apparently ants select foods to a great extent on the basis of their geometric and handling properties (Pulliam, 1975). In autumn and winter Arizona's ants remove whole seeds almost as fast as they are deposited.

A few species of granivorous ants do occur in the Monte, and harvesting rate of *Phalaris* seeds from our trays by ants is similar in both areas (Table 6-19). The difference occurs in mid-autumn when Catamarca ants were

TABLE 6-19 *Consumption of* Phalaris *Seeds from Feeding Trays (in grams consumed/grams offered)*

Arizona month	I	II	III	IV	V	VI	VII	VIII	IX	X	XI	XII
Catamarca month	VII	VIII	IX	I	XI	XII	I	II	III	IV	V	VI
Ants												
Larrea stands												
Arizona	—	0/225	—	—	—	—	68/375	—	—	261/480	30/225	5/225
Catamarca	—	0/270	—	0/280	12/960	0/700	0/520	—	—	—	91/300	—
Dry Wash												
Arizona	—	15/225	—	—	—	—	0/225	—	—	90/480	27/210	15/225
Catamarca	—	0/270	—	0/280	30/1200	21/600	128/600	—	—	—	114/400	—
Mammals												
Larrea stands												
Arizona	—	135/450	—	—	—	—	151/450	—	—	90/225	116/450	92/450
Catamarca	—	0/160	—	0/280	5/1200	2/750	4/560	—	—	—	0/200	—
Dry Wash												
Arizona	—	400/420	—	—	—	—	64/450	—	—	201/225	362/450	360/435
Catamarca	—	3/180	—	3/300	0/1200	2/750	20/200	—	—	—	0/200	—

taking a larger fraction of seeds than Arizona ants. Perhaps ants in Argentina, not having to compete with mammals, spread their activities out in time. More extensive sampling is needed to determine whether these differences are significant and whether they are sufficient to compensate for absence of mammalian impact in Argentina. Whether they do or not, it remains puzzling that Argentinian granivorous ants are not richer in species and more abundant than they are.

Birds

Although various seed-eating birds are found in deserts, birds rarely consumed seeds from our feeding trays, despite the fact that in at least one study plot such birds were the most conspicuous vertebrates. There was a tendency for Arizona birds to take more than Catamarca birds: 5.1 percent of 1,347 g offered and 2.8 percent of 1,335 g at Arizona wash and *Larrea* stations respectively, versus 1.0 percent of 2,640 g and 1.5 percent of 2,810 g in similar Catamarca stations. Nevertheless, because the rate of seed harvesting by birds in both continents is so small as to be similar in magnitude to our experimental error (see Table 6-20), there may be no real differences.

The seasonal variation in bird granivory was also less than expected. Although both deserts were studied during the cooler months, the period when finch-like birds are more granivorous than at any other time, our cool month data show very little increase in seed consumption in Arizona over the harvest month of October and a drop in Catamarca from the warm months of October, November, and December.

An experiment in which seed trays were left in one place for five to nine days and filled periodically demonstrated two things. First, birds were easily capable of taking canary seeds from the experimental apparatus. Second, after a few days birds began taking substantial quantities from trays in both habitats. Apparently the mode of operation of granivorous birds in the Sonoran Desert is that of mobile predators adept at finding and exploiting patches of superabundant seeds. Our general observations indicate that flocks

TABLE 6-20 *Percentage Consumption of* Phalaris *Seeds During Three Comparable Months, February (August), July (January), and November (May). (Arizona months are given first, followed by Catamarca in parentheses.)*

	Larrea stand		Dry wash	
	Arizona	Catamarca	Arizona	Catamarca
Ants	11.9	8.3	6.4	19.1
Mammals	29.8	0.4	62.6	4.0
Birds	5.0	1.2	7.3	0.3
Average % removed	15.6	3.3	25.4	7.8

of seed-eating birds are vagile and unpredictably dense in the Monte which fits with the pattern of seed predation in our experiments.

Based on his studies of arid grassland sparrows about 150 km from Silver Bell, H. R. Pulliam (pers. comm.) estimates that during a ten-hour winter day a sparrow must consume one seed of the average size available in the habitat about every three seconds to satisfy its basic metabolic needs. This seems possible only if it can find high density of seeds. Therefore, whether or not there are competing granivorous rodents, birds may be unable to exploit scattered seeds on the desert floor except possibly as supplements to an otherwise insectivorous diet.

Invertebrate Seed Predators

There are considerably more species of bruchids (pea weevils) in Catamarca than in Arizona (Kingsolver, in press), but little is known about their abundances and the number of species of plants they attack. In our project, we measured attack rates by bruchids on several species of *Prosopis*, especially *P. chilensis* and *P. flexuosa* in Catamarca and *P. velutina* in Arizona. Though meager, these data do not suggest significant differences in within-host species richness of bruchids between the two areas.

Collections of freshly fallen pods from twelve species of *Prosopis* in South America and three species in North America revealed a low (1–25 percent) rate of damage to seeds in newly mature pods, but there was considerable intraspecific variability (Solbrig and Cantino, 1975). The three species from South America belonging to the section *Strombocarpa* exhibited less damage than the remaining species in the section *Algarobia*, but the significance of this observation is not evident. Data on the course of bruchid infestations on fruits after they have fallen are available only for *P. flexuosa* in Argentina. They indicate a relatively constant percentage of damaged seeds during the first five weeks the pods are on the ground but an approximately linear increase in damage from the fifth to the fifteenth week. Again, there was a great deal of inter-tree variability, even between trees growing near one another. Under current circumstances this increase in bruchid attack does not normally occur because most pods are quickly eaten by mammals, chiefly by goats and horses in Catamarca and possibly cattle in Arizona. General rates of seed destruction might be higher in Catamarca than in Arizona, but our data are insufficient to tell this even for *Prosopis* (Solbrig and Cantino, 1975). Nothing is known about other genera.

Seasonality

Only three months of our data come from strictly comparable periods in the two deserts (Arizona's February, July, and November; Catamarca's August, January, and May). Because these deserts are so seasonal, it is important to distinguish real differences from artifacts of seasonal change. Table 6-20 shows the data from the three comparable months only. As regards birds and mammals, these more restricted data are very similar to the total data set. The ant data in the smaller sample indicate that ants in Catamarca dry washes have more impact than those in Arizona. Similarly, the creosote habitat shows nearly equivalent ant impacts in the two continents, whereas the whole set of data had suggested a much smaller ant impact in Catamarca. The primary reason for the change is that no data on ants are available from Catamarca to compare with Arizona in October. Thus most of the ants' harvesting activity in Arizona is excluded from the more restricted sample. It is unclear what the results would be if we had data from April in Catamarca. Even without the April sample, one may safely conclude ants are unlikely to make up for the absence of granivorous mammals in Catamarca. The average removed by all consumers from our trays during these three months was considerably higher in Arizona (Table 6-20).

Overall Comparison

Catamarca has much less rodent granivory, a richer bruchid fauna, and a poorer granivorous ant fauna than Arizona. Also, although birds seem similarly unimportant as granivores in both deserts, Catamarca harbors three species of parrots while Arizona has none.

The comparative fate of seeds in the two deserts is not easy to assess. At present, because of much lower rodent pressure and similar or lower pressure from ants, birds, and bruchids, it appears that seeds have a greater chance of surviving in Argentina. But if feral farm animals are preserving Argentine legume seeds from almost certain bruchid parasitism, then current conditions are not indicative of those natural to that system.

The reason for the absence of rodent granivores is probably historical. G. G. Simpson (1970) described a family of South American marsupials, the Argyrolagidae, which were convergent with the Heteromyidae. For some reason, probably associated with influx of North American predators near the time of the completion of the Panamanian isthmus (G. G. Simpson, 1950), this family of kangaroo-rat-like marsupials became extinct one or two million years ago. Considering the specialized kidneys and behavior patterns needed for mammalian granivory, we suspect that there has been insufficient time to reevolve granivorous rodents in South America.

Climatic explanations for the differences are less satisfying. The most prominent climatic difference between the deserts is the lack of winter rainfall in the Monte, but mammalian granivores are not dependent on either winter annuals or a more uniform distribution of seed production throughout the year. North America has varied desert climatic regimes, and all of them have rich faunas of granivorous rodents, especially heteromyids. This includes deserts like the Mohave where summer rainfall is absent and winter rainfall may not occur for several years in a row. It also includes parts of the

Chihuahuan Desert which have good summer rains but are dry in the winter. In fact, the more variable and unpredictable the environment, the more valuable is granivorous specialization. J. H. Brown (1973) has hypothesized that this is precisely the cause of the emphasis on granivory in arid North America; it should be even more so in the Monte.

If history explains the mammalian difference, and birds are unimportant in the two deserts for basic metabolic reasons, then why have the granivorous ants not increased in abundance in Argentina? And why have the bruchids done so well? We can only speculate.

Pulliam and Brand (1975) have found that birds, mammals, and ants experience little intertaxon granivorous competition because each is restricted to seeds of a certain phenotype and/or phenology. For example, seeds with awns are easily handled by ants, but not by birds (which prefer spherical seeds). Possibly seeds with some toxins are difficult for ants to consume, but they may not be protected from the detoxification capacity of a mammalian liver. Conversely, minuscule seeds may be taken by ants but not by mammals. If such differences or similar ones exist, then it is possible to view interactions between ants and mammals as mutualistic in the long term. Unless ants are important seed dispersal agents, plant seeds should evolve to be difficult for ants to utilize *if there are no mammals*. Moreover, in the absence of mammals seeds specialized in escape from mammals at the expense of defense against ants should be selected against. Thus, mammalian granivores exert selective pressures which, in evolutionary time, drive some seeds into the mandibles of ants. This notion is similar to one recently proposed by Charnov et al. (1976), who suggest that the foraging of one consumer should often force individual potential food animals into situations where they are less susceptible to that consumer but more susceptible to another one. The concept developed by Charnov et al. depends on mobile victims and can operate over short time spans whereas the present idea, which allows for fixed and nonplastic victim individuals, depends on enough time for evolutionary changes.

The scenario suggested by this theory is that three million years ago, South American deserts harbored granivorous biota much like that of present day North America. When the Argyrolagidae became extinct, granivorous ants either exterminated those plants whose seeds had been defended primarily against mammalian granivores, or caused them to evolve effective anti-ant characteristics. Richness and abundance of these ants declined because there were no counter selective pressures to prevent the evolution of excellent defenses of seeds against ants. (Inherent in this statement is an assumption that productivity and richness are positively correlated. For justification, see J. H. Brown, 1975. It also assumes that taxonomic richness is a better clue to the true impact of ants on seeds than our seed trials, which used a foreign seed selected because of its *appeal* to ants, birds, and mammals.) Bruchids infest fallen seeds until they are virtually all parasitized and because of their small sizes should be able to specialize more narrowly on their hosts than ants or mammals (see Hutchinson and MacArthur, 1959, and Rosenzweig, 1968a, for theory, and Janzen, 1971, for evidence that bruchids in some places actually can and do specialize to a very narrow extent). Hence bruchids and legumes undergo adaptive radiation.

This situation, while not ephemeral, is nevertheless not stable. Eventually, as mammalian granivores reevolve, the bruchids — not able to store seeds — once again become limited to the seeds they can consume before ants and mammals remove them. Moreover, they will decline to the richness which that productivity can support. Ant-susceptible seeds will reappear, and ants will simultaneously rediversify. The effect of large herbivores on bruchids and legumes could be much the same, because they reduce bruchid productivity (Solbrig and Cantino, 1975) by ingesting pods full of healthy seeds and reducing leaf surface areas making less energy available for seed production.

Unfortunately, the obvious method of testing the above explanation is morally unacceptable. Were heteromyids ever to be introduced to Catamarca, we predict a floral cataclysm. Many plants devoid of defense against rodent granivores would become extinct and carry their seed parasites and any other hangers-on to a similar fate. We must seek subtler methodology with less disastrous consequences.

FLOWERS –FLOWER VISITOR SYSTEM*

Action of Natural Selection on the Breeding System and Floral Characters

Because inbreeding (or asexual reproduction) involves a low energetic cost relative to outbreeding, and assures reproductive success, one might assume that it would be the dominant plant breeding system. In most areas, however, outcrossing taxa are more common than self-pollinating species. It is assumed that selection for outcrossing as a reproductive strategy is related to the fact that it results in more variable offspring than those produced by selfing and that, in most environments, the probability of survival is higher for variable than for uniform offspring (Williams, 1975). However, the degree of outcrossing versus selfing is often flexible and depends on plant life history, the strength of selection for variability, and the kinds and abundances of potential pollen vectors. Table 6-21 gives a generalized summary of the possible costs and benefits of various breeding systems and the use of different agents for pollen transfer. However, the relative costs versus benefits differ in different environments. We would, however, expect comparable selection for breeding systems and for the utilization of the same spectrum of pollinators in similar environments. Because of the restrictions imposed by hot desert environments, certain breeding systems and methods of pollen transfer appear to have a higher probability of success than others. Conse-

*By J. L. Neff, B. B. Simpson, and A. R. Moldenke.

TABLE 6-21 *Relative Benefits and Liabilities of Different Methods of Pollen Transfer*

Vector	Benefits	Liabilities
None = Selfing	Reduction or elimination of rewards and attractants High efficiency of fertilization	Reduced variability of offspring
Physical Environment (Wind or water)	No investment in rewards or attractants Permits outcrossing under conditions inimicable to biotic vectors	Ineffective in calm air. Transfer efficiency falls rapidly with distance Requires a large investment in male gametes (most of which are lost due to random dispersal)
Small Invertebrates	Modest investment in rewards per flower	Short cruising range of individual vectors Small pollen transfer per visit
Large Invertebrates	Long cruising radii of individual vectors Increased potential for pollen transfer per visit	Large investment in rewards per floral unit
Vertebrates	Very long cruising range Potential for transfer of large amounts of pollen per visit.	Very large investment in rewards necessary

quently, Table 6-22 attempts to examine the same array of costs and benefits indicated in Table 6-21 specifically in relation to hot desert habitats. Analysis of this table and an assessment of the life forms present in the study areas (Chapter 4) allows us to make some predictions about the breeding systems and pollination syndromes expected in hot desert environments.

Ephemeral species comprise an important component of the spring and summer flora of Silver Bell and a substantial part of the summer flora at Andalgalá. Selfing is highly correlated with the annual habit throughout the world and should correspondingly be high desert ephemerals. Annuals have only one opportunity to produce seeds and are presumably often facultative selfers because the ability to self-pollinate insures production of some off-spring even if they are not cross-pollinated. In addition, because of their short life span, the value of offspring variability may be less than for plants whose offspring encounter an unpredictable array of environmental changes over several years. In contrast, we expect most desert perennials to be under selection for outcrossing.

Within the framework of outcrossing, some methods of pollen transfer appear to be more probable in hot deserts than others. While wind is abundant in deserts, the use of wind as a pollination mechanism is enhanced by several characteristics associated with plant growth, namely, very close proximity of plants, synchronous flowering over large areas, reduced or absent foliage at the times of anthesis, and exposure of large, moist stigmatic surfaces that readily intercept pollen. Since desert shrubs are often widely

TABLE 6-22 *Relative Advantages and Disadvantages of Methods of Pollen Transfer in Hot Desert Environments*

Vector	Advantages	Disadvantages	In what plants expected
None – Selfing	Biotic and abiotic vector systems often unreliable due to unstable climatic pattern	No special disadvantage relative to other environments	Most prevalent in annuals. Facultative in all groups with the possible exception of the most "predictable" succulents and phreatophytes
Wind	Frequent strong winds Limited foliage present to obscure wind movements	Plants (particularly perennials) widely spaced Large stigmatic surfaces are vulnerable to desiccation during the hottest part of the year	Primarily in groups with growth and reproduction tuned to the cool seasons
Small Invertebrates	Warm temperatures favorable for flight. Nest (over-wintering) sites abundant	Period of activity often restricted by sharp diurnal fluctuations	Common in all groups. characterized by high density and/or low inter-plant distance (annuals)
Large Invertebrates	Warm temperatures favorable for flight. Nest (over-wintering) sites abundant	Period of activity often restricted by midday heat	In species or situations with relatively large interplant distances (perennials)
Vertebrates	Very long cruising range.	Foraging periods strongly restricted by midday heat. Heavy reward demand for moisture. Limited water availability will not permit a prolonged enough flowering period to sustain resident vector populations	Not expected

spaced, tend to bloom patchily, and exposed, large stigmas suffer from the desiccating effects of high temperatures, we would expect a low incidence of wind pollination relative to that found in more mesic temperate habitats. Similarly, we would expect a relative paucity of either vertebrates or social bees and wasps as common agents of pollen transfer. Both of these animal groups (assuming the vertebrates are resident community members) depend on long-term supplies of abundant nectar and, in some cases, also pollen. Because of low and temporally restricted precipitation in deserts, there is no long-term food supply abundant enough to support populations of either flower feeding social Hymenoptera or nectarivorous vertebrates. In contrast, nonsocial insects, particularly bees, wasps, and flies, should be ideal pollen vectors in hot deserts. These insects are favored by warm temperatures for maximum activity and dry, open areas for nest sites. Both of these conditions abound in hot deserts.

Therefore, at the two desert study areas we expected a general convergence of major pollen vectors and levels of inbreeding versus outbreeding in annuals and perennials. However, though plants may be utilizing the same general classes of pollinators in the two desert systems, there are a number of ways in which they might differ in terms of how they share pollen vectors. In any species, sexually reproducing individuals (assuming they are not obligate selfers) compete for pollen vectors that transfer the largest quantity of pollen from conspecific individuals. Plant characteristics that tend to maintain constancy of floral visits to conspecific individuals will be selectively advantageous. Such characteristics include specialized floral morphologies that allow easy recognition and help to reduce the preempting of floral rewards by other insects, or specialized rewards that are required by, or capable of being used by, only one or a few flower visitors. Another method of promoting constancy is by altering the time of floral production. If a flower is capable of being used by relatively generalized flower visitors but blooms when few other taxa are producing flowers, it will receive relatively constant service from pollinators. In addition the attractiveness of an individual is increased by increasing the number of flowers available and/or the amount of rewards per flower. However, the number of flowers produced and the amount of pollen and nectar (or other rewards) is, in part, determined by the amount of energy available when the plants are able to flower. Within the limits of energy available for production of flowers and their constituent rewards, intraspecific competition will tend to select those individuals that have attracted more successful pollen vectors. Within a species, such individuals are often those with the most impressive arrays of flowers and/or large amounts of rewards in each floral unit.

On the other side of the coin, an insect will not visit a flower unless, in the long run, it is advantageous to do so (Heindrich, 1975b). Essentially, animal-mediated pollination is a side effect of predation on floral products. The floral resources on which flower visitors feed are often provided by the plant only for the purpose of inducing and maintaining floral visitation. Such resources include floral parts, nectar, oils, and pollen. Within each of these rewards there are a host of possible variations, most of which are little understood. On energetic grounds flowers with the largest and most concentrated supplies of nectar would be the optimum flower for all nectivorous flower feeders. Likewise flowers producing the most pollen would be most heavily visited by all pollen-collecting bees. However, the availability of the nectar to insects of different sizes and with differing mouth parts, the presence and amount of amino acids in the nectar, the presence of toxic compounds in the nectar, and even the kinds of sugars can determine the desirability of nectar to different flower visitors. Likewise, floral parts are consumed only by certain groups of insects and oils can be harvested and metabolized only by a restricted number of specialized bees. Pollen itself appears to have, in addition to variation in size and consistency, a wide array of nutrients, vitamins, hormones, and other chemicals that determine its attractiveness to, and utilization by, different insects.

Thus flowers are not equivalent in the kinds of rewards they produce and their differences are not primarily related simply to the quantities of rewards. In general, similarities in both kinds and abundances of rewards between plant taxa are correlated with their degree of evolutionary relatedness although both floral diversification within plant families for different pollinators (Grant, 1976) and convergence of unrelated taxa for similar pollen vectors (Faegri and van der Pijl, 1971; Vogel, 1969) have both been documented. Similarly insects are not catholic in their choice of flowers and their preference rankings are not determined solely by the quantity of energy contained in different flowers.

Given the variation in floral morphology and resources, it is not surprising that potential pollen vectors vary in level of specificity to different plant taxa. The tightness or looseness of a given flower–flower visitor interaction is determined by a complex array of factors including the genetic constraints of both plant and animal as well as the severity of inter- and intraspecific competition for resources by flower visitors and for the more efficient transfer agents by the various plant taxa. At the outset of this study we expected, for several reasons, that the arrays of flower–flower visitor interactions in the two desert systems would be similar. First, about half the dominant species in the two areas are congeneric and would thus tend to have similar floral morphologies and reward structures. Second, the potential array of pollen vectors was similar in the two regions. Finally, because of the temporal restriction of water availability we expected flowering patterns to be comparable. We therefore predicted similarities in the breeding systems of the various components of the floras, patterns of flowering phenology, emphasis on different floral rewards, and, possibly, in the quantity of the total resource base available to flower feeders. Likewise, we initially predicted similarities in the number and classes of pollen vectors and convergent patterns in levels of specificity and foraging behavior. As discussed below, many of these predictions were not verified.

Patterns in Flowers and Floral Rewards

As we predicted, the annuals of the two desert scrub areas we investigated showed a high level of facultative selfing. In addition, more than any other group of plant species, they exhibited narrowly restricted relationships with potential pollinators (Table 6-23). Associated with this specificity are unique morphological features such as the large, showy corollas of *Eschscholzia mexicana* (NA), the small, narrow corolla tubes of *Cryptantha* spp. and *Gilia* spp. (both NA) and striking color patterns such as those found in *Sclerophyllax* sp. (SA) or *Phacelia* (NA). Still other annual taxa have flowers that open for only a short period of the day (e.g., *Mentzelia* (NA), *Malocothrix* (NA), *Oenothera* (NA)).

Because of the presence of winter rainfall at Silver Bell, our northern site supports a rich spring annual flora. These rains essentially charge the soil with moisture before early spring temperatures start to rise. Spring annuals begin to germinate in February and bloom through April. In a given season, the number of germinating and blooming individuals is determined both by the seed pool produced the previous springs and by the amount of winter rainfall immediately preceding the blooming period. This spring annual floral component is lacking at Andalgalá because there are only light, unreliable winter rains. The additional presence of a group of widely diverse plant species at Silver Bell relative to Andalgalá produces a higher resource base and is correlated with a greater diversity of flower visitors and higher proportion of specialized insect taxa at the northern site (Table 6-26).

The emphasis of our studies on plant breeding systems was, however, the perennial taxa. In these studies, we included all of the perennial species, except members of the Cactaceae, which were recorded as having a coverage or density value in any of the transect plots (see Chapter 4) of 1 percent or more. For all of these species the major pollen vectors, the breeding systems, and the reward structures were determined (Tables 6-24, 6-25).

As predicted, few of these species depend on vertebrates, and none on social Hymenoptera as pollen vectors. The one species in North America that relies heavily on hummingbirds as pollinating agents, *Fouquieria splendens,* blooms early in the spring when migrating populations of Costa's hummingbirds are present. None of the dominant plant taxa at Andalgalá is adapted to bird pollination. No species in either area reproduces exclusively by vegetative reproduction although three species at the northern site and one at the southern site produce underground rooting stems. Contrary to predictions, wind pollination was found in several dominants at Silver Bell. However, it was totally absent as a pollination mechanism among dominants near Andalgalá. Significant in this regard is the fact that all wind pollinated taxa bloom early in the year when temperatures are still cool (Chapter 4). A shift to early blooming is not possible at Andalgalá because there is little winter rainfall. Correlated with wind pollination is the presence of reduced, green unisexual flowers. Two wind-pollinated species at Silver Bell are monoecious and one is dioecious.

TABLE 6-23 *Seasonal Activity Patterns of Bees*

	Spring only		Summer only		Silver Bell Both spring and summer		Total	
Specialist	33	(14)*	34	(31)	4	(1)	71	(46)
Generalist	67		33		17		117	
Total	100		67		21		188	

					Bolsón de Pipanaco			
Specialist	20	(0)	6	((5)	6	(0)	32	(5)
Generalist	39		16		37		84	
Total	51		22		43		116	

Host plants of bee species present in both spring and summer

Andalgalá		Silver Bell	
Larrea	(4)	*Larrea*	(1)
Prosopis	(1)	*Prosopis*	(1)
Cacti	(1)	Cacti	(1)
		Euphorbia	(1)?

*Species feeding on annuals or herbaceous perennials are indicated by parentheses.

A comparison of the levels of self-compatibility exhibited by the dominant perennials studied shows that in this character also, the two areas strikingly differ (Table 6-26). Only one of fourteen North American species is self-compatible whereas almost half of the South America ones are self-compatible. However, of the self-fertile species at Andalgalá, only one, *Bulnesia retamo*, regularly self-pollinates in nature. Consequently, almost all perennials at both sites require an external agent for pollen transfer to set seed. Nevertheless, our results show that there is more divergence among North American than among South American perennials in respect to their utilization of alternative pollen vectors. Nine of fourteen dominants in the Sonoran area utilize insect vectors whereas all thirteen Monte species depend on insect pollination.

For those taxa utilizing insect vectors, we looked for evidence that features of their flowering had been influenced by competition for pollen vectors. The most obvious possibility was differences in floral morphology. However, the floral types found among dominants at Andalgalá fall into only two broad classes. One group, predominantly species of the lower bajadas and flats, consists of medium sized, open, "dish-shaped," regular or slightly zygomorphic, yellow flowers. Species which have this type of flowers include *Larrea divaricata, L. cuneifolia, Bulnesia retamo, Cercidium praecox, Tricomaria usillo, Zuccagnia punctata, Cassia aphylla,* and, to some extent,

TABLE 6-24 *Richness of Insect Species Visiting Flowers and Rewards Offered by Silver Bell Perennials*

Plant Taxon	Rewards offered	Relative richness of visitors*	Insect groups†
Acacia constricta	Little pollen no nectar	Low	Occasional pollen collecting bees.
Acacia greggii	Nectar	High	Preferred by large wasps; nectaring bees; major summer lep. species; bee flies.
Prosopis velutina	Pollen & nectar	High	[1] 60 bee species (6 common); wasps; beetles; small flies [2] low diversity
Cercidium floridum *Cercidium microphyllum* *Olneya tesota*	Pollen & nectar	Low	Primarily 3 bee species – one dominant "specialist," 2 generalists
Krameria spp.	Oils; some pollen	Low: 1–2 species	Exclusively female *Paracentris* bees.
Larrea tridentata	Pollen & nectar	Medium	[1] Primarily specialists; 10–12 common bees; [2] Several large polylectic bee species
Janusia gracilis	Oil	Low: 1–2 species	Exclusively female *Paracentris* bees
Jatropha cardiphylla	Nectar	Low	Occasional nectaring polylectic wasps: small leps; flies.
Simmondsia chinensis	–	0	Wind pollinated
Condalia spp.	Nectar	Medium	Primarily small solitary wasps and bees
Fouquieria splendens	Nectar (pollen)	Low	Hummingbirds; occasional large bees; sphyngid moths
Cacti Night blooming Ceroids	Nectar, pollen, floral tube	Low	At night, beetles, sphyngids (?) early morning, bees.
Day blooming (*Opuntia, Mammalaria, Echinocereus, Echinocactus*	Pollen & nectar	Low	Primarily 4–5 cactus specialists, about 7 other small bees.
Lycium andersoni	Pollen & nectar	Low	Primarily anthophorid bees; butterflies
Encelia farinosa	Nectar & pollen	Low	Butterflies & large syrphid flies
Ambrosia deltoidea	–	0	Wind pollinated

*Low = 0–5 species; Medium = 6–20 species; High = 21–50 species.
†1 = spring; 2 = summer blooms.

TABLE 6-25 *Richness of Insect Species Visiting Flowers and Rewards Offered by Perennial Plants of the Andalgalá Region*

Taxon	Rewards offered	Relative richness of visitors*	Insect groups†
Cassia aphylla	Pollen Floral parts	Low	Females of polylectic bee species; lepidopteran larvae; beetles
Tricomaria	Oils	Very Low	Essentially 2 species (females) of *Paracentris*.
Cercidium praecox	Nectar & pollen	Medium	Primarily larger polylectic bees; 1 rare Caesalp. specialist; beetles; solitary wasps; flies
Prosopis sect. *algarobia*	Pollen & nectar	Very High	Many bees (80+ sp., 15 specialists); lepidopterans; beetles; bee flies; wasps. 10–15 bee species common
Prosopis torquata	Nectar & pollen	High	Solitary bees; many lepidopterans in summer
Acacia furcatispina	Nectar	High	Preferred by large wasps; nectaring bees; major summer lepidopteran species; bee flies
Acacia aroma	Little pollen no nectar	Low	Occasional pollen collecting bees
Atamisquea	Nectar (pollen)	High	Major nectar plant after *Prosopis* blooms, solitary bees, wasps; bee flies; lepidopterans
Jatropha spp.	Nectar	Medium	Female solitary bees; wasps; muscoid flies
Bulnesia retama	Pollen & nectar	High	[1] Large early bees [2] Polylectic species
Larrea divaricata	Pollen & nectar	High	[1] Abundant zygophyll specialists; wasps [2] Wasps
Larrea cuneifolia	Pollen & nectar	High	[2] Solitary bees; polylectic species away from washes; wasps; bee flies.
Lantana	Nectar	Low	Primarily butterflies

*Low = 0–5 species; Medium = 6–20 species; High = 21–50 species.
† 1 = spring; 2 = summer blooms.

TABLE 6-26 *Characteristics of Reproductive Systems of Dominant Perennials.*

Species	Vegetative propagation	Moneocious	Dioecious	Self-incompatible
Silver Bell				
Cercidium floridum	−	−	−	+
Cercidium microphyllum	−	−	−	+
Prosopis velutina	−	−	−	+
Calliandra eriophylla	+	−	−	+
Acacia constricta	−	−	−	+
Acacia greggii	−	−	−	+
Krameria grayi	−	−	−	+
Larrea tridentata	−	−	−	+
Simmondsia chinensis	−	−	+	+
Jatropha cardiophylla	+	−	+	+
Fouquieria splendens	−	−	−	−
Ambrosia deltoidea	−	+	−	+
Ambrosia dumosa	−	+	−	+
Encelia farinosa	−	−	−	+
Total	2	2	2	13
Bolsón de Pipanaco				
Cassia aphylla	−	−	−	−
Cercidium praecox	−	−	−	+
Zuccagnia punctata	−	−	−	+
Prosopis torquata	−	−	−	+
Prosopis chilensis	−	−	−	+
Prosopis nigra	−	−	−	+
Acacia furcatispina	−	−	−	+
Acacia aroma†	−	−	−	+
Larrea cuneifolia	−	−	−	−
Bulnesia retamo	−	−	−	−
Trichomaria usillo	−	−	−	−
Jatropha macrocarpa	−	+	−	−
Total	0	1	0	7
Totals in both areas	1	3	2	20

*A χ^2 of the 2 × 5 contingency table shows that the numbers of species falling into each class of breeding system in the two desert scrub areas differ significantly from one another (p < 0.001, χ^2 = 26.73). The χ^2 value (4.338) between the number of self-compatible vs. self-incompatible species in the two areas is significant at the 0.05 level.

†The species appears to self-pollinate in nature.

Prosopis torquata. Of these species only *Tricomaria usillo* has an ultraviolet pattern displayed as a spot on the slightly larger petal. These flowers can loosely be considered as unspecialized "bee-flowers." However, although they appear relatively similar to us, they are certainly easily distinguished by insects.

The second general class of flowers common at Andalgalá is small, pale colored, and clustered into spherical or spicate inflorescences. Species with this floral morphology are most common along washes or on upper bajadas and include *Prosopis chilensis, P. flexuosa, Acacia furcatispina,* and *Mimosa ephedroides*.

While both of these floral syndromes are represented among the dominants at Silver Bell (with *Larrea tridentata* and *Cercidium microphyllum* and *C. floridum* in the first group and *Prosopis velutina* and *Acacia greggii* in the second), several others are also found. The brittle bush, *Encelia farinosa* has large discoid heads, *Olneya tesota* has purple "pea-shaped" flowers, and *Krameria grayi* and *K. parvifolia* have deep purple-pink zygomorphic flowers. Nevertheless, differences in floral morphology are important in maintaining constancy only if they are perceived as such and only if flowers are visited differently by pollinators. For example, although *Cercidium microphyllum* and *C. floridum* differ strikingly in floral morphology from *Olynea tesota* they share the same major pollen vector, *Centris pallida*. In this case, floral constancy is fostered by differences among the three taxa in habitat and blooming times. The two species of *Cercidium* have blooming peaks that are slightly skewed from one another. In addition, *C. microphyllum* is most common on bajadas whereas *C. floridum* is most abundant along washes. The ironwood (*O. tesota*) also occurs on bajadas, but has blooming peak substantially different (although, slightly overlapping) from that of *C. microphyllum*. Species such as *Fouquieria splendens* that use alternative vectors or *Krameria* spp. that offer specialized rewards bloom simultaneously. Flowers of the latter produce oils that are collected by females of the bee genus *Centris*. This oil is mixed with pollen collected from other species such as *Larrea tridentata* or *Cercidium* spp. Obviously, *Krameria* not only can bloom simultaneously with other taxa, but is obligated to do so.

Floral constancy can, therefore, be promoted even if flower visitors are relatively generalized if plant taxa diverge in blooming times or kinds of rewards produced. Among the dominant Argentine shrubs with five-parted yellow flowers, two (*Cassia aphylla* and *Tricomaria usillo*) produce special rewards. Like other members of the genus, *Cassia aphylla* secretes no nectar, but produces abundant pollen in anthers with terminal pores that require a specialized vibratory action to dislodge the pollen. Pollen of *Tricomaria usillo* is rarely collected, and the flowers produce no nectar. Similar to *Krameria* at the northern site, *Tricomaria* produces oils that are collected by female *Centris*. Both of these species, *Cassia aphylla* and *Tricomaria usillo,* must, therefore bloom at the same time as other species from which female bees can derive part or all of their nectar energy sources. The other taxa in the Andalgalá region with yellow, pentamerous flowers bloom in response to rainfall, but appear to differ in response time. The resultant blooming pattern is one in which species only slightly overlap in peak of flower production. As a result of this pattern, generalist pollinators can shift from one species to another (on a local basis) as they come into maximum bloom and thereby maintain partial floral constancy.

Having ascertained that the dominant perennial taxa in the two areas differ with respect to the utilization of major pollen vectors and the emphasis on distinctive floral morphology, blooming time, or specialized rewards as methods for the reduction of competition for pollen vectors, we attempted to determine if, on a community basis, the two areas were comparable in terms of the total resource base available for pollen and nectar feeders. We consequently made estimates of the yearly floral production (biomass), amount of total sugar, and quantity of pollen produced in three parts of the desert ecosystem: a pure *Larrea* flat, a lower, and an upper bajada. These results, shown in Table 6-27, indicate that on *Larrea* flats in the two areas where coverage is similar, the yearly floral biomass production is also similar. Barbour and Diaz (1973) had previously determined that on similar areas of microhabitat, the *Larrea* communities at the two sites were very similar in terms of vegetative structure. However, in terms of floral rewards, our estimates suggest that in comparable years, a hectare of *Larrea* in North America can produce about three times as much total sugar as a comparable hectare near Andalgalá. Pollen production appears to be nearly identical. If production by other species in the ecosystem are included, differences between the two areas are even greater. It is possible that, considering only the dominant, insect-visited perennial species, a hectare on an upper bajada near Silver Bell may produce four times as much floral biomass as a comparable hectare near Andalgalá. Moreover, the flowers in the northern area would produce four times as much pollen and ten times as much sugar as those in the southern area. If the annual component of the flora and the hummingbird-pollinated species at the northern site are added, these differences are further accentuated.

The most important proximate cause of the differences among perennials in floral biomass production and the potential resource base is probably the pattern of blooming of *Cercidium microphyllum*, *C. floridum*, and *Olneya tesota* at Silver Bell versus the somewhat comparable *C. praecox* and *Bulnesia retamo* near Andalgalá. Individuals of the three Arizona taxa are abundant, large, and mass flower early in the spring. Non-wash species at Andalgalá that "mass" flower bloom in summer and are relatively small and produce fewer flowers per unit time and per individual. It is true that *Bulnesia retamo*, perhaps our closest vegetative analogue to *Cercidum microphyllum* that occurs near Andalgalá has been extensively cut out in much of the Monte and replaced by weedy species such as *Acacia furcatispina*. Nevertheless, *Bulnesia retamo* does not exhibit the enormous mass flowering properties of the palo verdes (*Cercidium* spp.) in North America.

TABLE 6-27 *Estimate Floral Biomass, Total Sugar and Pollen Production of Dominant Perennials[a] on* Larrea *Flats*

	Floral biomass per hectare	Total sugar per hectare	Total pollen per hectare
	Larrea flat		
CATAMARCA			
17–20% coverage			
Plots 002 & 007	22–55 kg	1.1–2.9 kg	0.9–2.3 kg
ARIZONA			
16–19% coverage			
Plots 004 & 016	33–61 kg	1.04–2.3 kg	3.1–6.9 kg
	Lower Bajada		
CATAMARCA[b]			
1510 flat	22 kg	1.12 kg	961 gm
ARIZONA[c]	(21)	(1.1)	(902)
Plot 024			
	48 kg	1.7 kg	4.6 kg
	(31)	(1.0)	(3.0)
	Complex Upper Bajada		
CATAMARCA[d]			
Villavil	32 kg	1.4 kg	1.2 kg
	(23)	(1.2)	(.5)
ARIZONA[e]			
Plot 033	120 kg	4.4 kg	10.7 kg
	(30)	(.7)	(2.5)

[a]Includes only animal-pollinated species. Data were gathered in exceptionally wet years (1972 spring in Arizona, 1973/74 summer in Catamarca) and represent more or less maximum values. The plots listed were used for plant numbers per hectare and plant sizes. Phenology follows Yang and Abe (1973a,b,1974) and LeClair et al., 1973, LeClair and Brown, 1974). Numbers in parentheses exclude *Cercidium* in the total. from Simpson, 1977.

[b]Includes *Cercidium praecox, Cassia aphylla, Prosopis torquata, Larrea cuneifolia, Bulnesia retamo,* and *Tricomaria usillo.*

[c]Includes *Cercidium microphyllum, Prosopis velutina, Krameria grayi, Larrea tridentata,* and *Fouquieria splendens.* Data not available for *Olneya tesota.*

[d]Includes *Cercidium praecox, Prosopis torquata, Acacia furcatispina, Larrea cuneifolia, Bulnesia retamo, Tricomaria usillo,* and *Jatropha macrocarpa.*

[e]Includes *Cercidium microphyllum, Krameria grayi, Larrea tridentata, Fouquieria splendens, Jatropha cardiophylla,* and *Encelia farinosa. Olneya tesota* not included.

The Action of Natural Selection on Flower Visitors

Utilizers of the resources provided by flowers should exploit them to maximize their own fitness, making decisions unlikely to lead to maximization of fitness of the host plants. How utilizers accomplish this will depend largely upon the significance of floral resources in their particular life cycles. For many flower visitors, floral rewards are utilized primarily or even exclusively as sources of fuel for the flight muscles of the foraging adults. Among members of this group, nutritional characteristics of the rewards are presumably of minimal importance and the key variables affecting which flowers are to be visited are quantity and quality of energy resources available per flower, rate at which these resources can be extracted per visit, and traveling time between flowers. However, for flower visitors that utilize floral resources both as an adult fuel and for rearing of young, and for flower feeders for whom floral resources may play an important long-term role in body maintenance, energetic consideration are only part of the picture. For these animals floral rewards must provide a total diet including protein, lipids, vitamins and minerals. Pollens and, to more limited extent, nectars do frequently contain all these components, although there is considerable interspecific variation (Baker and Baker, 1973, 1975). Several studies have shown that different pollens may differ significantly in their nutritional value to bees (Maurzio, 1950; Haydak, 1970). Therefore, the composition and balance of floral rewards may often be of greater importance than rate of energy extraction in determining the value of a particular flower to an individual forager.

For those animals for which rate of ingestion of energy while foraging is of prime importance, the rules of simple optimal foraging as outlined in the first section of this chapter should apply. Understanding itineraries of different foragers will depend upon a knowledge of abundance and distribution of floral resources; relative accessibility and ease of extraction of the resources of each floral type by different foragers; and energetic requirements of each forager type. While differences in foraging itineraries are to be expected between different types of foragers due to morphological differences affecting ease of access to nectar supplies of different flowers, this class of forager should ignore utilizable nectar sources encountered while foraging only when flowers yielding high values of energy per unit time are abundant. Consequently, species requiring only energy will tend to be foraging generalists and as such will be evolutionarily difficult for flowers to "manipulate" to their own advantage.

As nutritional requirements become increasingly important, particularly among bees with their close dependence upon floral resources throughout their life cycles, increasing deviations from energy-based optimal foraging considerations are likely. In the absence of detailed knowledge of either reward chemistry or nutritional requirements of most flower feeders, individual foraging patterns may often be difficult to predict or understand. Another factor often of considerable significance for the foraging preferences of pollen-collecting animals is handling time and efficiency. There is wide variation between different plant taxa in pollen size, morphology, and mode of presentation. In many cases an array of morphological attributes optimal for collection and transport of one class of pollen may be suboptimal or even preclude utilization of alternate pollen hosts. Such considerations appear to have been of particular importance in the evolutionary history of bees (Hurd and Linsley, 1975), a group in which many members are characterized by high pollen host specificity (oligolecty). In any case, specialization is most likely, but by no means universal, among foragers for whom floral resources constitute the bulk of the diet for their entire life cycle.

If a specialist achieves increased efficiency or competitive ability in utilization of its preferred hosts, but at the expense of decreased efficiency in utilization of alternate hosts, then from an optimal foraging viewpoint, prevalence of specialist feeding habits is particularly unlikely in warm deserts. Due to climatic unpredictability, warm desert patterns of floral abundance and composition frequently vary considerably yearly and seasonally. Given unpredictably fluctuating food supplies, we might expect generalists capable of utilizing the widest possible array of host plants to prevail. However, several factors suggest that specialization is likely a result of adaptation to floral resources in desert environments, at least among bees. Temporal unpredictability may be slight from the point of view of bees since the same cues utilized by many plants for initiation of bloom, presumably temperature and moisture availability can also be utilized by flower feeders to trigger emergence. Second, flowering seasons in warm deserts tend to be brief, thus minimizing advantages accruing to social forms or long-lived individuals which necessarily must utilize a variety of host plants over a longer season. While flowering may in large measure be temporally predictable in warm deserts, nonetheless a strong element of quantitative unpredictability remains due to large fluctuation in floral abundance. This may be particularly important for univoltine, solitary bees since unlike floral abundance, forager abundance in these species depends largely upon foraging success of females in previous seasons because there is typically no recruitment within a given season. Therefore, solitary bees often have built-in lags between resource abundance and their abundance. A frequent outcome of such a system is periods of intense competition for scarce resources alternating with periods of virtually unlimited resource abundance. If this system favors maximizing minimum fitness (Templeton and Rothman, 1974), minimizing competition through specialization may be favored. Such specialization should entail not only divergence in hosts utilized but also, among species utilizing the same hosts, divergences in foraging times and foraging modes, the latter related to relative foraging efficiency at different levels of resource abundance.

The effects of desert heat and drought are at least partially alleviated for flower feeders since nectar provides a convenient moisture source. Nonetheless, number of adaptations are evident among desert flower feeders which have presumably been molded by pressures for optimizing foraging ability in environments characterized by daily and seasonal extreme temperature fluctuations. Such adaptations are particularly well illustrated among bees but are evident in numerous other desert flower feeders as well. Bees active at dawn or in the relatively cool early spring tend to be large bodied (to lose heat less rapidly) and frequently melanic or otherwise darkly colored for efficient absorption of solar radiation. Bees active during extreme midday heat tend to be much smaller and typically are of pale coloration, frequently with reflective oppressed grey or brown pubescence. In addition to the potential for minimizing heat load, such pale coloration may also serve as camouflage against predators by rendering the insects inconspicuous against pale desert soils.

Since convergence in community structure is dependent in large part on the presence of equivalent physical environments, differences are to be expected in community structure between our two areas when differences in the physical environments are evident. The most important difference between the two sites is the bimodal rainfall distribution in Arizona and unimodal pattern in Catamarca. As suggested in the previous section, this has important implications both for the annual floras and the phenologies of the perennial elements. The presence of two distinct periods favorable for flowering in Arizona coupled with distinctive temperature regimes has led to the development of distinct winter/spring and summer annual floras. This alone should permit a richer flower visiting fauna in Arizona than in Catamarca where only a summer annual bloom is possible. Similar differences are expected among components of the perennial floras which are dependent on rainfall for flowering in any given season.

The major classes of flower visitors of the two areas as well as the types of floral resources they utilize are shown in Table 6-28. While none of the major classes of flower visitors is unique to deserts, the overall similarity of the flower feeding faunas of the two areas is quite striking despite minimal overlap in terms of genera or species shared by the two regions.

Flowers and buds are opportunistically consumed by a number of small mammals in both areas although no quantitative data are available. None of the lizards of the Bolsón de Pipanaco are known to feed on flowers, but two species of the Sonoran desert (*Dipsosarus* and *Sauromalus*) do. None of these vertebrates are of any positive significance as pollinators. Of undoubtedly greater significance are the numerous chewing and sucking insects which feed on flowers in both regions; particularly larval Lepidoptera, adult Coleoptera, and Hemiptera. Since individual flowers are generally short lived in warm deserts, widespread host specificity among chewing insects of limited mobility feeding primarily on flowers is somewhat surprising. A rationale and some data are presented in the previous section on chewing herbivores. With few exceptions, these chewing and sucking insects are flower predators rather than pollinators. One clear exception is the beetles associated with *Prosopanche,* a holoparasitic perennial associated with *Prosopis* in Argentina. The

TABLE 6-28　*Major Flower Feeding Groups of Silver Bell and the Bolsón de Pipanaco*

Taxon	Relative abundance	Pollen	Nectar	Oils	Floral tissues
			Resources utilized		
HYMENOPTERA					
Apoidae (solitary bees)	+++	+++	+++[3]	++[5]	+[1]
Solitary wasps	++	+	++	0	0
Sphecidae	++	+	++	0	0
Eumenidae	++	+	++	0	0
Pompilidae	++	+	++	0	0
Scoloidea	++	+	++	0	0
Masaridae	+	+++	+++	0	
Formicidae – ants	++	0	++	0	++
DIPTERA					
Bombyliidae	+++	+	++	0	0
Syrphidae	+	+	++	0	0
Muscoidea	+	+	++	0	0[2]
LEPIDOPTERA					
Sphyngidae					
Geometridae	+				
Pieridae	to	+	++	0	++[2]
Libytheadae	+++				
Noctuidae					
COLEOPTERA					
Scarabaeidae	++				
Meloidae	to	++	++	0	++[4]
Buprestidae	+++				
OTHER INSECTS					
Hemiptera	++	0	+	0	+
Thysanoptera	++	+	+	0	+
VERTEBRATES					
Hummingbirds	++[7]	+	+++	0	0
Other birds					
(doves, etc.)	+	0	+	0	0
Bats	++[6,7]	++	+++	0	0
Small mammals	+	0	0	0	+
Lizards	+	0	0	0	+

[1] Petals, sepals, etc., used for nest construction
[2] Resource used by larvae only
[3] Particularly long-tongued Meloidae, Cantharidae
[4] Many families
[5] Larval food of *Centris*, collected by adults
[6] North American site only
[7] Transient visitors

+ = infrequently or rarely used
++ = commonly or sometimes used
+++ = abundant or a major resource
0 = not used

large, thick-walled, long-lived flowers possess a trap door device and are obligately pollinated by host specific beetles in which both adults and larvae feed on walls of flowers.

The most abundant group of flower-visiting vertebrates in both desert areas are nectar-feeding hummingbirds. As might be expected, none of the hummingbirds of either area are permanent residents but four to six species may be encountered in both areas as migrants with but a single species usually predominating. In Arizona the primary species is Costa's Hummingbird (*Calypte costae*) which frequently breeds in desert scrub regions during the spring bloom. Although Costa's utilizes a wide variety of flowers, its primary floral host is the red, tubular flowered ocotillo, *Fouquieria splendens,* a semi-succulent whose spring flowering is largely independent of winter rainfall patterns. Other spring migrants utilize essentially the same set of plants as Costa's while the smaller set of late summer or fall migrants utilize a variety of asclepiadaceous or convolvulaceous vines in addition to the sporadic summer ocotillo bloom.

At the Argentine site topography is such that migrant hummingbirds need not traverse the desert floor and none of the dominant shrubs or trees show any obvious adaptations for hummingbird pollination. The most regular hummingbird visitor, *Chlorostilbon aureoventris,* breeds in adjacent mountain canyons and descends to the desert to forage on such shrubs as *Bulnesia, Cercidium, Hyaloseris* and *Tecoma* when they are in bloom. Other migrants are frequently present in very early spring or late summer foraging about the long, tubular-flowered mistletoe, *Psittacanthus cuneifolius* which infests many riparian trees.

While avian floral utilization other than that by hummingbirds appeared to be minimal in Argentina, a variety of birds opportunistically utilizes the flowers of the ocotillo in Arizona while the white-winged dove is a frequent diurnal visitor of flowers of giant saguaro.

One final group of flower-feeding vertebrates, nectivorous bats, are found only at the Arizona site despite their presence through most of the American tropics. These migratory bats, chiefly *Leptonycteris nivalis* and *Chaeronycteris mexicana,* arrive in spring from their southern wintering grounds to forage upon pollen and nectar provided by the giant saguaro and various *Agave* species. The giant, nocturnally opening blossoms of the Argentina analogue of the saguaro, *Trichocereus terscheckii,* are exclusively insect-pollinated in the Andalgalá area.

Far more abundant and diverse than flower-visiting verebrates at either site are pollen and nectar feeding insects. Typical of flower feeding faunas throughout the world is the prevalence of Hymenoptera, Lepidoptera, and Diptera, with solitary bees, wasps, and beeflies being particularly abundant and diverse. A basic division in foraging patterns lies between the bees, who must harvest large amounts of floral resources to provision their larval cells, and other groups such as wasps, flies, and butterflies, who utilize floral resources primarily as an adult energy source. As male bees do not provision larval cells, they might be expected to fall into the latter group. However, since mating frequently occurs on host flowers foraging patterns often tend to parallel those of the female bees.

At both areas, numbers of species and of individuals of Lepidoptera were observed to fluctuate widely from year to year during the study period. Irregular outbreaks and periods of low density appeared to show no direct correlation with resource availability for either adults or larvae and may possibly be due to variation in parasite or predator pressure. As expected, adults of all species of this group studied appeared to be polyphagic in their floral host utilization patterns. The most extensively utilized plant taxa include mimosoid shrubs, various annual and perennial members of the Compositae and a variety of other shrubs such as *Lantana* or *Lippia* having flowers with relatively deep seated nectaries, that are commonly aggregated into heads or similar inflorescences.

Utilizing a different set of hosts are the larger, more active lepidopterans such as the long-tongued hawkmoths (Sphyngidae). Primarily nocturnal or crepuscular and with relatively high energy requirements, these large moths tend to frequent the large, pale, nectar-rich flowers of such nocturnally blooming species as *Habranthus, Nicotiana,* and various Bromeliaceae in Argentina and species of *Oenothera, Nicotiana,* and *Datura* in Arizona.

Another abundant group of nectar feeders prevalent at both sites in the bee flies (Bombyliidae). Their abundance is probably related to the abundance of Orthoptera and fossorial Hymenoptera, groups on which the larvae of many bombyliid species are nest or egg parasites. Like lepidopterans, adults tend to be polyphagic, but differences in foraging patterns are evident among species due to differences in mouthpart lengths. Very similar patterns are observed among another prominent and diverse group of flower visitors, the solitary wasps. Typical of nectar feeders, virtually all are polyphagic. Since the majority of species have relatively short mouthparts, they visit primarily plants with shallow flowers and readily accessible nectaries such as mimosoid legumes, various composites (*Baccharis* and *Tessaria*), most Euphorbiaceae along with a wide variety of annuals. A few specialized sphecoid wasps do possess elongate mouthparts allowing them access to deeply set nectaries of various members of the Compositae and Boraginaceae.

Clearly the dominant group of flower-feeding insects at both desert sites is bees with more than half the species of dominant perennials at each site being exclusively or predominately bee pollinated. Based on extensive field observations and collections of over 10,000 individuals, we found that both deserts have rich faunas of solitary bees (Table 6-23) while social forms are virtually absent. Excluding the recently introduced honeybee, (*Apis mellifera*), whose continued presence may be attributed to the local apiarists, no eusocial bees were found at Silver Bell while only queens of one bumblebee, *Bombus opifex,* were occasionally observed during early spring at Andalgalá, possibly immigrants from the neighboring mountains.

While the Arizona site is richer in bee species than the comparable area in the Bolsón de Pipanaco (188 vs. 116), the factors leading to this difference include more than differences in rainfall patterns. The most obvious and direct result of differences in rainfall patterns at the two sites is the presence of a rich spring annual flora in Arizona along with an associated rich fauna of specialist bees. These floral and faunal components are absent at Andalgalá where the spring bloom is essentially restricted to riparian perennials and succulents. Nonetheless, bee diversity at Andalgalá is actually highest during spring despite the very restricted set of potential floral hosts. Additionally, while only twenty-one species of nonparasitic bees (12 percent of the total) were active during both spring and summer blooms at Silver Bell, members of forty-three species (41 percent) were so at Andalgalá. More importantly, species of Monte bees with long flight seasons include such abundant species as *Centris brethesii, Svastrides zebra,* and various species of *Xylocopa* and *Megachile;* all robust species that are the chief pollinators of the majority of Monte perennials, plus many of the annuals. A possible basis for these extended periods of activity at Andalgalá is the presence of several subterranean river systems which permit low level but virtually continuous flowering by several species of riparian shrubs and trees throughout the dry spring and early summer. Such flowering patterns apparently provide a sufficiently continuous floral resource base for these large, wide-ranging polylectic bees to permit virtually continuous foraging activity along these riparian "refugia." At the Arizona site, in contrast, the hiatus in flowering activity between spring and summer blooms is usually total and extensive.

Large variations in bee species composition and abundance within a given site between different years made cross-community comparisons more difficult but a number of patterns of feeding specificity are evident. As might be expected given the similarities of the perennial floras, the numbers of specialist species associated with perennials at each of the two sites are quite similar with thirty-two at Andalgalá and twenty-nine at Silver Bell. The vast majority of these specialists are associated with members of the same set of plants at either study site (*Larrea, Prosopis,* or the Cactaceae, principally *Opuntia*). Additionally, in both areas the largest numbers of these specialist species and individuals associated with perennials are active during the spring bloom regardless of the pattern of rainfall.

As noted previously, the Arizona winter annual flora supports at least twenty-nine species of specialist bees at Silver Bell, faunal and floral elements absent at Andalgalá. Though summer rains are both greater and more predictable in Catamarca than Arizona, and the summer annual floras are remarkably similar, the number of both species and individuals of specialist bees associated with summer annuals is still far higher at Silver Bell than that found at Andalgalá (31 vs. 5). Although these summer annual specialists are associated with a greater number of hosts in Arizona than Argentina, a striking feature of the summer bee fauna at Silver Bell is the high degree of overlap resulting from many specialists utilizing the same host(s), particularly *Euphorbia* and *Pectis*. While a wide variety of explanations for these differences are possible, such as simple historical accident or differences in the intensity of competition, all possible explanations suffer from lack of data, problems of circularity, or both.

Chapter 7:

Degree of Convergence of Ecosystem Characteristics

·G.H. Orians, O.T. Solbrig

Adaptation involves complex interrelationships between organisms and environments. One goal of evolutionary studies is to determine these relationships as reflected in the phylogenetic history of organisms, and to discover rules that govern those relationships. It is useful to examine these interactions at several levels of complexity. First we can consider convergence of *single structures* among dissimilar phylogenetic stocks. For example, wings of flying organisms represent convergence for aerial locomotion. There can also be convergence in enough characters that the *taxa* are considered convergent, e.g., "organ-type" cacti in the New World, and "organ-type" euphorbias in the Old World. Finally, there can be convergence in *community characteristics,* such as species richness, productivity, or plant growth forms, as is the case in "chaparral" or "maqui" communities of Mediterranean ecosystems (di Castri and Mooney, 1973).

In previous chapters, theoretical arguments for or against convergence at several different levels in subtropical deserts of North and South America were advanced, and results of our field and laboratory studies were synthesized. In this chapter we assess overall convergence to throw light on patterns of convergence and nonconvergence and what they reveal about predictability of processes of natural selection.

Necessary Conditions for Convergence

We assume that natural selection acts on the inclusive fitness of individuals and not directly on populations, species or communities (Chapter 1). However, if the majority of members of two distant communities evolve similar functioning, there may be convergence in community structure as an *indirect* result of similarities in structure or behavior of individuals that form the community. For convergent evolution to take place in isolated regions with similar physical environments, there must be adequate rates of mutation and recombination for the required genic and chromosomal changes to occur within the available evolutionary time span. Also, gene flow from surrounding habitats must be low enough to permit adaptation to local conditions. To distinguish between convergence and parallel evolution of phylogenetically similar stocks, there must be substantial taxonomic differences in the biotas being compared. Nevertheless, the floras and faunas must have a modest degree of taxonomic similarity for convergence to be likely. For example, pigeons on islands have evolved to be ecologically and structurally much like pheasants, but land tortoises on oceanic islands have converged toward grazing mammals only to the extent that both eat leaves.

Most evolutionists implicitly assume that well-known mechanisms for modifying simple characteristics (Dobzhansky, 1970), such as wing color of moths, eye color or bristle number of *Drosophila,* or shell color of snails, are sufficient to account for the evolution of more complex adaptations. Some investigators, however, point to the difficulty of evolving complex adaptations and attempt to develop new theories to explain them (see Frazzetta, 1975, for a review of these problems). In particular, if one assumes that an adaptation requires only a modest number of different traits to appear or be modified more or less simultaneously, and that each of them is controlled by an independent gene, the probability of such changes occurring simultaneously is extremely small (Eden, 1967). The probability increases if the genes are not independent, if the number that need to be altered simultaneously is not great, or if the number of possible ancestors is large (Frazzetta, 1975).

For organisms to converge, they must be subjected to similar physical environments and the communities of plants and animals with which they interact must affect them in similar ways. Competition from different communities of organisms could favor different evolutionary pathways in spite of similar abiotic environments, thereby resulting in a failure to converge, or in only partial convergence. For example, if competitive and predation environments in an early stage of potential convergence are stringent, some mutants will not be favored because immediate losses in fitness override any potential gains, giving rise to "adaptive valleys" that act as barriers to evolutionary changes in certain directions. If competition and/or predation are relaxed, however, as often occurs on islands, barriers to evolutionary change may be much weaker. Part of our task is to predict which features of community organization should converge no matter what restraints are imposed by differences in patterns of competition and predation, and which features should be highly sensitive to these differences. Pointing out these problems does not, however, provide an adequate conceptual framework for thinking about complex adaptations. In spite of much writing on the matter (G. G. Simpson, 1953; Grant, 1963; Stebbins, 1974) a comprehensive predictive theory regarding convergent evolution is still lacking.

Our study concerns itself with convergence over relatively short geological time spans. Ages of the two deserts are such that surrounding regions were already populated by members of most major extant orders of terrestrial plants, invertebrates, and vertebrates when desert climates first began to develop. Thus, the amount of convergence required is minor relative to the overall changes that have occurred during the evolution of terrestrial organisms. On the other hand, adaptations shown by animals and plants to desert environments are considerable and involve significant changes in many important organs and organ systems. Accordingly they may be considered major convergences. Unfortunately, little is known regarding communities of plants and animals with which ancestors of the present biota had to compete.

Similarities and Differences in the Physical Environment

Climatic similarities at the same latitudes north and south of the equator result from patterns of solar energy impact due to the earth's size, shape, and orbit. However, sizes and locations of land masses and mountain ranges influence orogenic and marine circulation patterns and, hence, heat transfer. In addition, precipitation is strongly influenced by air motion and may operate relatively independently from temperature. Differences in climates at Tucson and Andalgalá are due in part to latitude, to differences in the amount of land mass in the north and south temperate zones, and to location and size of surrounding mountain ranges. South temperate climates are in general more maritime than north temperate ones, and the annual march of mean monthly temperatures at Andalgalá is less extreme than at Tucson (Chapter 2). In particular, summer temperatures are lower at Andalgalá, but for two reasons we believe this difference is insignificant to the features of organisms we have studied. First, midday summer temperatures are stressful to most organisms at both sites, and second, extreme maxima are similar at both sites.

The most significant difference between the two areas, and one we cannot ignore, is the greater proportion of annual precipitation that falls in winter at Tucson. It is already abundantly clear from data presented in preceding chapters that this difference has important effects on the plant community, and, through it, on the animal community. The most significant effects are lack of a winter annual flora in Andalgalá and differences in leafing and reproductive phenologies of dominant plants. We have probably identified the most important effects of this climatic difference and explicitly recognize them in the following discussion. Nevertheless, this introduces a significant source of bias which makes interpretation of other aspects of convergence or nonconvergence more difficult. In particular, it is difficult to avoid the temptation to explain all cases of nonconvergence as due to climatic differences, thereby exaggerating our perception of the extent of convergence that would have obtained had a better match of climates been possible.

With respect to the physical environment, both study areas have an array of habitats ranging from desert flats to steeper slopes and to washes. The Bolsón de Pipanaco is without external drainage, while the Avra Valley drains into the Gila River, but this difference does not appear to be significant for our purposes because our transects did not extend to the bottom of the Bolsón where the accumulation of salty water creates a very different environment. The current area of distribution of *Larrea* in North and South America is similar, about 10^6 km^2 on both continents. Nevertheless, histories of the two deserts over evolutionarily significant time exhibit some important differences. Pleistocene effects were not as dramatic around Tucson as in the Bolsón because of a lack of nearby mountains with glaciers and the absence of large pluvial lakes in the Avra Valley, both major Pleistocene features in the region of the Bolsón de Pipanaco. There is also evidence suggesting that drying occurred earlier in the North, but the record is poor in South America.

Perhaps more significant for our purpose is evidence from woodrat middens that *Larrea* may have arrived in North America no more than 10,000 years ago (Wells, 1975). Recent evidence suggests that this date must be revised backward (Difeo, pers. comm.) but even if *Larrea* had been in North

America several times that long, it is more recent there than in South America and differences in animals associated with it in the two deserts may reflect the short time they have had available to evolve with *Larrea* in Arizona.

Taxonomic Similarity of the Biota

To estimate convergence we must distinguish it from parallel adaptations of closely related taxa. As dealt with in some detail in Chapter 3, of the roughly 250 species of plants in 115 genera and 50 families at each site, there are 14 species (5.6 percent), 51 genera (44.3 percent), and 29 families (58 percent) in common. Of the species in common, six are widespread weeds, four from Europe and two from South America, five are annual herbs and grasses, and three are perennials. Thus, similarities at the species level are almost confined to ephemerals. The genera in common, on the other hand, are mostly herbaceous perennials (11) or shrubs and trees (15), with fewer annuals (4) and perennial succulents (3). In most cases the species involved are from different sections of the shared genera, the main exceptions being *Acacia, Prosopis, Cercidium, Larrea, Opuntia* and *Cereus,* in which at least some species are very closely related. However, these include most of the dominant shrubs and small trees of the two areas.

Among the fauna, taxonomic knowledge of invertebrates is so incomplete and our studies so fragmentary that comparisons can be made for only a few groups. Among grasshoppers, the Catamarca fauna is represented by five families or subfamilies, while Arizona has six. Of these, three are common to both areas, but only one genus is shared. Ten of the fourteen Catamarca species are members of nonshared families whereas twenty-two of twenty-five Arizona species are in shared families, all of which are poorly represented in Catamarca. Among ants, of approximately twenty-five species and fifteen genera at each site, only eight of twenty-two genera are shared and only two species are in common, but three of five families are shared. Among spiders, about 30 percent of genera are shared, but these include about 70 percent of all individuals collected at the two study sites.

Our knowledge of taxonomic similarity among vertebrates is much better. Among anurans, only one of seven families and one of eleven genera are shared, and the species in the only shared genus are rather distantly related. Three of five lizard families and one of nineteen genera are shared between the study areas. Among snakes, four of five families are shared, but only two of twenty-eight genera. Sixteen of thirty-five families of birds are shared, but only ten of ninety-eight species, all of which are widespread and not restricted to deserts. Similarly, among mammals seven of twenty-four families, seven of fifty-eight genera, and six of eighty-four species are shared, the latter also being widespread species found in many other habitats.

Thus, some similarities among plants and animals at the two sites are due to common ancestry. Nevertheless, since within many shared families and genera, species exhibit a variety of adaptations to varied habitats and modes of environmental exploitation, opportunities to detect convergence are more prevalent than might be suspected simply by comparing floral and faunal lists. In particular, the closest ecological equivalents are sometimes found in different families even though the families (or genera) themselves may be shared between the two sites. Such patterns constitute important indirect evidence of convergence.

An interesting example of convergence involving species in a shared genus is furnished by *Cercidium* (Leguminosae) and *Bulnesia* (Zygophyllaceae). *Cercidium* is a small genus of trees found primarily in western North America, extending down the Andes to Argentina (Carter, 1974). At Silver Bell, there are two species, one of which is *Cercidium microphyllum,* a large shrub or small tree, with gray-green bark and small leaves, found primarily in riparian habitats in lower bajadas. The second species, *C. floridum,* is a small tree with stout branches, green photosynthetic bark, and ephemeral leaves, also found in washes and lower bajadas. At Andalgalá only one species, *Cercidium praecox,* is found. Its morphology and ecological distribution are those of *C. floridum.* The ecological counterpart of *C. microphyllum* is *Bulnesia retamo,* which has a bark and branch structure like *C. microphyllum,* and occurs in similar habitats (Figures 7-1 and 7-2). *Bulnesia* is a small genus of primarily large tropical trees found in Venezuela, Colombia and the Chaco of Argentina and Paraguay (Hunziker and Poggio, in prep.). While the *Cercidium floridum-C. praecox* pair represents parallel or at best mildly convergent evolution, the *Cercidium microphyllum-Bulnesia retamo* pair is clearly a case of convergence from very dissimilar ancestors.

ASSESSMENT OF THE DEGREE OF CONVERGENCE BETWEEN SILVER BELL AND THE BOLSÓN DE PIPANACO

Since no systematic effort was made to study all aspects of the biology of species in the two systems, our analysis is incomplete. We can, however, make useful comparisons at several stages of convergence. Since the specific study sites were selected on climatic criteria and organisms were selected on the basis of interests of the investigators and not because we expected them to show convergence more than those not studied, available data should provide a fairly unbiased sample of the degree of convergence between systems. We consider convergence at three main levels: characteristics of individuals; niche characteristics and boundaries; and community patterns.

Convergence of Individual Characteristics

Many traits of organisms we have studied are recognizable as adaptations to one or more aspects of desert environments. They range from relatively

FIGURE 7-1. Cercidium microphyllum *(Leguminosae), a semi-aphyllous shrub common in washes and lower bajadas in the Avra Valley, Arizona. (Photo by O. T. Solbrig.)*

FIGURE 7-2. Bulnesia retamo *(Zygophyllaceae), a semi-aphyllous shrub common in washes and lower bajadas in the Bolsón de Pipanaco, Catamarca. (Photo by O. T. Solbrig.)*

simple features (color patterns, amount of nectar production) to complex ones that affect many morphological features (leaf size and shape, changes in kidney functioning, background mimicry, foraging behavior, and food selection). Because complex traits may necessitate many simultaneous physiological and morphological changes, they are perhaps less likely to converge than simpler traits.

Convergence of Species Niches

The existence of convergent ecologically equivalent species implies that requirements for environmental exploitation are so stringent that convergence is favored in enough ecologically significant traits that an intuitive, but subjective, judgment of species convergence is made. Therefore, such ecological equivalents are of special evolutionary interest.

Convergence in Community Patterns

Some component of community structure may be similar in two independently evolved systems even though no precise species equivalents can be identified. Examples might include species richness (within-habitat richness), energy flow, phenology, breeding seasons, energetic commitments to various activities, etc. Similarities in these patterns could result from compensatory adaptations of individual species niches which smooth out effects of different competitive and predation environments. This can happen even if all or most component species differ.

Theory relevant to convergence at these different levels is in its infancy. Because the physical environment of Silver Bell is very similar to that of the Bolsón de Pipanaco, some convergence is expected at all three levels if our general evolutionary model is correct (Chapter 1). Some nonconvergences probably result from differences in the physical environment, but ideally we would like to predict how much convergence should have occurred had there been sufficient time and if physical environments had been identical. This involves assessments of how interactions between organisms and their environment and among organisms themselves could favor different evolutionary pathways if the initial states are different.

Time is a major factor affecting the probability of occurrence of convergent evolution. Evolutionary changes can occur rapidly when conditions are right (Johnston and Selander, 1964) but, nonetheless, basic changes in morphology and physiology are likely to require thousands of generations. There has evidently been sufficient time in both North and South America for highly desert-adapted organisms to evolve from ancestors adapted to more mesic environments. However, the extensive faunal exchanges that occurred between the two continents when the Panamanian land bridge was formed resulted in extinctions and new selective pressures to which desert organisms may not yet have had time to respond evolutionarily.

For some types of organisms, adaptation to desert environments requires extensive physiological and morphological changes while for other organisms deserts present few conditions to which they are not already adapted. Of the physical attributes of desert environments, heat and lack of water are the most obvious and most frequently studied. More recently, however, it has become apparent that the constraints of desert heat may have been overemphasized. Many organisms, particularly those foraging on the soil surface, must avoid direct sunlight during the middle of the day, but, on the other hand, warm summer desert nights permit extensive nocturnal activity. The great diurnal range of temperatures in deserts may pose more serious problems since optimal or near-optimal temperatures for heterothermic organisms are likely to be present for only short periods during a typical day. Restricted activity periods may be of great ecological and evolutionary importance but there has yet been little study of their influence on patterns of community structure.

Lack of surface water most of the year and high negative soil water potentials pose serious problems for plants and for animals either requiring free water for some stage of their life cycles or which must lose substantial amounts of water when eliminating nitrogenous wastes. Not surprisingly, adaptations to deserts are more noticeable and seem to affect more features of physiology, morphology, and life cycles of amphibians and mammals than among other animal groups.

Because plants constitute a major part of a desert's structural environment, vegetation is a key component affecting the lives of desert animals. The openness of vegetation results in extensive penetration of sunlight to the soil surface, good visibility, and restricted availability of above-ground nest sites. On the other hand, the great life form richness of hot desert plants presents arboreal animals with an unusual variety of substrates on which to feed and hide. Low annual primary productivity, combined with high temperatures, results in rapid decomposition of fallen leaves and branches and a lack of accumulation of litter on the soil surface. For most groups of animals, these features of desert vegetation are more important selective pressures on attributes of individuals and community structure than are the purely physical features of desert environments.

Convergence at the level of community patterns is influenced both by the physical environment and by biological interactions. Features of vegetation such as total net productivity and life form richness are probably direct responses to the physical environment, while patterns of within and between habitat richness in animal taxa depend on plants, the richness of species in the taxa, and the history of their arrival. The ability of a species to colonize an area depends in part on which species are already present and, hence, how that species fits into the pattern of resource utilization and predator avoidance already in existence at the time of its arrival. Early-arriving species may strongly determine sizes and characteristics of prey available to subsequent invaders. Similarly, predators already present in an environment may prevent the establishment of a species that would be viable in their absence. Also, the nature of subsequent evolution of colonizing species may be strongly influenced by its associates from which it may diverge or toward which it may converge. The course of evolution in species-rich taxa should be influenced more by competition from coevolving species than in taxa with few species. Theorists generally believe that the larger the number of sympatric species, the larger the number of relevant dimensions to their interactions (Schoener, 1974). This may increase the probability of multiple evolutionary outcomes rather than precise convergence. Also, more species are expected in taxa living in what is for them a benign environment than in taxa living in harsher environments.

These tentative ideas can be used as a basis for examining patterns we discovered among plants and animals in the Monte and Sonoran Desert. We begin with an examination of convergence of species characteristics and possible convergent species pairs, and then deal with convergence in community patterns.

Species Comparisons on a Taxonomic Basis

Plants

For vegetative parts of higher plants, the physical environment is the main independent variable. Desert environments impose stringent constraints on plants (Chapter 4) necessitating complex physiological and morphological adaptations, but adaptations to dryness are also possessed by plants of more humid areas. Convergent species pairs are especially likely among plants because of the direct, powerful effects of the physical environment. Furthermore, the source biota in both areas was sufficiently large to provide a substantial species pool. However, differences in rainfall distribution at the two sites should have a strong direct effect on plants. We therefore expected to find close equivalents among woody perennials and among summer active plants but an absence of winter active ephemerals and herbaceous perennials at Andalgalá.

The reproductive biology of animal-pollinated plants, on the other hand, is strongly influenced by animals and cannot evolve primarily in response to the physical environment as might be expected for vegetative parts. Floral morphology, reward structure, and total commitment to reproduction will converge only if the animal communities exert similar selective pressures regardless of the physical environment's characteristics. However, since the potentially available flower visitor communities in our two study sites are very similar, we did expect some convergence in floral structures and patterns of floral rewards.

Adaptations to long periods of low moisture availability favor a constellation of morphological traits which includes cells that can withstand great negative water potentials, sunken stomata, trichomes lining the stomatal cavity, resin or waxy external leaf coatings, small diameter vessels, and small leaves. These traits are found in distantly related perennial plants in all the world's deserts, especially those that grow in the driest sites.

Associated with these individual traits are plant life forms which combine them in characteristic ways. In both deserts these life forms are present (ephemerals; deciduous summer-active perennials; deep-rooted phreatophytes; drought-enduring evergreen shrubs; and succulents) in roughly the same proportions and with similar distributions along moisture gradients (Chapter 4). Some equivalent species pairs such as the giant "saguaro" of Arizona (*Cereus gigantea*) and the "cardon" of Argentina (*Trichocereus terscheckii*) are very striking (Figures 7-3 and 7-4) because of the close correlation of most of their characteristics. However, most ecologically equivalent species pairs belong to the same genus (Table 7-1), which makes assessment of convergence impossible. Finally, plant communities show remarkable similarities in the parameters measured: coverture, biomass, diversity, abundance, and shrub height in response to a single variable (soil texture) in areas of comparable rainfall.

Other differences that remain without good explanation are the lack of a counterpart of ocotillo (*Fouquieria splendens*) and "cholla" type cacti in Argentina (Figures 7-5 and 7-6) and the different distribution within the deserts between the apparent ecological equivalents (on superficial morphology) *Agave* and *Yucca* spp. (Agavaceae) from Arizona and *Dyckia* and *Deuterochonia* (Bromeliaceae) from Argentina (Table 7-2). While the former commonly grow in open flats, the latter are found exclusively on steep rocky cliffs, like *Agave lechiguilla* in the Chihuahuan Desert.

In sum the convergence of individual morphological traits, ecologically equivalent species pairs, and community characteristics among plants is impressive, even though it is marred somewhat by the close phylogenetic affinity of portions of the floras. It was this morphological similarity that attracted the attention of early plant geographers and stimulated our study. We have been able to verify the similarities, to extend them to several community patterns, and to offer plausible causes for both convergences and some of the nonconvergences.

Anurans

The number of species of amphibians in a given environment is generally low, especially in arid and semi-arid regions. This, combined with the major

FIGURE 7-3. Trichocereus terscheckii *(Cactaceae), growing on rocky slopes near Andalgalá, Catamarca. (Photo by O. T. Solbrig.)*

FIGURE 7-4. Cereus gigantea *(Cactaceae) growing in Saguara National Monument West on slopes above the Avra Valley, Arizona. (Photo by O. T. Solbrig.)*

TABLE 7-1   *Examples of Convergent and/or Equivalent Pairs of Vascular Plants of the Monte and Sonoran Desert*

Monte	Sonoran Desert
Trichocereus terscheckii	*Cereus gigantea*
Acacia aroma	*Acacia constricta*
Cercidium praecox	*Cercidium floridum*
Bulnesia retamo	*Cercidium microphyllum*
Jatropha macrocarpa	*Jatropha cardiophylla*
Larrea cuneifolia	*Larrea tridentata*
Opuntia glomerata	*Opuntia fulgida*
Prosopis chilensis, P. flexuosa	*Prosopis velutina*

constraints on amphibian life cycles in desert regions, means that closely convergent species pairs are likely unless there are imposing barriers in the form of "adaptive valleys." Such barriers are not likely since some ponds in more humid regions are also temporary, and many amphibians in these regions are adapted for existence in ephemeral ponds and dry uplands. Adaptation to desert ponds is primarily a matter of adjusting to shorter periods of water availability.

Among anurans, five very similar species pairs were identified, and possibly more would be recognized if the remaining species were better known. Even so, this number of pairs represents 33 percent of the anuran fauna of the Monte and 42 percent of that of the Sonoran Desert. Correlated with the existence of species pairs is a set of twelve traits, enumerated in Chapter 5, that are common to most desert anurans in all parts of the world. The length of this list testifies to the consistency of natural selection on amphibians in desert environments. On the other hand, the use of uric acid rather than urea as the form of nitrogen excretion, which is common to all desert insects, birds, and reptiles, is known from only two species of anurans. This trait is not a desert adaptation in these other taxa since it is characteristic of species in all other habitats as well. Its relative rarity among anurans could be due either to the difficulty of evolving it or to the fact that selection might not actually favor this change as one might guess on first reflection. In desert areas there is probably little food for adult amphibians outside the rainy season even if they could tolerate the dryness. Survival might therefore be much better in an inactive state, and there would be little selection for uricotelism among species in which the adults live in water but bury themselves as soon as surface water disappears.

Mammals

Like anurans, mammals, because of their kidney physiology, find desert dryness more difficult to handle than do uricotelic animals. In addition, com-

FIGURE 7-5. Fouquieria splendens *(Fouquieriaceae), a green-stemmed shrub that produces flushes of leaves following rains. The individual shown is in leaf. Tucson Mountains, Arizona. (Photo by O. T. Solbrig.)*

FIGURE 7-6. Opuntia fulgida *(Cactaceae), a cholla belonging to the Cylindro-Opuntia section of its genus. Tucson Mountains, Arizona. (Photo by O. T. Solbrig.)*

TABLE 7-2 *Species of Plants with No Apparent Ecological Counterparts at the Two Study Sites*

Monte	Sonoran Desert
Acacia furcatispina	
	Ambrosia spp.
	Fouquieria splendens
Cassia aphylla	
Deuterochomia schreiteri	
	Agave spp. − *Yucca* spp.
	Olneya tesota
	Cylindro-Opuntia spp. (cholla types)
Trichomaria usillo	
	Encelia farinosa

pared to other taxa, there are relatively few species present in any one environment. Therefore, we expect many closely equivalent species pairs with a constellation of convergent characteristics related to adaptations to dryness and daytime summer desert heat. As documented in Chapter 5, however, there are few equivalent species pairs among the mammals of the two deserts (*Ctenomys-Thomomys; Octomys-Neotoma*), and the Monte lacks any rodent able to exist on a diet of dry seeds. Our predictions are borne out in other deserts of the world, however, and are also supported by the existence of fossil marsupial "rats" similar to kangaroo rats from Argentina. Therefore, we assume that the absence of this adaptive form in the Monte today is due to a historical accident (extinction of the marsupial "kangaroo rats") combined with insufficient time to reevolve replacements (Mares, 1975b, 1976). Some small Monte rodents do show convergence with North American heteromyids in many characteristics though none is as drought adapted as North American species.

Reptiles, Birds, and Insects

Insects, reptiles, and birds are in a sense physiologically preadapted to desert existence (Schmidt-Nielson, 1964), and there is no constellation of morphological or physiological traits that constitutes a unique adaptation to physical conditions imposed by deserts. Desert birds have the same normal operating temperatures (40-42° C) as nondesert birds and they begin panting at similar temperatures (42-43° C) (Bartholomew, 1960). Desert birds and reptiles have high rates of water loss when it is hot and all seem to require either water or succulent foods to maintain water balance (Schmidt-Nielsen, 1964). Therefore, if there are convergent species pairs, the major selective forces must have come from the biological environment, especially competitors and predators and how they interact with the physical environment, and the structural environment given by the photosynthetic plants which provide most of the food, foraging substrates, and hiding places.

Among reptiles we might expect closely similar species pairs because there are few species present in any one environment and few changes are needed to adapt to deserts. Five species pairs were recognized among both snakes and lizards representing 56 percent (Andalgalá) and 20 percent (Tucson) of the snakes.

Avifaunas in desert regions are richer than herpetofaunas, making convergent species pairs less likely, but since birds are trophically more diverse, comparisons are more meaningfully made among subsets of the total avifauna. The complex relationships birds have with their environment may favor alternative evolutionary outcomes at the level of species niches, but ecological equivalents are common among Mediterranean Scrub species (Cody, 1974). Also, enough genera or closely related genera are shared by the two sites to make parallel evolution rather than convergence an important avifaunal characteristic. Nevertheless, a number of striking convergent pairs, some of them involving species from distantly-related families, are readily recognizable (Table 7-3). These eight pairs represent 14.0 percent and 13.1 percent of the Avra Valley and Bolsón de Pipanaco avifaunas.

The richness of source areas and length of time available would seem to be sufficient for convergence among insects, but we did not expect it to be a striking phenomenon because species richness is high and few modifications are needed to exist in desert climates. In addition, a large number of independent variables influences insects, e.g., climate, food, plant structure, competitors, predators, also making similar species pairs unlikely. However, convergence in such features as background mimicry and dietary generalization or specialization should occur.

Among grasshoppers, there do not appear to be recognizable equivalent species in the two deserts, but convergence exists in a number of species traits. For example, there is a high degree of dietary specialization among desert grasshoppers (more than 25 percent of species in both areas feed exclusively on a single plant species or a few closely related species). Since grasshoppers in nearby grasslands in both North and South America tend to be generalized foragers (less than 5 percent of species feeding exclusively on one or a few closely related species), desert species can be considered convergent in this trait. In addition, at both Andalgalá and Tucson, 12 percent (one of eight and three of twenty-four, respectively) of grasshopper species are *Larrea* specialists. In both deserts polyphagous grasshoppers which feed on the ground eat a wider variety of plant species than those feeding arboreally, the food niche-width of vegetation-inhabiting species being about half that of ground-living species. There are also similarities in plant species completely avoided by grasshoppers in both deserts. These include species of *Euphorbia, Prosopis, Acacia,* and all cacti. None of the grass-feeding species in either area are oligophagous.

TABLE 7-3 *Convergent Species Pairs of Birds from Different Families**

Foraging mode	Monte	Sonoran Desert
Snatching and gleaning insects from foliage of shrubs	Lesser Wagtail-tyrant (*Stigmatura budytoides*) (Tyrannidae)	Black-tailed Gnatcatcher (*Polioptila melanura*) (Sylviidae)
Gleaning and probing for insects on foliage	Tufted Tit-spinetail (*Leptasthenura platensis*) (Furnariidae)	Verdin (*Auriparus flaviceps*) (Paridae)
Digging and probing on ground; gleaning from lower branches	Sandy Gallito (*Teledromus fuscus*) (Rhinocryptidae)	Thrasher (*Toxostoma* spp.) (Mimidae)
Gleaning and probing on and in crevices of bark	Short-billed Canastero (*Asthenes baeri*) (Furnariidae)	Cactus Wren (*Campylorhynchus brunneicapillus*) (Troglodytidae)
Pouncing on large insects and small vertebrates from elevated perches	Spot-winged Falconet (*Spiziapteryx circumcinctus*) (Falconidae)	Loggerhead Shrike (*Lanius ludovicianus*) (Laniidae)
Gleaning seeds and fruit from ground	Elegant Crested Tinimou (*Eudromia elegans*) (Tinamidae)	Gambel's Quail (*Lophortyx gambelii*) (Phasianidae)
General carrion feeding	Crested Caracara (*Polyborus plancus*) (Falconidae)	Raven (*Corvus corax*) (Corvidae)
	Chimango Caracara (*Milvago chimango*) (Falconidae)	White-necked Raven (*Corvus cryptoleucus*) (Corvidae)

*Convergence is judged on the basis of similarity of diet, manner of foraging, and type of substrates foraged on.

Convergences among ants in the two deserts are difficult to detect since parallel evolution cannot be ruled out. There is genuine convergence in psammophores, dissimilar structures which serve the same function for many different desert ants, but most other similarities are components of the basic biologies of the genera and tribes of ants which comprise the faunas. The many similarities among the spiders of the two sites also probably reflect the basic biologies of the dominant families rather than indicating any convergence to desert conditions.

Community Level Comparisons

Previous comparisons have dealt with characteristics of organisms believed to be the direct result of natural selection, strategies in our terminology. We now turn to a consideration of patterns of species richness, species packing, and production and utilization of total resources which, though clearly determined by traits we have already considered, are primarily only indirectly molded by natural selection. Consequently, their interpretation is more complex than for the previous traits, and it is more difficult to make unambiguous predictions. We have already indicated our reasons for rejecting the postulate that such patterns as total community productivity can be considered strategies (Chapter 1), but we nonetheless recognize that there *are* predictable patterns in productivity that must have explanations.

Species Richness Comparisons

As an environment accumulates species to some "saturation" level, within-habitat richness (alpha-richness) usually rises rapidly at first to its maximum value while between-habitat richness (beta-richness) initially rises more slowly and only increases to its final value long after alpha-richness has equilibrated. The generally accepted reason for this pattern is that intraspecific competition, which can be strong even when species richness is low, favors expanded use of habitats when interspecific competition is weak (Cody, 1974). The range of habitats occupied per species is gradually reduced by the addition of more species which increase the intensity of inter-specific competition. Normally this prediction is tested by comparing community structure for some taxonomic group, i.e., birds, in regions where, for historical reasons, fewer species are found in one area than another though both possess a similar array of habitats. Our two sites seem to meet most of these criteria. Habitat gradients are similar and surrounding communities provided a substantial pool of potential invaders of the deserts. Neither site is obviously an island for species we have examined, though the Bolsón might have been harder for mammals to reach following glaciation than was the Avra Valley (Chapter 3).

In Table 7–4 we present available data from the two deserts on species richness in taxa sufficiently well-studied to yield useful results. These represent species present in the general areas without specifying whether they occur together in the same sites. In fact, all of the data in Table 7–4 include species inhabiting the full range of desert habitats from dry flats to washes. Table 7–5 presents available data comparing richness changes along rainfall gradients where comparable measurements of both habitat and species presence are available. These data are more similar to the comparisons usually made of alpha- and beta-richness (usually referred to as diversity) in the ecological literature (MacArthur, 1965; Cody, 1970, 1974).

Considering first regional patterns in community richness, we can examine the expectation that species change-overs along geographical gradients should be greater in taxa with more species than in taxa with fewer species. This expectation is borne out for mammals where species change-overs are higher in Arizona where the mammal fauna is rich, than in Argentina where

TABLE 7-4   *Regional Comparisons of Species Richness in the Monte and Sonoran Deserts*

Taxon	Number of species in study area	
	Avra Valley	Bolsón de Pipanaco
Ants	25 spp.	25 spp.
Orthoptera	25	14
Bees	188	116
Anurans	12	14
Lizards	19	15
Snakes	24	14
Birds	57	61
Mammals	64	32
Vascular plants	250	250

TABLE 7-5   *Community Similarities Along a Habitat Gradient from Drier to Wetter Deserts*

	Taxon	Number of species found at		Number shared	Coefficient of community
		Andalgalá (wet)	Mendoza (dry)		
Argentina	Anurans	5	6	4	.667
	Snakes	15	14	12	.800
	Mammals	8	7*	7	.875

	Taxon	Tucson (wet)	Yuma (dry)	Number shared	Coefficient of community
Arizona	Anurans	7	4	4	.571
	Snakes	20	19	17	.850
	Lizards	13	13	11	.846
	Mammals	26	21	16	.615

*Valle de la Luna, San Juan Province (very dry).

the mammal fauna is poor in species. The opposite pattern is shown by orthoptera, however, and these data are particularly interesting since the extent of regional sampling of orthopterans is much greater than for other groups. The species richnesses are much higher in North American temperate habitats and yet the Argentine species are not more widespread than those in North America. Surprisingly, both within and between habitat species richnesses are lower in South America. For other taxa either insufficient data or insufficient differences in species richness make comparisons meaningless.

Data for comparative analysis of community patterns along local habitat gradients are fewer, being best for birds. In this taxon, species richness at the two study sites is similar (fifty-seven species in Arizona, sixty-one at Catamarca), so we should expect similar patterns of species change-overs along a gradient from a dry *Larrea* flat to a wash dominated by phreatophytic trees. A series of one-hectare sites in the Bolsón de Pipanaco and Avra Valley, ranging across the flat to wash gradient, were censused for breeding birds. These sites contained twenty-seven and twenty-six breeding species of non-raptorial birds respectively. The number of species of breeding birds increased at about the same rate in the two areas, as the relative amount of riparian habitat within the plots increased (Figure 7-7). The presumed cause of the relationship is that different and safer nest sites and new foraging opportunities are provided by riparian plant species which tend to be larger, to have more diverse bark and more spines and natural cavities than plants of the desert flats. This fits in well with the general observation that bird species diversity is predictable from a knowledge of foliage height diversity (MacArthur and MacArthur, 1961; MacArthur et al., 1966; Recher, 1969). However, in hot desert habitats structural characteristics of particular species of plants appear to be more important than in other habitats. In addition, since specific nest sites provided by few species of plants are often of major importance in deserts, the addition of just a few individuals of a spinescent shrub, for instance, may increase bird species diversity more than its effect on foliage height diversity would suggest (MacArthur, 1964; Tomoff, 1974). Birds of both deserts make extensive use of cacti and spinescent shrubs for nesting sites, including species that forage primarily or entirely on other substrates. Therefore, these data indicate a real convergence in desert bird community structure toward a pattern distinct from that found in more mesic habitats.

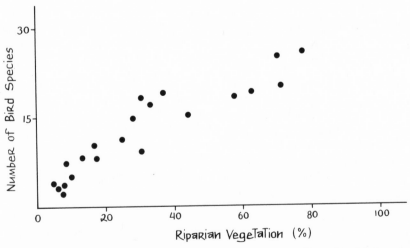

Figure 7-7. *Relationship between number of species of breeding birds and the amount of cover provided by plants other than* Larrea *in the Bolsón de Pipanaco.*

Data on plant community structure and species richness are available for transects along moisture and soil texture gradients. At both the Bolsón de Pipanaco and Avra Valley there is a strong correlation between soil particle size and species diversity, crown coverage, and mean distance between plants. There is also a highly significant positive correlation between total plant coverage and species diversity. These results strongly suggest that the complexity of soil-plant-water relations increases as the fraction of particles in the rock and gravel fraction of the soil increases. This must affect water penetration and storage and thereby increase the number of different soil-water resources available to plants in these deserts (Chapter 4).

These similarities are presumably the result of strong selection on individual species for response to soil water regimes, but this does not mean that exact replacement species are necessarily involved. For example, the close equivalents, *Larrea cuneifolia* in Argentina and *Larrea tridentata* in Arizona do not behave identically along moisture gradients. The density of *Larrea* drops with increasing moisture in Arizona but peaks at the middle of the gradient in Catamarca. Also, the Arizona site had fewer *Larrea* shrubs less than 50 cm in height, and there was a marked single peak in creosote shrub heights. In Catamarca at comparable positions along the gradient there are many more small shrubs and a generally broader range of shrub heights with no marked peak. Despite these differences, however, community parameters of species diversity and coverage were very similar in the two areas, suggesting some compensatory evolution among the component species in response to the exact characteristics of their associates.

Resource Utilization Comparisons

Though detailed studies of resource utilization were not made on all animal groups we studied, enough information is available for most taxa to permit at least crude comparisons between the two deserts and with deserts elsewhere in the world.

Reptiles

Among reptiles there is a predominance of nocturnal activity among snakes in both areas, though lizards are primarily diurnal, but this pattern is probably true of snakes and lizards elsewhere in hot climates. Both herbivores and carnivores (insectivores) are represented among the lizards of both deserts in contrast to more humid environments where herbivorous lizards are rare outside the tropics or subtropics. Interestingly, though there is striking convergence in lizard community structure between Chile and California, there are herbivorous lizards in Chilean chaparral but not in Californian chaparral (Fuentes, 1976). However, the diets of the snakes of the two areas are very different. Few birds and mammals are taken by Monte snakes, while mammal-eaters are an important component of the Sonoran Desert snake fauna. This difference probably reflects the absence of granivorous rodents in Catamarca, the overall lower abundance of small mammals in the Monte compared to the Sonoran Desert, and the large sizes of many Monte rodents. Among both snakes and lizards there are several arboreal species in Arizona but none in Catamarca. The reason for this difference is not clear.

From the extensive work of Pianka (1966, 1967, 1969, 1971, 1973) detailed information is available on lizard community structure in the Kalahari Desert of Africa and a variety of Australian deserts. In the general area of the Silver Bell Bajada, seventeen species of lizards are found but Pianka never found more than nine to eleven species on any one uniform plot in Arizona. Sixteen species of lizards are recorded for the Monte but only nine occur at Andalgalá, though twelve are found in Valle de la Luna and near Mendoza City. In contrast, in the Kalahari Desert twelve to eighteen ($\overline{X}$ = 15) species can be found together, while eighteen to forty ($\overline{X}$ = 29) live together in the Australian deserts (Table 7-6). There are more species of arboreal and subterranean lizards in Africa, Australia, and South America than in North America.

A major difference in lizard diets in different deserts is that termites are prominent in diets of Kalahari lizards (41.3 percent of all prey items compared to 16.5 percent and 15.9 percent in North America and Australia, respectively). In contrast, vertebrates are a major part of lizard diets in Australia (24.8 percent) compared to North America (7.8 percent) and the Kalahari (2.3 percent). Comparable figures are not available for the Monte, but the scarcity of termites around Andalgalá and the absence of large carnivorous lizards suggests that lizard diets there are more similar to those in the Sonoran than to the other two deserts. Monte lizards are more like Sonoran lizards than Kalahari or Australian lizards in the small number of nocturnal species. In Australia in particular, the richness of nocturnal species approaches that of diurnal species.

TABLE 7-6 *Some Aspects of Lizard Community Structure in Several Hot Deserts**

Category	Sonoran this study	Sonoran Pianka (1973)	Monte overall	Monte Andalgalá	Kalahari (ave. of 10 study sites)	Australia (ave. of 8 study sites)
Diurnal, terrestr.	12	7	11	5	6	14
Diurnal, arboreal	3	2	1	1	2	3
Nocturnal, terr.	2	1	2	2	4	8
Nocturnal, arb.	0	0	0	0	2	3
Fossorial	0	0	2	1	1	1
Totals	17	10	16	9	15	29
Range		(9–11)			(12–18)	(18–40)

*Data for Australia and the Kalahari Desert from Pianka, 1973.

Pianka (1973) explained some of the striking differences among lizard communities in different deserts on the basis of interactions with other vertebrates. There are proportionally more species of ground-dwelling insectivorous birds in the Kalahari Desert than in Australia (Pianka and Huey, 1971) suggesting greater potential competition among birds and lizards there. By combining study plots Pianka found that the number of bird species increases faster than the number of lizard species in North America and the Kalahari, while the number of lizard species increases faster than the number of birds species in Australia. There are few migratory birds in Australia compared to the Kalahari and Sonoran deserts, and lack of competition from migrants may provide additional foraging opportunities for lizards in Australia. Similarly, the prevalence of nocturnal species in Australia may be causally related to the paucity of mammals and snakes. Indeed, several species of large Australian varanid and pygopodid lizards are ecological equivalents of mammals and snakes, respectively. These patterns can plausibly be explained in other ways but they do suggest that interclass interactions among vertebrates may have been evolutionarily important in molding several aspects of community structure and may prevent closer convergence than would otherwise be the case.

Mammals

As is true in deserts all over the world, most mammals in the Monte and Sonoran deserts are nocturnal and place their nests underground. The proportion of carnivores in the mammalian community is high in both areas. The most striking difference, as indicated above, is the total absence of obligate granivores at Catamarca, where 20 percent of the mammalian fauna of the Silver Bell area belongs to this group.

Birds

Convergence in the structure of bird communities in grasslands and Mediterranean climates in various parts of the world has been examined in detail by Cody (1974). In all grasslands there are usually three or four raptors, including one *Falco* (bird hawk) and one *Buteo* (mammal hawk). Cody also found precise ecological equivalents in terms of their micro-habitat selection, food harvested, and foraging behavior between birds in Kansas and Chile.

In comparisons among birds of the Mediterranean scrub of Chile and California Cody found that Chilean species are, on the average, more widely distributed on habitat gradients than are California species but almost every species has a clear ecological counterpart. Among supposed ecological counterparts, body sizes ($r = 0.66$), bill sizes ($r = 0.61$), and mean foraging heights ($r = 0.85$) are very similar. Fewer ecological counterparts are recognizable among desert birds, supporting the conjecture that species convergence is less likely in communities where a taxon has more species.

Comparisons of Monte and Sonoran Desert birds with those of similar deserts in Australia and the Kalahari are shown in Table 7-7. The Monte and Sonoran data represent total species lists for the overall study areas while the data of Pianka and Huey (1971) represent averages of nine study plots in the Kalahari and eight in Australia. Therefore, the most meaningful comparisons are of the percentages of the total avifauna in the four general categories. These proportions are generally similar except that there are more arboreal herbivores and fewer ground herbivores in the Monte than in other deserts. Birds actually harvest seeds at about the same rate in the Monte and Sonoran deserts but fewer species are involved and the Monte also lacks the great influx of wintering finches so characteristic of the Sonoran Desert. Arboreal herbivores are represented by parrots and leaf-cutters, both absent in the Sonoran and Kalahari deserts, though there are desert parrots in Australia.

In general, bird communities in hot deserts are richer than those of grasslands and Mediterranean scrub and they contain different kinds of species. For example, the waders characteristic of grasslands disappear as woody plants become a prominent part of the vegetation, and though there are passerines in both environments, the number of arboreal species increases greatly as woody plants are added. These are not surprising differences but they do indicate that similarities in desert bird communities are not simply reflections of general similarities in bird communities in all habitats.

Resource Utilization Communities

Another method of evaluating convergence at two sites is to examine types of resources and communities utilizing them without respect to taxonomic affinities of the resources or their utilizers. We have such data for herbivores, seed eaters, and flower visitors that can be used to test for convergence in resources and in patterns of their utilization.

TABLE 7-7 *Some Aspects of Bird Community Structure in Hot Deserts of the World**

Foraging Category	Monte		Sonoran		Kalahari†		Australian††	
	N spp.	%	N spp.	%	N. spp.	%	N spp.	%
Ground, herbivores	5	8	11	20	6.1	28	7.4	29
Ground, carnivores	21	34	23	40	7.3	34	4.8	18
Arboreal, herbivores	7	12	1	2	0.7	2	2.0	7
Arboreal, carnivores	28	46	22	38	8.3	36	12.4	46

*Kalahari and Australian data from Pianka and Huey, 1971.
† Average of nine study plots.
†† Average of eight study plots.

Plant-Herbivore Relationships

To the best of our limited knowledge, chemical defenses of vascular plants involve functionally similar chemicals in Catamarca and Arizona. Evidence suggests that annuals and perennials have, respectively, converged on different types of defenses and levels of commitment to them. Patterns of defense were predicted on the basis of temporal and spatial availability of plant resources and probable levels of grazing associated with them (Chapter 6). Assumptions about patterns of grazing on desert annuals were tested in Argentina. The major differences in availability of resources to herbivores are caused by rainfall difference at the two sites. Herbivores eating annuals are more generalized in their diets at both sites than are herbivores eating perennials, as predicted, but this pattern is not a specifically desert-related one, being expected in all environments.

There are also similarities in seasonal patterns of activity of different herbivore types correlated with moisture contents of leaves, ambient temperatures, and susceptibility of herbivores to desiccation. If this pattern is actually confirmed by additional data from other sites, it represents a significant convergence of general importance for the structure of plant-herbivore communities. It is, however, not a specifically desert-related phenomenon either as it appears to be true in more mesic environments as well.

Flower–Flower Visitor Relationships

Annual gross photosynthesis per hectare is probably similar on the two sites and the relative advantages to investing in vegetative growth and reproduction should be comparable. In addition the same types of potential pollinators exist at the two sites. Therefore we expected the fraction of the total production devoted to floral resources by the dominant perennials to be similar in the two deserts regardless of plant species involved. This expectation was not confirmed. A *Larrea* flat in Arizona with a comparable density and coverage of shrubs was estimated to produce about the same amount of pollen but three times as much sugar as an equivalent site in Catamarca. Lower bajada sites in Arizona were estimated to produce four times the floral biomass, ten times the amount of sugar, and four times the amount of pollen as comparable sites in Catamarca. If production of floral resources by annuals and hummingbird-pollinated species is added to these figures, the difference becomes even greater.

We expected few vertebrate-pollinated flowers in either desert because desert climates are favorable for insects while dry air evaporates the larger amounts of nectar required to attract vertebrates. The Arizona site has one hummingbird-pollinated and one bat-pollinated plant, while Catamarca has none among the plant species comprising more than 1 percent of the total cover per hectare. There is also little wind pollination among shrubs, though

again there are several wind-pollinated species in Arizona and none in Catamarca. This difference is related to the lack of winter rains in Catamarca,
since wind-pollinated species in Arizona all bloom in early spring when winds
are strong and temperatures less favorable for insects. Associated with the
higher incidence of wind-pollination in Arizona, there are more plant species
with either separate sexes or separation of male and female flowers on the
same plant.

We also expected more diverse flower types among dominant perennials
in Catamarca since the period of flowering is unimodal, and all plants are
potentially competing for vectors during that restricted time span. This expectation was also not borne out. Most flowers at Catamarca fall into one of
two classes, generalized yellow flowers or pale flowers clustered into spherical
or spicate inflorescences. These same two floral types are represented in Arizona, but there are many others as well.

Predictions concerning flower visitors must be based on knowledge (or
expectations) of the kinds of rewards available to them. As indicated above,
reward structure in the two areas is substantially different, in total production, allocation, and temporal pattern of allocation. Nevertheless, some general patterns are expected as a result of constraints imposed on timing of
flowering by the shortness of rainy periods in both deserts. In particular, we
expected a prevalence of solitary bees in both areas because flowering periods
are too short to permit the buildup and maintenance of the larger units of the
social bees. This pattern is characteristic of both deserts, the flower-visiting
community being dominated by solitary Hymenoptera and Bombyliidae
(Diptera). The bombyliids are presumably common because their larvae are
parasitic on orthopterans and hymenopterans, both of which are common in
deserts.

Because of the great diurnal range of temperatures in deserts during the
flowering season, we also expected and found bees visiting flowers in early
morning to be larger and darker than those visiting flowers during the middle
of the day.

Given the strongly bimodal flowering pattern in Arizona, major differences in the community of flower visitors were expected. Flowers are
available at two different times of year, and temperatures are also very different during those two blooming periods, being cool (even cold at night) in
late winter and early spring but very hot during summer. Therefore, we
expected both a greater richness in flower visitors in Arizona and that the
pollinator species common during late winter and spring would be different
from those active during the summer flowering period. Some seasonal differences in pollinators were expected at Catamarca, but the number and
reliability of late winter and early spring flowers is so low that evolution of
specialized bee species for that period is less likely. As expected, there is a
much greater richness of bees in Arizona than in Catamarca, much of which is
associated with the early spring ephemerals in Arizona. Furthermore, only

19 percent of the bees in Arizona are active during both blooming periods whereas 36 percent of the bee species in Catamarca are active throughout the flowering season.

Theoretically, resources that are less predictable in space and time should be more difficult to specialize on than more predictable resources, other things being equal, and herbivore foraging patterns are in accordance with this expectation. The same arguments, if applied to floral resources would predict more specialization among bees visiting perennial plants with great longevity and long blooming times than among bees visiting short-lived ephemerals with restricted bloom times. However, because of the mutualistic interactions among floral resources and flower visitors, greater specialization on ephemeral resources is likely among flower visitors and this is, indeed, the case. Fourteen species of specialized bees visit winter annuals in Arizona and another nineteen species are specialists on summer annuals. Five bee species at Catamarca are also specialists on summer annuals. In comparison, very few of the bees visiting shrubs or herbaceous perennials are restricted to a single species, and many visit a wide variety of shrubs, especially among species with generalized yellow flowers. The prevalence of specialized bees on annuals can be explained in at least two ways. First, plants may actually be highly predictable to bees because they both respond to the same environmental cues. This explanation can account for the timing of activity but is insufficient to explain the high degree of specialization observed. A second and complementary hypothesis assumes that there are qualitative differences in the nutritional characteristics of floral rewards of different species with which bees have co-evolved. Specialization might be most likely to evolve among solitary bees since floral resources constitute the sole food throughout the life history and not just carbohydrate source for adults as is the case with other groups of flower visitors. For example, no bombyliid species is a specialist on a single flower species.

Seed–Seed Eater Relationships

Given comparable total primary productivity and similar levels of plant competition, one would expect comparable expenditure of energy on seeds in both communities. Seed characteristics, however, are strongly influenced by the structure of the seed-predator community since traits that decrease the probability of loss to one kind of predator may increase the probability of losses to another. Also, the intensity of competition at the seedling stage affects optimal seed sizes. Therefore, details of seed characteristics should not be predictable from the physical environment alone unless the biotic community exerts similar pressure in the areas being compared.

There is a major difference between seed predator communities in Arizona and Catamarca: the absence of obligate granivorous rodents in the

Monte (Chapter 6). Data indicate that larger seeds are better food sources for rodents than smaller ones because rodents can obtain more energy per unit time spent foraging and handling them (Rosenzweig and Sterner, 1970). Therefore, if larger seeds are preferred, rodents are selective agents favoring smaller seed sizes (C. C. Smith, 1970, 1975). Birds are likely to act similarly, but ants are not, since larger seeds are more difficult for them to harvest and carry back to the nest. Therefore, if there is heavy seed predation by birds and mammals, smaller seed sizes should be favored, while if there is heavy mortality from ants, larger seed sizes would be optimal.

In addition, if predation rates on seeds are in general lower in an area, then more seeds should survive to germination time, and competition among seedlings should be more severe. This in turn favors larger seeds since the reserves available to a seedling should be positively correlated with its early competitive ability. Both of the above arguments predict larger seed sizes in the Monte than in the Sonoran Desert but data are lacking to test the prediction.

Unfortunately, the implications of differences in the communities of seed predators were not grasped in time for the necessary seed collections to be made, and we lack data with which to test the different selective roles of seed predator communities at our two sites. It is interesting that this major difference in seed predators does not seem to have resulted in any striking differences in richness or distribution of plant species and life form types. We expect differences in seed and seedling characteristics, but these remain to be investigated in the future.

Carnivores

Though the characteristics of leaves, flowers, and seeds are so different that the organisms exploiting them are mostly distinct, there is much more overlap among carnivores on these three groups of plant tissue eaters. Most species of birds and lizards prey regularly on insects belonging to two or more of the three groups just mentioned. Predators on small mammals do not discriminate among granivores, herbivores, or insectivores at either site. It is only among predatory invertebrates that specialization occurs and this specialization involves foraging modes rather then prey specificity. For example, some crab spiders are specialists on flower visitors, and solpugids probably take primarily herbivorous insects resting on the stems and leaves in Catamarca. Even so, many invertebrate predators, such as mantids and hunting spiders, encounter prey of many different types and do not appear to be restricted to any of the three feeding guilds of herbivores.

The reason for this greater overlap among carnivores is probably due to a combination of several factors. First, the density of their prey is less than for herbivores, and, hence, conditions favoring specialization on particular prey types are less likely to occur. Second, many prey from different feeding guilds intermingle while they are hiding. Many leaf-eating insects rest on substrates other than leaves where their associates are more likely to be utilizers of different resources. Waiting at flowers for visitors is the one case in which specialization on a specific guild is likely among carnivores. Finally, there is no reason to expect that members of any one guild are likely to fall into a single group with respect to their ranking to some carnivore. For a hawk, high-ranked prey are likely to include a mixture of herbivores, granivores, and insectivores. A warbler or titmouse is likely to have a similar pattern of prey ranking so that even when prey are relatively abundant and diets correspondingly restricted, there is no reason to expect this restriction to be within a single prey guild.

Therefore carnivores everywhere should be good generalists and desert species are unlikely to reveal any evolutionarily surprising characteristics.

CONCLUSIONS

In general, our results indicate that plants show striking convergences in individual morphological and physiological traits. In addition, there are a number of closely matched species pairs, though many of these are congeneric and hence reflect parallel evolution rather than convergence. At the level of community structure, patterns of distribution of total plant biomass, life form types, and spacing and density of shrubs are all remarkably similar. However, features of plants related to their interactions with animals are less similar at the two sites. Floral morphology and total investment in floral rewards are not the same in the two deserts, though anti-herbivore chemicals do appear to be similar in comparable plants.

We interpret these patterns to mean that those features of organisms most strongly affected directly by the physical environment are more convergent than those in which there is, in addition, a strong component of adaptation to biological interactions with competitors or predators. The complexity of these interactions, combined with the fact that the exact nature of selective pressures are likely to differ if the initial biotas are different, leads to greater likelihoods of alternative evolutionary results.

This conclusion is further strengthened by an examination of patterns of convergence and nonconvergence among animal taxa. Those animals most strongly affected by the physical environment, such as anurans, are highly convergent in terms of individual adaptive traits and equivalent species pairs. The same was expected for mammals but not found. In this case, however, we accept a historical explanation because equivalent mammals appear to have evolved in the past in South America but went extinct during the Pleistocene. Insufficient time has elapsed for a new group of granivorous rodents to evolve. Strong convergence is apparently characteristic of desert rodents in all other hot deserts of the world.

One final pattern that appears to emerge from our data is that taxa with few species are more likely to contain convergent species pairs than those with many species. The existence of only a few sympatric species in a taxon presumably indicates that there are only a few ways for an animal of that general form of organization and life history to exist in an environment. Strong selection from both the physical environment and associated biota are the most likely reasons for this restriction, and these pressures should generate strong selection for convergence. On the other hand, the existence of many species in a taxon living in a general region indicates many viable strategies for that kind of organism and a greater possibility that the evolutionary outcome will be molded more by biological interactions with fewer constraints from the physical environment. As we have already argued, biological interactions are more likely to lead to alternative stable states.

All of these conclusions are advanced tentatively since there are many difficult problems in deciding whether or not convergence has occurred and how much. Also, our sample sizes are small, and we do not know how generally applicable are the patterns we have observed. This points to a need for additional studies in hot deserts on other continents where the physical environments of Silver Bell Bajada and the Bolsón de Pipanaco can be approximated and where the biotas are more distinct taxonomically than those we studied. We have already used insights derived from a knowledge of these other deserts when interpreting our results. Such data were important in the selection of the original project and in adding breadth to our interpretations about convergence (or the lack of it) among mammals, anurans, lizards, and birds. Since the power of "natural experiments" to explain processes in the real world is partly a function of the number of experiments examined, comparable studies on other continents can be expected to yield new insights and contribute to strengthening or rejecting those we now hold.

Nevertheless, we have not exhausted the information that can usefully be extracted from our two sites. Our results have suggested a number of new theories relating to convergence and where and why it is to be expected. These theories can be tested with more complete data on the taxa we studied and by extending studies to other taxa. In particular, we have taken only tentative first steps in developing a predictive theory for patterns of convergence at higher levels of community structure. Both the power of our current theories and the strength of our data in this area are weak, even if our collective insights have been improved by our studies.

The critical problems we faced in predicting community level patterns from theories based on natural selection acting on traits of individuals is not peculiar to convergent evolution studies but is, rather, central to all community studies in ecology. Predictive theories about community structure and functioning are nearly absent in ecology. We believe that the general experimental design employed in our project may have general usefulness for the development of several kinds of predictive theory for communities. Natural experiments are a powerful tool in this type of analysis, and many predictions are best tested when the physical environment can be held as constant as possible. Nature has not been overly generous in providing opportunities to match physical environments in distant lands, but more opportunities exist than have been exploited. We predict that the probability of finding ecologists at work where we can identify a suitable natural experiment will increase in the future, to the benefit of ecological theory at all levels of community organization.

APPENDIX A

Shared Plant Genera in Transect Areas

Family	Genus
Sinopteridaceae:	*Notholaena*
Gnetaceae:	*Ephedra*
Graminae:	*Aristida**
	*Bouteloua**
	*Chloris**
	*Eragrostis**
	Panicum
	Setaria
	*Sporobolus**
Ulmaceae:	*Celtis*
Loranthaceae:	*Phoradendron*
Chenopodiaceae:	*Atriplex*
Amaranthaceae:	*Amaranthus*
Nyctaginaceae:	*Allionia**
	*Boerhavia**
Portulacaceae:	*Portulaca*
Ranunculaceae:	*Clematis*
Papaveraceae:	*Argemone*
Cruciferae:	*Sisymbrium*
Leguminosae:	*Acacia*
	Cassia
	Cercidium
	Prosopis
Geraniaceae:	*Erodium**
Zygophyllaceae:	*Kallstroemia*
	Larrea
	*Tribulus**
Rhamnaceae:	*Condalia*
Euphorbiaceae:	*Jatropha*
	Euphorbia
	Tragia
Malvaceae:	*Abutilon*
	Sphaeralcea
	Sida
Sterculiaceae:	*Avenia*
Loasaceae:	*Mentzelia*
Cactaceae:	*Opuntia*
	Cereus
Asclepiadaceae:	*Gonolobus*
Convolvulaceae:	*Ipomoea*
Hydrophyllaceae:	*Nama*
	Phacelia
Verbenaceae:	*Lippia*

APPENDIX A (Continued)

Shared Plant Genera in Transect Areas

Family	Genus
Solanaceae:	*Solanum**
	Lycium
	Nicotiana*
	Datura
Compositae:	*Baccharis*
	Verbesina*
	Senecio
	Zinnia

*Share common species.

APPENDIX B

Shared Plant Species on Study Sites

Family	Species	Habit	Distribution
Graminae:	Aristida adscensionis	Annual	Cosmopolitan – abundant in Argentina
	Bouteloua aristidoides	Annual	New World – abundant in Argentina & Arizona
	Bouteloua barbata	Annual	New World – abundant in Argentina & Arizona
	Chloris virgata	Annual	New World – abundant in Pipanaco & Avra Valley.
	Eragrostis cillianensis	Annual	Introduced from Europe –
	Sporobolus pyramidatus	Perennial	Cosmopolitan
Nyctaginaceae:	Boerhavia coccinea	Perennial	Widespread in New World – abundant in Argentina
	Allionia incarnata	Annual	Cosmopolitan – abundant in Argentina & Arizona
Geraniaceae:	Erodium cicutarium	Annual	Cosmopolitan –
Zygophyllaceae:	Larrea divaricata-	Shrub	Amphitropical disjunct –
	L. tridentata*		
	Tribulus terrestris	Annual	Introduced from Europe – Occasional in both areas
Solanaceae:	Nicotiana glauca	Shrub	Introduced in Arizona from South America
	Solanum elaeagnifolium	Perennial	Cosmopolitan
Compositae:	Verbesina encelioides	Perennial	New World – Abundant in Argentina

*Sibling species.

APPENDIX C

Plant Species Studied in the Analysis of Desert Bajada Gradients; (R) = riparian species.

Northern Site (U.S.A.) Arizona — Silver Bell Bajada	Southern Site (Argentina) Catamarca — Bajada Joyango
Abutilon californicum	
Abutilon incanum	
Acacia constricta	*Acacia aroma*
Acacia greggii	*Acacia furcatispina*
Allionia incarnata	
Allium macropetalum	*Amaryllis* sp.
Ambrosia ambrosioides	
Ambrosia deltoidea	
Ambrosia dumosa	
Anemone tuberosa	
Aplopappus spinulosus	
Aplopappus tenuisectus	
Aristida ternipes	*Aristida mendocina*
Aristolochia watsoni	
	Atamisquea emarginata
Atriplex canescens	*Atriplex lampa*
Atriplex polycarpa	
Ayenia pusilla	
Baccharis glutinosa	
Baccharis sarothroides	
Baileya multiradiata	
	Blumenbachia sp.
	Boerhaavia paniculata
Bouteloua curtipendula	
Bouteloua gracilis	
Bouteloua rothrocki	
Brickellia coulteri	*Buddleja tucumanensis*
	Bulnesia retamo
Calliandra eriophylla	
Carlowrightia arizonica	
Cassia covesi	*Cassia aphylla*
Celtis tala	
Cercidium floridum	*Cercidium praecox*
Cercidium microphyllum	
Cereus giganteus	*Cereus aethiops*
Cereus greggii	
	Chloris castilloniana
Clematis drummondi	
Commicarpus scandens	
Condalia lycioides	
Condalia spathulata	

APPENDIX C (Continued)

Northern Site (U.S.A.) Arizona – Silver Bell Bajada	Southern Site (Argentina) Catamarca – Bajada Joyango
	Cordobia argentia *Cottea pappophyroides* *Cressa* sp.
Dalea parryi (R)	
	Deuterochonia schreiteri
Dichelostemma pulchellum	*Digitaria californica*
Ditaxis lanceolata	
	Dyckia velazcana
Dyssodia porophylloides	
Echinocereus fendleri	
	Echinopsis sp.
Encelia farinosa	
Ephedra nevadensis	*Ephedra triandra*
Ephedra trifurca	
Eriogonum inflatum	
Erioneuron pulchellum	
Euphorbia arizonica	
Euphorbia melanadenia	
Euphorbia polycarpa	
Ferocactus wislizeni	
	Flourensia campestris
Fouquieria splendens	
Funastrum heterophyllum	
	Geoffroea decorticans
Gonolobus parvifolius	
	Grahamia bracteata *Gymnocalycium bodenbenderi*
	Habranthus jamesoni *Heliotropium mendocinum*
Herissantia crispa	
Heteropogon contortus	
Hibiscus coulteri	
Hibiscus denudatus	
Hyptis emoryi	
	Ibicella parodi
Janusia gracilis	
Jatropha cardiophylla	*Jatropha excisa* *Jatropha grossidentata* *Jatropha macrocarpa*
Krameria grayi	
Krameria parvifolia	

APPENDIX C (Continued)

Northern Site (U.S.A.) Arizona — Silver Bell Bajada	Southern Site (Argentina) Catamarca — Bajada Joyango
Larrea tridentata	*Larrea cuneifolia* *Larrea divaricata* (R)
Lippia wrighti *Lycium* cf. *berlandieri*	*Lycium chilensis* *Lycium ciliatum* *Lycium spathulata* *Lycium tenuispinosum*
Mammillaria fasciculata *Mammillaria microcarpa* *Menodora scabra*	*Mammillaria* sp. *Mimosa ephedroides* *Mimosa farinosa*
Muhlenbergia porteri	
Nicotiana glauca (R, introd) *Nicotiana trigonophylla* *Notholaena standleyi*	*Nicotiana glauca* (R)
Olneya tesota *Opuntia acanthocarpa* *Opuntia arbuscula* *Opuntia bigelovi* *Opuntia fulgida* *Opuntia leptocaulis* *Opuntia phaeacantha* *Opuntia spinosior* *Opuntia versicolor*	*Opuntia glomerata* *Opuntia strobiliformis* *Opuntia sulphurea*
	Pappophorum mucronulatum *Parodia* sp.
Pellaea longimucronata *Penstemon parryi* *Perezia nana* *Perezia wrighti*	
	Philibertia gilliesi
Physalis hederaefolia *Physalis versicolor* *Polygala macradenia*	
	Portulaca confertifolia *Portulaca* cf. *echinosperma* *Portulaca pilosa*
Prosopis velutina	*Prosopis chilensis* *Prosopis flexuosa* *Prosopis torquata* *Pseudabutilon stuckerti*
Psilostrophe cooperi	
Selaginella arizonica	

APPENDIX C (Continued)

Northern Site (U.S.A.) Arizona – Silver Bell Bajada	Southern Site (Argentina) Catamarca – Bajada Joyango
Setaria macrostachya	*Setaria argentina* *Setaria leucopila* *Setaria mendocina*
Siphonoglossa longiflora *Sphaeralcea ambigua* *Sphaeralcea laxa* *Sporobolus cryptandrus* *Stephanomeria pauciflora*	*Sphaeralcea* sp.
	Suaeda divaricata
	Talinum polygaloides *Tillandsia duratti* *Tillandsia hieronymii* *Tillandsia myosura* *Tillandsia recurvata*
Tragia nepetifolia *Trichachne californica*	*Tragia hieronymii*
	Trichloris crinita *Tricomaria usillo* *Trichocereus terscheckii*
Tridens muticus *Trixix californica* *Tumamoca macdougali*	
	Ximenia americana
	Zephyranthes longistila
Zinnia pumila	
	Zuccagnia punctata

APPENDIX D

List of Acridoid Species Believed to Be Endemic to North and South American Larrea *deserts. Desert Species that Also Occur Widely in the Grasslands Are Not Included.*

North America	South America
Tanaoceridae	
Tanaocerus koebelei	
Mohavacris timberlakei	
Romaleinae	Romaleinae
Tytthotyle maculata	*Diponthus argentinus*
Dracotettix monstrosus	
Acridinae	Acridinae
Cibolacris parviceps	*Euplectrotettix ferrugineus*
Goniatron planum	
Ligurotettix coquilletti	
Astehelius sp.	
Bootettix argentatus	
Acantherus piperatus	
Paropomala pallida	
Achurum sumichrasti	
Pedioscirtetes maculipennis	
Oedipodinae	Oedipodinae
Derotmema haydenii	*Trimerotropis pallidipennis*
Trepidulus rosaceous	
Trimerotropis californica	
Trimerotropis cristata	
Conozoa sulcifrons	
Aeoloplus tenuipennis	
Aeoloplus chenopodii	
Anconia integra	
Xeracris minimus	
Coniana snowi	
Lactista oslari	
Catantopinae	
Netrosoma nigropleura	
	Ommexechidae
	Calcitrena muculosa
	Neuquenina fictor
	Tetrixocephalus willemsei
	Ommexechidae sp. 1
	Ommexechidae sp. 2
	Proscopiidae
	Anchocoema subalata
	Astroma riojanum
	Astroma compactum
	Astroma sp. 1
	Astroma sp. 2

TOTAL:

25 species	13 species

APPENDIX E

Bee Faunas of North and South American Study Sites

Family	Subfamily	Andalgalá N	% Fauna	Silver Bell N	% Fauna
COLLETIDAE		28	24.1	11	5.8
	Colletinae	18		9	
	Diphaglossinae	4		+	
	Hylaeinae	+		2	
	Xeromellisinae	6		−	
HALICTIDAE		8	06.9	29	15.4
	Dufoureinae	−		6	
	Halictinae	8		20	
	Nomiinae	−		3	
OXAEIDAE		1	00.9	1	0.5
ANDRENIDAE		12	10.3	58	30.9
	Andreninae	−		8	
	Panurginae	12		50	
MELITTIDAE		−	0.0	1	0.5
FIDELIIDAE		−	0.0	−	.0
MEGACHILIDAE		29	25.0	42	22.3
	Lithurginae	1		1	
	Megachilinae	28		41	
ANTHOPHORIDAE		36	31.0	46	20.7
	Anthophorinae	31		39	
	Nomadinae	2		6	
	Xÿlocopinae	3		1	
APIDAE		2	1.7	+	0.0
	Apinae	*		*	
	Bombinae	2		+	
Total species		116		188	

+ Indicates present at adjacent desert scrub study sites but absent at main site.
− Indicates absent in region.
* Apinae represented by *Apis mellifera* at both sites but excluded from table.

APPENDIX F

Genera of Spiders and Scorpions Known to Occur at the Study Sites or in Adjacent Areas

Order & Family	Catamarca — La Rioja	Arizona — California
ARANEAE (SPIDERS)		
Orthognatha		
Pycnothelidae	Lycinus	
Actinopodidae	Actinopus	
Theraphosidae	Grammostola	Aphonopelma
Labidognatha		
Filistatidae	Filistata	Filistata
Dictynidae	Dyctyna	Dictyna
Sicariidae	Sicarius	
Scytodidae	Scytodes	Scytodes
Loxoscelidae		Loxosceles
Diguetidae	Diguetia	Diguetia
Plectreuridae		Plectreurys
Caponiidae		Orthonops
Pholcidae	Pholcus	Pholcus
Theridiidae	Latrodectus	Latrodectus
		Euryopis
	Steatoda	Steatoda
	Anelosimus	
Linyphiidae		Ceratinella
Araneidae		Argiope
	Mastophora	
	Metepeira	Metepeira
	Neosconella	
		Neoscona
	Parepeira	
		Araneus
	Wixia	
		Eustala
Agelenidae		Agelenopsis
Hersiliidae	Tama	
Mimetidae		Mimetus
Zodariidae	Gliesella	
	Leprolochus	
	Hyltoniella	
Lycosidae	Lycosa	Lycosa
Oxydopidae	Oxyopes	Oxyopes
		Hamataliwa
		Peucetia
Gnaphosidae		1 species
Homalonychidae		Homalonychus
Clubionidae		Megamyrmicion?
	Corinna	
		Castianeira
		Syspira

APPENDIX F (Continued)

Order & Family	Catamarca – La Rioja	Arizona – California
Anyphaenidae	Anyphaena	
	1 species	1 species
Ctenidae	Xenoctenus	
Sparassidae	1 species	1 species
Selenopidae	Selenops	
Thomisidae	Misumenops	Misumenops
	Petricus	
	Paracleonemis	
		Titanebo
	Tmarus	Tmarus
		Apollophanes
		Philodromus
Salticidae	Attulus	
		Phidippus
	Cerionesta	
		Sassacus
		Metaphidippus
		Pseudicius
	Phiale	
		Pellenes
	Evophrys	
SCORPIONIDA (SCORPIONES)		
Buthidae		Centruroides
Vejovidae		Hadrurus
		Vejovis
		Parausoctonus
Bothriuridae	Timogenes	
	Brachistosternus	
	Vachonia	
	Bothriurus	
SOLPUGIDA (SOLPUGIDS)		
Ammotrechidae	Oltacola	
	Mummucina	several species
	Pseudocleobis	
Eremobatidae		Eremorhax
		Eremobates
		Scolopendra
PSEUDOSCORPIONIDA (PSEUDOSCORPION)		
	1 species	1 species

APPENDIX G

Composition of the Vertebrate Faunas of the Two Deserts

Family	Monte		Sonoran Desert		Shared	
	No. Genera	No. Species	No. Genera	No. Species	Genera	Species
FROGS and TOADS (AMPHIBIA)						
Pelobatidae	–	–	1	2	–	–
Leptodactylidae	4	9	–	–	–	–
Ceratophrynidae	2	4	–	–	–	–
Bufonidae	1	1	1	7	1	–
Hylidae	–	–	1	1	–	–
Ranidae	–	–	1	1	–	–
Microhylidae	–	–	1	1	–	–
LIZARDS (LACERTILIA)						
Amphisbaenidae	1	1	–	–	–	–
Gekkonidae	1	2	1	1	–	–
Iguanidae	2	9	10	16	–	–
Teiidae	3	3	1	1	1	–
Helodermatidae	–	–	1	1	–	–
SNAKES (SERPENTES)						
Leptotyphlopidae	1	1	1	1	1	–
Boidae	–	–	1	1	–	–
Colubridae	7	9	13	16	–	–
Viperidae	2	3	1	5	1	–
Elapidae	1	1	1	1	–	–
TURTLES (CHELONIA)						
Testudinidae	1	1	2	2	–	–
BIRDS (AVES)						
Rheidae	1	1	–	–	–	–
Tinamidae	1	1	–	–	–	–
Cathartidae	2	2	2	2	2	2
Accipitridae	3	3	3	3	2	1
Falconidae	3	4	1	1	1	1
Phasianidae	–	–	1	1	–	–
Cariamidae	1	1	–	–	–	–
Columbidae	3	3	2	3	1	–
Psittacidae	2	2	–	–	–	–
Cucullidae	–	–	1	1	–	–
Tytonidae	1	1	1	1	1	1
Strigidae	4	4	4	5	4	4
Caprimulgidae	2	2	2	2	–	–
Apodidae	1	1	1	1	–	–
Trochilidae	1	1	1	1	–	–
Picidae	3	3	3	3	2	–
Dendrocolaptidae	2	2	–	–	–	–
Furnariidae	6	8	–	–	–	–
Rhinocryptidae	2	2	–	–	–	–
Tyrannidae	6	7	2	3	1	1
Alaudidae	–	–	1	1	–	–
Hirudinidae	1	1	1	1	1	–
Corvidae	–	–	1	2	–	–

APPENDIX G (Continued)

Family	Monte		Sonoran Desert		Shared	
	No. Genera	No. Species	No. Genera	No. Species	Genera	Species
Paridae	–	–	1	1	–	–
Troglodytidae	–	–	3	3	–	–
Mimidae	1	2	2	5	1	–
Sylviidae	–	–	1	1	–	–
Ptilogonatidae	–	–	1	1	–	–
Laniidae	–	–	1	1	–	–
Vireonidae	–	–	1	1	–	–
Parulidae	–	–	1	1	–	–
Icteridae	1	3	3	4	1	–
Thraupidae	1	1	1	1	–	–
Emberizidae	5	6	4	6	–	–
Carduelidae	–	–	1	1	–	–
MAMMALS (MAMMALIA)						
Didelphidae	2	2	1	1	1	–
Soricidae	–	–	1	1	–	–
Emballonuridae	–	–	1	1	–	–
Desmodontidae	1	1	–	–	–	–
Phyllostomatidae	–	–	3	3	–	–
Natalidae	–	–	1	1	–	–
Vespertilionidae	3	4	7	12	3	2
Molossidae	2	3	2	5	1	2
Dasypodidae	3	3	–	–	–	–
Leporidae	–	–	2	4	–	–
Sciuridae	–	–	2	3	–	–
Geomyidae	–	–	1	1	–	–
Heteromyidae	–	–	2	8	–	–
Muridae	2	4	5	8	–	–
Chinchillidae	1	1	–	–	–	–
Caviidae	3	3	–	–	–	–
Ctenomyidae	1	1	–	–	–	–
Erethizontidae	–	–	1	1	–	–
Canidae	1	2	3	4	–	–
Procyonidae	–	–	2	2	–	–
Mustelidae	3	3	4	4	1	–
Felidae	1	3	2	4	1	2
Tayassuidae	–	–	1	1	–	–
Cervidae	–	–	1	2	–	–

APPENDIX H

Species of Anurans in the Sonoran and Monte Deserts

Family	Species	
	Sonoran	Monte
Pelobatidae	*Scaphiopus couchi* *Scaphiopus hammondi*	
Bufonidae	*Bufo woodhousei* *Bufo cognatus* *Bufo alvarius* *Bufo punctatus* *Bufo retiformis* *Bufo microscaphus* *Bufo mazatlanensis*	*Bufo arenarum*
Hylidae	*Pternohyla fodiens*	
Ranidae	*Rana* sp. (*pipiens* group)	
Leptodactylidae		*Leptodactylus ocellatus* *Leptodactylus bufonius* *Leptodactylus mysticeus* *Leptodactylus latinasus* *Odontophrynus occidentalis* *Odontophrynus americanus* *Pleurodema nebulosa* *Pleurodema cinerea* *Physalaemus biligonigerus*
Ceratophrynidae		*Ceratophrys ornata* *Ceratophrys pierotti* *Lepidobatrachus llanensis* *Lepidobatrachus asper*
Microhylidae	*Gastrophryne olivacea*	

APPENDIX I

Species of Snakes at Two Sites Along a Transect in the Monte and the Sonoran Desert (+ indicates species present, - indicates species absent)

	MONTE DESERT	
Species	Andalgalá	City of Mendoza
Leptotyphlops borrichianus	+	+
Clelia occipitolutea	+	+
Elapomorphus bilineatus	-	+
Elapomorphus tricolor	+	-
Leiamadophis sagittifer	+	+
Lystrophis semicinctus	-	+
Oxyrhopus rombifera	+	+
Philodryas burmeisteri	+	+
Philodryas patagoniensis	+	+
Philodryas psammophideus	+	+
Pseudotomodon trigonatus	+	+
Phimophis vittatus	+	-
Lygophis lineatus	+	-
Micrurus frontalis	+	+
Bothrops neuwiedi	+	+
Bothrops ammodytoides	+	+
Crotalus durissus	+	+

	SONORAN DESERT	
	Tucson	Yuma
Leptotyphlops humilis	+	+
Lichanura trivirgata	-	+
Phyllorhynchus browni	+	-
Phyllorhynchus decurtatus	+	+
Masticophis flagellum	+	+
Salvadora hexalepis	+	+
Pituophis melanoleucus	+	+
Arizona elegans	+	+
Rhionochelus lecontei	+	+
Lampropeltis getulus	+	+
Thamnophis marcianus	+	+
Sonora semiannulata	+	+
Chionactis occipitalis	+	+
Chilomeniscus cinctus	+	+
Hypsiglena torquata	+	+
Micruroides euryxanthus	+	-
Trimorphodon lambda	+	+
Crotalus tigris	+	-
Crotalus atrox	+	+
Crotalus scutulatus	+	+
Crotalus cerastes	+	+
Crotalus mitchelli	-	+

APPENDIX J

Species Composition of Lizards at Three Sites Along a Transect in the Monte and Sonoran Desert. (+ indicates species present; – indicates species absent). Coefficients of community: Andalgalá-San Juan = 0.538; San Juan-Mendoza = 0.533; Andalgalá-Mendoza = 0.500; Tucson-Ajo = 0.909; Ajo-Yuma = 0.533; Tucson-Yuma = 0.600.

	MONTE DESERT		
	Andalgalá	San Juan	Mendoza
Homonota underwoodi	+	+	+
Homonota horrida	+	+	+
Liolaemus darwini	+	+	+
Liolaemus goetschi	–	+	+
Liolaemus marmoratus	+	+	+
Liolaemus sp. 1	+	+	–
Liolaemus sp. 2	–	+	–
Liolaemus sp. 3	–	–	+
Liolaemus gracilis	–	+	+
Leiosaurus bardensis	–	–	+
Leiosaurus catamarcensis	+	+	+
Cnemidophorus longicaudus	+	+	+
Teius teyou	+	+	+
Tupinambus rufescens	–	+	+
Amphisbaena angustifrons	+	?	+

	SONORAN DESERT		
	Tucson	Ajo	Yuma
Coleonyx variegatus	+	+	+
Sauromalus obesus	+	–	+
Dipsosaurus dorsalis	+	+	+
Callisaurus draconoides	+	+	+
Uma notata	–	–	+
Crotaphytus collaris	+	+	+
Crotaphytus wislizeni	+	+	+
Sceloporus magister	+	+	+
Urosaurus graciosus	–	–	+
Uta stansburiana	+	+	+
Phrynosoma platyrhinos	–	–	+
Phrynosoma solare	+	+	–
Phrynosoma m'calli	–	–	+
Cnemidophorus tigris	+	+	+
Heloderma suspectum	+	+	–

APPENDIX K

Species and Subspecies of Mammals Occurring in the Avra Valley and Bolsón de Pipanaco.

Avra Valley	Bolsón de Pipanaco

ORDER: MARSUPIALIA
Family: Didelphidae

Didelphis marsupialis virginiana	*D. albiventris pernigra*
	Marmosa pusilla pallidior

ORDER: INSECTIVORA
Family: Soricidae

Notiosorex crawfordi crawfordi

ORDER: CHIROPTERA
Family: Desmodontidae

	Desmodus rotundus

Family: Phyllostomatidae

Macrotus waterhousei
Choeronycteris mexicana
Leptonycteris n. nivalis

Family: Vespertilionidae

Myotis y. yumanensis	*M. levis*
M. velifer brevis	
M. c. californicus	
M. evotis apache	
M. t. thysanodes	
Lasionycteris noctivagans	
Pipistrellus hesperus apus	
Eptesicus fuscus pallidus	*Eptesicus sp.*
Lasiurus borealis teliotis	*L. b. varius*
L. c. cinereus	*L. c. villosissimus*
Plecotus townsendii	*Histiotus m. montanus*
Antrozous p. pallidus	

Family: Molossidae

Tadarida brasiliensis mexicana	*T. brasiliensis*
T. femorosacca	
T. molossa	*T. molossa*
Eumops perotis californicus	
E. underwoodi	unidentified molossid

ORDER: EDENTATA
Family: Dasypodidae

	Chaetophractus v. vellerosus

APPENDIX K (Continued)

Avra Valley	Bolsón de Pipanaco

ORDER: LAGOMORPHA   xmxmxm
Family: Leporidae

Lepus a. alleni
L. californicus eremicus
Sylvilagus floridanus holzneri
S. audubonii arizonae

ORDER: RODENTIA
Family: Sciuridae

Spermophilus spilosoma canescens
S. tereticaudus neglectus
Ammospermophilus h. harrisi

Family: Geomyidae

Thomomys bottae modicus

Family: Hetermoyidae

Perognathus f. flavus
P. amplus taylori
P. b. baileyi
P. penicillatus pricei
P. i. intermedius
Dipodomys spectabilis perblandus
D. m. merriami
D. o. ordii

Family: Muridae

Onychomys t. torridus   *Eligmodontia typus puerulus*
Reithrodontomys m. megalotis   *Phyllotis darwini ricardulus*
R. f. fulvescens   *P. g. griseoflavus*
Peromyscus e. eremicus   *P. species*
P. m. merriami
P. maniculatus sonoriensis
Sigmodon hispidus cienegae
Neotoma a. albigvla

Family: Caviidae

Microcavia australis maenas
Galea m. musteloides
Dolichotis patagonum centricola

APPENDIX K (Continued)

Avra Valley	Bolsón de Pipanaco

Family: Ctenomyidae

Ctenomys fulvus coludo

Family: Erethizontidae

Erethizon dorsatum couesi

ORDER: CARNIVORA
Family: Canidae

Canis latrans mearnsi	*Dusicyon culpaeus andinus*
C. lupus baileyi	*D. griseus gracilis*
Vulpes macrotis arsipus	
Urocyon cinereoargenteus scottii	

Family: Procyonidae

Bassariscus astutus arizonensis
Procyon lotor mexicanus

Family: Mustelidae

Taxidea taxus	*Lyncodon patagonicus thomasi*
Spilogale putorius gracilis	*Galictes c. cuja?*
Mephitis macroura milleri	*Conepatus chinga budini*
Conepatus mesoleucus venaticus	

Family: Felidae

Felis onca arizonensis	*F. c. puma*
F. concolor azteca	*F. y. ameghinoi*
P. yagouaroundi cacomitli	*F. geoffroyi salinarum*
Lynx rufus baileyi	

ORDER: ARTIODACTYLA
Family: Tayassuidae

Dicotyles tajacu sonoriensis

Family: Cervidae

Odocoileus hemionus crooki
O. vierginianus couesi

APPENDIX L

Species of Rodents in Three Xeric Monte Localities. Coefficients of community: Andalgalá = Valle de la Luna = 0.667; Valle de la Luna-Mendoza = 0.875; Andalgalá-Mendoza = 0.875.

Andalgalá (8)	Valle de la Luna (7)	Mendoza (7)
Eligmodontia typus	*Eligmodontia typus*	*Eligmodontia typus*
Phyllotis darwini	*Phyllotis darwini*	*Phyllotis darwini*
Phyllotis grisseoflavus	*Phyllotis griseoflavus*	*Phyllotis griseoflavus*
Phyllotis sp.		
Microcavia australis	*Microcavia australis*	*Microcavia australis*
Galea musteloides	*Galea musteloides*	*Galea musteloides*
Dolichotis patagonum	*Dolichotis patagonum*	*Dolichotis patagonum*
Ctenomys fulvus	*Ctenomys fulvus* (?)	*Ctenomys* sp.
	Octomys mimax	

APPENDIX M

Species of Lagomorphs and Rodents Found at Three Arid Localities in the Sonoran Desert. Coefficients of community: Tucson-Gila Bend = 0.577; Gila Bend-Yuma = 0.762; Tucson-Yuma = 0.643. Numbers in parentheses are total species per site.

Tucson (26)	Gila Bend (16)	Yuma (21)
Lepus alleni		
L. californicus	*Lepus californicus*	*Lepus californicus*
Sylvilagus auduboni	*Sylvilagus auduboni*	*Sylvilagus auduboni*
S. floridanus		
Sciurus griseus		
Spermophilus spilosoma		
S. tereticaudus	*Spermophilus tereticaudus*	*Spermophilus tereticaudus*
Ammospermophilus harrisi	*Ammospermophilus harrisi*	*Ammospermophilus harrisi*
Thomomys bottae	*Thomomys bottae*	*Thomomys bottae*
Perognathus flavus		*Perognathus longimembris*
P. amplus	*Perognathus amplus*	*P. amplus*
P. baileyi		*P. baileyi*
P. penicillatus	*P. penicillatus*	*P. penicillatus*
P. intermedius	*P. intermedius*	*P. intermedius*
Dipodomys spectabilis	*Dipodomys deserti*	*Dipodomys deserti*
D. merriami	*D. merriami*	*D. merriami*
D. ordii		
Onychomys torridus	*Onychomys torridus*	*Onychomys torridus*
Reithrodontomys megalotis	*Reithrodontomys megalotis*	*Reithrodontomys megalotis*
R. fulvescens		
Peromyscus eremicus	*Peromyscus eremicus*	*Peromyscus eremicus*
P. maniculatus	*P. maniculatus*	*P. maniculatus*
P. merriami		
Sigmodon hispidus		
Neotoma albigula	*Neotoma albigula*	*Neotoma albigula*
Erethizon dorsatum	*Erethizon dorsatum*	*Erethizon dorsatum*

APPENDIX N

The Mammal Faunas (Exclusive of Bats) of the Monte Desert (Andalgalá Area), Sonoran Desert (Tucson Area), and the Eastern Deciduous Forest (Linesville, Pennsylvania). Time of Activity: C = crepuscular; D = diurnal; N = nocturnal; B = active either day or night; X = activity seasonally variable. Nest Placement: A = above ground; G = ground surface; U = underground; C = catholic. Food: G = granivore; H = herbivore; O = omnivore; M = microomnivore; I = insectivore; C = carnivore.

	Time of Activity	Nest Placement	Food	Common name
Monte Fauna				
Didelphis albiventris	N	C	O	opposum
Marmosa pusilla	N	U	I	mouse opossum
Chaetophractus vellerosus	X	U	O	armadillo
Eligmodontia typus	N	U	M	gerbil mouse
Phyllotis darwini	N	U	M	leaf-eared mouse
Phyllotis griseoflavus	N	U	M	leaf-eared mouse
Phyllotis sp.	N	U	M	leaf-eared mouse
Microcavia australis	D	U	H	cavy
Galea musteloides	D	U	H	cavy
Dolichotis patagonum	C	U	H	Patagonian "hare"
Ctenomys fulvus	B	U	H	tuco-tuco
Dusicyon culpaeus	N	–	C	fox
Dusicyon griseus	N	U	O	fox
Lyncodon patagonicus	N	U	C	weasel
Galictes cuja	N	U	C	weasel
Conepatus chinga	N	U	O	skunk
Felis concolor	N	–	C	mountain lion
Felis yagouaroundi	N	–	C	jaguarundi
Felis geoffroyi	N	–	C	Geoffroy's cat
Sonoran Desert				
Didelphis marsupialis	N	C	O	opossum
Notiosorex crawfordi	B	G	I	shrew
Lepus alleni	C	G	H	jackrabbit
Lepus californicus	C	G	H	jackrabbit
Sylvilagus auduboni	C	G	H	cottontail
Sylvilagus floridanus	C	G	H	cottontail
Spermophilus spilosoma	D	U	M	ground squirrel
Spermophilus tereticaudus	D	U	M	ground squirrel
Ammospermophilus harrisi	D	U	M	ground squirrel
Thomomys bottae	B	U	H	gopher
Perognathus flavus	N	U	G	pocket mouse
Perognathus amplus	N	U	G	pocket mouse
Perognathus baileyi	N	U	G	pocket mouse
Perognathus penicillatus	N	U	G	pocket mouse
Perognathus intermedius	N	U	G	pocket mouse
Dipodomys spectabilis	N	U	G	kangaroo rat
Dipodomys merriami	N	U	G	kangaroo rat

APPENDIX N (Continued)

	Time of Activity	Nest Placement	Food	Common name
Dipodomys ordii	N	U	G	kangaroo rat
Onychomys torridus	N	U	I	grasshopper mouse
Reithrodontomys megalotis	N	U	M	harvest mouse
Reithrodontomys fulvescens	N	U	M	harvest mouse
Peromyscus eremicus	N	U	M	field mouse
Peromyscus merriami	N	U	M	field mouse
Peromyscus maniculatus	N	U	M	field mouse
Sigmodon hispidus	N	U	H	cotton rat
Neotoma albigula	N	G	H	pack rat
Erethizon dorsatum	N	U	H	porcupine
Canis latrans	N	–	C	coyote
Canis lupus	N	–	C	wolf
Vulpes macrotis	N	U	O	fox
Urocyon cinereo-argeneus	N	G	C	fox
Bassariscus astutus	N	U	C	ringtail
Procyon lotor	N	–	O	racoon
Taxidea taxus	N	–	C	badger
Spilogale putorius	N	U	C	skunk
Mephitis macroura	N	U	C	skunk
Conepatus mesoleucus	N	U	O	skunk
Felis onca	N	–	C	jaguar
Felis concolor	N	–	C	mountain lion
Felis yagouaroundi	N	–	C	*jaguarundi*
Lynx rufus	N	–	C	bobcat
Dicotyles tajacu	C	–	O	peccary
Odocoileus hemionus	C	–	H	deer
Odocoileus virginianus	C	–	H	deer

Pennsylvania

	Time of Activity	Nest Placement	Food	Common name
Didelphis marsupialis	N	O	C	opossum
Sorex cinereus	B	G	I	shrew
Sorex palustris	B	U	I	shrew
Sorex fumeus	B	G	I	shrew
Blarina brevicauda	B	G	I	shrew
Condylura cristata	B	U	I	mole
Parascalopus breweri	B	U	I	mole
Sylvilagus floridanus	C	G	H	cottontail
Lepus americanus	C	G	H	hare
Tamias striatus	D	U	M	chipmunk
Marmota monax	D	U	H	marmot
Sciurus carolinensis	D	A	M	squirrel
Sciurus niger	D	A	M	squirrel
Tamiasciurus hudsonicus	D	A	M	squirrel
Glaucomys volans	N	A	N	flying squirrel
Castor canadensis	D	U	H	beaver
Peromyscus maniculatus	N	U	M	field mouse
Peromyscus leucopus	N	U	M	field mouse
Clethrionomys gapperi	B	U	H	vole

APPENDIX N (Continued)

	Time of Activity	Nest Placement	Food	Common name
Microtus pennsylvanicus	B	U	H	vole
Ondatra zibethicus	D	U	H	muskrat
Napeozapus insignis	N	U	M	jumping mouse
Vulpes fulva	N	U	O	fox
Urocyon cinereoargenteus	N	G	O	fox
Ursus americanus	D	–	O	bear
Procyon lotor	N	–	O	racoon
Mephitis mephitis	N	U	O	skunk
Mustela rixosa	N	U	C	weasel
Mustela frenata	B	U	C	weasel
Felis concolor	N	–	C	mountain lion
Lynx rufus	N	–	C	lynx
Odocoileus virginianus	N	–	H	deer

APPENDIX O

A List of Ant Taxa Known to Have Been Collected in Catamarca, Argentina. The right-hand column notes the source for inclusion on this list; a = recorded in Kempf (1972); b = collected in the present study (December 1973 and January 1974). Species preceded by an asterisk are those collected at a 5 hectare study site at km 1512 near Andalgalá.

Subfamily PONERINAE
  1. *Pachycondyla striata*   a
  2. *Hypoponera clavatula*   a
  3. *Hypoponera opaciceps* var. *pampana*   a
Subfamily ECITONINAE
  4. *Neivamyrmex bruchi*   a
  5. *Neivamyrmex diversinodis*   a
  6. *Neivamyrmex lieselae*   a
  7. *Neivamyrmex pertyi*   a
  8. *Neivamyrmex raptans*   a
  9. *Neivamyrmex shuckardi*   a
 10. *Neivamyrmex spinolai*   a
 11. *Neivamyrmex sulcatus*   a
*12. *Neivamyrmex swainsoni*   a,b
Subfamily PSEUDOMYRMECINAE
 13. *Pseudomyrmex maculatus*   a
  *   *Pseudomyrmex sp.*   b
Subfamily MYRMICINAE
*14. *Pogonomyrmex brevibarbis*   b
      Pogonomyrmex brevibarbis niger   a
 15. *Pogonomyrmex cunicularius*   a,b
 16. *Pogonomyrmex inermis*   a
 17. *Pogonomyrmex laticeps*   a
 18. *Pogonomyrmex longibarbis*   a
 19. *Pogonomyrmex rastratus*   a
      Pogonomyrmex rastratus var. *pulchellus*   a
 20. *Pogonomyrmex vermiculatus*   a
 21. *Ephebomyrmex naegelii*   a
 22. *Pheidole bergi*   a
      Pheidole bergi pulliventris   a
*23. *Pheidole fallax*   a,b
 24. *Pheidole seeldrayersi*   a
*25. *Pheidole spininodis*   a,b
      Pheidole spininodis var. *lucifuga*   a
      Pheidole spininodis var. *solaris*   a
*26. *Pheidole triconstricta*   b
 27. *Crematogaster bruchi*   a
 28. *Crematogaster rudis*   a
  *   *Crematogaster sp. 1*   b
  *   *Crematogaster sp. 2*   b
 29. *Solenopsis angulata huasanensis*   a
 30. *Solenopsis granivora*   a

APPENDIX O (Continued)

31.	*Solenopsis minutissima*	a
32.	*Solenopsis nigella*	a
33.	*Solenopsis oculata*	a
34.	*Solenopsis saevissima richteri*	a
*	*Solenopsis sp. 1*	b
*	*Solenopsis sp. 2*	b
35.	*Oligomyrmex bruchi*	a
36.	*Zacryptocerus bivestitus*	a
37.	*Zacryptocerus bruchi*	a
*38.	*Zacryptocerus jheringi*	a,b
*39.	*Zacryptocerus liogaster*	a,b
*	*Zacryptocerus sp.*	b
*40.	*Cyphomyrmex transversus*	b
*41.	*Trachymyrmex jheringi*	b
42.	*Trachymyrmex tucumanus*	a,b
*43.	*Acromyrmex aspersus*	b
*44.	*Acromyrmex lobicornus*	a,b
	Acromyrmex lobicornis var. *ferrugineus*	a
45.	*Acromyrmex lundi*	a
*46.	*Acromyrmex silvestrii*	a,b
	Acromyrmex silvestrii bruchi	a
*47.	*Mycetophlax bruchi*	a,b
48.	*Mycetophylax cristulatus* var. *emmae*	a
*49.	*Mycetophylax emeryi*	b
	Mycetophylax emeryi var. *arenicola*	a
	Mycetophylax emeryi var. *fortis*	a
	Mycetophylax emeryi weiseri	a
50.	*Atta saltensis*	a
Subfamily DOLICHODERINAE		
*51.	*Forelius albiventris*	a,b
52.	*Forelius breviscapus* var. *obscuratus*	a
53.	*Forelius chalybaeus*	a
*54.	*Forelius grandis*	a,b
	Forelius grandis var. *basalis*	a
55.	*Forelius nigriventris*	a
56.	*Forelius rufus*	a
*57.	*Dorymyrmex ensifer*	a,b
58.	*Dorymyrmex flavescens*	a
59.	*Dorymyrmex joergenseni*	a
	Dorymyrmex joergenseni var. *albipes*	a
	Dorymyrmex joergenseni var. *azulensis*	a
*60.	*Dorymyrmex morenoi*	a,b
*61.	*Dorymyrmex planidens*	a,b
62.	*Dorymyrmex bruchi*	a
	Dorymyrmex bruchi var. *ebeninus*	a
*	*Dorymyrmex sp.* nr. *bruchi*	b
63.	*Araucomyrmex baeri*	a
*64.	*Araucomyrmex exsanguis*	a,b
	Araucomyrmex exsanguis var. *carbonarius*	a
	Araucomyrmex exsanguis sordidus	a
*65.	*Conomyrma bitubera*	b
66.	*Conomyrma breviscapis*	a

APPENDIX O (Continued)

67.	*Conomyrma carettei*	a
*	*Conomyrma sp. 1*	b
*	*Conomyrma sp. 2*	b
68.	*Conomyrma wolffhuegeli*	a
Subfamily FORMICINAE		
69.	*Brachymyrmex bruchi*	a
	Brachymyrmex bruchi var. *rufipes*	a
*70.	*Brachymyrmex patagonicus*	a,b
71.	*Myrmelachista elongata*	a
*72.	*Camponotus blandus*	b
*73.	*Camponotus mus*	a,b
74.	*Camponotus bonariensis*	a
	Camponotus bonariensis var. *tucumanus*	a
	Camponotus banariensis weiseri	a
75.	*Camponotus bruchi*	a
	Camponotus bruchi lysistratus	a
*76.	*Camponotus punctulatus*	a,b
	Camponotus punctulatus var. *tenuibarbis*	a
	Camponotus punctulatus andigena	a
	Camponotus punctulatus andigena var. *heliades*	a
	Camponotus punctulatus andigena var. *nigriscapus*	a
77.	*Camponotus substitutus* var. *pullulus*	a

APPENDIX P

A List of Ant Species Collected at a 5 Hectare Study Site (site 002, Barbour and Diaz, 1973) in the Avra Valley near Silver Bell, Arizona, in August 1973.

Subfamily PONERINAE
  1. *Odontomachus clarus*
Subfamily MYRMICINAE
  2. *Pogonomyrmex pima*
  3. *Pogonomyrmex rugosus*
  4. *Aphaenogaster cockerelli*
  5. *Veromessor pergandei*
  6. *Pheidole cerebrosior*
  7. *Pheidole gilvescens*
  8. *Pheidole hyatti*
  9. *Pheidole sciophila*
  10. *Pheidole subdentata*
  11. *Pheidole xerophila tucsonia*
  12. *Pheidole n.sp.?*
  13. *Monomorium minimum*
  14. *Solenopsis xyloni*
  15. *Crematogaster depilis*
  16. *Cyphomyrmex wheeleri*
  17. *Acromyrmex versicolor*
  18. *Trachymyrmex desertorum*
  19. *Trachymyrmex smithi neomexicanus*
Subfamily DOLICHODERINAE
  20. *Iridomyrmex pruinosum*
  21. *Forelius foetidus*
  22. *Conomyrma insana*
Subfamily FORMICINAE
  23. *Myrmecocystus flaviceps*
  24. *Paratrechina melanderi*
  25. *Camponotus festinatus*
  26. *Camponotus ocreatus*
  27. *Camponotus sayi*

APPENDIX Q

A Generic Comparison of the Ant Faunae of Catamarca and Arizona and of One Study Site in Each. Data in the columns are numbers of species. An asterisk indicates that the genus is not known from the geographic region (southern North America or southern South America) containing the study area. Data on generic distributions were taken largely from Brown (1973).

	Catamarca	Arizona	Bolsón de Pipanaco site	Avra Valley site
PONERINAE				
Amblyopone	–	1	–	–
Pachycondyla	1	–	–	–
Ponera	*	1	*	–
Hypoponera	2	4	–	–
Odontomachus	–	1	–	1
CERAPACHYINAE				
Cerapachys	–	1	–	–
DORYLINAE				
Neivamyrmex	9	16	1	–
PSEUDOMYRMECINAE				
Pseudomyrmex	2	2	1	–
MYRMICINAE				
Myrmica	*	8	*	–
Paramyrmica	*	1	*	–
Pogonomyrmex	7	11	1	2
Ephebomyrmex	1	–	–	–
Stenamma	*	3	*	–
Aphaenogaster	*	6	*	1
Veromessor	*	3	*	1
Pheidole	5	26	3	7
Rogeria	–	1	–	–
Crematogaster	2	15	2	2
Monomorium	*	3	*	1
Solenopsis	6	6	2	1
Oligomyrmex	1	–	–	–
Myrmecina	*	1	*	–
Macromischa	*	1	*	–
Leptothorax	–	11	–	–
Xiphomyrmex	*	1	*	–
Zacryptocerus	4	1	3	–
Strumigenys	–	1	–	–
Smithistruma	–	1	–	–
Cyphomyrmex	1	2	1	1
Trachymyrmex	2	4	1	2
Acromyrmex	4	1	3	1
Mycetophylax	3	*	2	*
Atta	1	1	–	–

APPENDIX Q (Continued)

	Catamarca	Arizona	Bolsón de Pipanaco site	Avra Valley site
DOLICHODERINAE				
Liometopum	*	2	*	—
Iridomyrmex	—	2	—	1
Forelius	6	1	2	1
Dorymyrmex	6	*	3	*
Araucomyrmex	2	*	1	*
Conomyrma	4	2	3	1
Tapinoma	—	1	—	—
FORMICINAE				
Acropyga	—	1	—	—
Brachymyrmex	2	1	1	—
Myrmelachista	1	*	—	*
Camponotus	6	18	3	3
Paratrechina	—	3	—	1
Prenolepis	*	1	*	—
Lasius	*	8	*	—
Acanthomyops	*	7	*	—
Myrmecocystus	*	10	*	1
Formica	*	17	*	—
Polyergus	*	1	*	—

APPENDIX R

Type of Photosynthetic System of Monte Plants

Family	Species	Anatomy	C_{13}/C_{12}	Phot. Syst.
Acanthaceae	*Justicia campestris*	Nv		C3
Amaranthaceae	*Gomphrena maritima*	Kv		C4
	Gomphrena tomentosa	Kv	12.60	C4
	Gomphrena martiana	–	13.88	C4
Anacardiaceae	*Lithraea ternifolia*	Nv		C3
	Schinus piliferus	Nv		C3
	Schinus bumelioides	Nv		C3
Apocynaceae	*Aspidiosperma quebracho-blanco*	Nv		C3
	Vallesia glabra	Nv		C3
Asclepiadaceae	*Philibertia gilliesii*	Nv		C3
	Morrenia odorata	Nv		C3
Borraginaceae	*Heliotropium campestre*	Nv		C3
	Heliotropium catamarcense	Nv		C3
	Heliotropium mendocinum	Nv		C3
Calyceraceae	*Calycera calcitrapa*	Nv		C3
Capparaceae	*Atamisquea emarginata*	Nv		C3
Chenopodiaceae	*Atriplex argentina*	Kv		C4
	Atriplex lampa	Ka		C4
	Suaeda divaricata	Ka		C4
Compositae	*Baccharis salicifolia*	Nv		C3
	Baccharis pulchella	Nv		C3
	Bidens subalternans	Nv		C3
	Eupatorium patens	Nv		C3
	Eupatorium arnottianum	Nv		C3
	Flaveria bidentis	Kav		C4
	Flourensia campestris	Nv		C3
	Flourensia tortuosa	Nv		C3
	Helenium donianum	Nv		C3
	Hyaloseris rubicunda	Na		C3
	Mikania urticaefolia	Nv		C3
	Proustia cuneifolia	Nv		C3
	Senecio gilliesianus	Nv	23.88	C3
	Senecio subulatus	Nv		C3
	Tessaria absinthioides	Nv		C3
	Tessaria dodoneaefolia	Nv		C3
	Trichocline incana	Nv		C3
	Verbesina enceliodes	–	24.65	C3
	Wedeliella incarnata	–	13.31	C4
	Xanthium spinosum	Nv		C3
Euphorbiaceae	*Jatropha peiranoi*	Nv		C3
	Jatropha excisa	Nv		C3
	Jatropha macrocarpa	–	22.69	C3
	Acalypha lycioides	Nv		C3
	Ditaxis jablonszkiyana	Nv		C3
	Euphorbia catamarcensis	Kv		C4
	Tragia hieronymi	Nv		C3
Hydrophyllaceae	*Nama dichotomum*	Nv		C3
	Nama undulatum	Nv		C3

APPENDIX R (Continued)

Family	Species	Anatomy	C_{13}/C_{12}	Phot. Syst.
Leguminosae	*Acacia aroma*	–	27.20	C3
	Geoffroea decorticans	–	23.06	C3
	Zuccagnia punctata	–	23.07	C3
Loasaceae	*Mentzelia grisebachii*	Nv		C3
Malphigiaceae	*Tricomaria usillo*	–	23.12	C3
Malvaceae	*Pseudoabutilon longepilosum*	Nv		C3
	Sida argentina	Nv		C3
	Sphaeralceae brevipis	Nv		C3
Nyctaginaceae	*Boerhavia coccinea*	Kv	13.45	C4
	Bougainvillea stipitata	Nv		C3
	Bougainvillea spinosa	Nv		C3
Olacaceae	*Ximenia americana*	Nv	23.54	C3
Santalaceae	*Jodina rhombifolia*	Nv		C3
Portulacaceae	*Portulaca echinosperma*	Ka		C4
Solanaceae	*Cestrum parqui*	Nv		C3
	Grabowskia boerhaavigefolia	Nv		C3
	Grabowskia duplicata	–	22.43	C3
	Lycium ovalilobum	Nv		C3
	Lycium ciliatum	Nv		C3
	Lycium cestroides	Nv		C3
	Nicotiana petunioides	Nv		C3
	Nicotiana glauca	Nv		C3
	Nicotiana noctiflora	Nv		C3
	Nierembergia gracilis	Nv		C3
	Nierembergia browallioides	Nv		C3
	Petunia axillaris	Nv		C3
	Sclerophylax cynocrambe	Nv		C3
	Solanum chacoensis	Nv		C3
	Solanum eleagnifolium	Nv		C3
	Solanum stuckertii	Nv		C3
	Solanum evacanthum	Nv		C3
Verbenaceae	*Aloysia gratisima*	Nv		C3
	Glandularia hookeriana	Nv		C3
	Junellia juniperina	Nv		C3
	Lantana xenica	Nv		C3
	Lippia grisebachiana	Nv		C3
	Lippia integrifolia	Nv		C3
Zygophyllaceae	*Bulnesia bonariensis*	–	25.36	C3
	Bulnesia retamo	–	22.04	C3
	Kallstroemia tribuloides	Kv	14.11	C4
	Larrea cuneifolia	Nv		C3
	Plectocarpa rougesii	Nv		C3
	Porlieria microphylla	Nv		C3
	Sericodes sp.	–	24.65	C3
	Tribulus terrestris	Kv	13.11	C4

APPENDIX S

Sources for Weather Data

United States and Mexico.
U.S. Weather Bureau. 1962. *Monthly normals of temperature, precipitation, and heating degree days, 1931-1960.* Decennial census of the United States climate, no. 81 (separates for each state). Washington, D.C.: Government Printing Office.
U.S. Weather Bureau. 1963. *Local climatological data, Tucson.* Washington, D.C.: Government Printing Office.
U.S. Weather Bureau. 1965. *Climatic summary of the United States, supplement for 1951 through 1960.* Decennial census of the United States climate, no. 86 (separates for each state). Washington, D.C.: Government Printing Office.
U.S. Weather Bureau. 1965. *World Weather Records 1951-60, Volume 1, North America.* Washington, D.C.: Government Printing Office.
C. W. Thornthwaite Associates. 1964. *Average climatic water balance data of the continents, Part VII United States.* Centerton, N.J.: Laboratory of Climatology.
J. R. Hastings. 1964. *Climatological data for Baja California.* Tucson: University of Arizona.
J. R. Hastings. 1964. *Climatological data for Sonora and Northern Sinaloa.* Tucson: University of Arizona.
Estado de Chihuahua. 1967? *Boletin Meteorologico, Boletin No. 7.*

Argentina
ESSA (1966) *World weather records 1951-60, Volume 3, South America, West Indies, the Caribbean.* Washington, D.C.: Government Printing Office.
Servicio Meteorológico Nacional. 1969. *Estadisticas climatológicas, 1951-1960* (3a, edición corregida). Buenos Aires.

APPENDIX T

List of Participants in Desert Project of the Structure of Ecosystems Subprogram*

Solbrig, Otto T., Project Director, Harvard University

Bailey, Harry P., University of California, Riverside

Bawa, Kamaljit, Harvard University

Barbour, Michael G., University of California, Davis

Birkhead, William S., University of Texas, Austin

Blair, W. Frank, University of Texas, Austin

Bogart, James P., University of Texas, Austin

Bohnstedt, Charles, University of Texas, Austin

Brown, Gordon, Harvard University

Cantino, Phillip, Harvard University

Carman, Neil, University of Texas, Austin

Cates, Rex G., University of New Mexico

Cross, John, University of Arizona

Dement, William, Stanford University

Diaz, David, University of California, Davis

DiFeo, Dan, University of Texas, Austin

di Tada, Ismael, Universidad de Córdoba, Argentina

Enders, Frank, University of Texas, Austin

Goldstein, Guillermo, Universidad de Buenos Aires, Argentina

Greegor, David, University of Arizona

Hulse, Arthur C., Indiana University of Pennsylvania

Hunsaker, Don, II, San Diego State University

Hunt, James, University of Missouri, St. Louis

Hunziker, Juan, University of Buenos Aires, Argentina

Hurd, Paul D., Jr., Smithsonian Institution, Washington, D.C.

Joern, Anthony, University of Texas, Austin

Kingsolver, John M., U.S. Dept. of Agriculture, Washington, D.C.

LeClaire, Jerry, Harvard University

Linsley, Gordon E., University of California, Berkeley

Lowe, Charles H., University of Arizona

Mabry, Tom J., University of Texas, Austin

Mares, Michael A., University of Pittsburgh

Michelbacher, A. E., University of California, Berkeley

Moldenke, Andrew, University of California, Santa Cruz

Morello, Jorge, Universidad de Buenos Aires, Argentina

Naranjo, Carlos A., Universidad de Buenos Aires, Argentina

Neff, Jack, University of California, Santa Cruz

Orians, Gordon H., University of Washington

Otte, Daniel, Philadelphia Academy of Science

Palacios, Ramon A., Universidad de Buenos Aires, Argentina

Poggio, Lidia, Universidad de Buenos Aires, Argentina

Reppun, Paul, Harvard University

APPENDIX T (Continued)

Rhoades, David F., University of Washington

Rodriguez, Eloy, University of Texas, Austin

Rosenzweig, Michael L., University of Arizona

Ross, Herbert H., University of Georgia

Roughgarden, Jonathan, Stanford University

Sage, Richard D., University of California, Berkeley

Sanderson, Stewart, University of Texas, Austin

Schultz, John C., Dartmouth College

Seeligmann, Peter, Instituto Miguel Lillo, San Miguel de Tucuman, Argentina

Selander, R. B., University of Illinois

Simpson, Beryl B., Smithsonian Institution, Washington

Stange, Lionel, Instituto Miguel Lillo, San Miguel de Tucuman, Argentina

Teran, Arturo, Instituto Miguel Lillo, San Miguel de Tucuman, Argentina

Timmermann, Barbara, Harvard University

Tomoff, Carl S., University of Arizona

Turner, B. L., University of Texas, Austin

Van der Velde, University of Texas, Austin

Vervoorst, Frederico, Instituto Miguel Lillo, San Miguel de Tucuman, Argentina

Willink, Abraham, Instituto Miguel Lillo, San Miguel de Tucuman, Argentina

Yang, Tien Wei, University of Arizona

*University affiliation at time of work

REFERENCES

Abbot, K. D. 1971. Water economy of the canyon mouse *Peromyscus crinitus stephensi.* Comp. Biochem. Physiol. *38A*:37-52.

Abdel Rahman, A. A. 1953. Studies in the water economy of Egyptian desert plants. IV. Establishment and competition. Bull. Desert Inst. Egypt. *3*:84-92.

Abdel Rahman, A. A., and K. H. Batanouny. 1965. Vegetation and root distribution in the different microhabitats in Wadi Hof. Bull. Desert Inst. Egypt. *15*:55-66.

Aguilar, F. P. G. 1968. Nota sobre los escorpiones de Lima. Anal. Cientif. Univ. Agrar., Lima, Perú *6*:165-172.

Aguilar, F. P. G., and M. A. Mendez G. 1971. La "Araña chata del nido de arena," *Sicarius peruensis* (Keyserling), 1880. I. Caracteristicas morfológicas y ecológicas. Primer. Congr. Lationamer. Entomol., 143-156.

Alexander, R. D. 1974. The evolution of social behavior. Ann. Rev. of Ecol. and Syst. *5*:325-383.

Andersen, K. W. 1973. Renal efficiencies in five species of *Peromyscus.* Ph.D. thesis, University of New Mexico, Albuquerque.

Anderson, D. J. 1967. Studies on structure in plant communities. V. Pattern in *Atriplex vesicaria* communities in south-eastern Australia. Aust. J. Bot. *15*:451-458.

Anderson, D. J. 1971. Pattern in desert perennials. J. Ecol. *59*:555-560.

Anderson, J. F. 1974. Responses to starvation in the spiders *Lycosa lenta* (Hentz) and *Filistata hibernalis* (Hentz). Ecology *55*:576-585.

Andrewartha, H. G., and L. C. Birch. 1954. The Distribution and Abundance of Animals. Univ. of Chicago Press, Chicago, Ill.

Anonymous. 1964. Soils of the Western United States. Joint regional publication by the Agrl. Experiment Stations of the Western States Land-Grant Universities and Colleges with Cooperative Assistance by the Soil Conservation Service of the U.S.D.A.:11-16.

Auer, V. 1960. The Quaternary history of Fuego-Patagonia. Proc. R. Soc., B *152*:507-516.

Axelrod, D. I. 1939. A miocene flora from the western border of the Mohave Desert. Carnegie Inst. Wash. Pub. *516*:2-129.

Axelrod, D. I. 1941. The concept of ecospecies in tertiary paleobotany. Proc. Nat. Acad. Sci. USA *27*:545-551.

Axelrod, D. I. 1948. Climate and evolution in western North America during Middle Plesiocene time. Evolution *2*:127-144.

Axelrod, D. I. 1950. Evolution of desert vegetation in Western North America. Carnegie Inst. Publ. *590*:217-306.

Axelrod, D. I. 1956. Mio-Pliocene floras from west-central Nevada. Univ. Calif. Publ. Geol. Sci. *33*:1-321.

Axelrod, D. I. 1957. Late Tertiary floras and the Sierra Nevadan uplift. Bull. Geol. Soc. Amer. *68*:19-46.

Axelrod, D. I. 1958. Evolution of the Madro-Tertiary geoflora. Bot. Rev. *24*:433-509.

Bailey, H. P. 1956. Two grid systems that divide the entire surface of the earth into quadrilaterals of equal area. Trans. Amer. Geophys. Un. *37* (2):628-635.

Bailey, H. P. 1958. A simple moisture index based upon a primary law of evaporation. Geografiska Annaler *3-4*:196-215.

Bailey, H. P. 1966. The mean annual range and standard deviation as measures of dispersion of temperature around the annual mean. Geografiska Annaler *48A*:183-194.

Baker, H. G., and I. Baker. 1973. Amino acids in nectar and their evolutionary significance. Nature *241*:543-545.

Baker, H. G., and I. Baker. 1975. Studies of nectar constitution and pollinator-plant coevolution, pp. 100-140. *In* L. Gilbert and P. H. Raven (eds.), Animal and Plant Coevolution, Univ. Texas Press, Austin, Texas.

Balderrama, N., and H. Maldonado. 1973. Ontogeny of the behavior in the praying mantis. J. Insect. Physiol. *19*:319-336.

Barbour, M. G. 1968. Germination requirements of the desert shrub *Larrea divaricata.* Ecology *49*:915-923.

Barbour, M. G. 1969. Age and space distribution of the desert shrub *Larrea divaricata.* Ecology *50*:679-685.

Barbour, M. G. 1973. Desert dogma reexamined: Root/shoot productivity and plant spacing. Am. Midl. Nat. *89*:41-57.

Barbour, M. G., and D. V. Diaz. 1973. *Larrea* plant communities on bajada and moisture gradients in the United States and Argentina. Vegetatio *28*:335-352.

Barbour, M. G., D. V. Diaz, and R. W. Breidenbach. 1974. Contributions to the biology of *Larrea* species. Ecology *55*:1199-1215.

Barghoorn, E. S. 1951. Age and environment: a survey of North American Tertiary floras in relation to paleoecology. Jour. Paleontology *25*:736-744.

Bartholomew, G. A. 1960. The physiology of desert birds. Anat. Rec. *137*:338.

Bate-Smith, E. C., and C. R. Metcalf. 1957. Leucoanthocyanins. 3. The nature and systematic distribution of tannins in dicotyledenous plants. J. Linn. Soc. Bot. *55*:669-705.

Beatty, J. A. 1961. The spiders and scorpions of the Santa Catalina Mountain area, Arizona. M. S. thesis. Dept. of Zoology, Univ. of Arizona, Tucson.

Bell, R. H. V. 1970. The use of the herb layer by grazing ungulates in the Serengeti, pp. 111-124. *In* A. Watson (ed.), Animal Populations in Relation to Their Food Resources. Brit. Ecol. Soc. Symp. #10.

Birand, H. 1961. Relations entre le development des raciues et des parties aeriennes chez certain plantes xerophytes et leur resistance a la secheresse, pp. 175-182. *In* Plant-water Relationships in Arid and Semi Arid Conditions, UNESCO, Paris.

Blair, W. F. (ed.). 1972. Evolution in the Genus *Bufo*. University of Texas Press, Austin, Texas.

Blair, W. F. 1976. Adaptations of anurans to equivalent desert scrub of North and South America, pp. 197-221. *In* D. W. Goodall (ed.), Evolution of Desert Biota. Univ. of Texas Press, Austin and London.

Boyer, J. S. 1973. Response of metabolism to low water potentials in plants. Phytopathology *63*:466-472.

Bragg, A. N. 1940a. Observations on the ecology and natural history of Anura. I. Habits, habitat, and breeding of *Bufo cognatus* Say. Amer. Natur. *74*: 322-349.

Bragg, A. N. 1940b. Observations on the ecology and natural history of Anura. II. Habits, habitat, and breeding of *Bufo woodhousii woodhousii* (Girard) in Oklahoma. Amer. Midl. Natur. *24*:306-321.

Bray, W. L. 1898. On the relation of the flora of the lower Sonoran zone in North America to the flora of the arid zones of Chile and Argentine. Bot. Gazette *26*:121-147.

Bristowe, W. S. 1929. The distribution and dispersal of spiders. Proc. Zool. Soc. Lond. *1929*:633-657.

Bristowe, W. S. 1939. The Comity of Spiders. Roy Soc., London. Two volumes.

Brown, H. A. 1967. High temperature tolerance of the eggs of a desert anuran, *Scaphiopus hammondii.* Copeia *1967*:365-370.

Brown, J. H. 1968. Adaptation to environmental temperature in two species of woodrats, *Neotoma cinerea* and *N. albigula.* Misc. Publ. Mus. Zool. Univ. Michigan *135*:1-48.

Brown, J. H. 1973. Species diversity of seed-eating rodents in sand dune habitats. Ecology *54*:775-787.

Brown, J. H. 1975. Geographical ecology of desert rodents, pp. 315-341. *In* M. L. Cody and J. Diamond (eds.), Ecology of Species Communities. Belknap Press of Harvard Univ. Press, Cambridge, Mass.

Brown, J. H., J. J. Grover, and D. W. Davidson, 1975. A preliminary study of seed predation in desert and montane habitats. Ecology *56*:987-992.

Brown, J. L. 1966. Types of group selection. Nature *211*:870.

Brown, R. W. 1934. Recognizable species of the Green River flora. U.S. Geol. Survey Prof. Paper *185*:45-77.

Bryson, R. A., and F. K. Hare (eds.). 1974. Climates of North America. Vol. 11 of the World Survey of Climatology. Elsevier, New York.

Buckman, H. O., and N. C. Brady. 1974. The Nature and Properties of Soils. MacMillian and Co., New York.

Budyko, M. I. 1956. The heat balance of the earth's surface (English translation by N. Stepanova, 1958, Office of Technical Services, U.S. Dept. of Commerce), Washington.

Budyko, M. I. 1974. Climate and Life. Academic Press, New York.

Burt, W. H., and R. P. Grossenheider. 1964. A Field Guide to the Mammals. Houghton Mifflin Co., Boston.

Cabrera, A. 1957. Catálogo de los mamíferos de America del Sur. I. (Metatheria-Unguiculata-Carnivora). Rev. Museo Argentino Cienc. Natur. "Bernardino Rivadavia", Zool. 4:1-307.

Cabrera, A. L. 1956. Esquema fitogeográfico de la República Argentina. Rev. Mus. La Plata (n.s.) Bot. 8:87-168.

Cabrera, A. L. 1971. Fitogeografía de la República Argentina. Bol. Soc. Arg. Bot. 14:1-42.

Caminos, R. 1972. Sierras pampeanas de Tucuman, Catamarca, La Rioja y San Juan, pp. 42-79. In A. F. Leanza, Geología Regional Argentina. Acad. Nac. Cienc., Córdoba.

Campbell, D. H. 1943. Continental Drift and Plant Distribution. Privately printed.

Cannon, W. A. 1911. The root habits of desert plants. Carnegie Inst. Wash. Year Book 18.

Capitanelli, R. 1972. Geomorfologia y clima de la provincia de Mendoza. Bol. Soc. Arg. Bot. 13(Suppl.):15-48.

Carpenter, R. E. 1966. A comparison of thermoregulation and water metabolism in the kangaroo rats Dipodomys agilis and Dipodomys merriami. Univ. California Publ. Zool. 78:1-36.

Carter, A. M. 1974. Evidence for the hybrid origin of Cercidium sonarae (Leguminosae: Caesalpinoideae) of northwestern Mexico. Madroño 22: 266-272.

Cates, R. G., and D. F. Rhoades. 1977. Prosopis Leaves as a Resource for Insects. In B. Simpson (ed.), Mesquite: Its biology in two desert scrub ecosystems. US/IBP Synthesis Series, vol. 4. Dowden, Hutchinson & Ross, Inc., Stroudsburg, Pa.

Cei, J. M. 1956. Nueva lista sitematica de los batracios de Argentina y notas Sobre su biologia y ecologia. Invest. Zool. Chilenas 3:31-68.

Cei, J. M. 1959. Ecological and physiological observations on polymorphic populations of the toad, Bufo arenarum Hensel from Argentine. Evolution 13:532-536.

Chaney, R. W. 1940. Tertiary forests and continental history. Bull. Geol. Soc. Amer. 51:469-488.

Chaney, R. W. 1944. Summary and conclusions. In Pliocene Floras of California and Oregon, Carnegie Inst. Wash. Publ. 553:353-373.

Charnov, E. L. 1976. Optimal foraging: attack strategy of a mantid. Amer. Nat. 110:141-151.

Charnov, E. L., G. H. Orians, and K. Hyatt. 1976. The ecological significance of resource depression. Am. Nat. 110:247-259.

Charnov, E. L. and W. M. Schaffer. 1973. Life-history consequences of natural selection: Cole's result revisited. Amer. Nat. *107*:791–793.

Chew, R. M. 1961. Ecology of the spiders of a desert community. J. N. Y. Ent. Soc. *69*:5–41.

Clark, T. H. and C. W. Stern. 1968. Geological Evolution of North America. Ronald Press, New York.

Clark, W. K. 1951. Ecological life history of the armadillo in the eastern Edwards Plateau region. Amer. Midl. Natur. *46*:337–358.

Clarke, B. 1968. The evidence for apostatic selection. Heredity *24*:347–352.

Cloudsley-Thompson, J. L. 1960. Adaptive functions of circadian rhythms. Cold Spring Harbor Symp. Quant. Biol. *25*:345–355.

Cloudsley-Thompson, J. L. 1962. Microclimates and the distribution of terrestrial arthropods. Ann. Rev. Entom. *7*:199–222.

Cloudsley-Thompson, J. L. 1975. Adaptations of arthropods to arid environments. Ann. Rev. Entom. *20*:261–283.

Cody, M. L. 1970. Chilean bird distribution. Ecology *51*:455–464.

Cody, M. L. 1974. Competition and the Structure of Bird Communities. Princeton Monographs in Population Biology, No. 7. Princeton Univ. Press, Princeton, New Jersey.

Cohen, D. 1967. Optimizing reproduction in a randomly varying environment when a correlation may exist between the conditions at the time a choice has to be made and the subsequent outcome. J. Theor. Biol. *16*:1–14.

Cohen, D. 1966. Optimizing reproduction in randomly varying environment. J. Theor. Biol. *12*:119–129.

Cott, H. B. 1940. Adaptive Coloration in Animals. Oxford Univ. Press, New York.

Czajka, W. 1966. Tehuelche pebbles and extra-Andean glaciation in east Patagonia. Quaternaria *8*:245–252.

Darwin, C. 1859. On the Origin of Species by Means of Natural Selection. J. Murray, London.

Daubenmire, R. F. 1974. Plants and Environment; A Textbook of Plant Autecology. 3rd ed., Wiley, New York.

Davis, P. H., and V. H. Heywood. 1963. Principles of Angiosperm Taxonomy. Oliver and Boyd, Edinburgh.

Di Castri, F., and H. A. Mooney (eds.). 1973. Mediterranean Type Ecosystems. Springer-Verlag, Berlin.

Dietz, R. S., and J. C. Holden. 1970. Reconstruction of Pangea: Breakup and dispersion of continents, Permian to present. J. Geophys. Res. *75*:4939–4956.

Dixon, A. F. G. 1970. Quantity and availability of food for a sycamore aphid population, pp. 271–286. *In* A. Watson (ed.), Animal Populations in Relation to Their Food Resources. Brit. Ecol. Soc. Symp. #10.

Dixon, W. J. (ed.). 1970. BMD biomedical computer programs. Univ. California Publ. Automatic Computations, No. 2.

Dobzhansky, T. 1970. Genetics of the Evolutionary Process. Columbia Univ. Press, New York.

Doutt, J. K., C. A. Heppenstall, and J. E. Guilday. 1966. Mammals of Pennsylvania. Pennsylvania State Game Commission.

Dowling, H. G. 1956. Geographic relations of Ozarkian amphibians and reptiles. Southwestern Natur. *1*:174–189.

Durham, J. W. 1950. Cenozoic marine climates of the Pacific coast. Bull. Geol. Soc. Amer. *61*:1243–1264.

Durham, J. W. 1959. Palaeoclimates. Phys. Chem. Earth *3*:1–16.

Eden, M. 1967. Inadequacies of neo-Darwinian evolution as a scientific theory, pp. 5–19, 109–111. *In* P. S. Moorehead and M. M. Kaplan (eds.), Mathematical Challenges to the Neo-Darwinian Interpretation of Evolution. Wistar Inst. Symp., Monogr. 5.

Enders, F. 1974. Vertical stratification in orb-web spiders (Araneidae, Araneae) and a consideration of other methods of coexistence. Ecology *55*: 317–328.

Enders, F. Submitted. The influence of hunting manner on prey size, particularly in spiders with long attack distances (Fams. Araneidae, Linyphiidae, and Salticidae). Amer. Nat. *109*:737–763.

Enders, F. 1976. Possible biomechanical basis for guilds of insectivores. Submitted to Forma et Functio.

Enders, F. In press. Size, food finding, and Dyar's constant. Environ. Entom.

Engler, A. 1876. Uber die geographische Verbreitung der Zygophyllaceen in Verhaltniss zu ihner systematischen Pliederung Abh. K. Akad. Wiss. Berlin *1876* (2):1–36.

Epenshade, E. (ed.) 1970. Goode's World Atlas. 13th edition. Rand McNally, Chicago.

Estes, R. 1970. Origin of the recent North American lower vertebrate fauna: an inquiry in the fossil record. Forma et Functio *3*:139–163.

Evenari, M., L. Shanan, and N. Tadmor. 1971. The Neger, the Challenge of a Desert. Harvard Univ. Press, Cambridge, Mass.

Faegri, K., and L. van der Pijl. 1971. The Principles of Pollination Ecology. Pergamon Press, Oxford.

Feeny, P. P. 1970. Seasonal changes in oakleaf tannins and nutrients as a cause of spring feeding by winter-moth caterpillars. Ecology *51*:656–681.

Fenneman, N. M. 1931. Physiography of Western United States. McGraw-Hill, New York.

Feruglio, E. 1957. Los glaciares de la Cordillera Argentina. GEAEA (Soc. Arg. Estudios Geogr.) 7:1–86.

Feth, J. H. 1961. A new map of western coterminous United States showing the maximum known or inferred extent of Pleistocene lakes. U.S. Geol. Survey Prof. Paper *424-B*:B110–B112.

Fisher, R. A. 1958. The Genetical Theory of Natural Selection. Dover Publ., New York.

Fitch, H. S., P. Goodrum, and C. Newman. 1952. The armadillo in the Southeastern United States. J. Mammal. *33*:21–37.

Flint, R. F. 1971. Glacial and Quaternary Geology. Wiley & Sons, New York.

Frazetta, T. H. 1975. Complex Adaptations in Evolving Populations. Sinauer Associates, Sunderland, Mass.

Freeland, W. J., and D. H. Janzen. 1974. Strategies in herbivory by mammals: the role of plant secondary compounds. Amer. Nat. 108:269-289.

Fuentes, E. R. 1976. Ecological convergence of lizard communities in Chile and California. Ecology 57:3-17.

Gates, D. M. 1968. Transpiration and leaf temperature. Ann. Rev. Plant Physiol. 19:211-238.

Gentry, A. H. 1974. Flowering phenology and diversity in tropical Bignoniaceae. Biotropica 6:64-68.

Gerth, H. 1941. Die Tertiärfloren des südlichen Südamerika und die angebliche Verlagerung des Südpols während dieser Periode. Geol. Rund 32:321-336.

Gertsch, W. J. 1949. American Spiders. Van Nostrand Co., New York.

Gilbert, L. E. 1971. Butterfly-plant coevolution: Has Passiflora adenopoda won the selectional race with heliconiine butterflies? Science 172:585-586.

Goetsch, W., and E. Lawatsch. 1944. Beitraege zur Biologie und Vertebreitung südamerikanischer Walzenspinnen. Zool. Anz. 144:75-90.

Gordillo, C. E., and A. N. Lencinas. 1972. Sierras pampeanas de Córdoba y San Luis, pp. 1-39. In A. F. Leansa (ed.), Geologia regional Argentina. Córdoba, Acad. Nac. de Ciencias.

Graham, A. 1973. History of the arborescent temperate element in the northern Latin American biota, pp. 301-314. In A. Graham (ed.), Vegetation and Vegetational History of Northern Latin America. Elsevier, New York.

Grant, V., 1949. Pollination systems as isolating mechanisms in angiosperms. Evolution 3:82-97.

Grant, V. 1976. Isolation between Aquilegia formosa and A. pubescens: A reply and reconsideration. Evolution 30:625-628.

Grant V. E. 1958. The regulation of recombination in plants. Cold Springs Harbor Symposium in Quantitative Biology 23:337-363.

Grant V. E. 1963. The Origin of Adaptations. Columbia University Press, New York.

Gray, J. 1964. The emerging pollen picture in the American Northwest, pp. 21-30. In L. Cranwell (ed.), Ancient Pollen Floras. University of Hawaii Press, Honolulu.

Greegor, D. H., Jr. 1975. Renal capabilities of an Argentine desert armadillo. J. Mammal. 56:626-632.

Grisebach, A. 1845. Report on the progress of geographical and systematic botany. Ray Society, No. 16:418-493.

Hadley, N. F. 1972. Desert species and adaptation. Amer. Sci. *60*:338-347.

Hadley, N. F., and S. C. Williams. 1968. Surface activities of some North American scorpions in relation to feeding. Ecology *49*:726-734.

Haffer, J. 1970. Geologic-climatic history and zoogeographic significance of the Uraba region in northwestern Colombia. Caldasia *10*:603-636.

Hall, E. R., and K. R. Kelson. 1959. The Mammals of North America. Ronald Press Co., New York. 2 Vols.

Hamilton, W. J., III. 1973. Life's Color Code. McGraw-Hill, New York.

Hand, I. F. 1937. Review of the United States Weather Bureau solar radiation investigations. Monthly Weather Review *65*:415-441.

Harrington, H. J. 1962. Paleographic development of South America. Bull. Am. Ass. Pet. Geol. *46*:1773-1814.

Haurwitz, B., and J. M. Austin. 1944. Climatology. McGraw-Hill, New York.

Haydak, M. H. 1970. Honey bee nutrition. Ann. Rev. Entom. *15*:143-156.

Heindl, L. A. 1959. Introduction, pp. 1-4. *In* L. A. Heindl (ed.), Southern Arizona guidebook II. Ariz. Geol. Soc., Tucson, Ariz.

Heindrich, B. 1975a. Bee flowers: a hypothesis on flower variety and blooming times. Evolution *29*:325-334.

Heindrich, B. 1975b. The role of energetics in bumblebee-flower interrelationships, pp. 141-158. *In* L. E. Gilbert and P. H. Raven (eds.), Coevolution of Animals and Plants. Univ. of Texas Press, Austin, Texas.

Heindrich, B., and P. Raven. 1972. Energetics and pollination ecology. Science *176*:597-602.

Henning, W. 1966. Phylogenetic Systematics. University of Illinois Press, Urbana, Illinois.

Hershkovitz, P. 1962. Evolution of neotropical cricetine rodents (Muridae) with special reference to the phyllotine group. Fieldiana, Zoology *46*: 1-524.

Heusser, C. J. 1961. Some comparisons between climatic changes in northwestern North America and Patagonia. Ann. N.Y. Acad. Sci. *95*:642-657.

Hinds, D. S. 1973. Acclimitazion of thermoregulation in the desert cottontail, *Sylvilagus audubonii*. J. Mammal. *54*:708-728.

Hoffmann, G. 1960. Die mittleren jahrlichen und absoluten Extremtemperaturen der Erde, Teil II Ergebnisse. Meteorologische Abhandlungen, Vol. 8, Institut fur Meteorologie and Geophysik der Freien Universitat Berlin.

Hoffstetter, R. 1972. Relationships, origins and history of the ceboid monkeys and caviomorph rodents. A modern reinterpretation. Evol. Biol. *6*:323-347.

Holling, C. S. 1959. The components of predation as revealed by a study of small mammal predation of the European Pine Sawfly. Can. Ent. *91*: 293-320.

Holling, C. S. 1965. The functional response of predators to prey density and its role in mimicry and population regulation. Mem. Ent. Soc. Can. *45*: 5-60.

Holling, C. S. 1966. The functional response of invertebrate predators to prey density. Mem. Ent. Soc. Can. *48*:1-85.

Horn, H. S. 1971. The Adaptive Geometry of Trees. Princeton Univ. Press, Princeton, N.J.

Hudson, J. W., and D. R. Deavers. 1973. Metabolism, pulmocutaneous water loss and respiration of eight species of ground squirrels from different environments. Comp. Biochem. Physiol. *45A*:69-100.

Humboldt, A. F. von. 1849. Aspects of Nature in Different Lands and Different Climates: With Scientific Elucidations. Longman, Brown, Green, and Longmans, London. 2 vols.

Hunt, J. H. 1973. Comparative ecology of our communities in Mediterranean regions of California and Chile. Ph.D. thesis, University of California, Berkeley, California.

Hunt, J. H., and R. R. Snelling. 1975. A checklist of the ants of Arizona. Ariz. Acad. Science *10*:20-23.

Hunziker, J. H., R. A. Palacios, A. G. de Valesi, and L. Poggio. 1972. Species disjunctions in *Larrea*: evidence from morphology, cytogenetics, phenolic compounds, and seed albumins. Ann. Mo. Bot. Gard. *59*:224-233.

Hunziker, J. H., et al. (In press). *Larrea tridentata* x *divaricata* hybrids.

Hurd, P. D. Jr., and E. G. Linsley. 1975. The principal *Larrea* bees of the southwestern United States. Smithsonian Contr. to Zool. *193*:1-74.

Hutchinson, G. E., and R. H. MacArthur. 1959. A theoretical ecological model of size distributions among species of animals. Amer. Nat. *93*:117-125.

Janzen, D. H. 1968. Host plants as islands in evolutionary and contemporary time. Amer. Nat. *102*:592-595.

Janzen, D. H. 1971. Escape of *Cassia grandis* L. beans from predators in time and space. Ecology *52*:964-979.

Janzen, D. H. 1973. Host plants as islands. II. Competition in evolutionary and contemporary time. Amer. Nat. *107*:786-790.

Johansen, K. 1961. Temperature regulation in the nine-banded armadillo. Physiol. Zool. *34*:126-144.

Johnston, I. M. 1940. The floristic significance of shrubs common to North and South American deserts. J. Arnold Arb. *21*:356-363.

Johnston, R. F., and R. K. Selander. 1964. House Sparrow: rapid evolution of races in North America. Science *144*: 548-550.

Just, T. 1952. Fossil floras of the southern hemisphere and their phytogeographical significance. Bull. Am. Mus. Nat. Hist. *99*:189-203.

Kalmbach, E. R. 1943. The armadillo in relation to agriculture and game. Game and Fish Oyster Comm., Austin, Texas.

Kanter, H. 1948. La cuenca de Andalgalá en la Argentina. Univ. Nac de Tucumán, Inst. Estud. Geográficos. Monografia 2:1-34.

Karr, James R., 1971. Structure of avian communities in selected Panama and Illinois habitats. Ecol. Monogr. 41:207-233.

Kaston, B. J. 1948. Spiders of Connecticut. State Geol. and Nat. Hist. Survey. Conn. Bull. No. 70.

Kenagy, G. J. 1972. Saltbush leaves: excision of hypersaline tissue by a kangaroo rat. Science 178:1094-1096.

Kenagy, G. J. 1973. Adaptations for leaf eating in the Great Basin Kangaroo Rat, Dipodomys microps. Oecologia (Berl.) 12:383-412.

Kessler, A. 1963, Über Klima und Wasserhaushalt des Altiplano (Bolivien, Perú) während des Hochstandes der letzen Vereisung. Erdkunde 17:165-173.

Kettlewell, H. B. D. 1958. A survey of the frequencies of Biston betualria and its melanic forms in Great Britain. Heredity 12:51-72.

King, T. J., and S. R. J. Woodell. 1973. The causes of regular pattern in desert perennials. J. Ecol. 61:761-765.

Kingsbury, J. M. 1964. Poisonous Plants of the United States and Canada. Prentice-Hall, New York.

Kingslover, J. M., C. D. Johnson, S. R. Swier and A. R. Teran, 1977. Prosopis fruits as a resource for invertebrates, pp. 108-122. In B. B. Simpson (ed.) "Mesquite: Its Biology in Two Desert Ecosystems." Dowden, Hutchinson & Ross, Inc., Stroudsburg, Pa.

Klein, D. R. 1970. Food selection by North American deer and their response to over-utilization of preferred plant species, pp. 25-46. In A. Watson (ed.), Animal Populations in Relation to Their Food Resources. Brit. Ecol. Soc. Symp. #10.

Kluge, A. G. 1966. A new pelobatine frog from the Lower Miocene of South Dakota with a discussion of the evolution of the Scaphiopus-Spea complex. Contrib. Sci. Los Angeles County Mus. 113:1-26.

Kluge, M. and K. Fisher. 1967. Über Zusammenhäuge Zwischen dem CO_2-Austausch und der Abgabe von Wasserdampf durch Bryophyllum daigermontianum Berg. Planta 77:212-223.

Knost, S. J., and J. S. Rovner. 1975. Scavenging by wolf spiders (Araneae: Lycosidae). Amer. Midl. Nat. 93:239-244.

Koford, C. B. 1968. Peruvian desert mice: water independence, competition, and breeding cycle near the equator. Science 160:552-553.

Koppen, W. 1900. Versuch einer Klassifikation der Klimate, vorzugsweise nach ihren Beziehungen zur Planzenwelt. Geographische Zeitschrift, 6:593-611, 657-679.

Koppen, W. 1917. Klassifikation der Klimate nach Temperatur, Niederschlag und Jahreslauf. Petermanns Mitteilungen, pp. 193-203, 243-248.

Kottlowski, F. E., M. E. Cooley, and R. V. Ruhe. 1965. Quaternary ecology of the Southwest, pp. 287–298. *In* H. E. Wright and D. G. Frey, The Quaternary of the United States. Princeton Univ. Press, Princeton, N.J.

Kozlowski, T. T. 1968–1972. Water Deficits and Plant Growth. Academic Press, New York. 3 vols.

Kramer, P. J. 1969. Plant and Soil Water Relationships, a Modern Synthesis. McGraw-Hill, New York.

Kruuk, H. 1972. The Spotted Hyena. University of Chicago Press, Chicago.

Lack, D. 1954. The Natural Regulation of Animal Numbers. Oxford Clarendon Press, Oxford.

Larcher, W. 1969. The effect of environmental and physiological variables on the carbon dioxide gas exchange of trees. Photosynthetica *3*:167–198.

LeClaire, J., and G. Brown. 1974. Summary of qualitative phenology data. Origin and Structure of Ecosystems, IBP Technical Report 74-9, unpaged.

LeClaire, J., P. Reppun, and P. Cantino. 1973. Summary of qualitative phenology data. Origin and Structure of Ecosystems, IBP Technical Report 73-2, unpaged.

LeClaire, P. Reppun and P. Cantino. 1974. Summary of qualitative phenology data. Origin and Structure of Ecosystems, IBP Technical Report 74-3, unpaged.

Leighly, J. 1953. Dry climates: their nature and distribution. Special Publication Number 2, Research Council of Israel, pp. 3–18.

Levins, R. 1968. Evolution in Changing Environments: Some Theoretical Explanation. Princeton Univ. Press, Princeton, N.J.

Lewontin, R. C. 1970. The units of selection. Ann. Rev. of Ecol. and Syst. *1*:1–18.

Linsley, E. G., J. W. McSwain, and P. H. Raven. 1964. Comparative behavior of bees and Onagraceae. III. *Oenothera* bees of the Mojave Desert, California. Univ. Calif. Publ. Entomol. *33*:59–98.

Lowe, C. H., and D. S. Hinds. 1971. Effect of paloverde (*Cercidium*) trees on the radiation flux at ground level in the Sonoran Desert in winter Ecology *52*:916–922.

Lowe, C. H., and V. J. Vance. 1955. Acclimation of the critical thermal maximum of the reptile *Urosaurus ornatus.* Science *122*: 73–74.

Ludwig, J. A. In press. Distributional adaptations of roots in deserts. *In* J. K. Marshal (ed.), The Below Ground Ecosystem.

Lunt, O. R., J. Lety, and S. B. Clark. 1973. Oxygen requirements for root growth in three species of desert shrubs. Ecology *54*:1356–1362.

Mabry, T. J., J. H. Hunziker, and D. R. DiFeo, Jr. (eds.) 1977. Creosote Bush: Biology and Chemistry of *Larrea* in New World Deserts. US/IBP Synthesis Series, vol. 6. Dowden, Hutchinson & Ross, Inc., Stroudsburg, Pa.

MacArthur, R. H. 1964. Environmental factors affecting bird species diversity. Amer. Nat. *98*:387–397.

MacArthur, R. H. 1965. Patterns of species diversity. Biol. Rev. *40*:510–533.

MacArthur, R. H. 1972. Geographical Ecology: Patterns in the Distribution of Species. Harper and Row, New York.

MacArthur, R. H., and J. H. Connell. 1966. The Biology of Populations. John Wiley and Sons, New York.

MacArthur, R. H., and J. W. MacArthur. 1961. On bird species diversity. Ecology *42*:594-598.

MacArthur, R. H., and E. R. Pianka. 1966. On optimal use of a patchy environment. Amer. Nat. *100*:603-609.

MacArthur, R. H., H. Recher, and M. Cody. 1966. On the relation between habitat selection and species diversity. Amer. Natur. *100*:319-332.

McClanahan, L., Jr. 1964. Osmotic tolerance of the muscles of two desert-inhabiting toads. *Bufo cognatus* and *Scaphiopus couchi.* Comp. Biochem. Physiol. *12*:501-508.

McClanahan, L., Jr. 1967. Adaptations of the spadefoot toad, *Scaphiopus couchi,* to desert environments. Comp. Biochem. Physiol. *20*:73-99.

McClanahan, L. Jr. 1972. Changes in body fluids of burrowed spadefoot toads as a function of soil potential. Copeia 1972:209-216.

McCook, H. C. 1890. American Spiders and Their Spinning Work. Allen, Land and Scott, Philadelphia. 3 Vols.

MacDougal, D. T. 1908. Botanical features of North American deserts. Carnegie Inst. Wash. Publ. 99:1-111.

MacGinitie, H. D. 1953. Fossil plants of the Florissand bids, Colorado. Carnegie Inst. Wash. Publ. 599:1-180.

MacMillen, R. E. 1964. Population ecology, water relations, and social behavior of a southern California semidesert rodent fauna. Univ. California Publ. Zool. *71*:1-59.

MacMillen, R. E. 1972. Water economy of nocturnal desert rodents, pp. 147-174. *In* G. M. O. Maloiy (ed.), Comparative Physiology of Desert Animals. Academic Press, New York.

MacMillen, R. E., R. V. Bandinette, and A. K. Lee. 1972. Water economy and energy metabolism of the sandy inland mouse, *Leggadina hermannsburgensis.* J. Mammal. *53*:529-539.

MacMillen, R. E., and A. K. Lee. 1967. Australian desert mice: Independence of exogenous water. Science *158*:383-385.

MacMillen, R. E., and A. K. Lee. 1969. Water metabolism of Australian hopping mice. Comp. Biochem. Physiol. *28*:493-514.

Mares, M. A. 1973a. Climates, mammalian communities and desert rodent adaptations: an investigation into evolutionary convergence. Ph.D. thesis. Univ. Texas, Austin.

Mares, M. A. 1973b. Desert rodent ecology. Acta Zoologica Lilloana *30*: 207-225.

Mares, M. A. 1975a. Observations on Argentine desert rodent ecology, with emphasis on water relations of *Eligmodontia typus,* pp. 155-175. *In* I. Prakash and P. K. Ghosh (eds.), Rodents in Desert Environments. Junk W., The Hague.

Mares, M. A. 1975b. South American mammal zoogeography: evidence from convergent evolution in desert rodents. Proc. Nat. Acad. Sci., USA *72*:1702-1706.

Mares, M. A. 1976. Convergent evolution of desert rodents: multivariate analysis and zoogeographic implications. Paleobiology 2:39-63.

Margolis, S. V. and J. P. Kennett. 1971. Cenozoic paleoglacial history of Antarctica recorded in subantarctic deep-sea cores. Amer. Jour. Sci. 271:1-36.

Martin, P. S., and P. J. Mehringer. 1965. Pleistocene pollen analysis and biogeography of the Southwest, pp. 433-451. In H. E. Wright and D. G. Frey, The Quaternary of the United States. Princeton Univ. Press, Princeton, N.J.

Mayhew, W. W. 1965. Adaptations of the amphibian, Scaphiopus couchi, to desert conditions. Amer. Midl. Natur. 74:95-109.

Mayhew, W. W. 1968. Biology of desert amphibians and reptiles, pp. 195-356. In G. W. Brown (ed.), Desert Biology, Vol. 1. Academic Press, New York. York.

Maynard Smith, J. 1965. The evolution of alarm calls. Amer. Nat. 99:59-63.

Medawar, P. B. 1957. The Uniqueness of the Individual. Methuen, London.

Meeuse, B. J. D. 1961. The Story of Pollination. Ronald Press Co., New York.

Meidner, H., and T. A. Mansfield. 1968. Physiology of Stomata. McGraw-Hill, London.

Meigs, P. 1953. World distribution of arid and semiarid homoclimates. UNESCO reviews of research on arid zone hydrology, Paris, pp. 203-209.

Mello-Leitao, C. de 1941. Las arañas de Córdoba, La Rioja, Catamarca, Tucuman, Salta, y Jujuy. Rev. Mus. de la Plata (N.S.) 2:99-198.

Melton, M. A. 1965. The geomorphic and paleoclimatic significance of alluvial deposits in southern Arizona. J. Geol. 73:1-38.

Menendez, C. A. 1972. Paleofloras de la Patagonia, pp. 129-184. In M. J. Dimitri (ed.), La región de los Bosques Andino-Pateginicos. Col. Cient. INTA, Buenos Aires.

Michener, Charles D. 1940. The distributional history of North American Bees. Proceedings of the Sixth Pacific Science Congress, 4:297-303.

Migahid, A. M., and A. A. Abdel Rahman. 1953. Studies in the water economy of Egyptian desert plants. III. Observations on the drought resistance of desert plants. Bull. Desert Inst. Egypt. 3:59-83.

Mooney, H. A. 1972. The carbon balance of plants. Ann. Rev. Ecol. and Syst. 3:315-346.

Mooney, H. A., and E. L. Dunn. 1970. Convergent evolution of Mediterranean-climate evergreen sclerophyll shrubs. Evolution 24:292-303.

Mooney, H. A., O. T. Solbrig, and B. B. Simpson. 1977. Phenology, morphology, physiology. In B. Simpson (ed.), Mesquite: Its Biology in Two Desert Scrub Ecosystems. US/IBP Synthesis Series, vol. 4, Dowden, Hutchinson & Ross, Inc., Stroudsburg, Pa.

Morello, J. 1958. La provincia fitogeográfica del Monte. Opera Lilloana II, Tucuman, Argentina.

Morello, J. 1955a. Estudios botánicos en las regiones áridas de la Argentina I. Rev. Agr. No Argentino 1(1):385-524.

Morello, J. 1955b. Estudios botanicos en las regiones aridas de la Argentina II. Rev. Agr. No Argentiono *1*(2):301-370.

Morello, J. 1972. Variables enstructurales de la Vegetacion del Monte (Argentina) y Desierto Sonorense (E.U.A.). Primer Congreso Latinoamericano de Botánica, Mem. Symp.:359-364.

Mosquin, T. 1971. Competition for pollinators as a stimulus for the evolution of flowering time. Oikos *22*:398-402.

Mulkern, G. B., K. T. Preuss, H. Knutson, A. F. Hagen, J. B. Campbell, G. D. Lambley. 1969. Food habits and preferences of grassland grasshopper North Central Great Plains. Agr. Exp. St. of N. Dakota St. Univ. Bull. *481*:1-32.

Muma, M. H. 1966a. Feeding behavior of North American Solpugida (Arachnida). Fl. Entom. *49*:199-216.

Muma, M. H. 1966b. The life cycle of *Eremobates durangonus* (Arachnidae: Solpugidae). Fl. Entom. *49*:233-242.

Muma, M. H. 1974. Solpugid populations in south-western New Mexico. Fl. Entom. *57*:385-392.

Newlands, G. 1973. Zoogeographical factors involved in the trans-Atlantic dispersal pattern of the genus *Opisthacanthus* Peters (Arachnida: Scorpionidae). Ann. Transvaal Mus. *28*:91-98.

Norgaard, E. 1956. Environment and behaviour of *Theridion saxatile*. Oikos *7*:159-192.

Noy-Meir, I. 1973. Desert ecosystems: environment and producers. Ann. Rev. Ecol. and Syst. *4*:25-51.

Oechel, W. E., B. R. Strain, and W. R. Odening. 1972. Tissue water potential, photosynthesis. ^{14}C-labeled photosynthate utilization, and growth in the desert shrub *Larrea divaricata* Cav. Ecol. Monogr. *42*:127-141.

Oelberg, K. 1956. Factors affecting the nutritive value of range forage. J. Range Mgmt. *9*:220-225.

Olsen, R. W. 1973. Shelter-site selection in the white-throated woodrat, *Neotoma albigula*. J. Mammal. *54*:594-610.

Orians, G. H. 1969. The number of bird species in some tropical forests. Ecology *50*:783-801.

Orians, G. H., and O. T. Solbrig. 1977. A cost income model of leaves and roots with special reference to arid and semi-arid areas. Am. Nat. (in press).

Otte, D. 1972. Environmentally induced color dimorphisms in grasshoppers. Anal. Ent. Soc. Am. *65*:1154-1161.

Otte, D. 1974. Effects and functions in the evolution of signalling systems. Ann. Rev. of Ecol. and Syst. *5*:383-417.

Otte, D. 1977. Species richness pattern of New World desert grasshoppers in relation to plant diversity. J. Biogeogr. (in press).

Otte, D., and A. Joen. 1977. On feeding patterns in desert grasshoppers and the evolution of specialized diets. Proc. Acad. Nat. Sci. (Phila) (in press).

Paine, R. T., and R. L. Vadas. 1969. Calorific values of benthic marine algae and their postulated relation to invertebrate food preference. Marine Biology 4:79-86.

Parker, J. 1968. Drought resistance mechanisms, pp. 195-238. In T. T. Kozlowski (ed.), Water Deficits and Plant Growth, Vol. 1. Academic Press, New York.

Parkhurst, D. F., and O. L. Loucks. 1972. Optimal leaf size in relation to environment. J. Ecol. 60:505-537.

Pascual, R. 1970. Evolución de comunidades, cambios faunísticos y integraciones biocenoticas de los vertebrados cenoziocos de Argentina. Actas. IV Congr. Latinoamer. Zool. Caracas, Venezuela:991-1088.

Patterson, B., and R. Pascual. 1968. Evolution of mammals on southern continents. V. The fossil mammal fauna of South America. Quat. Rev. Biol. 43:409-451.

Patterson, B., and R. Pascual. 1972. The fossil mammal fauna of South America, pp. 247-309. In A. Keast, F. C. Erk, and B. Glass (eds.), Evolution Mammals, and Southern Continents. State Univ. of New York, Albany.

Pearcy, R. W., O. Bjorkman, A. T. Harrison, and H. A. Mooney. 1971. Photosynthetic performance of two desert species with C4 photosynthesis in Death Valley, California. Carnegie Gust. Wash. Yearls. 70:540-550.

Peirano, A. 1957. Observaciones generales sobre la tectonica y los depositos terciarios del cuadrangulo 26°S - 64° 30'0 − 28° 30' S − 67° 0 en el noreste Argentino. Acta Geol. Lilloana 1:61-144.

Penman, H. 1947. Natural evaporation from open water, bare soil, and grass. Proceedings, Royal Society, Series A, 193:120-145.

Petriella, B. 1972. Estudio de maderas petrificados del terciario inferior del area de Chubut central. Rev. Mus. La Plata (N.S.) Pal. 6:159-254.

Pianka, E. R. 1966. Convexity, desert lizards, and spatial heterogeneity. Ecology 47:1055-1059.

Pianka, E. R. 1967. On lizard species diversity: North American flatland deserts. Ecology 48:333-351.

Pianka, E. R. 1969. Habitat specificity, speciation and species density in Australian desert lizards. Ecology 50:498-502.

Pianka, E. R. 1971. Lizard species density in the Kalahari Desert. Ecol. 52: 1024-1029.

Pianka, E. R. 1973. The structure of lizard communities. Ann. Rev. Ecol. & Syst. 4:53-74.

Pianka, E. R., and R. B. Huey. 1971. Bird species density in the Kalahari and Australian deserts. Koedoe 14:123-130.

Polanski, J. 1957. Sobre algunos métodos paleográficos de la investigación del Cuartario pedemontano de Mendoza. Ass. Geol. Arg. Rev. 12:211-232.

Postma, R. 1973. Automap II, Environmental Systems Research Institute, Redlands, California.

Pulliam, H. R. 1974. On the theory of optimal diets. Amer. Natur. 108:59-74.

Pulliam, H. R. 1975. Coexistence of sparrows: a test of community theory. Science 189:474-476.

Pulliam, H. R., and M. R. Brand. 1975. The production and utilization of seeds in plains grassland of southeastern Arizona. Ecology *56*:1158-1166.

Rand, A. S. 1967. Predator-prey interactions and the evolution of aspect diversity. Atas do Simposio sobre a Biota Amazonica *5*:73-83.

Rapport, D. J. 1971. An optimization model of food selection. Amer. Nat. *105*:575-587.

Raven, P. H. 1963. Amphitropical relationships in the floras of North and South America. Quart. Rev. Biol. *38*:151-177.

Raven, P. H., and D. I. Axelrod. 1974. Angiosperm biogeography and past continental movements. Ann. Mo. Bot. Garden *61*:539-673.

Recher, H. F. 1969. Bird species diversity and habitat diversity in Australia and North America. Amer. Natur. *103*:75-80.

Rehr, S. W., P. P. Feeny, and D. H. Janzen. 1973. Chemical defense in Central American non-ant acacias. J. Anim. Ecol. *42*:405-416.

Rhoades, D. F. 1977a. Integrated antiherbivore, antidesiccant, and ultraviolet-screening properties of creosotebush resin. Biochem. Ecol. and Syst. (in press).

Rhoades, D. F. 1977b. The anti-herbivore chemistry of *Larrea*. *In* T. J. Mabry, J. H. Hunziker, and D. R. DiFeo, Jr. (eds.), Creosote Bush: Biology and Chemistry of *Larrea* in New World Deserts. US/IBP Synthesis Series, vol. 6. Dowden, Huntchinson & Ross, Inc., Stroudsburg, Pa.

Rhoades, D. F., and R. G. Cates. 1976. Toward a general theory of plant antiherbivore chemistry. Recent Advances in Phytochemistry *10*:168-213.

Richter, P. O. 1958. Biology of the Scarabaeidae. Ann. Rev. Entom. *3*:311-334.

Ricklefs, R. E., and K. O'Rourke. 1975. Aspect diversity in moths: a temperate-tropical comparison. Evolution *29*:313-324.

Robinson, M. H. 1969. Defenses against visually hunting predators, pp. 225-229. *In* T. H. Dobzhanski, M. K. Hecht, W. C. Steere (eds.), Evolutionary Biology. Appleton-Century-Crofts, New York.

Rodin, L. E., and N. I. Bazilevich. 1967. Production and Mineral Cycling in Terrestrial Vegetation. (English translation by G. E. Fogg) Oliver and Boyd, London.

Roig, V. G. 1969. Termorregulación en *Euphractus sexcinctus* (Mammalia, Dasypodidae). Physis *29*:27-32.

Roig, V. G. 1971. Observaciones sobre termoregulación en *Zaedyus pichiy*. Acta Zoologica Lilloana *28*:13-18.

Romer, A. S. 1966. Vertebrate Paleontology. University of Chicago Press, Chicago, Illinois.

Root, Richard B. 1967. The niche exploitation pattern of the Blue-Gray Gnatcatcher. Ecol. Monogr. *37*:317-350.

Rosen, R. 1967. Optimality Principles in Biology. Buterworths, London.

Rosenzweig, M. L. 1968a. The strategy of body size in mammalian carnivores. Amer. Midl. Natur. *80*:299-315.

Rosenzweig, M. L. 1968b. Net primary productivity of terrestrial communities: prediction from climatological data. Amer. Nat. *102*:67-74.

Rosenzweig, M. L., B. Smigel, and A. Kraft. 1975. Patterns of food, space and diversity, pp. 241-276. *In* I. Prakash and P. K. Ghosh (eds.), Rodents in Desert Environments. Junk, W., The Hague.

Rosenzweig, M. L., and P. W. Sterner. 1970. Population ecology of desert rodent communities: Body size and seed-husking as bases for heteromyid coexistence. Ecology *51*:217-224.

Rosenzweig, M. L., and J. Winakur. 1969. Population ecology of desert rodent communities: Habitats and environmental complexity. Ecology *50*:558-572.

Ruibal, R. 1962. Osmoregulation in amphibians from heterosaline habitats. Physiol. Zool. *35*:133-147.

Ruibal, R., L. Tevis, Jr., and V. Roig. 1969. The terrestrial ecology of the spadefoot toad *Scaphiopus hammondii.* Copeia 1969:571-584.

Ruiz Huidobro, O. 1965. Hidrogeología del Valle de Santa Maria. (Prov. de Catamarca, Argentina). Rev. Ass. Geol. Arg. *20*:29-66.

Salisbury, E. J. 1942. The Reproductive Capacity of Plants. G. Bell & Sons, London.

Sarmiento, G. 1972. Ecological and floristic convergences between seasonal plant formations of tropical and subtropical South America. J. Ecol. *60*: 367-410.

Savory, T. H. 1964. The Arachnida. Academic Press, London.

Schaffer, W. M. 1974. Selection for optimal life histories: the effects of age structure. Ecology *55*:291-303.

Schaffer, W. M., and M. D. Gadgil. 1975. Selection for Optimal Life Histories in Plants, pp. 142-157. *In* M. L. Cody and J. M. Diamond (eds.), Ecology and Evolution of Communities. The Belknap Press of Harvard University, Cambridge, Mass.

Schimper, A. F. W. 1903. Plant-geography Upon a Physical Basis. Clarendon Press, Oxford, England.

Schmidt-Nielsen, B., and R. O'Dell. 1961. Structure and concentrating mechanism in the mammalian kidney. Amer. J. Physiol. *200*:1119-1124.

Schmidt-Nielsen, B., K. Schmidt-Nielsen, A. Brokaw, and H. Schneiderman. 1948. Water conservation in desert rodents. J. Cell. Comp. Physiol. *32*:331-360.

Schmidt-Nielsen, K. 1964. Desert Animals. Physiological Problems of Heat and Water. Clarendon Press, Oxford.

Schmidt-Nielsen, K., T. J. Dawson, H. T. Hammel, D. Hinds, and D. C. Jackson. 1965. The jack rabbit — a study in its desert survival. Hval. Skrif. Norske Videnskaps, Akad. Oslo *48*:125-142.

Schmoller, R. R. 1970. Terrestrial desert arthropods: fauna and ecology. The Biologist *52*:77-98.

Schoener, T. W. 1971. Theory of feeding strategies. Ann. Rev. Ecol. Syst. *2*:369-404.

Schoener, T. W. 1974. Resource partitioning in ecological communities. Science *185*:27-39.

Schwarzbach, M. 1963. Climates of the Past. (Trans. by R. O. Muir) Van Nostrand Co., Ltd., New York.

Schwerdtfeger, W. (ed.) (in press). Climates of Central and South America, Vol. 12 of World Survey of Climatology. Elsevier, New York.

Sellers, W. D. 1964. Potential evapotranspiration in arid regions. J. of Applied Meteorology *3*:98-104.

Shantz, H. L. 1927. Drought resistance and soil moisture. Ecology *8*:145-157.

Shepard, D. 1968. A two-dimensional interpolation function for computer mapping of irregularly spaced data. Paper No. 15, Geography and the properties of surfaces series, Harvard Laboratory for Computer Graphics and Spatial Analysis.

Shoemaker, V. H., D. Balding, R. Ruibal, and L. L. McClanahan, Jr. 1972. Uricotelism and low evaporative water loss in a South American frog. Science *175*:1018-1020.

Shoemaker, V. H., L. McClanahan, Jr., and R. Ruibal. 1969. Seasonal changes in body fluids in a field population of spadefoot toads. Copeia 1969:585-591.

Shoemaker, V. H., and L. L. McClanahan. 1973. Nitrogen excretion in the larvae of a land-nesting frog. (*Leptodactylis bufonius*). Comp. Biochem. Physiol. *44A*:1149-1156.

Shreve, F. 1951. Vegetation and Flora of the Sonoran Desert. Carnegie Inst. of Wash. Publ. 591, Vol. 1.

Shreve, F., and T. D. Mallery. 1933. The relation of caliche to desert plants. Soil Science *35*:99-113.

Shreve, F., and I. L. Wiggins, 1964. Vegetation and Flora of the Sonoran Desert. Stanford Univeristy Press, Stanford, California. 2 Vols.

Simpson, B. B. (ed.) 1977a. Mesquite: Its Biology in Two Desert Scrub Ecosystems. US/IBP Synthesis Series, vol. 4. Dowden, Hutchinson & Ross, Inc., Stroudsburg, Pa.

Simpson, B. B. 1977b. Breeding systems of dominant perennial plants of two disjunct warm desert ecosystems. Oecologia *27*:203-226.

Simpson, G. G. 1949. The meaning of evolution. Yale Univ. Press, New Haven, Conn.

Simpson, G. G. 1950. History of the fauna of Latin America. Am. Sci. *38*:361-389.

Simpson, G. G. 1953. The Major Features of Evolution. Columbia Univ. Press, New York.

Simpson, G. G. 1970. The Argyrolagidae, extinct South American marsupials. Bull. Mus. Comp. Zool. *139*:1-86.

Slatyer, R. O. 1967. Plant-water Relationships. Academic Press, New York.

Sloan, A. J. 1964. Amphibians of San Diego County. Occas. Paps. San Diego Soc. Nat. Hist. *13*:1-42.

Smith, C. C. 1970. The coevolution of pine squirrels (*Tamiasciurus*) and conifers. Ecol. Monogr. *40*:349–371.

Smith, C. C. 1975. The coevolution of plants and seed predators. *In* L. E. Gilbert and R. H. Raven (eds.), Coevolution of Animals and Plants. Univ. of Texas Press, Austin.

Smith, F. E. 1972. Spatial heterogeneity, stability, and diversity in ecosystems. *In* E. S. Deevey (ed.), Growth by Intussusception. Trans. Conn. Acad. Arts and Sci. *44*:310–335.

Sokal, R. R., and P. H. A. Sneath, 1973. Numerical Taxonomy. W. H. Freeman and Co., San Francisco.

Solar Energy Laboratory. 1966. World distribution of solar energy. University of Wisconsin, Engineering Experiment Station, Report No. 21.

Solbrig, O. T. 1972. New approaches to the study of disjunctions with special emphasis on the American amphitropical desert disjunctions, pp. 85–100. *In* D. D. Valentine (ed.), Taxonomy, Phytogeography and Evolution. Academic Press, London and New York.

Solbrig, O. T. 1973. The floristic disjunctions between the Monte in Argentina and the Sonoran Desert in Mexico and the United States. Ann. Mo. Bot. Gard. *59*:218–223.

Solbrig, O. T. 1976. The origin and floristic affinities of the South American temperate desert and semidesert regions, pp. 7–49. *In* D. W. Goodal (ed.), Evolution of Desert Biota. University of Texas Press, Austin, Texas.

Solbrig, O. T., and P. D. Cantino. 1975. Reproductive adaptations in *Prosopis* (Leguminosae). J. Arnold Arb. *56*:185–210.

Southwood, T. R. E. 1961. The number of species of insects associated with various trees. J. Anim. Ecol. *30*:1–8.

Southwood, T. R. E. 1972. The insect/plant relationship – an evolutionary perspective. *In* H. F. van Emden (ed.), Insect/Plant Relationships. Blackwell, London.

Stebbins, G. L. 1974. Flowering plants. Evolution Above the Species Level. The Belknap Press of Harvard University Press, Cambridge, Mass.

Stevens, P. S. 1974. Patterns in Nature. Little, Brown, Boston.

Stocker, O. 1956. Die Durreresistenz, pp. 696–741. *In* O. Stocker (ed.), Encyclopedia of Plant Physiology, Vol. 3. Springer-Verlag, Berlin.

Strain, B. 1970. Field measurements of tissue water potential and carbon dioxide exchange in the desert shrubs *Prosopis juliflora* and *Larrea divaricata*. Photosynthetica *4*:118–122.

Strong, D. R. 1974. Rapid asymptotic species accumulation in phytophagous insects: the pests of cacao. Science *185*:1064–1066.

Sutton, O. G. 1961. The Challenge of the Atmosphere. Harper and Bros., New York.

Szarek, S. R. and I. P. Ting. 1974. Seasonal patterns of acid metabolism and gas exchange in Opuntia basilaris. Plant Physiol. *54*:76–81.

Talbot, M. 1943. Population studies of the ant, *Prenolepis imparis* Say. Ecology *24*:31–44.

Taljaard, J. J. 1967. Development, distribution, and movement of cyclones and anticyclones in the Southern Hemisphere during the IGY. J. of Applied Meteorology 6:973-987.

Tapia, A. 1935. Pilcomayo. Ministerio de Agricultura de la Nación, Dir. Minas y Geologia Bol. 40:1-124.

Templeton, A. R., and E. D. Rothman. 1974. Evolution in heterogeneous environments. Am. Nat. 108:409-428.

Tevis, L., Jr. 1958. Interrelations between the harvester ant Veromessor pergandei (Mayr) and some desert ephemerals. Ecology 39:695-704.

Thornthwaite, C. 1933. Climates of the earth. Geographical Review 23: 633-655.

Thornthwaite, C. 1945. Report of the committee on transpiration and evaporation, 1943-1944. Transactions of 1944, Part V, pp. 672-829.

Thornthwaite, C. 1948. An approach toward a rational classification of climate. Geographical Review 38:55-94.

Thornthwaite, C., and J. Mather. 1957. Instructions and tables for computing potential evapotranspiration and the water balance. Laboratory of Climatology, Centerton, N.J.

Tinbergen, N., B. J. D. Meeuse, L. K. Boerema, and W. Varossieau. 1942. Die Balz des Samtfalters, Eumensis semele (L). Zs. Tierpsychol. 5:182-226.

Tinkle, D. W. 1967. The life and demography of the side-blotched lizard, Uta stansburiana. Misc. Publ. Mus. Zool. Univ. Michigan 132:1-182.

Tomoff, C. S. 1974. Avian species diversity in desert scrub. Ecology 55: 396-403.

Tretzel, E. 1955. Intragenerische isolation und interspezifische Konkurrenz bei Spinnen. Z. Morph. Oekol. Tiere 44:43-162.

Turekian, K. K. (ed.). 1971. The Late Cenozoic Glacial Ages. Yale Univ. Press, New Haven.

Turnbull, A. L. 1973. Ecology of the true spiders (Araneomorphae). Ann. Rev. Entom. 18:305-348.

Turner, C. 1970. The Andes of Northwestern Argentina. Geol. Rund 59: 1028-1063.

Turner, R. M. 1963. Growth in four species of Sonoran desert trees. Ecology 44:760-765.

Ueckert, D. N., and R. M. Hansen. 1971. Dietary overlap of grasshoppers on sandhill rangeland in NE Colorado. Oecologia 8:276-295.

Van der Hammen, T. 1961. The quaternary climatic changes of northern South America. Ann. N.Y. Acad. Sci. 95:676-683.

Van der Hammen, T. 1972. Historia de la vegetación y el medio ambiente del Norte Sud Americano, pp. 119-134. Memorias de Symposia, Primer Congresso Latino Americano y Mexicano de Botanica, December 3-9, 1972.

Van Devender, T. R. 1974. The late Wisconsin biotic communities of the Sonoran Desert of Arizona: the fossil packrat midden record (Abstract). Bull. Ecol. Soc. Amer. 55:27.

Van Loon, H. 1964. Mid-season average zonal winds at sea level and at 500 mb south of 25 degrees South, and a brief comparison with the Northern Hemisphere. J. of App. Meteor. *3*:554-563.

Van Loon, H. 1965. A climatological study of the atmospheric circulation in the Southern Hemisphere during the IGY, Part I: July 1, 1957-March 31, 1958. J. of Applied Meteorology *4*:479-491.

Van Loon, H. 1967. A climatological study of the atmospheric circulation in the Southern Hemisphere during the IGY, Part II. J. of Applied Meteorology *6*:803-815.

Varley, G. C. 1939. Frightening attitudes and floral simulation in praying mantids. Proc. Roy. Entomol. Soc., London (A) *14*:91-96.

Vervoorst, F. 1954. El Bosque de algarrabos de Pipanaco (Catamarca). Ph.D. thesis. Universidad de Buenos Aires.

Vervoorst, F. 1972. Plant communities in the Bolsón de Pipanaco. USIBP, Proj. Origin and Structure of Ecosystems, Progress Report 73-3.

Viana, M. J., and G. J. Williner. Evaluación de las faunas entomologica y aracnológica de las provincias cuyanas y centrales de la Republica Argentina. (Tercera Comunicación). Acta. Cien. Ser. Entom. Observ. Nac. Fis. Cosmica, Inst. Entom., San Miguel (Bs. AS, Argentina), No. 9.

Vogel, S. 1969. Flowers offering fatty oil instead of nectar. Abstracts XI Int. Bot. Congr., Seattle, p. 229

Volkheimer, W. 1971. Aspectos paleoclimatiológicos del Terciario Argentino. Revta. Mus. Cienc. Nat. B. Rivadavia, Paleontol. *1*:243-262.

Vuilleumier, B. S. 1971. Pleistocene changes in the fauna and flora of South America. Science *173*:771-780.

Walker, E. P. 1964. Mammals of the World. John Hopkins Press, Baltimore. 3 vols.

Walter, H. 1963. The water supply of desert plants, pp. 191-205. *In* A. J. Rutter and F. H. Whitehead (eds.), The Water Relationships of Plants. John Wiley and Sons, Inc., New York.

Walter, H. and E. Stadelman. 1974. A new approach to the water relations of desert plants, pp. 213-274. *In* G. W. Brown (ed.) Desert Biology. Academic Press, New York.

Watkins, N. D., J. Keany, M. T. Ledbetter, T-C. Huang. 1974. Antarctic glacial history from analyses of ice-rafted deposits in marine sediments: new model and initial tests. Science *186*:533-536.

Wells, P. V. 1966. Late Pleistocene vegetation and degree of pluvial climatic change in the Chihuahuan Desert. Science *153*:970-975.

Wells, P. V. 1975. Post-glacial origin of the present Chihuahuan Desert less than 11,500 years ago. *In* Biological Resources of the Chihuahuan Desert (no pagination). Nat. Park Service, Washington, D.C.

Wells, P. V., and C. D. Jorgensen. 1964. Pleistocene wood rat middens and climatic change in Mohave Desert: a record of Juniper woodlands. Science *143*:1171-1174.

Went, F. W. 1949. Ecology of desert plants. II. The effect of rain and temperature on germination and growth. Ecology *30*:1-13.

Went, F. W. 1955. The ecology of desert plants. Sci. Amer. *192*:68-75.

Werner, F. G., W. R. Enns, and F. H. Parker. 1966. The Meliodae of Arizona. Tech. Bull. 175. Agricultural Experiment Station, University of Arizona, Tucson, Arizona.

Whittaker, R. H., and W. A. Niering. 1963. Vegetation of the Santa Catalina mountains, Arizona. Ecology *46*:429-452.

Williams, C. B. 1964. Patterns in the Balance of Nature and Related Problems of Quantitative Ecology. Academic Press, London.

Williams, G. C. 1966. Adaptation and Natural Selection. Princeton Univ. Press, Princeton, N.J.

Williams, G. C. 1975. Sex and Evolution. Princeton Monographs in Population Biology #8. Princeton Univ. Press, Princeton, N.J.

Williams, S. C. 1970. Coexistence of desert scorpions by differential habitat preference. Pan-Pacif. Entom. *46*:254-267.

Wilson, E. C. 1962. A resume of the geology of Arizona. Ariz. Bur. Mines Bull. 171.

Wilson, E. D. and R. T. Moore. 1959. Structure of Basin and Range Province in Arizona, pp. 89-104. *In* L. A. Heindl (ed.), Southern Arizona Guidebook II. Arizona Geol. Soc., Tucson, Ariz.

Wilson, E. O. 1971. The Insect Societies. Belknap Press of Harvard Univ. Press, Cambridge, Massachusetts.

Wood, A. E. and B. Patterson. 1971. Relationships among hystricognathous and hysticomorphous rodents. Mammalia *34*:628-639.

Woodell, S. R. J., H. A. Mooney, and A. J. Hill. 1969. The behavior of *Larrea divaricata* (Creosote bush) in response to rainfall in California. J. Ecol. *57*:37-44.

Wright, A. H., and A. A. Wright. 1949. Handbook of Frogs and Toads. Cornell Univ. Press, Ithaca, New York.

Wright, S. 1932. The roles of mutation, inbreeding, crossbreeding, and selection in evolution. Proc. 6th Intern. Congr. Genet. *1*:356-366.

Yang, T. W., and Y. Abe. 1973a. Summary of qualitative phenology data. Origin and Structure of Ecosystems, IBP Technical report 73-1, unpaged.

Yang, T. W., and Y. Abe. 1973b. Summary of qualitative phenology data. Origin and Structure of Ecosystems, IBP Technical report 73-18, unpaged.

Yang, T. W. and Y. Abe. 1974. Phenology of *Larrea divaricata* in the Tucson Region. Am. J. Bot. *61* (5. Supp):69

Yang, T. W., and C. H. Lowe, Jr. 1956. Correlation of major vegetation climaxes with soil characteristics in the Sonoran Desert. Science *123*:542.

Zimmerman, M. H., and C. L. Brown. 1971. Trees, Structure and Function. Springer-Verlag, N.Y.-Berlin.

Zweifel, R. G. 1956. Two pelobatid frogs from the Tertiary of North America and their relationship to fossil and recent forms. Amer. Mus. Novitates *1762*:1-45.

Zweifel, R. G. 1968. Reproductive biology of anurans of the arid southwest, with emphasis on adaptation of embryos to temperature. Bull. Amer. Mus. Nat. Hist. *140*:1-64.

Scientific Name Index

Abutilon, 256
Abutilon californicum, 259
Abutilon incanum, 259
Acacia, 65, 72, 73, 87, 88,
171, 229, 240, 256
Acacia aroma, 74, 83, 86, 87, 89,
125, 187, 194, 212, 237, 259,
287
Acacia constricta, 83, 86, 88, 89,
211, 213
Acacia furcatispina, 86, 89, 212,
213, 214, 215, 216, 239, 257
Acacia greggii, 72, 74, 83, 86, 88,
89, 210, 213, 214, 259
Acalypha lycioides, 286
Acanthaceae, 286
Acantherus piperatus, 263
Acanthomyops, 58, 285
Accipitridae, 287
Achurum piperatus, 263
Achurum sumichrasti, 263
Acridinae, 181, 263
Acromyrmex, 148, 284
Acromyrmex aspersus, 281
Acromyrmex lobicornis, 150, 281
Acromyrmex lundi, 281
Acromyrmex silvestrii, 150, 281
Acromyrmex striatus, 150
Acromyrmex versicolor, 283
Acropyga, 285
Actinopodidae, 265
Actinopus, 265
Aeoloplides, 145
Aeoloplus chenopodii, 263
Aeoloplus tenuipennis, 263
Agavaceae, 74
Agave, 235, 239
Agave lechuguilla, 235
Agelenidae, 265
Agelenopsis, 265
Alaudidae, 267
Allionia, 256

Allionia incarnata, 53, 147, 258,
259
Allium macropetalum, 259
Alnus, 15
Aloysia gratisima, 287
Amaranthaceae, 286
Amaranthus, 256
Amaryllis, 259
Amblyopone, 284
Ambrosia, 91, 239
Ambrosia ambrosioides, 259
Ambrosia deltoidea, 86, 88, 89, 93,
211, 213, 259
Ambrosia dumosa, 73, 74, 93, 213,
259
Ammexechidae, 263
Ammospermophilus harrisi, 273,
276, 277
Ammotrechidae, 266
Amphisbaena angustifrons, 114,
129, 135, 271
Amphisbaenidae, 267
Anacardiaceae, 286
Anchocoema subalata, 144, 263
Anconia, 145
Anconia integra, 263
Andrenidae, 264
Andreninae, 264
Anelosimus, 265
Anemone tuberosa, 259
Anthidium, 59
Anthophoridae, 59, 264
Antrozous pallidus, 272
Anyphaena, 155, 266
Anyphaenidae, 266
Aphaenogaster, 148, 284
Aphaenogaster cockerelli, 283
Aphonopelma, 153, 154, 265
Apinae, 264
Apis mellifera, 58, 222
Apocynaceae, 286
Apodidae, 267

315

318   Index

Subject Index